Studies in Economic Transition

General Editors: **Jens Hölscher**, Reader in Economics, University of Brighton; and **Horst Tomann**, Professor of Economics, Free University Berlin

This series has been established in response to a growing demand for a greater understanding of the transformation of economic systems. It brings together theoretical and empirical studies on economic transition and economic development. The post-communist transition from planned to market economies is one of the main areas of applied theory because in this field the most dramatic examples of change and economic dynamics can be found. The series aims to contribute to the understanding of specific major economic changes as well as to advance the theory of economic development. The implications of economic policy will be a major point of focus.

Titles include:

Lucian Cernat
EUROPEANIZATION, VARIETIES OF CAPITALISM AND ECONOMIC PERFORMANCE IN CENTRAL AND EASTERN EUROPE

Irwin Collier, Herwig Roggemann, Oliver Scholz and Horst Tomann (*editors*)
WELFARE STATES IN TRANSITION
East and West

Bruno Dallago and Ichiro Iwasaki (*editors*)
CORPORATE RESTRUCTURING AND GOVERNANCE IN TRANSITION ECONOMIES

Bruno Dallago (*editor*)
TRANSFORMATION AND EUROPEAN INTEGRATION
The Local Dimension

Hella Engerer
PRIVATIZATION AND ITS LIMITS IN CENTRAL AND EASTERN EUROPE
Property Rights in Transition

Saul Estrin, Grzegorz W. Kolodko and Milica Uvalic (*editors*)
TRANSITION AND BEYOND

Hubert Gabrisch and Rüdiger Pohl (*editors*)
EU ENLARGEMENT AND ITS MACROECONOMIC EFFECTS IN EASTERN EUROPE
Currencies, Prices, Investment and Competitiveness

Iraj Hashi, Paul J.J. Welfens and Anna Wziatek-Kubiak (*editors*)
INDUSTRIAL COMPETITIVENESS AND RESTRUCTURING IN ENLARGED EUROPE
How Accession Countries Catch Up and Integrate in the European Union

Oleh Havrylyshyn
DIVERGENT PATHS IN POST-COMMUNIST TRANSFORMATION
Capitalism for All or Capitalism for the Few?

Jens Hölscher (*editor*)
FINANCIAL TURBULENCE AND CAPITAL MARKETS IN TRANSITION COUNTRIES

Jens Hölscher and Anja Hochberg (*editors*)
EAST GERMANY'S ECONOMIC DEVELOPMENT SINCE UNIFICATION
Domestic and Global Aspects

Mihaela Kelemen and Monika Kostera (*editors*)
CRITICAL MANAGEMENT RESEARCH IN EASTERN EUROPE
Managing the Transition

Emil J. Kirchner (*editor*)
DECENTRALIZATION AND TRANSITION IN THE VISEGRAD
Poland, Hungary, the Czech Republic and Slovakia

David Lane (*editor*)
THE TRANSFORMATION OF STATE SOCIALISM
System Change, Capitalism or Something Else?

David Lane and Martin Myant (*editors*)
VARIETIES OF CAPITALISM IN POST-COMMUNIST COUNTRIES

Tomasz Mickiewicz
CORPORATE GOVERNANCE AND FINANCE IN POLAND AND RUSSIA

Tomasz Mickiewicz
ECONOMIC TRANSITION IN CENTRAL EUROPE AND THE COMMONWEALTH OF INDEPENDENT STATES COUNTRIES

Milan Nikolic
MONETARY POLICY IN TRANSITION
Inflation Nexus Money Supply in Postcommunist Russia

Julie Pellegrin
THE POLITICAL ECONOMY OF COMPETITIVENESS IN AN ENLARGED EUROPE

Stanislav Poloucek (*editor*)
REFORMING THE FINANCIAL SECTOR IN CENTRAL EUROPEAN COUNTRIES

Gregg S. Robins
BANKING IN TRANSITION
East Germany after Unification

Johannes Stephan
ECONOMIC TRANSITION IN HUNGARY AND EAST GERMANY
Gradualism and Shock Therapy in Catch-up Development

Johannes Stephan (*editor*)
TECHNOLOGY TRANSFER VIA FOREIGN DIRECT INVESTMENT IN CENTRAL AND EASTERN EUROPE

Hans van Zon
THE POLITICAL ECONOMY OF INDEPENDENT UKRAINE

Adalbert Winkler (*editor*)
BANKING AND MONETARY POLICY IN EASTERN EUROPE
The First Ten Years

Studies in Economic Transition
Series Standing Order ISBN 0-333-73353-3
(*outside North America only*)

You can receive future titles in this series as they are published by placing a standing order. Please contact your bookseller or, in case of difficulty, write to us at the address below with your name and address, the title of the series and the ISBN quoted above.

Customer Services Department, Macmillan Distribution Ltd, Houndmills, Basingstoke, Hampshire RG21 6XS, England

---

Also by David Lane

VARIETIES OF CAPITALISM IN POST-COMMUNIST COUNTRIES
(*co-editor with Martin Myant*)

THE RISE AND FALL OF STATE SOCIALISM
POD"EM I UPADOK GOSUDARSTVENNOGO SOTSIALIZMA

RUSSIAN BANKING: Evolution, Problems and Prospects (*editor*)

THE LEGACY OF STATE SOCIALISM AND THE FUTURE OF TRANSFORMATION (*editor*)

THE POLITICAL ECONOMY OF RUSSIAN OIL (*editor*)

THE TRANSITION FROM COMMUNISM TO CAPITALISM: Ruling Elites from Gorbachev to Yeltsin (*co-author with Cameron Ross*)

The Transformation of State Socialism

System Change, Capitalism or Something Else?

Edited by

David Lane

palgrave
macmillan

First published 2007 by
PALGRAVE MACMILLAN
Houndmills, Basingstoke, Hampshire RG21 6XS and
175 Fifth Avenue, New York, N.Y. 10010
Companies and representatives throughout the world

PALGRAVE MACMILLAN is the global academic imprint of the Palgrave Macmillan division of St. Martin's Press, LLC and of Palgrave Macmillan Ltd. Macmillan® is a registered trademark in the United States, United Kingdom and other countries. Palgrave is a registered trademark in the European Union and other countries.

ISBN-13: 978-0-230-52088-2 hardback
ISBN-10: 0-230-52088-X hardback

This book is printed on paper suitable for recycling and made from fully managed and sustained forest sources. Logging, pulping and manufacturing processes are expected to conform to the environmental regulations of the country of origin.

A catalogue record for this book is available from the British Library.

Library of Congress Cataloging-in-Publication Data
The transformation of state socialism: system change, capitalism or something else? / edited by David Lane.
p. cm.
Includes bibliographical references and index.
ISBN 0-230-52088-X (alk. paper)
1. Europe, Eastern--Economic conditions--1989- 2. Former Soviet republics--Economic conditions. 3. Post-communism--Europe, Eastern. 4. Post-communism--Former Soviet republics. I. Lane, David Stuart.
HC244. T698614 2007
330.947--dc22

2007018264

10 9 8 7 6 5 4 3 2 1
16 15 14 13 12 11 10 09 08 07

Printed and bound in Great Birtain by
Antony Rowe Ltd, Chippenham and Eastbourne

Contents

List of Tables

List of Figures

List of Appendices

Acknowledgements

This book is the consequence of a specially convened conference held at the University of Cambridge under the auspices and support of the Centre for Research in the Arts, Social Sciences and Humanities. We acknowledge the support in this venture provided by the Leverhulme Trust, the British Academy, the Centre for Latin American Studies and Emmanuel College.

We gratefully acknowledge permission to use copyright material from the following: EBRD for reproduction of data in Chapters 1 and 12.

Notes on the Contributors

Susan Eckstein is Professor of Sociology at Boston University and former president of the Latin American Studies Association. Her publications include *What Justice? Whose Justice? Fighting for Fairness in Latin America* (2003, co-editor) and *The Struggle for Social Rights in Latin America* (2002, co-editor). She is currently writing a book on the changing Cuban diaspora and its transnational impact.

Philip Hanson is Emeritus Professor of the Political Economy of Russia and Eastern Europe, University of Birmingham, and Associate Fellow, Chatham House. His books include *Regional Economic Change in Russia* (2000, co-edited with Michael Bradshaw) and *The Rise and Fall of the Soviet Economy* (2003). His academic articles have appeared in a number of journals, including *Europe-Asia Studies, Eurasian Geography and Economics, Economy and Society* and *European Economic Review*.

Lawrence P. King is Reader at the Department of Sociology, University of Cambridge and a fellow of Emmanuel College. Most of his published work has focused on foreign direct investment, privatization and industrial restructuring in central eastern Europe and Russia. His books include *The Basic Features of Postcommunist Capitalism* (2001) and *Theories of the New Class: Intellectuals and Power* (2004).

Soyoung Kwon is currently a fellow at the Centre for Asia Pacific Studies in Kyung Hee University in Seoul, Korea. Her interest mainly focused on changes in North Korea in terms of leadership, politics and foreign relations as well as its implications for future development in North Korea; EU–DPRK relations; and security in north-east Asia and multilateral diplomacy. Her recent publications include 'Survival of the North Korean Regime and Changing Legitimation Modes', Cornell University, The Mario Einudi Center for International Studies Working Paper Series 07-2005; 'EU's Critical Engagement Course towards North Korea', with Glyn Ford, *Journal of National Unification* (Vol. 22, Yeongnam University, 2006).

David Lane is Senior Research Associate in the Faculty of Social and Political Sciences at the University of Cambridge. He is currently the recipient of a Leverhulme Trust Research award on class and transformation in Ukraine and Russia. He also is the holder of a British Academy network award on elites and the European Union. His recent books include: *Varieties of Capitalism in Post-Communist Countries* (2007, editor with Martin Myant, and contributor) and *The Legacy of State Socialism* (2002, editor and contributor).

Nick Manning is Professor of Social Policy and Sociology in the School of Sociology and Social Policy, University of Nottingham. His recent books include: *Work and Welfare in the New Russia* (2000, with Nataliya Tikhonova and Ovsey Shkaratan); *Poverty and Social Exclusion in the New Russia* (2004, edited with Nataliya Tikhonova). Currently he is being funded by INTAS to study health and health policy in Russia.

Satoshi Mizobata is Professor and Vice-Director at the University of Kyoto, Kyoto Institute of Economic Research. His research areas are the Russian and East European economies, focusing on the enterprises and market structure, and the comparative analysis of corporate governance. He is editor of *The Journal of Comparative Economic Studies* in Japan. His recent works include: 'Bank Sector Restructuring', in D. Lane (ed.), *Russian Banking* (2002), 'The Impact of EU Integration on Corporate Governance Reforms in Russia', Kyoto University (The Twenty-first Century COE Program), in *The Wider Europe: Institutions and Transformation* (2005), The Association for Comparative Management eds., *Business and Society* (2006, in English and Japanese).

Martin Myant is Professor in the Paisley Business School, University of Paisley. He has written extensively on the economic and political history of east-central Europe, particularly the Czech Republic, and on the transformation of economic systems after 1989. Among his recent publications are *The Rise and Fall of Czech Capitalism: Economic Development in the Czech Republic since 1989* (2003) and *Varieties of Capitalism in Post-Communist Countries* (2007, jointly edited with David Lane).

Mario Nuti is Professor of Comparative Economic Systems at the University of Rome 'La Sapienza'. He studied in Warsaw and at Cambridge University. He has lectured at Cambridge and the European University, Florence, and at Birmingham where he was Director of CREES. He has been an economic advisor to the European Commission, Brussels, on relations with eastern Europe, a consultant to several international organizations and to the governments of Poland, Belarus and Uzbekistan. He is the author of many publications mainly on the economics of workers' participation and on economic reform and transition in eastern Europe.

David Ost is Professor of Political Science at Hobart and William Smith Colleges in New York, and occasional visiting professor at the Central European University. His most recent book, *The Defeat of Solidarity: Anger and Politics in Postcommunist Europe* (2005), won the 2006 Ed Hewett Prize of the American Association for the Advancement of Slavic Studies. He has written for publications such as *East European Politics and Society*, *Theory and Society*, *Politics and Society*, *European Journal of Social Theory* and *The Nation*.

Rudi Schmidt is Professor of Sociology and has held university and research posts at the universities of Berlin, Erlangen and Jena. His research interests include the sociology of work, industrial relations, the modernization of industry and production systems and transition in east-central Europe. Recent publications include 'Eastern Germany's Incorporation into the Federal Republic', in David Lane and Martin Myant (eds), *Varieties of Capitalism in Post-Communist Countries* (2007).

Ovsey Shkaratan is Professor at the State University, Higher School of Economics, Moscow. His recent publications include: *Work and Welfare in the New Russia* (2000, in co-authorship with N. Manning and N. Tikhonova); *Gosudarstvennaya sotsial'naya politika i strategiyi vizhivaniya domokhozyaystv* (2003, in co-authorship with N. Manning, T. Sidorina and N. Tikhonova); *Rossiyskiy poryadok: Vector peremen* (2004); *Social'naya stratifikatsiya Rossiyi i Vostochnoy Evropi: sravnitel'niy analiz* (2006, in co-authorship with V. Ilyin).

David Stuckler has a Master's degree in Public Health from Yale University and is a doctoral student at the Department of Sociology, University of Cambridge. He has recently published in *Nature-Medicine, Public Health* and *Cancer Research*.

Peggy Watson is a senior researcher in the Faculty of Social and Political Sciences at the University of Cambridge. She writes on health, feminism and post-communist transformations. Recent published work includes: 'Stress and Social Change in Poland' in *Health and Place*; 'Rethinking Transition: Gender, Globalism and Class', in *Going Public: Feminism and the Shifting Boundaries of the Private Sphere*, edited by Joan W. Scott and Debra Keates (2004), as well as essays in *Generational Consciousness, Narrative, and Politics*, edited by June Edmunds and Bryan Turner (2002).

Stephen White is Professor of International Politics and a Senior Associate of the School of Central and East European Studies at the University of Glasgow. He is the chief editor of the *Journal of Communist Studies and Transition Politics*, and has recently published *Putin's Russia and the Enlarged Europe* (2006, with Roy Allison and Margot Light), *Politics in Europe* (with others 2007), and *Developments in Central and East European Politics 4* (2007, with Judy Batt and Paul G. Lewis).

Jeanne L. Wilson is a Professor of Political Science at Wheaton College in Norton, Massachusetts, and a research associate at the Davis Center for Russian and Eurasian Research at Harvard University. Her research interests include the politics of transition in China and Russia and Russian–Chinese relations. Recent publications include: 'Emerging Capitalism in Russia and China: Implications for Europe' (with Sheila M. Puffer and Daniel J. McCarthy), *European Journal of International Management* (No. 1, May 2007); and *Strategic Partners: Russian–Chinese Relations in the Post-Soviet Era* (2004). Currently, she is working on a research project examining the impact of internationalization on domestic policy in Russia and China.

1

Introduction: Outcomes of Transformation

David Lane[1]

When, on 25 February 1986, Mikhail Gorbachev launched the programme of perestroika, he presided over what was known as the 'world socialist system'. This was made up of a core of 16 established states located in central and eastern Europe, Asia and Latin America. In addition, there were seven African states which defined themselves as 'Marxist-Leninist'. These societies all had in common a centrally planned economy, a hegemonic communist party and a comprehensive state-based system of social welfare, science and education. They had large, well-organized armed forces and the USSR was equipped with nuclear weapons. State socialism was a world system and a competitor to capitalism.

Perestroika was a policy of radical reform to introduce market relations, to create conditions for opening up the USSR to world competition, to lessen central controls and to encourage a more pluralistic political system with greater public electoral participation. It was a policy intended to move from détente with the Western powers to an entente with them. A major objective, to ensure peace and prosperity for the communist bloc, was to bring the socialist states into the world order. It was a strategy which was to inspire political and economic reformers in the central European communist states and to impress the leaders of the Western capitalist states.

The consequences in the USSR were unintended: there was a rapid decline of economic growth accompanied by high levels of inflation and rising public disenchantment. The spread of electoral democracy to the socialist states of Europe led to instability. Three years after launching the Soviet reform programme, in September 1989 in Poland, the political movement Solidarity overwhelmingly defeated the communists in an open election. Anti-communists came to power and in the following two years further electoral defeats followed in all the other eastern European countries. The impact of Gorbachev's perestroika was collapse of the European communist system, which had severe repercussions on the communist states and their allies outside. In Europe, the home of Marxism and Leninism, the promise of communism as an alternative social and political system to capitalism evaporated.

This book considers the effects of this collapse: not only in the European states, but also in China, Cuba, North Korea and the responses and adjustments of other countries of the Third World. The contributors to this book reflect on the outcomes of the transformation – the extent to which alternative economically capitalist and politically pluralist societies have been constructed and the degree to which the legacy of communism persists. The former state socialist societies offer not a single form of 'transition to capitalism and democracy' but various formations: some more successful than others, some more reformed than others. By 2007, ten of the former communist countries of central and eastern Europe had become members of the European Union (EU). In so doing they had, at least formally, fulfilled the conditions of the *acquis communautaire* which accredit them with the status of modern capitalist democratic states. Other countries claim the formal features of reform while retaining the networks of state socialism. Some remain substantially 'unreformed' and still subscribe, though in an attenuated form, to a socialist type of society. We consider how they have adapted to the fall of the core socialist states and their prospects for further adaptation and adjustment.

Outlooks and outcomes

Following the collapse of communist political hegemony in the European states, most economic reformers conjectured that the Soviet Union and other state socialist societies were politically and ideologically bankrupt and presented a *tabula rasa* on which an advanced form of capitalism could be created. It was assumed that the legacy of the previous regime could be neutralized relatively quickly and that a move to private property, markets and democracy would be ensured through the introduction of the appropriate institutional forms copied from Western practice coupled to positive political leadership.[2] Economic reformers thought that the major social institutions in the old system were completely flawed and that their reform was impossible. The economy was defective because a system of planning and state ownership could not and did not work.[3]

A comprehensive reform process was called for, involving privatization concurrently with destatization, the creation of market competition and price liberalization; the exposure of home industries to foreign competition and full open currency exchange.[4] A priority was placed on privatization which would create the basis of a business class having a stake in the new system, thereby weakening any attempts to revert to statism. Following these economic changes, in a pluralistic society would evolve classes and interests providing the basis of a healthy competitive electoral democracy, which would be 'crafted' from the top by the new self-emancipated elites.

An alternative way to consider the transformation is that based on a path-dependency approach which places considerable weight on the ways that people and institutions are socially embedded in society. Values and norms are socially based and these may continue independently of changes of elites or of the introduction of formally new institutions. A principal difference between these two paradigms is that the path-dependent theorists do not consider post-communist societies to have emerged from a unitary 'totalitarian' or 'socialist' mould. Rather, each state socialist society had unique characteristics. They were mixtures of traditional, oligarchic societies with 'socialistic' welfare state elements. Whereas the system transfer theorists viewed state socialism through the prism of an organic systemic type of totalitarianism[5], this school distinguishes more complicated sets of exchanges.

Such writers take a more sceptical view of the possible effects of 'radical' political change: while the formal institutions may be replaced, the expectations of people and the processes inherited from the past may either continue or be reconstituted.[6] Here the focus is not only on the ability of the new elites to 'craft democracy', to surmount the legacies and institutions left by the old regime. It is considered problematic whether any desired 'system transfer' can effectively copy Western institutions and implant private property, markets, parliaments and competitive elections. A transition from above will not work if the social and institutional preconditions are not in place, including the values and norms of the population.

The chapters in this book illustrate the range of adaptation, malformations and non-adjustments which have taken place. While the central European countries have moved successfully to capitalism and electoral democracy (polyarchy) others have not.

In Chapter 2, Stephen White reminds us that the number of people who lived under communist governments in 2006 was almost as big as it was in 1989. It may be premature to dismiss the transformations in central and parts of eastern Europe as a triumph of capitalism involving, in Francis Fukuyama's words, '... the universalisation of Western liberal democracy as the final form of human government'.[7] Moreover, White points out that in the 1990s 'more than half the adult population of the entire region [of central and eastern Europe] had a positive view of the communist economic system'. Even in the areas of the former German Democratic Republic, a country in which, as Rudi Schmidt (Chapter 7 below) points out, had conditions 'ideal' for system change, popular reaction has not been favourable to the changes which have ensued. Populations in the Czech Republic and Poland may be more favourable to the new economic and political systems but those further east are sceptical. These attitudes are not only the consequence of the previous socialization of communist values, but also reflect dissatisfaction with the outputs of the new regimes.

The shift from state socialism

In the European societies, major reforms occurred between 1991 and 1994: there was significant privatization of property, a major decline of the communist parties and the rise of a competitive party electoral system. Appendix 1.1 lists post-communist countries for four selected years (1989, 1995, 2000, 2006) for four key components[8] of economic change: large-scale privatization (LSP), small-scale privatization (SSP), enterprise restructuring (EnRe) and price liberalization (Pli). The measurement scale for the indicators ranges from 1 to 4+, where 1 represents little or no change from a centrally planned economy and 4+ represents the standards of an industrialized market economy. The reform scores reflect the assessments of EBRD country economists.[9]

Figure 1.1 summarizes these measures for these four key years. Figure 1.1(a) shows the average changes over all 29 countries; Figures 1.1(b)–(d) detail four European countries discussed in some detail in later chapters of this book (Belarus, Czech Republic, Poland, Russia). The major changes took place in the early transition period between 1993 and 1995. Poland started at a higher position than 1 in 1989 when it already had small private enterprises and some price liberalization; also Bosnia, Croatia, Macedonia, Hungary, Montenegro and Slovenia all had at least one positive score over 1 (see details in Appendix 1.1). The Czech Republic and Hungary carried out the most rapid changes, followed later by Russia and Poland. Belarus, it will be noted, unlike the other countries highlighted here, reverted after 1995. By 2006, the overall economic transition, however, is below the levels of the advanced Western industrial countries – even on the formal criteria used by the EBRD. Figure 1.1(a) shows that price liberalization has been most widespread and enterprise restructuring has changed least from the Soviet period.

These data illustrate that by 2000 the foundation of reform (or lack of reform) had been laid in the European and post-USSR countries. In order to plot the extent of the political and economic changes as they affect all the former state socialist societies, I have utilized the work of the Fraser Institute which includes both economic and political indexes. It also has the advantage, unlike the EBRD reports, of including China, Cuba and North Korea.

Figure 1.2 shows the differentiation of post-communist states at the end of the twentieth century – some ten years after the start of transformation.[10] Two major indexes of economic and political transition are considered. The Fraser Institute's Economic Freedom of the World 2000[11] ranks countries on a 10-point scale (0 the least free, 10 the most free).[12] On political freedoms, Freedom House has devised two measures in terms of the levels of political rights and civil liberties.[13] It must be kept in mind that these indexes measure the values and norms of Western societies, especially those of the Anglo-American type of capitalism; also the measures may not be strictly comparable given the problems of data collection in various countries. Nevertheless, they are useful and bring out differences between various countries and groups of countries which is our concern here.

The trajectory of transformation has led to three main groups of countries in terms of economic and political freedom. First: those with political rights and civil liberties sharing many features with advanced Western societies ('Great political reform' on Figure 1.2). Second: an intermediary group of countries constituted of those which have made some progress towards political liberalization.

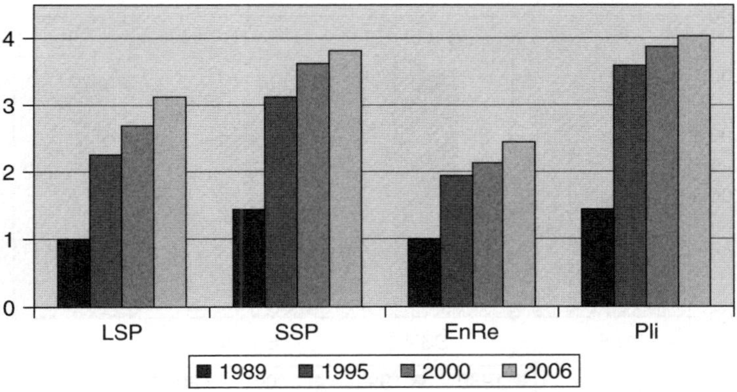

(a) All European post-socialist countries

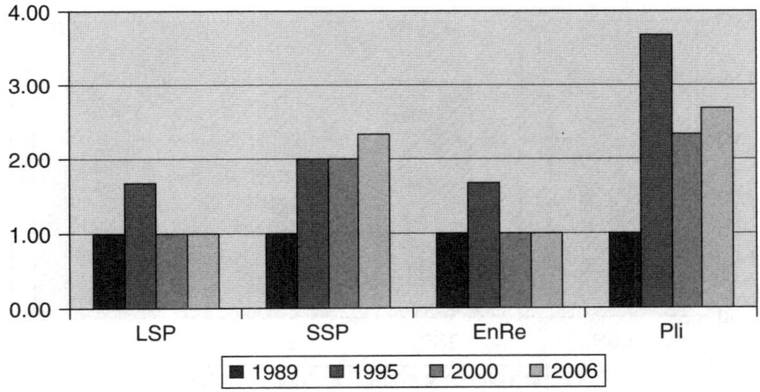

(b) Belarus

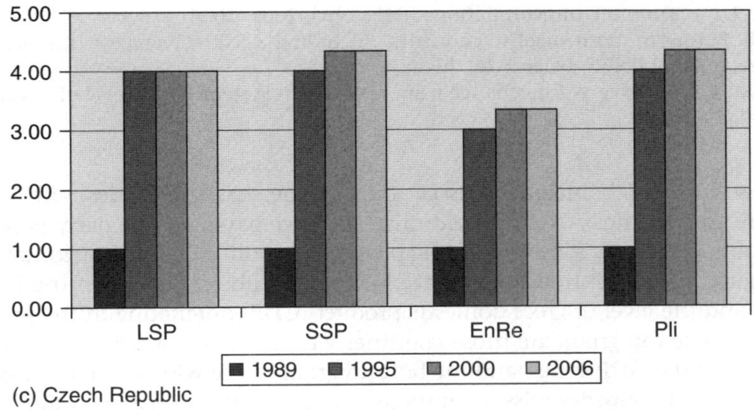

(c) Czech Republic

Figure 1.1 *(Continued)*

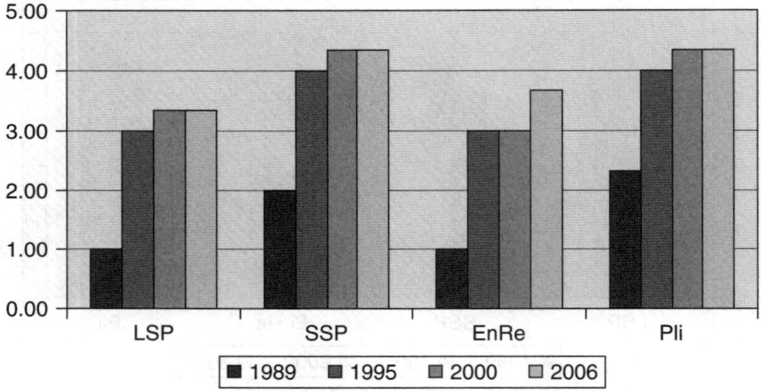

(d) Poland

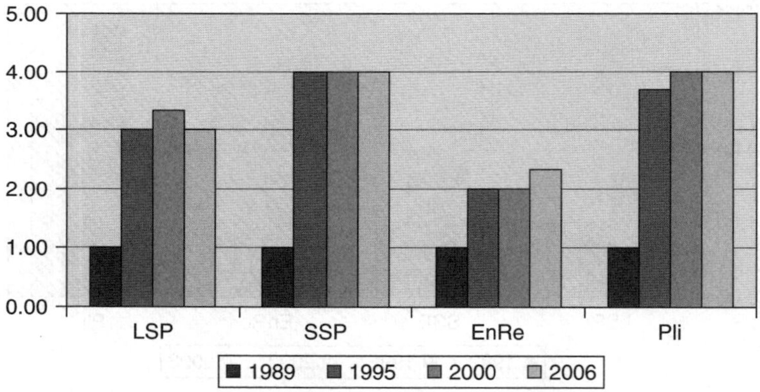

(e) Russia

Figure 1.1 Economic transformation: 1989, 1995, 2000, 2006
(a) all European post-socialist countries, including USSR: (averages); (b) Belarus; (c) Czech Republic; (d) Poland; (e) Russia.
Legend: 1 = no or very little change from communist system; 4+ = level of advanced capitalist country

This sector, which includes Russia and Ukraine, has similarities with Latin American countries. The third group are regimes having a one-party political regime and a largely state-owned and planned economy. On the horizontal axis of Figure 1.2 are plotted the extent of economic liberalization on the Fraser scale and the level of gross domestic product (GDP) originating in the private sector.[14] The top group are those countries with an index of 6 or more on the Fraser and the GDP scales, and the bottom group those with an index under 4 on both. (For countries missing in these sources, I have estimated a value.)

GREAT POLITICAL REFORM		Romania	Hungary Czech Republic Estonia Latvia Lithuania Slovenia Poland Slovakia
PARTIAL POLITICAL REFORM		Bulgaria Ukraine Georgia Russia Croatia Armenia Moldavia Mongolia Macedonia	
LITTLE OR NO POLITICAL REFORM	North Korea Turkmenistan Belarus Cuba	Tajikistan Kyrgyzstan Uzbekistan Kazakhstan Azerbaijan Bosnia	China
	LITTLE OR NO ECONOMIC REFORM	*PARTIAL ECONOMIC REFORM*	*GREAT ECONOMIC REFORM*

Figure 1.2 Political and economic transformation: after ten years of reform

Study of Figure 1.2 shows a very high correlation between economic and civil freedoms. Only one country stands out with an asymmetric relationship between economic and political – that is China which has carried out significant market reforms and is a major player in world economic markets. The top right-hand corner is composed of states which joined the EU in 2004: Hungary, the Czech Republic, Estonia, Latvia, Lithuania, Slovenia, Poland and Slovakia. Romania and Bulgaria, in the 'partial transformation' at this time, joined in 2007. Those with insignificant political and economic change (North Korea, Turkmenistan, Belarus, Cuba and Vietnam) have remained so right up to 2007. And another set of central Asian states, previously in the USSR, Tajikistan, Kyrgyzstan, Uzbekistan, Kazakhstan and Azerbaijan, have maintained features of the previous Soviet system to a considerable degree.

By 2002, privatization[15] of 50 per cent or more of large-scale companies had taken place in only 6 of the 27 countries, another 14 had achieved a 25 per cent level; for small-scale privatization, the figures were much higher: 21 had reached the levels of advanced industrial economies, and another 4 had comprehensive programmes ready for implementation. However, even for the most advanced countries, there is still a considerable level of state ownership and production. By 2004, the new members of the EU have an average of 72.5 per cent of GDP originating from the private sector, south-east Europe following with an average of 65 per cent and the CIS with only 50 per cent (Russia and Ukraine were just above 60 per cent), whereas Belarus was just over 20 per cent.[16] While these EBRD data are useful in comparative work, they hide important differences in the definition and reality of privatization in different countries. Certain forms of the market transition involved 'mixed property' which is not considered in the EBRD classifications. Mixed property is private property in which the state (as one of the proprietors) holds a share of the assets. These figures of state ownership (and control is even wider) reflect the reality of the notion of 'etacratism' suggested by Ovsey Shkaratan in Chapter 8. He contends that there is a deeper set of values underlying the lower level of private ownership in some of the post-Soviet states. People have a different view towards the private ownership of wealth; private ownership of productive assets may be legal but it is widely considered to be illegitimate. This is not just a socialist value, but one, in Russia, predating the Bolshevik period. Such values were subscribed to in the core republics of the USSR, though less so in the Baltic states and the central European ones.

One important conclusion from this analysis is that the list of 'unreformed' countries should include those like Belarus and Turkmenistan; others mentioned above are hybrid systems, with many economic institutions and processes little changed from the previous Soviet period.

These conclusions seriously compromise the idea that a rapid move could be made (even if they would be welcomed by some) from the state socialist system. Rather than a consolidation of 'capitalist economic democracy' espoused by the system transfer school above, a consolidation of a 'hybrid' type of regime seems to be characteristic of a large number of states: societies with some aspects of a market system, but many of the values, processes and institutions remaining from the Soviet period. Those that are more in keeping with the neo-liberal perspective are the states which have joined the EU.

The EU may have been an important influence in the transformation of these societies and is discussed below by Philip Hanson (Chapter 5). His chapter shows that while there remain considerable differences between the new members of the EU, they nevertheless have adopted many of the forms of the Anglo-American form of capitalism, rather than the more corporatist 'continental' form of capitalism.[17] Desire to 'rejoin Europe' was mediated by the conditionality of the Copenhagen Treaty, by which the new member states had to show that conditions were compatible with those of the EU: this boosted the move to marketization, private property, financial liberalization and a reduction in state management of the economy.

Economic development: the move to privatization and markets

Prior to the transformation process, it was widely predicted that, when the burdens of communist rule and central planning were disposed of, the economies would grow and wealth creation would increase. However, the impact of policies had a negative effect; even by 2002, most of the transition countries were at a lower level of GDP than they were at the beginning of the reform period. Seven countries (Poland, Slovenia, Albania, Hungary, Slovakia, Uzbekistan and the Czech Republic) had exceeded the 1989 level,[18] 13 countries achieved between 70 and 95 per cent of their former level, and 7 countries (Russia, Azerbaijan, Tajikistan, Serbia, Ukraine, Moldova and Georgia) had fallen to between 38 and 65 per cent of the former figure.

Figure 1.3 shows the GDP and economic growth of the post-communist countries (and some other countries for comparison) in 2005. Here one notes a wide range of developments. Just three countries are in the bracket of high-income countries as far as GDP per capita is concerned (Slovenia, Hungary and the Czech Republic). Most are in, or just above, the income levels of middle-income countries. Only a few – Ukraine, China, Georgia, Azerbaijan – are below; and three – Kyrgyzstan, Uzbekistan and Tajikistan – are at the level of low-income countries.

As far as economic growth is concerned there appears to be no close relationship between countries which have more developed market and private property relations than others. Russia, Belarus, Kazakhstan, Serbia and China all appear in the groups with a higher than 6 per cent growth in 2005. (Others include the new EU member states of Estonia, Lithuania, Latvia and Slovakia). In analysing the outputs of the post-socialist states one must bear

GDP per capita 2005 (US$)					
Over 10,000	*European Monetary Union*	Slovenia *High-income countries*	Hungary, Czech Republic		
8,000–10,000			Croatia	Estonia	
4,000–8,000		Poland		Lithuania Russia Slovakia	Latvia
2,000–4,000			Albania Bosnia Bulgaria Romania	Belarus Kazakhstan Serbia *Middle-income countries*	
1,000–2,000		Ukraine		China Georgia	Azerbaijan
0–999	Kyrgyzstan Tajikistan			Uzbekistan	
Economic growth (%)	**0–1.99**	**2–3.9**	**4–5.9**	**6–9.9**	**Over 10**

Figure 1.3 Economic growth and per capita GDP: post-communist countries, 2005
No data on: Moldova, Cuba, N. Korea
Source: Economic Indicators 2005, World Bank 2006, http://devdataworldbank.org/data, accessed 8 Dec 2006

in mind that they represent countries at different levels of economic, social and political development.

Martin Myant's contribution (Chapter 6) deals in some detail with developments in one of the more successful new members of the EU, the Czech Republic. He shows the dependency of this state on inward investment. While it had a positive heritage for the development of capitalism (relatively high skill levels, a favourable geographical location, and membership of the EU), the country lags behind the industrial western European states. It has not advanced to join the core states of the world economy. Dependence on foreign companies has limited the autonomous development of Czech companies.

Human development

While economic growth and income per capita are important economic considerations, evaluation should also consider the changes in social development. The Human Development Index is a composite ranking based on a number of factors: life expectancy at birth, adult literacy, primary and tertiary education enrolment, as well as gross domestic product per capita.[19] Figure 1.4 lists the countries of the socialist bloc by country ranking in 1990 – at the start of the transformation process. The highest country (Japan) had a rank of 1. This we may take as a benchmark of levels before the collapse of state socialism in Europe. Three Western countries are cited for comparison (USA ranked 7, Denmark 12 and West Germany 14). Czechoslovakia, ranked 27, followed by Hungary 30, and the USSR 31 had the highest level of human development of the socialist countries. At this time all the European

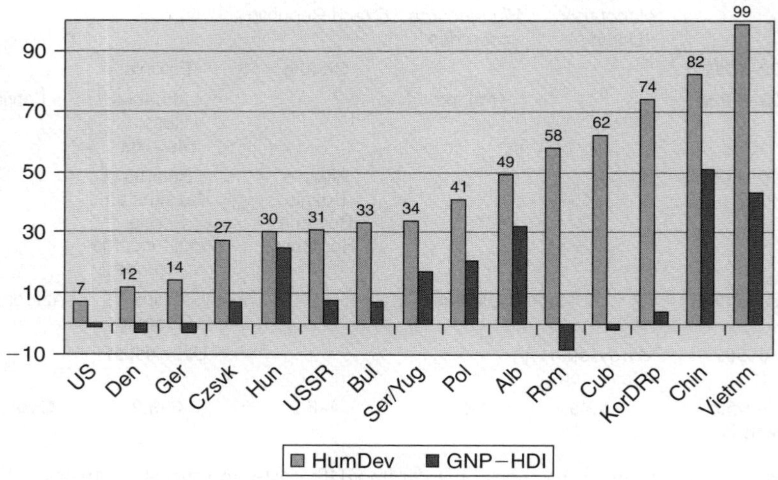

Figure 1.4 Human Development Index and deviation from GDP, 1990

socialist countries (except Romania) were in the 'high human development category' – comprising 53 countries (Romania was 58). Non-European socialist countries were in the medium development echelon: Cuba (62), North Korea (74) and China (82); only Vietnam was in the 'low human development' category (99). The USSR at this time included many previously rural undeveloped republics of central Asia, and the rankings of the European republics would certainly be higher than 31.

A second feature of Figure 1.4 is the index of deviation of HDI from GDP. This is simply the rank of GDP per capital minus the HDI rank: a positive figure indicates that HDI is higher than GDP per capita. Excepting Romania and Cuba, the figure shows the higher performance of the socialist countries measured by the HDI rank compared to the GDP rank. The three top capitalist countries cited all have negative measures. The average of the top 15 advanced capitalist countries in 1990 was +3, and these included the leading European welfare states (e.g. Sweden +3); the coefficient would have been even lower if Australia were excluded (having an index of +12). The average for the socialist bloc (including Vietnam, China and North Korea) was 37.5. For the European socialist countries it was lower, 13, but still more than four times as great as the leading capitalist states. The difference is accounted for by the greater transfer of resources by the socialist governments to human welfare. The poor did relatively better in the socialist countries than in the capitalist ones. From a developmental perspective, the socialist states (with the notable exception in this case of Cuba) were successful in channelling a high proportion of GDP into education and health, while concurrently reducing the propensity of the population to consume.

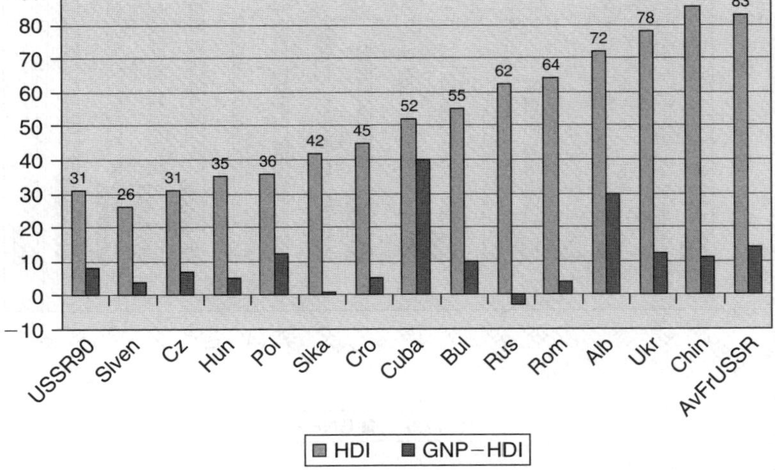

Figure 1.5 Human Development Index and deviation from GDP, 2003

How then did the transformation process affect human development? Figure 1.5 considers country rankings in the year 2003. Remember: the lower the ranking, the higher the level of human development. The data are not strictly comparable because the number of states in 2003 was greater than in 1990. The disintegration of the USSR led to another 14 states being formed: in total there were 160 in 1990 and 177 in 2003. Even allowing for this difference, Figure 1.5 shows the relative position of the state socialist societies and for comparison, it includes the USSR in 1990. There are three major groups. First, the central European societies which maintained or even bettered their relative positions: Slovenia, Hungary, Czech Republic, Poland. Poland, for example, in 2003 was ranked 36, compared to 41 in 1990. Cuba has risen from 62 to 52, and China (bearing mind the increase in states) had kept its relative position: 82 in 1990 and 85 in 2003.

Second are the countries of the former USSR: these have suffered a considerable relative decline in levels of human development. These are illustrated in Figure 1.6 which enumerates the ranking of the former republics of the USSR as well as the USSR in 1990. I have also calculated the average of all the former republics in 2003 which acts as a comparison with the figure for the USSR in 1990.

The USSR ranked 31 in 1990; the areas of the former USSR had fallen to an average of 83 in 2003. The central Asian republics and Ukraine all had positions higher than 60 (Ukraine 78 and Tajikistan 122). The Russian Federation was now ranked at 62 and Belarus 67. The Baltic states were all much higher than the USSR average (Estonia 38, Lithuania 39 and Latvia 48). Compared to their

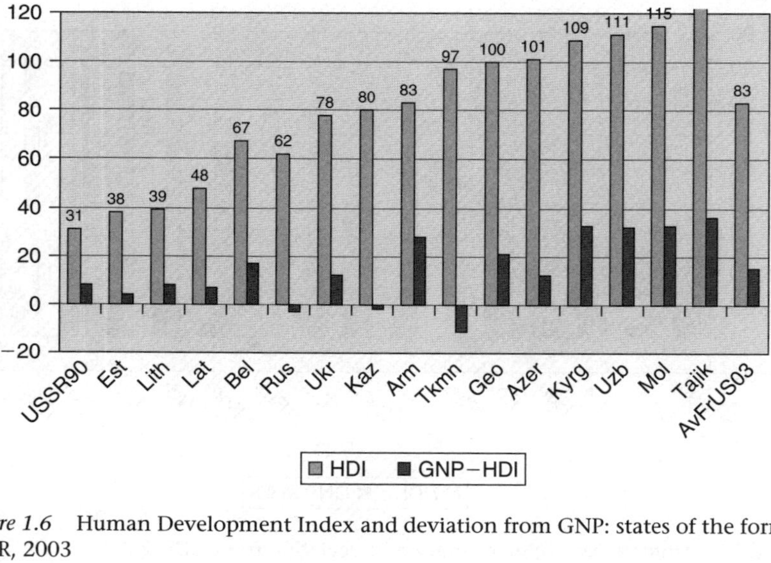

Figure 1.6 Human Development Index and deviation from GNP: states of the former USSR, 2003

relative position in 1990, only Estonia and Lithuania had survived relatively well – though below the previous USSR ranking. Bearing in mind that the Baltic states had the highest standards in the USSR, one might charitably conclude that they just maintained their relative position, though the Russian Federation had greatly worsened. The Caucasus had also fallen well below even the level of the Russian Federation; Armenia was now 83 (just below Ecuador) and Georgia 100 (just below Iran). Georgia had a particularly significant decline, as it was one of the most developed republics in the USSR.

When we consider GNP minus HDI, we find some differences in the two time periods (see Figure 1.7). There were two groups of countries: Cuba which had a negative GDP–HDI of −2 in 1990, now moved to a positive one of 40, Romania also had a similar increase from −8 to +4, and Bulgaria had a modest increase from 7 to 10; the countries of the former USSR actually increased in their index from +8 to +15. For all the other countries there was a contraction in the index. If we exclude Cuba, the average falls from 18 in 1990 to 12 in 2003. Figure 1.7 sums the former republics of the USSR in 2003 into one category to compare with the USSR in 1990. The data are arranged with the deviations in 1990 falling from left to right. What seems to have happened is that the countries which experienced greater marketization had *declines* in their HDI, those which had less marketization actually increased the gap between HDI and GDP. China, Russia, Hungary and Poland had significant negative changes. The central Asian republics of the USSR had highly positive rankings of HDI over GNP: Kyrgyzstan 33, Uzbekistan 32, Tajikistan 36; Moldova had 33, Belarus 17 and Georgia 21. These figures are also affected by the considerable decline in GNP, and the carry-over effects from the previous socialist period. These findings are probably the root causes for the 'nostalgia'

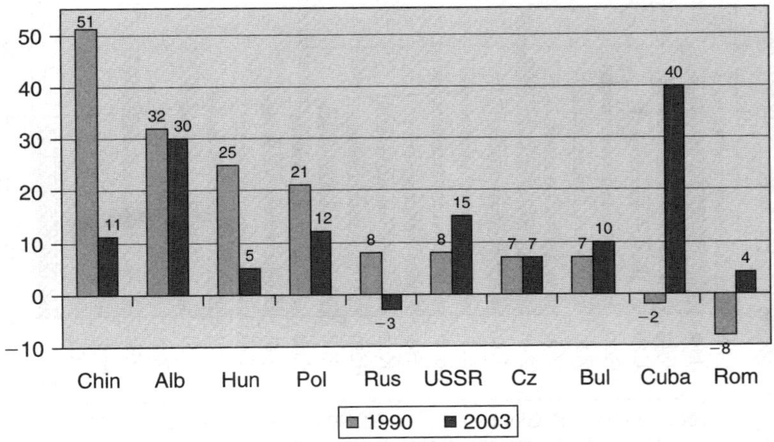

Figure 1.7 GNP – HDI 1990, 2003: state socialist countries

for state socialism referred to in Chapter 2 by Stephen White. In these countries, many groups of the population – white-collar state employees, professionals such as doctors, the scientific intelligentsia, as well as the poor, were relatively better off under state socialism.

Inequality

While the level of national income and rate of economic growth are important economic variables, so also is the distribution of income. The state socialist societies were equalitarian in income distribution and had relatively little poverty: the two major causes of gross income inequality under capitalism are unequal private ownership of productive assets (giving rise to 'unearned income') and unemployment. The state socialist countries had neither of these, though inequality derived from bureaucratic position. One of the objectives of the reform programme was not only to increase wealth but also to redistribute in such a way as to provide economic incentives to encourage initiative. Figure 1.8 details the Gini indexes for two periods: the first before 1994 (most of the data are for the year 1992); the second for the period after 1999 (most of the data are for 2001 and 2002).[20] Gini indexes show the ratio of the richest group to the poorest: a figure of 0 represents perfect equality (everybody receives the same), whereas 100 perfect inequality (the rich receive the total, the poor nothing). (Sometimes an index as a proportion of 1 is used – as in Nick Manning's chapter below.) The Gini index measures income inequality which ignores other forms of income (state provision of education, health care, housing) (see Chapter 9 by Nick Manning); income,

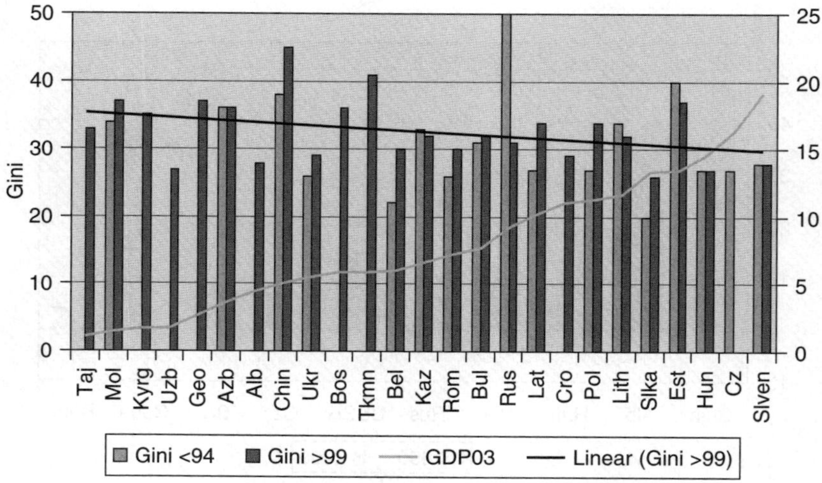

Figure 1.8 Gini indexes <1994, >1999, GDP 2003

however, is the major component of inequality and allows comparisons to be made. Figure 1.8 lists data available for post-socialist countries and is arranged with the countries in ascending order of GDP for 2003, shown by the right-hand axis (measuring thousands of dollars per capita). The downward-sloping line is the trend for the Gini index for the years post-1999 and is linked to the left-hand axis.

The data show considerable inequalities. Inequality has risen: before 1994 (though after the fall of state socialism), the average for all the post-socialist countries was 30.9 rising to 32.7 in the period after 1999, when three countries had indexes over 40: China, Turkmenistan and Russia. Cuba also experienced a rise in inequality – as indicated in Chapter 13 below, the Gini coefficient rose from 22 in 1986 to 41 in 1999. Excepting for countries such as the USA (41) and capitalist developing societies, such as Brazil (59), most industrialized Western countries are in the 20s (Germany 28, Denmark 25). Only nine of the post-socialist countries were 30 or under: Uzbekistan, Albania, Ukraine, Belarus, Croatia, Slovenia, Slovakia, Hungary and the Czech Republic. There is a mix here of 'unreformed' (Belarus and Ukraine) and 'reformed' countries (Hungary, Czech Republic).

The correlation between GDP and the Gini index 1999, indicated by the trend line, is −0.36 – the higher the GDP, the lower the inequality. For an earlier period I calculated the relationship between the Gini index and ranking of privatization: there was a mildly negative correlation of −0.18[21] – the lower the level of privatization, the higher the level of inequality. But in Russia, a relatively high level of privatization gave rise to very high levels of inequality. The index for Russia was well above the trend line in the earlier period but has fallen during the period of Putin's presidency. Primary materials exporting countries (Azerbaijan, Turkmenistan, Moldova and Russia) all have (or have had) high levels of income inequality. This is probably due to the low labour costs involved in oil and gas industries, as well as the high levels of income accruing to owners. Only countries (such as Norway) which strongly regulate oil profits, avoid the excessive concentration of wealth derived by a small number of wealthy owners. The high inequality levels in Moldova, Georgia and China are probably associated with the very low income levels of some workers as well as the large numbers of unemployed. Nick Manning takes up further the problems of inequality in Chapter 9, where he focuses on the experience of Russia. Factors which influence the extent of inequality include the large differentials between the private and the state sectors. The latter are characterized by wage arrears and pay restraint, even during period of inflation – both neo-liberal policies of restricting state expenditure.

We may conclude that the transformation has led to higher differentials than in the socialist period and that these levels are higher than in the advanced Western states (with the exception of the USA). They are negatively correlated with GNP, and in this respect follow Western capitalist countries. The 2004 new members of the EU all have relatively lower levels of inequality – this of course being related to the higher average level of GDP. The post-socialist central European societies have also been more successful in creating a prosperous middle class which is notably lacking in Russia. For the really polarized societies, Nick Manning illustrates the hopelessness of people who find themselves in poverty. Here some of his examples provide a backdrop to the high levels of mortality described by Larry King and David Stuckler in Chapter 11.

Health provision and unemployment

In addition to the level of GDP and its distribution, health and level of mortality are important indexes of effective economic adaptation. Equity is not only related to income distribution but also is conditioned by how states cope with employment and poverty. One of the major characteristics of the previous state socialist societies was the comprehensive provision of a state-financed and delivered health system. The post-communist societies have attempted in different ways to graft private provision onto the state systems. Current heath expenditure[22] classified by public and private sources is shown on Figure 1.9[23] which also illustrates differences with advanced capitalist societies (USA, UK, Denmark and Germany).

Study of Figure 1.9 shows a wide range of public and private provision in the former state socialist societies. Nevertheless, the post-socialist countries have a higher level of public health provision and a lower level of private provision than other countries *at the same level of development*. There are four major groupings: first, a group of states with higher public provision of

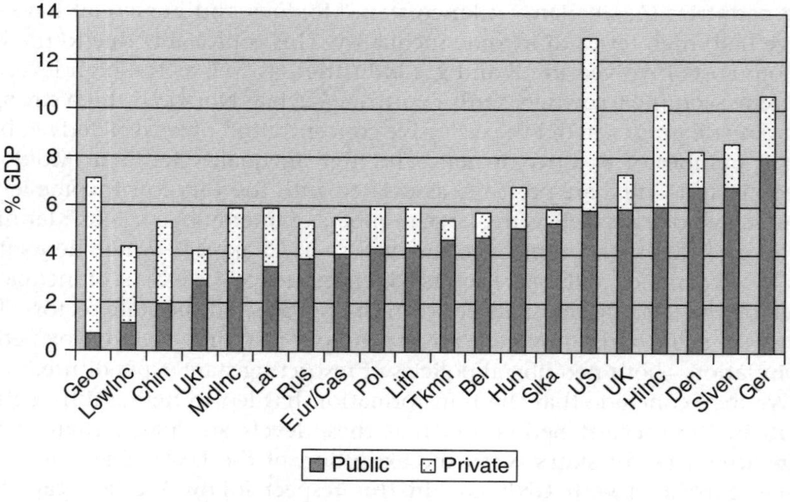

Figure 1.9 Public and private health provision

health services than high-income countries: these are the central European countries of Slovenia and the Czech Republic. Second, a cluster with public provision above the middle-income countries: Slovakia, Macedonia, Hungary, Estonia, Belarus, Turkmenistan, Lithuania, Poland, Russia, Latvia, Armenia and Bosnia (not all shown on the figure). A third group is below the public provision of middle-income countries – Bulgaria, Ukraine, Serbia, Moldova. Finally comes a cluster with very low public provision – even below that of low-income countries: Kazakhstan, Uzbekistan, Kyrgyzstan, Albania, Romania, Tajikistan, Georgia, Azerbaijan and China. A distinctive feature of provision for the first two groups is that all these countries had lower provision of private services than the average in both high-income and middle-income countries. Public health expenditure correlates very highly with level of gross national income: the Pearson r is 0.82 (calculation based on all post-socialist countries).

For the former state socialist countries with high levels of spending on public health, the level of private expenditure falls considerably. The difference between the average of high-income countries' expenditure on private and public provision is very much less in the former state socialist societies than in Western societies at medium to high levels of income. This difference, however, may be due to lower costs of health services in the former socialist countries (lower salaries of physicians, and lower prices of drugs). The low-income post-socialist countries, generally, have higher private health expenditure than public expenditure: Uzbekistan, Kyrgyzstan, Tajikistan and Georgia have even higher proportions of private expenditure on health. Clearly, here people with the money to do so have to spend it on health. There is a negative correlation between GNI and private health spending of −0.264. Overall, relatively higher spending on *public* health indicates the footprint of the socialist welfare state.

Peggy Watson (Chapter 10) shows on the basis of her research in Poland the inadequacy of health service delivery which has been grafted onto the previous comprehensive (though inadequate) health system. She points to a greater differentiation in the health system driven by market and class forces. By giving the individual responsibility under conditions where many groups of individuals do not have the resources to exercise that responsibility, the neo-liberal strategy creates serious health hazards for the poorer groups in the population. Market transformation, therefore, 'ignores justice, need and equality'. The conditional capacities of people are conditioned by their market position and has led to a negative evaluation of health provision after the reforms. She points to the fact that health service provision started from a different basis from that in the Western democracies. In the latter, public health widened citizen rights and limited class inequalities, whereas in the post-socialist societies, they started from a base in which there was a relative equality in the first place. The shift to the inequality of the market has anchored rights in property and created class rights which are reflected in the unequal provision of health services.

Unemployment is a consequence not only of economic conditions but is also mediated by state policy which may influence wages either through minimum wage policies or through income support of the unemployed. It is exceedingly difficult to procure data for *long-term* unemployment. UNDP collected a number of figures for 2003.[24] As a proportion of the labour force, the United States was one of the lowest with only 0.7 per cent unemployed, the UK 1.2 per cent; Germany had a rate of 4.6 per cent (one of the highest of western European countries) – no doubt due to the difficulties of absorbing into employment citizens from the former German Democratic Republic. The former state socialist societies cited had very much higher rates: the Czech Republic 3.9 per cent, Hungary 2.5 per cent, Poland 9.8 per cent and Slovakia 10.7 per cent (no other data are available).[25] When we consider registered unemployment, there are marked differences in levels of unemployment in European states. We might distinguish, however, between three major divisions. At one end of the scale are post-socialist countries similar to the USA and UK with relatively low average (registered) unemployment of under 10 per cent of the working population. Such countries include Slovenia, the Czech Republic, Hungary; at the other end are those similar to Mediterranean countries (like Spain) – rates of unemployment are over 15 per cent in Lithuania, Poland, Slovakia and Bulgaria.[26] Such high levels have persisted over time and are indicative of lack of job creation as well as low labour mobility.

The creation of new jobs through foreign direct investment is probably a positive feature for the central European countries (particularly Hungary and the Czech Republic). Structural problems of the economy, general economic slowdown, destruction of many industries and agriculture, plus the immobility of the population, are contributory factors in the eastern areas.

Mortality

One measurement of the effects of human development and health care on people's lives may be derived from an index of the probability of persons dying before the age of 60. In the UK, of people born between 2000 and 2005, only 8.7 per cent are likely to die before the age of 60; in Germany the figure is 8.8, in Sweden 7.2; the USA is one of the highest in the developed world – 11.8 per cent.[27] The rates for the post-communist societies, on which data are available, are very much higher. They are shown in Figure 1.10. Only Albania (11.4) and Slovenia (11.8) rank with the highest OECD country (USA) at 11.8 per cent; Hungary is 18.3, Poland 15.1; Russia and Ukraine are 31.6 and 31 respectively. In other words, just under a third of babies born in Russia and Ukraine between 2000 and 2005 have a probability of dying before reaching the age of 60.

The experience of the post-communist countries is very mixed with respect to life expectancy. As Larry King and David Stuckler point out in Chapter 11, 15 years after the beginning of transformation, 11 out of 25 countries have

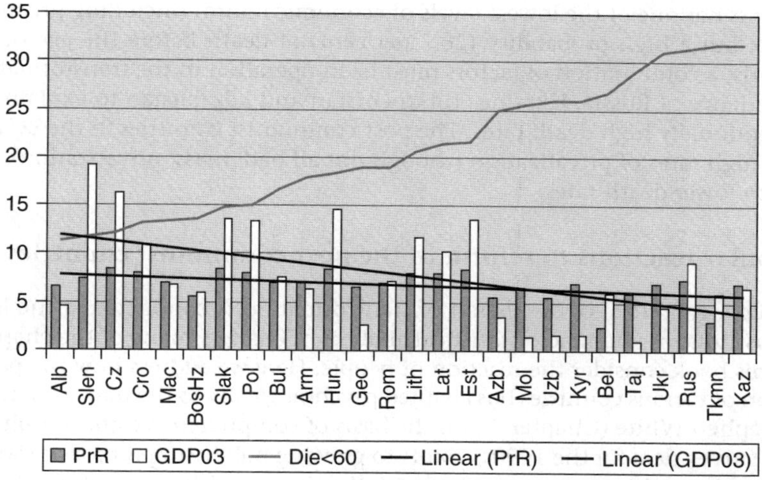

Figure 1.10 Probability of dying before age 60: rank of privatization and GDP, 2003
Legend: PrR, privatization rank; GDP03, level of privatization in 2003; Die < 60, likelihood of dying before 60 as proportion of age cohort born 2000–5
Privatization: EBRD, *Transition Report* 2003 rank
Probability at birth of surviving to the age of 60 years: *Human Development Report* 2005 (data for percentage of cohort born 2000–5)
GDP: *Human Development Report* 2005, data for 2003 (US$ PPP)
Pearson r = death : privatization – 0.44; Death : GDP = −0.51

failed to retain even their pre-transition levels of life expectancy; and they contend that the declines in some of the post-communist countries represent 'a peacetime mortality crisis unparalleled in modern history'.

Reasons for this decline include the deterioration of the health services brought about by constraints on government spending; many of the factors mentioned above – unemployment, the rise of a significant proportion of the population in poverty and stress consequent on the destabilizing effects of transformation policies – are discussed in some detail in the chapter by King and Stuckler (Chapter 11). They argue that effect of large-scale *mass* privatization is at the root of the increase in the mortality rate in Russia. On the basis of the data above, I compared the level of privatization with the death rates and found a negative correlation of −0.44: that is, in countries with a higher level of privatization (of all types), the lower the chance of dying. What also affects the death rate is the level of GDP: the correlation between the probability of death and GDP was −0.51; the higher the GDP, the lower the chance of dying.

At one end, Albania is exceptional: it does not have a particularly high rate of privatization nor a high level of GDP, but its citizens have the highest chance (of the post-socialist states) of reaching age 60. At the other end of the scale, Russia has high privatization and higher GDP, but a very high death rate.

Belarus has one of the lowest levels of economic reform (including privatization), but a high probability (26.7 per cent) of death before the age of 60. Clearly, a combination of factors must be in operation in the transformation experience of Russia, Ukraine, Turkmenistan and Kazakhstan to explain the exceptionally high death rates. The post-communist countries in the EU also had high rates of privatization (though not all had 'mass' privatization), but much lower death rates.

Popular reactions to reform in the post-communist countries

While a great deal of discussion of transformation is conducted at the level of institutions and macro statistical analysis of change, many of the chapters in this book consider the reaction of people. Here we address how the population of various countries has adapted psychologically to the transformation.

Stephen White (Chapter 2), on the basis of comprehensive public opinion poll survey data for the 1990s, points to growing public support for the Soviet way of doing things in comparison with the situation following reform. While there is a generally positive attitude to the political changes, the social and economic shortcomings of the transformation have led to public disapproval. These surveys show that significant proportions of the population find life worse, not better, under post-Soviet conditions. There is particularly support for the Soviet-era provision of employment, economic stability, equality and public order. In Russia and Ukraine, White finds that the current regime performance is regarded as being even worse than under state socialism. Post-communist rule is associated with crime and corruption, is considered to be remote, irresolute and weak, it is 'short-sighted, bureaucratic ... parasitic, illegal ... and incompetent'. Significant proportions of the population even complain that they have 'less influence over the making of public policy than they enjoyed in the communist period, in spite of the introduction of competitive elections ...'. Western-type competitive democracy is not widely regarded positively in Belarus, Ukraine and Russia. While most people in these countries thought a return to Soviet rule is unlikely, there is an increasing respect for the principles on which Soviet rule was based: the positive role of the state over employment, provision of welfare and public management.

Rudi Schmidt (Chapter 7) outlines the changes that have taken place in the provinces of the former German Democratic Republic, now absorbed as a constituent part of the German Federal Republic. The conditions for a successful transition to democracy and capitalism were ideal in the former GDR: there was wide backing for reunification, the people were highly educated and motivated; more importantly, the host country, West Germany, was rich, politically stable and economically successful and willing to accept the financial burdens of transformation. The country too was able to offer 'ready-made' institutions to put in place and had the means to do so. After an initial period of popular euphoria, Schmidt points to unfavourable popular reactions to developments. These were consequent on the high levels of unemployment, deindustrialization and the imposition of 'foreign' personnel and institutions. People became passive and alienated: even by 1993, he writes, people increasingly identified with the former GDR rather than a unified Germany. We have here the formation of a 'retrospective GDR identity'.

As in other states described below by Stephen White, David Ost and David Lane, the reality of the new market relations and competitive party politics fell short of expectations. This cannot be explained solely in terms of material deprivation, for the massive economic transfers from the Federal Republic to the GDR gave a higher standard of living than in other post-communist countries. Schmidt shows that there was a fundamental disharmony between the values of the host society and those internalized in the GDR. Many of the new German citizens found that a market society did not provide the kinds of personal satisfaction claimed by its advocates; consequently, the successor communist parties have received considerable public backing.

A similar theme is raised both by David Ost's and David Lane's essays (Chapters 4 and 3 respectively). They contend that many people personally disadvantaged by the conditions of transformation still have positive sentiments towards the market and reform. Ost points out that an ideology of 'bad capitalism' defines the unpopular market reality. What people aspire to, he argues, is a successful 'good capitalism' which has been denied them by the reformers. The peculiar conditions of neo-liberal reform policies have incorporated the traditional left wing into the right wing, accepting the rhetoric of neo-liberal conditions of reform and private property. The causes of economic and general discontent are defined in terms of 'identity' politics – the butt of discontent is projected against the weak, ethnic minorities, rather than against those manipulating political power. This has occurred, Ost contends, because of the association of public property and non-market relations with the anti-democratic character of the former communist order. Private property then is a constituent part of a truly democratic society which can only be brought about by a transition to capitalism. To oppose the market and private property is labelled derogatively as 'populist' and 'anti-democratic'. Market ideas are popular, its reality not so; the 'hidden hand' of the market does not provide benign guidance and control of the economy, but is guided by that of the swindler plundering public funds. Hence, Ost points out that the corruption of the market, rather than the market itself, is regarded as the cause of public disenchantment.

Lane's chapter also addresses the question of the movers of transformation. He claims that in addition to other social 'identities', classes are crucial in the transformation process: they define the winners in the privatization policy as new owners of assets as a source of wealth. Based on survey reports, he contends that in central and eastern Europe, class is a crucial indicator for a wide range of inequalities and conditions. In Ukraine and Russia, class identification is closely linked to attitudes to transformation and political outlook. Like Ost, he notes the absence of a widely based movement opposed to the reform process. A lack of class consciousness deflects political opposition to focus on non-class actors as sources of social and political problems. But, despite the widespread suffering caused by reforms, there is still a belief that liberal recipes of marketization and privatization could work, if properly implemented.

The studies by White, Schmidt, Watson, Ost and Lane indicate an underlying social and political malaise at the root of many of the post-communist countries. Such disenchantment might be indicative of latent revolutionary forces against the whole reform process, which could spring to life, as in the 'Orange Revolution': the important proviso is that sufficient organizational and ideological energy have to be available. A lack of counter-reform opposition is partly explained by the association of private property and the market with the desired state of democracy, and the space occupied by civil society organizations which are ideologically neo-liberal in form, supporting the existing strategy of reforms.

The state socialist survivors

While transformation of the European states has dominated discussion, little attention has been given to the effects of the fall of European state socialism on other states constituting the 'socialist world'. Here we need to address questions about the driving motors of the reform of the socialist systems: whether similar factors are at work, whether system change has simply been delayed, or whether there are fundamental differences between the survivors and the transformed European socialist states.

Satoshi Mizobata (Chapter 16) considers the wider effects of the collapse of the European socialist states. Unlike African countries, the Asian ones have positively adapted their economies to post-communist conditions. He points out that changes in their economies predated the fall of the communist bloc. The IMF and other agencies had already played an important stabilizing role, which enabled conditions for foreign investment which in turn absorbed the 'transformation shock'. Foreign financial and economic assistance to Vietnam, for example, exceeded that of the USSR and, even before 1990, Vietnam had a socialist-oriented market economy. The Asian countries were experiencing a dual transformation: one from underdevelopment to a modern economy with a move from a socialist economy to a market one. China pursued modernization then marketization, whereas Vietnam carried out marketization, then modernization. The pace of change and the process of adaptation were much slower. As they moved gradually to marketization and the institution of private property, they developed a 'non-Anglo-American' version of capitalism. North Korea was quite exceptional among the Asian countries. It was dependent on the socialist bloc for energy, technology and markets. The country suffered a 'remarkable shock' consequent on the fall of the USSR which is detailed by Soyoung Kwon in Chapter 14.

The African continent was negatively influenced by the collapse of the USSR. African countries with a 'socialist orientation', Mizobata considers, had accepted to a much greater extent the Soviet economic model and were dependent on economic assistance. They were less able to accept the conditions laid down for aid by the United States – democratization and economic liberalization – and by the World Bank for 'good governance'. With the decline of the Soviet bloc, Africa became less important to the West politically, and economic aid could be suspended consequent on the non-fulfilment of political conditions.

As outlined in Chapter 12 by Mario Nuti, Belarus poses the question as to whether a reformed 'market socialism' could be a 'resilient' and 'sustainable' alternative to capitalism. Belarus avoided the disorganization and chaos of transformation and moved to what Nuti calls 'a command economy without central planning'. Its economic performance has been much superior to many of the reformed economies of the former Soviet Union. Its neighbour, Russia, provided a very poor transformation example. He shows that Belarus has had real rises in national income; moreover, the country has had low unemployment, a favourable Gini index and little poverty. Political coordination is maintained by the Communist Party whose power is little changed from the Soviet system. In place of state planning, the economy has moved to the market, thus eliminating the 'shortage economy' and suppressed inflation. It has maintained public ownership. The state remains the collective entrepreneur and production regulator, and prioritizes investment. Nuti considers whether such a model could have been applied to the 'entire ex-Soviet area'. The market could have been used to allocate resources without shifting the ownership of assets from the public sector to private ownership. A key condition, however, is the support afforded by Russia's natural energy resources which, consequent on international trade, are needed to sustain the economies. It becomes problematic, however, when one considers the long-term prospects: can Belarus (and could the states of the former USSR) sustain its (their) economic performance in the long run, concurrent on exclusion from the world system? This remains a problem which is outside the parameters of this book.

China was not dependent on the European socialist states. The country had long ago taken an independent course from the USSR: it had successfully entered the world economy, had a very high rate of economic growth and was a stable political order. As Jeanne Wilson points out in Chapter 15, developments in other communist countries were utilized in debates about the course of development in China itself and she illustrates this point by contrasting the positions of Chinese reformers and conservatives. From an economic point of view, the fall of state socialism in Europe had little effect on China. Many in the political elites saw the collapse as justifying China's own economic reforms. The USSR, it was claimed, had delayed entering the world economy and therefore was excluded from the most advanced forces of production. Chinese policy in entering the global economic market was vindicated.

More importantly, perhaps, Gorbachev's policy of 'glasnost' (openness) was seen as a politically destabilizing course, leading to political disintegration. This was used to legitimate the suppression of protesting groups in Tiananmen Square. As Wilson points out, the failure of Gorbachev's political policy – the attempt to install 'a humanitarian democratic socialism' – became a 'compelling negative example' and weakened those who wished to adopt similar policies in China. One element in the collapse of the European communist regimes was the role of national and ethnic identities, and Chinese policy makers called for greater autonomy for them as well as the promotion of regional economic development. The Chinese leadership, however, was confronted with the consequences of the collapse: the phenomenon of the 'coloured' revolutions. These were seen as an attempt by the USA to foment regime change through support of political groups to establish pro-US regimes. The Chinese response here was to restrict developments which sought to allow greater penetration of Western media, and to exert greater supervision of NGOs. For the Chinese leadership, the fall of European state socialism justified their own form of market socialism and legitimated the continuing hegemony of the Communist Party.

Developments in the Democratic People's Republic of Korea (DPRK) are addressed by Soyoung Kwon in Chapter 14. She points out that the country preserves many of its previous features: a formal hegemonic single party, an official dominant ideology, a dominant state sector and public ownership. She notes that, unlike the European state socialist countries, the ruling elites have been closed for a long period and succession has followed a kin-based trajectory. The collapse of the European socialist states certainly had a negative influence on North Korean society. It has been accompanied by military threats emanating from the USA. Response has been to rely on a 'military first' ideology. However, this should not deflect attention from changes in the economy which have taken place since 2001. Moderate economic reforms have occurred which are similar in character to those in the early days of perestroika in the USSR and in China. There has been a moderate shift to markets both in retail trade and for labour, foreign exchange rates have been made more realistic. While there has been a rise in legitimate family businesses, the formation of economic zones, and a move to profit maximization in enterprises, state control and ownership of the economy have been maintained. Kwon's prognosis is that Korea will adopt the Chinese and Vietnamese type of reforms: development of a type of market socialism. Three factors impede more radical reforms. First, internally there is an absence of a managerial 'counter-elite' which could shift the economy in the direction of private property. The political leadership has kept power within a kin-based personal network. Second, the country has been under military threat which has strengthened military interests and made the ruling elite less willing to experiment with reform. Third, the experience of the European post-socialist countries, as detailed in this book, have not led to significant economic advances in public welfare.

Like North Korea, Cuba also faced significant economic disruption and contraction following the fall of the USSR: it lost its main partners in aid, trade and investment which had helped secure Cuban independence in the face of the Cold War embargoes presented by the USA. While Cuba initially experienced significant economic decline, politically it remained robust and introduced only marginal reforms. Susan Eckstein in Chapter 13 shows how Cuba survived with the help of remittances sent by expatriate Cubans in the USA. This, however, is a double-edged sword. The remittances themselves have destabilizing effects on the regime. The receipt of large sums of dollars has led to a dollarization of the currency. Social and economic life became 'transnationalized'. The peso economy is undermined which, in turn, reduces the motivation to work and to seek education. The recipients of remittances are largely middle class and white which leads to the growth of class distinction. The Gini coefficient has risen from 22 to 41 between 1986 and 1999. More important perhaps is the erosion of the moral order of socialism. Dollarization undermines the welfare economy, it encourages a consumption ethic and an Americanization of culture. Ironically, perhaps the economic and other sanctions put in place by the USA may prove less effective in undermining the Cuban economy than the remittance economy fuelled by expatriate dollars. While the internal infrastructure of Castro's Cuba remains intact, there is a moral decay which may undermine the system. Without the support of the former socialist bloc, Cuba is an example of the fact that one cannot build socialism in one country, particularly if it is surrounded by a hostile world power.

Conclusion

Twenty years after the inauguration of perestroika by Gorbachev, we witness not the renewal of the world system of state socialism, but its succession in Europe by different forms of capitalist market societies, and hybrid market-administered economies elsewhere. In analysing these changes one has to bear in mind that the internal economic and political transformations have taken place under conditions of increasing globalization and internationalization. The movement to the market in many countries preceded the economic restructuring associated with the political changes following 1989. International financial organizations, such as the IMF and World Bank, were able to exert enormous influence over developing economies. The ideological sphere is also dominated by neo-liberalism – a belief in the relatively unrestricted role of the market under conditions of private property, profit maximization, stable currencies and free trade. The fall of the planned economies has accelerated the spread of neo-liberalism.

There are three major outcomes of transformation: a definite shift to capitalism, the formation of hybrid regimes and non-reform. As illustrated in Figure 1.11, three components of transformation are defined: ownership of assets, type of political power, form of economic coordination. A revolution to capitalism occurs when: there occurs the privatization of the economy, a polyarchic system of political power and the market acting as the major coordinator of the economy; an unreformed system maintains effective state power in these three dimensions; most of the post-communist societies are hybrid regimes with a mixture of state ownership, state control of political power and economic coordination. Market-socialist regimes – such as Belarus and China – are a particular type of hybrid regime. They lack the political coordination provided by polyarchy (electoral democracy), though they have allowed both the functioning of the market economic mechanism and elements of private ownership.

The economic and social legacy of each state socialist society shaped its character after the collapse. Those countries in central Europe bordering on the EU (Poland, Slovenia, Slovakia, Hungary, German Democratic Republic and Czech Republic) have all transformed more effectively than those in the former USSR. They have higher levels of GNP and more secure and stable parliamentary systems. These countries were less favourably politically disposed towards the communist system epitomized by the USSR, making the replacement of state socialism easier. The external factors were also favourable for systemic change. The promise of membership of the EU required the fulfilment of economic, political and social conditions to bring them into line with those of the EU. The advantages offered by the EU in terms of economic help, and the promise of future 'levelling up' to western European standards, legitimated the transition to private property, markets and electoral democracy.

These changes have not been without costs. Even in the most successful countries, significant sections of the population have suffered unemployment, greater uncertainty, stress and loss of identity. For many (not all) nostalgia for the benefits of state socialism has *increased*: a retrospective identity with socialism has developed. Writers in this book point to the weaknesses of the new post-communist regimes; however, there is still widespread support for reform and little likelihood of a reversion to the former socialist system.

	POLITICAL POWER			
ASSETS	**Polyarchy/Plural**	**Mixed**	**State**	*ECONOMIC COORDINATION*
Private	*REVOLUTION TO CAPITALISM*			*Market*
Mixed		*HYBRID REGIME*	*MARKET-SOCIALIST*	*Mixed*
State			*UNREFORMED*	*State*

Figure 1.11 Outcomes of transformation: three types of regimes

People aspire to 'good capitalism', effective markets leading to wealth creation and prosperity. Whether the trajectory of world capitalism and globalization, which has led to growing polarization of rich and poor, both within and between countries, can deliver yet remains to be seen.

The countries to the east of Poland have had a relatively slow move to the market and electoral democracy. These include the large and populous countries of Russia and Ukraine, which have had a relatively unsuccessful transition to capitalism. They have, however, made significant inroads into state property and have developed market relations, especially in the retail sector. All these countries (with the exception of Belarus) have experienced much higher levels of poverty and some extreme income differentials. Most have weak pluralistic political structures, with dominant elites and weak civil societies. They are hybrid regimes having elements of capitalism but retaining many of the features of state socialism.

A significant number of countries have adapted to the fall of the European socialist countries by maintaining significant institutions of the state socialist era. China, Cuba, North Korea, Belarus and the former Soviet republics of central Asia have kept their political institutions and personnel fairly intact. Even here, however, the world economic system is having effects. In both Cuba and China, the norms of socialism are being weakened, income inequalities have grown to levels of capitalist states. North Korea is beginning economic reforms which are likely to follow the path of China. The types of reform in eastern Europe are unlikely to be followed. They represent, as one of the contributors to this volume has put it, 'a compelling negative example'. In these countries a strong state prevails and they lack electoral democracy and a polyarchic system of political power. It seems likely that a shift to a Western-type capitalist system is unlikely and that post-state socialist societies will consolidate into 'hybrid' types of regimes.

Appendix 1.1 Economic transformation in former state socialist countries (Europe and USSR) 1989, 1995, 2000, 2006. Large-scale privatization, small-scale privatization, enterprise restructuring and price liberalization

	Large-scale privatization	*Small-scale privatization*	*Enterprise restructuring*	*Price liberalization*
Albania				
1989	1.00	1.00	1.00	1.00
1995	2.00	4.00	2.00	3.67
2000	2.67	4.00	2.00	4.33
2006	3.00	4.00	2.33	4.33
Armenia				
1989	1.00	1.00	1.00	1.00
1995	2.00	2.67	2.00	3.67
2000	3.00	3.33	2.00	4.33
2006	3.67	4.00	2.33	4.33

(Continued)

Appendix 1.1 (continued)

Azerbaijan				
1989	1.00	1.00	1.00	1.00
1995	1.00	1.00	1.67	3.67
2000	1.67	3.33	1.67	4.00
2006	2.00	3.67	2.00	4.00
Belarus				
1989	1.00	1.00	1.00	1.00
1995	1.67	2.00	1.67	3.67
2000	1.00	2.00	1.00	2.33
2006	1.00	2.33	1.00	2.67
Bosnia and Herzegovina				
1989	1.00	3.00	1.00	2.67
1995	1.00	2.00	1.00	1.00
2000	2.00	2.33	1.67	4.00
2005	2.67	3.00	2.00	4.00
2006	2.67	3.00	2.00	4.00
Bulgaria				
1989	1.00	1.00	1.00	1.00
1995	2.00	3.00	2.00	2.67
2000	3.67	3.67	2.33	4.00
2006	4.00	4.00	2.67	4.33
Croatia				
1989	1.00	3.00	1.00	2.67
1995	3.00	4.00	2.00	4.00
2000	3.00	4.33	2.67	4.00
2005	3.33	4.33	3.00	4.00
2006	3.33	4.33	3.00	4.00
Czech Republic				
1989	1.00	1.00	1.00	1.00
1995	4.00	4.00	3.00	4.00
2000	4.00	4.33	3.33	4.33
2006	4.00	4.33	3.33	4.33
Estonia				
1989	1.00	1.00	1.00	1.00
1995	4.00	4.00	3.00	4.33
2000	4.00	4.33	3.00	4.33
2006	4.00	4.33	3.67	4.33
FYR Macedonia				
1989	1.00	3.00	1.00	2.67
1995	2.00	4.00	2.00	4.00
2000	3.00	4.00	2.33	4.00
2005	3.33	4.00	2.33	4.33
2006	3.33	4.00	2.67	4.33
Georgia				
1989	1.00	1.00	1.00	1.00
1995	2.00	3.00	2.00	3.67

(Continued)

Appendix 1.1 (continued)

2000	3.33	4.00	2.00	4.33
2005	3.67	4.00	2.33	4.33
2006	3.67	4.00	2.33	4.33
Hungary				
1989	1.00	1.00	1.00	2.67
1995	4.00	3.67	3.00	4.33
2000	4.00	4.33	3.33	4.33
2006	4.00	4.33	3.67	4.33
Kazakhstan				
1989	1.00	1.00	1.00	1.00
1995	2.00	3.00	1.00	4.00
2000	3.00	4.00	2.00	4.00
2006	3.00	4.00	2.00	4.00
Kyrgyzstan				
1989	1.00	1.00	1.00	1.00
1995	3.00	4.00	2.00	4.33
2000	3.00	4.00	2.00	4.33
2006	3.67	4.00	2.00	4.33
Latvia				
1989	1.00	1.00	1.00	1.00
1995	2.00	4.00	2.00	4.33
2000	3.00	4.33	2.67	4.33
2006	3.67	4.33	3.00	4.33
Lithuania				
1989	1.00	1.00	1.00	1.00
1995	3.00	4.00	2.00	4.00
2000	3.00	4.33	2.67	4.00
2006	4.00	4.33	3.00	4.33
Moldova				
1989	1.00	1.00	1.00	1.00
1995	3.00	3.00	2.00	3.67
2000	3.00	3.67	2.00	3.67
2006	3.00	3.67	2.00	4.00
Mongolia				
1989	1.00	1.00	1.00	1.00
1995	1.00	2.67	1.67	3.33
2000	2.00	3.67	2.00	4.33
2006	3.00	4.00	2.00	4.33
Montenegro				
1989	1.00	3.00	1.00	2.67
1995	1.00	3.00	1.00	2.67
2000	1.67	2.00	1.00	3.67
2006	3.33	3.00	2.00	4.00
Poland				
1989	1.00	2.00	1.00	2.33
1995	3.00	4.00	3.00	4.00
2000	3.33	4.33	3.00	4.33
2006	3.33	4.33	3.67	4.33

(Continued)

Appendix 1.1 (continued)

Romania				
1989	1.00	1.00	1.00	1.00
1995	2.00	2.67	2.00	4.00
2000	3.00	3.67	2.00	4.33
2006	3.67	3.67	2.67	4.33
Russian Federation				
1989	1.00	1.00	1.00	1.00
1995	3.00	4.00	2.00	3.67
2000	3.33	4.00	2.00	4.00
2006	3.00	4.00	2.33	4.00
Serbia				
1989	1.00	3.00	1.00	2.67
1995	1.00	3.00	1.00	2.67
2000	1.00	3.00	1.00	2.33
2006	2.67	3.67	2.33	4.00
Slovak Republic				
1989	1.00	1.00	1.00	1.00
1995	3.00	4.00	3.00	4.00
2000	4.00	4.33	3.00	4.00
2006	4.00	4.33	3.67	4.33
Slovenia				
1989	1.00	3.00	1.00	2.67
1995	2.67	4.00	2.67	3.67
2000	3.00	4.33	2.67	4.00
2006	3.00	4.33	3.00	4.00
Tajikistan				
1989	1.00	1.00	1.00	1.00
1995	2.00	2.00	1.00	3.33
2000	2.33	3.33	1.67	3.67
2006	2.33	4.00	1.67	3.67
Turkmenistan				
1989	1.00	1.00	1.00	1.00
1995	1.00	1.67	1.00	2.67
2000	1.67	2.00	1.00	2.67
2006	1.00	2.00	1.00	2.67
Ukraine				
1989	1.00	1.00	1.00	1.00
1995	2.00	2.00	2.00	3.67
2000	2.67	3.33	2.00	4.00
2006	3.00	4.00	2.00	4.00
Uzbekistan				
1989	1.00	1.00	1.00	1.00
1995	2.67	3.00	2.00	3.67
2000	2.67	3.00	1.67	2.67
2006	2.67	3.33	1.67	2.67

(Continued)

Appendix 1.1 (continued)

Average (all countries)				
1989	1.00	2.90	1.89	3.23
1995	2.37	2.97	1.92	3.25
2000	2.31	2.95	1.89	3.21
2006	2.31	2.95	1.89	3.21

Averages calculated by author, other data from: EBRD Transition Indicators 2006. WWW/ebrd/com/country/econo/stats. Accessed 4 December 2006

Notes

1 Acknowledgement is made to the Leverhulme Trust which supported the author's research project Transformation of State Socialism, grant F/01 034/A.

2 See, for example, David Lipton and Jeffrey Sachs, 'The Strategy of Transition' in David Kennett and Marc Lieberman, *The Road to Capitalism: Economic Transformation in Eastern Europe and the Former Soviet Union* (Fort Worth: Dryden Press, 1992), pp. 350–4. Originally published as 'Creating a Market Economy in Eastern Europe: the Case of Poland', *Brookings Papers on Economic Activity*, vol. 1, 1990. Washington, DC: Brookings Institution.

3 See particularly the views of J. Kornai, *From Socialism to Capitalism* (London: The Social Market Foundation, 1998) and B. Kaminski, *The Collapse of State Socialism* (Princeton University Press, 1991).

4 See David Lipton and Jeffrey Sachs, 'Creating a Market Economy in Eastern Europe: the Case of Poland', *Brookings Papers on Economic Activity*, vol. 1, 1990. Extract in Kennett and Lieberman, *The Road to Capitalism*, pp. 350–4.

5 K. Von Beyme, for example, emphasizes that the state socialist societies were '*a uniform socialist political system* which was unique in European constitutional history'. *Transition to Democracy in Eastern Europe* (Basingstoke: Macmillan, 1996), p. 20.

6 A good example of this is Stark's account of privatization, see David Stark, 'Recombinant Property in East European Capitalism', *American Sociological Review*, 101, 4 (Jan. 1996) 993–1027.

7 Francis Fukuyama, 'The End of History?' *The National Interest*, Summer (1989) 3–4.

8 EBRD Transition Indicators 2006. www.ebrd/com/country/econo/stats. Accessed 4 December 2006.

9 For methodology, see www.ebrd/com/country/econo/stats

10 This chart is based on D. Lane, 'Trajectories of Transformation: Theories, Legacies, Outcomes', in D. Lane (ed.), *The Legacy of State Socialism and the Future of Transformation* (Lanham: Rowman and Littlefield, 2002), p. 19.

11 www.fraserinstitute.ca

12 This index considers government consumption as a proportion of total consumption, the ratio of transfers and subsidies to GDP, the number, composition and share of output by state-operated enterprises, government investment as a share of total investment, the use of price controls, the rates of top marginal tax thresholds, duration and use of military conscription, growth rate of money supply, level of inflation, access to foreign currency bank accounts, exchange rate controls, risk of property confiscation, risk of government cancelling contracts, revenue derived from taxes on international trade, variation on tariff rates, share of

trade sector covered by non-tariff restrictions, size of the trade sector, percentage of bank deposits held in privately owned banks, share of total domestic credit allocated to the private sector, determination of interest rates by market forces, and access to a country's capital markets by foreign capital. Summarized from Appendix 2, Explanatory Notes and Data Sources. Data here refer to 1997. EBRD, *Transition Report 1999* (EBRD: London, 1999), p. 24. In interpreting these data, one should note that in some countries, privately owned companies may still have considerable state ownership, especially in large-scale industry. For other indexes, see also Philip G. Roeder, 'The Revolution of 1989: Post Communism and the Social Sciences', *Slavic Review*, 58, 4 (1999) 743–55.

13 Political rights include the right of adults to vote and compete for public office and for 'elected representatives to have a decisive vote on public policies'. Civil liberties include the rights to 'develop views, institutions and personal autonomy' independently of the state. Freedom House, Freedom in the World 1998/99, website www.freedomhouse.org. Rankings (on a 1–7 point scale) are shown on Figure 1.2: I have reversed the rankings given by Freedom House to make symmetric with the economic ratings: hence the lower the rank the higher the level of freedom.

14 GDP derived from: EBRD, *Transition Report, 1998* (London: HMSO), Table 2.1.

15 Data here and following taken from: EBRD, *Transition Report 2003* (London: EBRD, 2003), p. 16. The definition of a 'private' company includes companies which are not part of the state sector, but they certainly include companies in which various government agencies (local authorities, ministries) hold stakes.

16 *Transition Report 2006* (London: EBRD, 2006), Table 1.1.

17 For details see the chapters in David Lane and Martin Myant (eds), *Varieties of Capitalism in Post-Communist Countries* (New York: Palgrave Macmillan, 2007).

18 EBRD, *Transition Report 2003*, p. 18.

19 *Human Development Report 2005*. www.hdr.und.org/reports/global/2005 (reference for 2005). In the following tables, the issues for 2001 (referring to the year 2000) and 2005 (referring to 2003) have been utilized. There is also a hardback publication, UNDP, *Human Development Report 1991* (New York and London: Oxford University Press, 1991).

20 Sources used are: *Human Development Reports* for 2002 and 2005. *Human Development Reports* are published annually for the United Nations Development Programme (UNDP) (New York: OUP, 2002). Similar title and publisher for 2005. IBRD, *World Development Report 1996* (New York: Oxford University Press, 1996), Table 5.

21 David Lane, 'Emerging Varieties of Capitalism in Former State Socialist Societies', *Competition and Change*, 9, 3 (September 2005) 238–9.

22 These data on health are derived from a section of my article, 'Emerging Varieties of Capitalism', pp. 240–3.

23 *World Development Report 2004*, pp. 256–7.

24 UNDP *Human Development Report 2005*, pp. 230–1. www.hdr.undp.org/reports/global/HDR 2005. Accessed November 2006.

25 UNDP, *Human Development Report 2005*, p. 230. www.hdr.undp.org/reports/global/2005/pdf/HDR05. Accessed November 2006.

26 For more detail see Lane, 'Emerging Varieties of Capitalism', pp. 240–2.

27 See UNDP, Human Development Indicators, *Human Development Report 2005*, pp. 230–1.

Part I

Social Forces and Transformation

2

Communist Nostalgia and its Consequences in Russia, Belarus and Ukraine

*Stephen White**

'Communism – world tour, 1917–1989', declared the T-shirts. It was a judgement that reflected the dramatic changes that had just taken place in central and eastern Europe as long-established communist systems gave way to coalitions or in some cases to regimes that were headed by political dissidents like Vaclav Havel, a prisoner earlier the same year, or the Polish Prime Minister Tadeusz Mazowiecki, a prisoner in the early 1980s. By 1991 communist rule had ended in the USSR itself, and the union had dissolved into its 15 constituent republics. All, apparently, had changed, and changed utterly.

This was, of course, a hasty and incomplete judgement. For a start, communist rule continued elsewhere: in Cuba, and parts of Asia. Taking into account the enormous and increasing number that lived in the People's Republic of China, there were almost as many who lived under communist rule in 2006 as had lived under communist rule in a rather larger number of regimes in 1989: 1.4 billion, which was more than a fifth of the world's entire population, as compared with 1.6 billion in 1989. This was scarcely the 'end of history'. And there were many more who lived under post-communist rule as formerly ruling parties changed their name, dropped their claims to a political monopoly and contested elections, in some cases with great success: in Bulgaria and Hungary, in Lithuania, Mongolia, Poland and elsewhere.

Nor was it entirely clear what kind of change had taken place at the end of the 1980s. For the Russian President Boris Yeltsin, speaking immediately after the collapse of the attempted coup of August 1991, the Russian people had 'thrown off the shackles of seventy years of slavery' and were on their way to a 'parliamentary democracy'.[1] Others, however, were more doubtful, including the sociologist Tat'yana Zaslavskaya. In her view, there were several objections to the view that a fundamental social revolution had taken place. One of them was that the new ruling group consisted overwhelmingly of the former *nomenklatura*, while in central and eastern Europe it was 'oppositional social forces' that had come to power.[2]

The USSR, moreover, remained a popular institution, and not just for Russians. There was a turnout of 80 per cent in the referendum that took place in March 1991 on its continuation as a 'renewed federation of equal sovereign republics in which the human rights and freedoms of people of every nationality [would] be fully guaranteed'. More than 76 per cent voted in favour across the entire country; Belarusians (83 per cent) were even more enthusiastic than Ukrainians (70 per cent) and Russians (71 per cent). There was little popular resistance to the attempted coup in August 1991, and little support for the hasty and probably unconstitutional decision to terminate the USSR the following December – an 'elite pact' of a rather peculiar kind, conducted by a Russian president, Boris Yeltsin, who was in no position to reason clearly (according to participants he was 'so drunk he fell out of his chair'),[3] and who had in any case no prior commitment to the dissolution of the union.[4] Levels of support for the principle of a union state have consistently been very high; in our 2005 survey, for instance, 66 per cent largely or entirely agreed that the demise of the USSR had been a 'catastrophe', and 76 per cent thought the CIS member countries should reconstitute a single state or at least cooperate more closely.

Substantial numbers, indeed, continue to insist that it would have been better if the Soviet system had remained, and in the form it had acquired before perestroika. About half of those who were asked by the Levada Centre in January 2005, for instance, thought it 'would have been better if everything had stayed the way it was before 1985'. Why? Because 'we were a big, united country', and 'there was order' (both 26 per cent); in addition, there was 'certainty in the future' (24 per cent) and 'prices were low and stable' (20 per cent). As for perestroika, just 21 per cent thought it had been a positive development, but nearly three times as many (56 per cent) took the opposite view;[5] Gorshkov and Petukhov found similarly that 28 per cent were positive about perestroika, but 63 per cent negative.[6] And even if there were many who believed that perestroika had, all the same, been necessary, it should have been conducted in a different way: 'without destroying the socialist order' (33 per cent), or indeed 'not at all' (20 per cent), or by 'firmly developing market relations in the economy, but not rushing the development of democracy' (19 per cent).[7]

In Russia at least, the changes that had taken place were clearly more complicated than a 'transition to democracy': it was hardly a transition, not necessarily to democracy, led by a section of the regime itself. Russians, understandably, often preferred to use the neutral term 'the collapse of the union' (*raspad soyuza*).

Assessing communist nostalgia

The research literature has generally been in no doubt that communist nostalgia is a significant presence in post-communist politics, particularly in Russia. There has been less agreement about how it can be measured, and about its larger significance; in particular, what kind of linkage exists between a positive assessment of the communist past, a negative view of the post-communist present, and a restorationist view of the future. Haerpfer is one of those who posits a direct equivalence in a study covering 15 central and eastern European countries over the 1990s, making extensive use of a 'heaven and hell' scale in which past, present and future regimes are evaluated between +100 and −100. More than half the adult population of the entire region had a positive view of the communist economic system (the average was 54 per cent in 1998); support was highest of all in Belarus and Ukraine, at 78 and 90 per cent respectively. There was evidence here of 'increasing nostalgia for the economic stability of the past, when compared with the speed of economic changes and economic instability since 1989'.[8]

There was slightly less support, but still close to a majority across the entire region (47 per cent), for the communist system of government, which was an increase on the level of support it had received in 1991 (36 per cent). Again, there was a wide range, from Poland (30 per cent) to Ukraine (82 per cent), and from central and southern to eastern Europe. Levels of support were generally highest in the former Soviet republics; the level of support that appeared to exist in Ukraine for the communist system of government appeared in particular to represent a 'serious warning about the fragility of democracy and the potential risks of non-democratic alternatives eventually taking over ... if the political dissatisfaction of the Ukrainian electorate cannot be halted'.[9] There were also positive views about communism: across the entire region, 10 per cent thought it was a 'good way of running things', and another 46 per cent thought it was at least 'tolerable'; the lowest levels of support were once again in the Czech Republic and Poland, the highest levels in Belarus and Ukraine (16 and 59 per cent respectively), and Serbia.

What, then, about a communist restoration? A reverse change of this kind had the support of 18 per cent across the region in 1994, increasing to 24 per cent in 1998; levels of support were lower than this in central Europe (19 per cent), and lowest of all in the Baltic (6–7 per cent), but somewhat higher in south-eastern Europe (up from 21 per cent in 1994 to 28 per cent in 1998), and higher again in the former Soviet republics. The wish for a communist restoration, evidently, was 'not vanishing, but, on the contrary, growing during the process of political transformation'.[10] Once again, the highest levels of all were in Ukraine, where support for a communist restoration had increased steadily over the decade up to 51 per cent in 1998. This appeared to represent 'quite a strong indicator of an extremely high level of discontent with the [current] political system in the Ukraine, and an indicator of the risk of a collapse of democracy and market economy in this country with all the potential consequences of such a breakdown and of the possible attempt to reinstate Communism'.[11]

A more differentiated view has been presented by Ekman and Linde in a study that distinguishes the various elements of a complex and multidimensional phenomenon and pays more attention to causality. Was communist nostalgia, in particular, 'an indication of genuine non-democratic values among the post-communist citizens, acquired as the result of political socialization in the old, communist system?' Or was it 'quite simply brought about by a perceived output deficit, and related to a general discontent with the democratic system's *performance* ability?' There was a further dimension that was less easy to measure but no less important, a 'retrospective image of the "good old days"' that was more likely to emerge when post-communist citizens – for instance, East Germans – found themselves obliged to adjust to a different way of life at the same time as their previous life experience was defined as worthless. 'Literally over a single night, all the things that had been taken for granted were no longer valid'; the natural result was a 'serious identity crisis' that was reflected in 'confusion and frustration'.[12]

Ekman and Linde drew their evidence from the New Europe Barometer, covering ten countries in central and eastern Europe but none of the former Soviet republics outside the Baltic; they also used the Eurobarometer. Other cross-national exercises, as they noted, had relatively few items that were directly related to system support, and none that asked specifically about a return to communist rule.[13] Their exercise covered the period from 1993 to 2001, at which point levels of nostalgia as they defined it ranged from 15 to 30 per cent and were tending to increase still further, even in countries that were generally seen as consolidating democracies such as the Czech Republic.[14] Levels of nostalgia were lower in the three Baltic republics, almost certainly because communist rule was associated with a loss of national sovereignty, but there was more support than in central and eastern Europe for the view that it would be 'better to get rid of parliament and elections and have a strong leader who [could] quickly decide everything'.[15] This was evidence that lower levels of communist nostalgia did not automatically mean higher levels of support for liberal democracy.

If nostalgia was mostly a matter of socialization, it would have been reasonable to expect older generations to be more 'nostalgic' than their younger counterparts, who had experienced only the decline and demise of communist rule. But communist nostalgia might also be a response to the performance of post-communist governments; in this respect it would be less reasonable to expect age-related differences, and more reasonable to expect a generalized dissatisfaction. On the whole, it was the second proposition that was more strongly supported by the evidence. Younger respondents were less likely to favour a return to communist rule, and more likely to reject authoritarian alternatives (including military rule and a 'strong man' as well as communist rule). But there were increasing levels of nostalgia among younger as well as older respondents, which suggested that nostalgia was 'mainly output-oriented'. It followed that communist nostalgia did not necessarily represent a threat to the post-communist order; nor did it necessarily covary with a rejection of liberal democracy.[16]

Munro focuses on post-communist Russia in the same context, using the 2005 New Russia Barometer. He distinguishes between nostalgia (generalized approval of the communist past), reaction (the wish to see it return), and the belief (for better or for worse) that it will eventually do so. Overall, 70 per cent of Russians had a positive view of the Soviet system, which was well above the level of support in the new post-communist members of the European Union (54 per cent), and tending to increase further; and 41 per cent were in favour of a return to communist rule, as compared with 15 per cent in the new EU member countries. But very few (16 per cent) thought a return to communist rule was a serious prospect.[17] Taken as a whole, the evidence was generally most supportive of a 'persistence scenario', in which the values of the communist past were a more powerful determinant of political behaviour than economic or political performance, social structure or cognitive differences, but a diminishing determinant, as they affected attitudes to the past and present more than to the future.[18]

Others have been less sanguine, seeing communist nostalgia – and attitudes to Stalin in particular – as a serious 'impediment to Russian democratization'. Support for transparency, the rule of law and free elections, Mendelson and Gerber suggest, can be 'greatly inhibited by the power of historical legacies', and 'widely held, uncritical views of the past' can exercise a substantial and continuing influence on political and social development. Younger Russians, for instance, were more inclined to attribute the dramatic events in Ukraine at the end of 2004 to Western intelligence, and more sympathetic to Stalin (a fifth said they would vote for him if he was a candidate for high office, and more than half saw him as wise leader).[19] Nostalgia for Stalin, they wrote elsewhere,

> is not simply a relic that will die out with the older generation. And as long as young Russians remain ignorant about or have positive feeling towards a murderous dictator who institutionalized terror throughout their country, they are unlikely to mobilize behind calls for greater justice, human right, or transparency – factors critical to Russia's transformation into a modern democratic society.[20]

In what follows we seek to advance the discussion in several ways. We look, first of all, at Russia, Belarus and Ukraine, three Slavic republics that together account for about three-quarters of the territory and half the population of what used to be the Soviet bloc. Like others, we use evidence drawn from an extended period of time, from 1993 up to 2006. But unlike many, we examine the dimensions of nostalgia within as well as between national societies. Perhaps most important, we also disaggregate 'communist rule' into its various components. There have certainly been suggestions in the survey-based literature that Russians wanted a 'socialism that worked', without its inefficiencies but otherwise not very different; or a 'more democratic Soviet system', without its restrictions on elections and minority rights.[21]

These objectives may not have been realistic, but they did at least suggest a more differentiated view of the Soviet past, 'with all its pluses and minuses'. Looking to the future, we also examine the association between communist nostalgia and voting behaviour, using post-election surveys in Russia and Ukraine (details are provided in Appendix 2.1). If nostalgia has implications for contemporary politics, it is here above all that we should expect to find it.

Looking backwards

Russians, Belarusians and Ukrainians certainly have a differentiated view of the former regime, if our survey evidence is any guide. We asked, first of all, what ordinary members of the society thought were the 'best' and 'worst' features of the communist system of the recent past. The evidence is set out in Figures 2.1 and 2.2. Across the three countries, it was guaranteed employment that was seen as the most positive feature of the old regime, particularly in Russia and Ukraine. There was also approval for the way in which the former regime had maintained stable relations between the various nationalities,

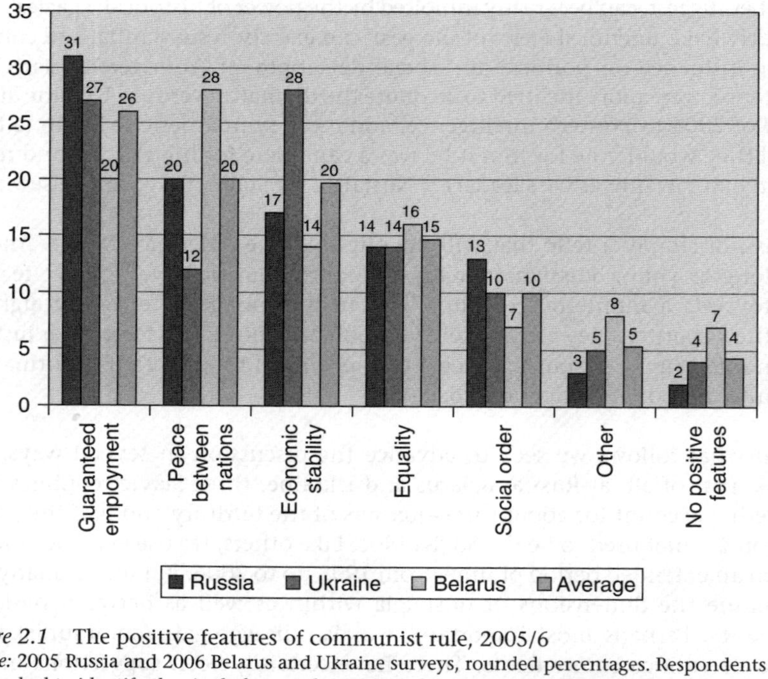

Figure 2.1 The positive features of communist rule, 2005/6

Source: 2005 Russia and 2006 Belarus and Ukraine surveys, rounded percentages. Respondents were asked to identify the single feature they regarded as the most positive in the previous governmental system; if they replied that they could not remember the Soviet period, they were told that we were interested not in their personal experience but in their perception of what life was like in the USSR, and the question was repeated

especially in Belarus (oddly perhaps, in that it was the least ethnically divided of the three societies). Economic stability was also important, especially in Ukraine (where it was seen as the most important of all the positive features of the Soviet system). Substantial numbers, in addition, approved of the way in which the Soviet system had maintained a measure of social equality, and public order. There were in fact very few who could find no positive features at all in the former regime.

There was a substantial measure of agreement, equally, about the features of the old regime that were least acceptable. In every case it was 'excessive bureaucracy' that was seen as its main shortcoming; but 'economic stagnation' was almost as important, at least in Russia and Belarus. Violation of human rights was in third place, and relatively more important in Ukraine than in the other two countries. Corruption and environmental pollution were mentioned by rather fewer, and about one in ten thought the old system had no negative features at all. We asked identical questions in Russia alone in 1993 as well as 2005; the results are set out in Table 2.1. Slightly more, in 2005, drew attention to the equality that had at least nominally characterized the communist period, and slightly fewer thought it had no positive features. On the negative side, bureaucracy was the main perceived

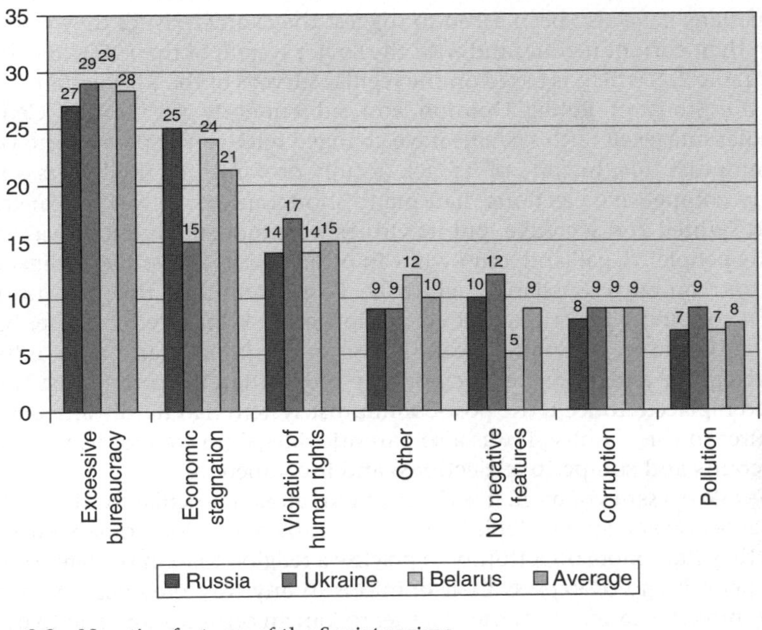

Figure 2.2 Negative features of the Soviet regime
Source: As Figure 2.1; respondents were asked to identify the single most negative feature of the previous governmental system

Table 2.1 'Best' and 'worst' features of communist rule in Russia, 1993 and 2005

	Best features			*Worst features*	
	1993	*2005*		*1993*	*2005*
Job security	29	31	Too much bureaucracy	32	27
Inter-ethnic peace	24	20	Oppressed human rights	17	14
Economic stability	22	17	Corruption	15	8
Law and order	12	13	None	13	10
More equality	7	14	Pollution	12	7
None	7	2	Economic stagnation	11	25

Source: 1993 and 2005 Russia surveys, responses in percentages; don't knows and failures to respond account for residuals. Respondents were asked to identify one positive and one negative feature.

shortcoming of the Soviet system in both cases, but economic stagnation became relatively more important, and human rights slightly less so. The formal attributes of democracy played a relatively minor part in both positive and negative assessments: it was social and economic achievements that accounted for most of the favourable judgements, and social and economic shortcomings that – at least by 2005 – accounted for most of the criticisms.

Russians have also been asked to suggest the characteristics they associate with their current regime, and with the Soviet system of the 1970s and 1980s (see Table 2.2, which is based on the regular surveys of the All-Russian Centre for the Study of Public Opinion and subsequently the Levada Centre). Popular images of both systems have changed relatively little over the years. Communist rule, in spite of its lack of fully or – until its final years – even partly competitive elections, had many shortcomings: it was bureaucratic, short-sighted and secretive. But its virtues were more apparent. It was 'close to the people', 'legal' and 'our own' – in other words, accessible, indigenous, and (for ordinary Russians) legitimate. Post-communist rule, by contrast, was associated with crime and corruption more than anything else; but it was also remote, irresolute, weak (less so under Putin than under Yeltsin), short-sighted and more bureaucratic – by 2005 – than the communist system it had replaced. Indeed, the post-communist system had hardly any positive features in this inquiry; it was also parasitic, illegal (in spite of its independent courts and competitive elections) and incompetent.

We asked a series of more specific questions about particular freedoms in the Soviet period and after it (Table 2.3). There is little doubt, for ordinary Russians, that they have more opportunity to practise a religion than in the late communist period, and to express their opinions in any way they wish. Similarly, they think it is easier to choose whether to join an organization, and to decide whether or not to take part in politics (in the communist period, it was often suggested, everything that was not banned was compulsory); but they think

Table 2.2 The 'most characteristic' features of communist and post-communist rule in Russia, 1998 and 2005 (percentages)

	Soviet rule, 1970s–1980s			*Post-communist rule, 1990s–2000s*	
	1998	*2005*		*1998*	*2005*
Close to the people	36	34	Criminal, corrupt	63	62
Legal	32	28	Remote, alien	41	42
'Our own', familiar	32	26	Irresolute	32	29
Bureaucratic	30	30	Weak, powerless	30	20
Strong, firm	27	30	Short-sighted	28	25
Short-sighted	23	21	Bureaucratic	22	39
Authoritative, respected	21	24	Parasitic	18	15
Secretive, closed	17	13	Illegal	12	16
Just	16	21	Unprofessional	12	12
Honest, open	14	13	Limited	11	8
Criminal, corrupt	13	12	Educated, intelligent	6	13

Source: Adapted from *Ekonomicheskie i sotsial'nye peremeny*, 3 (1998) 57 and *Vestnik obshchestvennogo mneniya*,1, 81 (January–February 2006) 10, showing all qualities that were reported by at least 10% of respondents in either year. Figures for 2001 have also been reported.

there has been no more than a modest improvement in the protection of citizens from the threat of illegal arrest. Most strikingly of all, ordinary people have (in their own view) much less influence over the making of public policy than they enjoyed in the communist period, in spite of the introduction of competitive elections, the rule of law and freedom of speech, although the largest proportion of all think there has simply been no change; and they think they are much less likely to be treated fairly and equally by government.

These, moreover, were not just Russian responses (Table 2.4). Across the three republics, Russians, with some justification, were the most likely to believe they had secured more freedom of speech than they had enjoyed in the communist period, and they were also the most likely to take the view that they had more opportunity to choose whether or not to join an organization. With Belarusians, they were the most likely to believe they had secured more freedom of conscience. Belarusians, perhaps surprisingly, were the most likely to believe they had secured more opportunity to decide whether or not to take part in politics; very similar proportions across the three countries thought they were less likely to suffer an illegal arrest. But again, there was much less evidence of a positive change in the relationship between citizens and government. On the contrary, in every case almost twice as many thought they had *less* influence over government than they had enjoyed in the communist period, and up to four times as many thought they were *less* likely to be treated equally and fairly by government

Table 2.3 Freedoms under communist and post-communist Rule in Russia, 2001 and 2005

	Much better		*Somewhat better*		*Stayed the same*		*A bit worse*		*Much worse*	
	2001	*2005*	*2001*	*2005*	*2001*	*2005*	*2001*	*2005*	*2001*	*2005*
Religious life	52	59	27	26	12	11	1	1	1	1
Join organization	45	44	31	33	10	13	2	3	1	1
Take part in politics	44	45	25	30	17	17	2	2	2	1
Freedom of speech	45	39	32	36	12	18	3	3	2	2
Freedom from illegal arrest	11	17	13	25	34	33	9	9	10	8
Influence public policy	4	6	10	13	47	44	10	16	18	17
Equal treatment	–	4	–	7	–	38	–	21	–	23

Source: 2001 and 2005 Russian surveys, rounded percentages; don't knows and non-responses account for residuals. The question about equal treatment was not asked in 2001; a question about freedom of travel (better for 48%, worse for 30%) was not asked in 2005. Question wording was: 'Compared with the Soviet period, have the following become easier or more difficult?'; options were respectively 'For everyone to freely resolve questions of his/her religious life', 'To join any organization', 'To decide freely whether or not to take part in political life', 'For everyone to freely express what they think', 'People can live without worrying about illegal arrest', 'For ordinary people to influence government policy', and 'Government deals with all citizens equally and fairly'.

Table 2.4 Changing opportunities compared to Soviet times, 2005/6

	Belarus		*Russia*		*Ukraine*	
	Agree	*Disagree*	*Agree*	*Disagree*	*Agree*	*Disagree*
Everyone has freedom of religious life	86	6	85	1	29	4
Everyone is free to decide whether or not to participate in political life	73	10	30	4	34	5
There is no need to fear illegal arrest	49	23	42	16	45	28
Everyone has freedom of speech	48	25	75	5	44	13
You can join any organization	38	13	77	4	43	7
Officials treat citizens equally	27	38	11	44	26	62
Ordinary people can influence government policy	26	46	19	33	32	52
(Ns)*	1000		2000		1600	

* Total number of respondents.
Source: 2005 Russia and 2006 Belarus and Ukraine surveys, rounded percentages; 'neither' accounts for residuals. Question wording was 'Compared with Soviet times do you agree or disagree that …?'

(the difference in this respect was less marked in Belarus than in the other two countries).

Taking everything together, did our respondents, on the whole, regret the demise of the USSR? The evidence is set out in Figure 2.3. Russians clearly did so, by more than two to one; but a plurality in the other two countries took the opposite view. For Russians, 'the USSR' is in effect the Soviet system, with all its positive and negative features. But for Belarusians and Ukrainians, it was also a time in which their countries had been union republics and not independent states, in spite of their representation in the United Nations. To regret the demise of the USSR was in effect to regret the end of a period in which they had been ruled from Moscow, not by their own elected institutions; not to regret its demise was in effect to affirm the importance of national sovereignty, without necessarily implying a rejection of the economic and political system that had prevailed in Soviet times. There was, of course, an association: those who regretted the demise of the USSR were the most likely to favour the Soviet system, and vice versa. But evidence of this kind is further confirmation of the need to disaggregate: a 'nostalgic' view of the USSR was not the same as a positive view of the Soviet system, and a negative view of the USSR, particularly outside Russia, did not necessarily mean a rejection of the principles on which it had been governed.

Who – more than others – bemoaned the demise of the USSR? On the evidence of our 2005 and 2006 surveys (Table 2.5), gender made relatively little

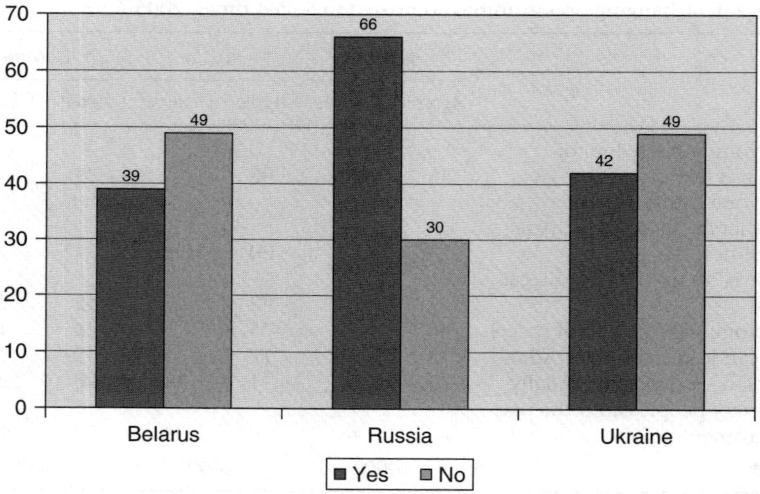

Figure 2.3 Attitudes to the demise of the USSR, 2005/6
Source: 2005 Russia and 2006 Belarus and Ukraine surveys, rounded percentages; don't knows and non-responses account for residuals. Question wording was: 'Do you agree or not with the following statement, "It is a great misfortune that the USSR no longer exists"?'

Table 2.5 Attitudes to the demise of the USSR by socio-economic characteristics, 2005/6

	Belarus		*Russia*		*Ukraine*	
	Regret	*Don't regret*	*Regret*	*Don't regret*	*Regret*	*Don't regret*
Socio-economic characteristics						
Male	40	51	**62**	**33**	39	**52**
Female	39	48	**69**	**27**	44	**48**
Under 30 years	**22**	**64**	**44**	**47**	**25**	**62**
60 or older	**57**	**32**	**82**	**15**	**57**	**37**
Urban	38	53	66	30	44	49
Rural	40	46	67	28	37	51
Primary education	48	**36**	**82**	**16**	**56**	**35**
Higher education	37	56	62	33	**34**	**60**
Low income	**51**	**36**	**76**	**20**	**53**	**36**
High income	32	**59**	**54**	**40**	29	**65**
Total	39	49	66	30	42	50

Source: 2005 Russia and 2006 Belarus and Ukraine surveys; don't knows and no answers account for residuals. Question wording as in Figure 2.3. Cells highlighted in bold show a statistically significant association between the two variables, judged by the values of adjusted residuals.

difference, but age had strong effects, and in the expected direction; across all the variables we considered, its effects were the most consistent and substantial. Residence also made little difference, but education was another powerful predictor, and in the expected direction. So was self-assessed income, which tended in each of three countries to reduce levels of regret and to raise levels of indifference. It was, of course, to be expected that former members of the Communist Party in each of the three countries would be more likely to regret the demise of the USSR than others, and this was the case. In Belarus, 39 per cent of the entire sample regretted the demise of the USSR, but 56 per cent of those who had been members of the Communist Party; in Russia the corresponding figures were 66 per cent of the entire sample but 79 per cent of those who had been party members, and in Ukraine, 42 and 71 per cent. There were similar but smaller differences between the entire sample and those whose immediate family had been party members.

Looking forwards

Did communist nostalgia, however it was defined and measured, have any implications for policy preferences in the post-communist period? Was it an abstract, perhaps romanticized view of the recent past that had no particular consequences, or was it a distinct position that could be directly linked to domestic and foreign choices, and to electoral behaviour? We consider first of all the connection with domestic regime choices (Figure 2.4). Belarusians were the only ones who preferred 'the political system as it is today' to other choices – but their system as it currently existed was already close to what a Soviet system had been, with an authoritarian leadership and a state that continued to play a dominant role in the economy. For Russians and Ukrainians, it was a 'more democratic Soviet system' that came first, ahead of either the Soviet system as it had existed in the past or a Western-style pluralist democracy. In Russia, there was more support for the unreformed Soviet system than for Western democracy; in Belarus and Ukraine it was the other way round. But nowhere did Western-style democracy attract the support of as many as a quarter of our respondents, and in Russia it was even less popular than the political system that presently exists.

As we might have expected, these regime choices were themselves associated with views about the demise of the USSR. For instance, 66 per cent in Russia regretted the demise of the USSR, but 90 per cent of those who favoured the restoration of a Soviet system of government and 74 per cent of those who favoured a 'more democratic Soviet system'. Soviet nostalgia was rather less marked among those who favoured the current political system (48 per cent of whom regretted the demise of the USSR), or Western-style democracy (41 per cent). There was less regret about the demise of the USSR in Belarus and Ukraine, as we have seen (39 and 42 per cent respectively); but again, those who took this view were more likely than others to favour the

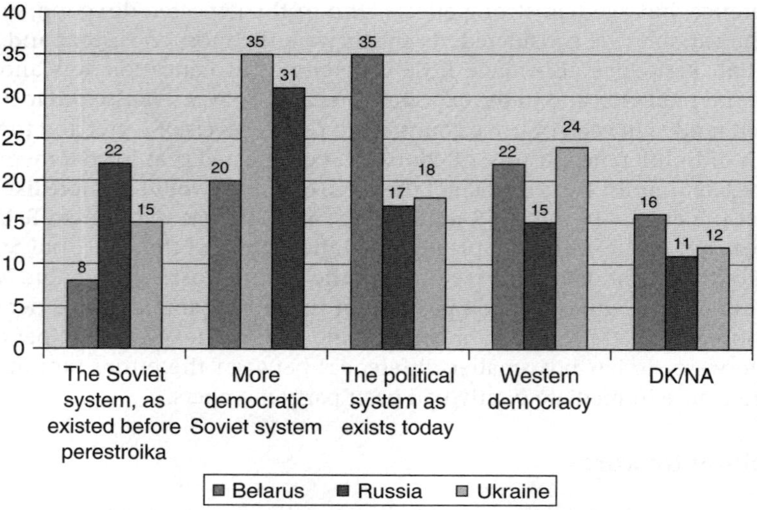

Figure 2.4 Political system preferences, 2005/6
Source: 2005 Russia and 2006 Belarus and Ukraine surveys, rounded percentages. Question wording was: 'Which of the following political systems would be the most suitable for [country]? The Soviet system that existed in our country before perestroika; the Soviet system, but in a different, more democratic form; the political system that exists today; democracy of the Western kind; neither'

restoration of a Soviet system of government (84 and 87 per cent respectively of those who took this view were also 'nostalgics'), and more likely to favour a 'more democratic Soviet system' (62 and 55 per cent respectively). Soviet nostalgia was notably less, as in Russia, among those who favoured the current political system, or Western-style democracy (22 and 17 per cent respectively; a fuller cross-tabulation is set out in Table 2.6).

We also examined views about the main dimensions of economic policy. In Figure 2.5 we show the pattern of opinion in each of the three countries, expressed in terms of the difference between 'Soviet' and 'market' responses. Unlike views about the political system, responses in this case were generally less supportive of the practices of the recent past. In Belarus there was a 'Soviet' majority for only one of the five questions, the one that related to state ownership as compared with private enterprise in the management of an enterprise. In Russia and Ukraine there was also majority support for the proposition that the state should assume the main responsibility for the welfare of the family; in Belarus there was a more 'Catholic' response, in that responsibilities of this kind were thought to be more properly entrusted to the family itself. In all other respects – whether earnings should be limited, whether higher pay was better than guaranteed employment and whether there should be higher prices but a wider choice of goods – it was the 'market'

Table 2.6 Correlating the demise of the USSR and policy attitudes, 2005/6

	Belarus			*Russia*			*Ukraine*		
	Regret	*Don't regret*	*Total*	*Regret*	*Don't regret*	*Total*	*Regret*	*Don't regret*	*Total*
Political system preferences									
The Soviet system before perestroika	**17**	**1**	8	**31**	**7**	22	**32**	**3**	15
A more democratic Soviet system	**32**	**12**	20	**39**	**27**	35	**41**	**22**	31
The present political system	**27**	**39**	35	**12**	**27**	17	**9**	**26**	18
Western-style democracy	**12**	**33**	22	**10**	**27**	15	**10**	**38**	24
Economic system preferences									
A Soviet-type economy	**39**	**19**	27	**41**	**19**	34	**36**	**16**	25
A market economy	**31**	**53**	43	**27**	**49**	34	**34**	**53**	44
Foreign policy preferences									
The CIS should unite into a single state	**34**	**7**	19	**53**	**20**	42	**35**	**5**	18
The CIS should cooperate more closely	56	57	58	**36**	**52**	41	**55**	**64**	61
Cooperation should remain at present levels	**10**	**31**	21	**7**	**18**	11	**9**	**24**	17
There should be less cooperation within CIS	0	1	1	2	3	2	1	3	2
The CIS should be dissolved	**4**	**1**	2	**3**	**7**	4	**1**	**5**	3

Source: 2005 Russia and 2006 Belarus and Ukraine surveys, column percentages. Question wording was 'Do you regret the demise of the Soviet Union?'; don't knows and non-responses account for residuals. Cells highlighted in bold show a statistically significant association between the two variables, judged by the values of adjusted residuals.

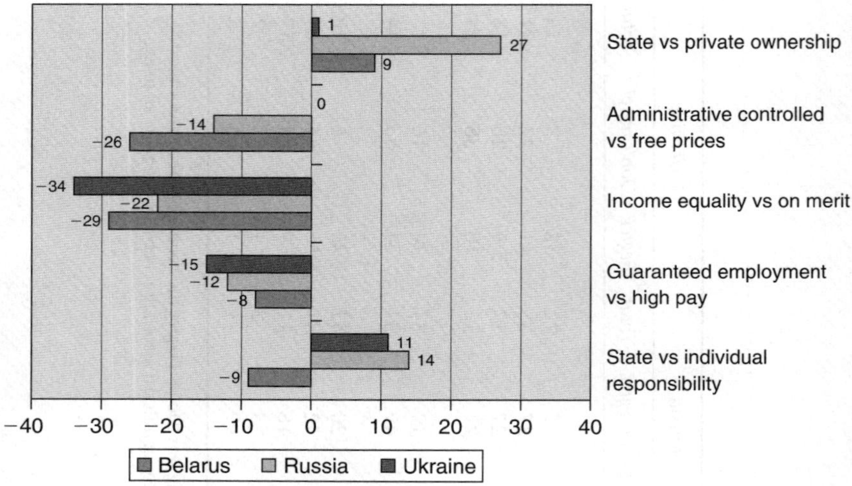

Figure 2.5 Economic system preferences, 2005/6
Source: 2005 Russia and 2006 Belarus and Ukraine surveys, 'Soviet' minus 'market' responses, rounded percentages. Question wordings were: 'State ownership is the best way to manage an enterprise OR Enterprises are better managed by private entrepreneurs'; 'It's better when there are a lot of goods in the shops even if they are dear OR It's better when the state keeps prices low even if there are not a lot of goods in the shops'; 'People's incomes should not vary very much OR Everyone should receive as much as they earn'; 'It's better to work where you aren't fired even if you are paid less OR It's better to work where they pay well even if you can be easily dismissed'; 'People themselves should be responsible for the well-being of their family OR The state should ensure that every family lives normally'

choices that had majority support. A 'nostalgic' choice of political system was evidently compatible with a very different view of the most desirable basis for managing a post-communist economy.

Was this also true at the individual level? Were 'communist nostalgics', for instance, more likely to resemble each other than other members of the mass public in their own country? And did they take a different view about economic ownership and management than those who did not regret the demise of the USSR? The differences, in fact, were very marked. In Russia, for instance, 59 per cent favoured state ownership of enterprises, but 75 per cent of those who largely or entirely agreed that the demise of the USSR had been a disaster. And if just 37 per cent preferred prices that were low even if the choice of goods was less extensive, 75 per cent of those who regretted the demise of the USSR took this view. Patterns of opinion in Belarus and Ukraine were less 'Soviet' in both respects and the differences were smaller, but here again 'nostalgics' were more likely than others (for instance) to favour state ownership, and to prefer low prices even if the choice was limited (30 and 40 per cent respectively took this view, but 50 and 46 per cent respectively of those who believed the demise of the USSR had been a disaster).

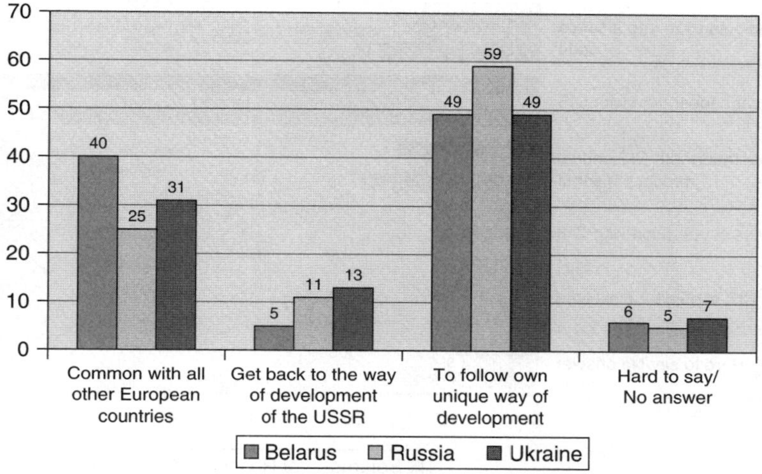

Figure 2.6 Foreign policy orientations, 2005/6
Source: 2005 Russia and 2006 Belarus and Ukraine surveys, rounded percentages. Question wording: 'Which historical path do you think [country] should follow: the common path for the contemporary world of European civilization; it should return to the path that was being followed by the Soviet Union; follow its own specific path; hard to say; no answer?'

In international affairs, there was a general inclination to follow 'our own path' rather than a pro-Western or pro-Soviet orientation (Figure 2.6). But a broadly European orientation was much more popular than one that sought to reconstitute the relationships of the Soviet period, and most of all in Belarus. At the same time there was strong support in all three countries for a closer association with the other members of the Commonwealth of Independent States, which brings together all the former Soviet republics with the exception of the Baltics (Figure 2.7). Russians were the most likely to favour a full-scale reintegration, and hardly less likely to favour a closer relationship with the other members. But there was majority support in the other two countries for a closer relationship, and very little support in any of the three countries for a reduction in the intensity of relations within the CIS or indeed its dissolution. These were views that had their origin in a variety of circumstances, not just in 'communist nostalgia'; for instance, of those who thought the CIS should become a unitary state, a higher proportion had at least one family member living in one of the other CIS countries.

There was, nonetheless, a close relationship between regretting the demise of the USSR and a commitment, in effect, to re-establish it in the form of a unitary state based on the CIS. In Russia, 39 per cent favoured the re-establishment of a unitary state, but 49 per cent of those who regretted the demise of the USSR, and 58 per cent of those who 'entirely agreed' its demise was to be

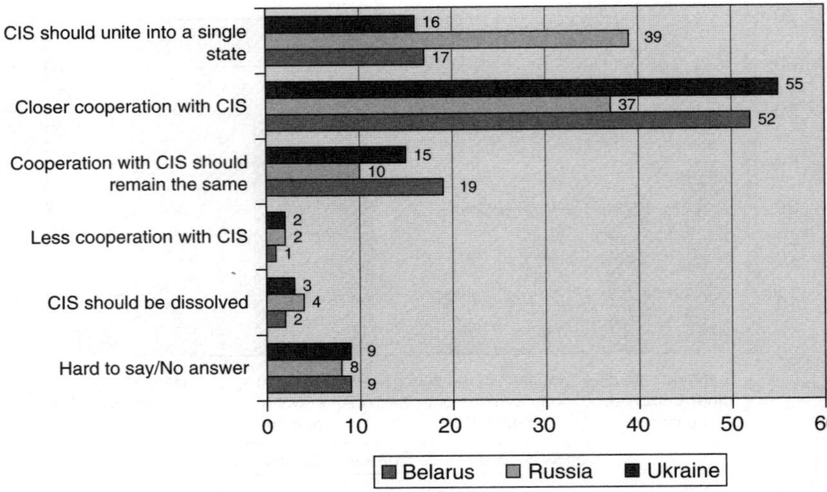

Figure 2.7 Foreign policy and the Commonwealth of Independent States, 2005/6
Source: 2005 Russia and 2006 Belarus and Ukraine surveys, rounded percentages. Question wording was: 'Some people think the republics of the former USSR that are members of the CIS should cooperate more closely with each other, or even unite in a single state. Others think the relations between the CIS countries are close enough already. Some think the CIS should simply be dissolved. Which view comes closest to your own? The CIS countries should unite in a single state; the CIS countries should cooperate more closely than at present, but remain independent states; the CIS countries should cooperate at their present level; the CIS should continue to exist, but its member countries should cooperate less than at present; the CIS should be dissolved; don't know; hard to say'

regretted. There was less support for a unitary state in Belarus and Ukraine, but again, it was much more likely to be the view of nostalgics. We set out these relationships and others in Table 2.6, indicating those that are statistically significant in bold type. In fact, nearly every relationship is significant: between regretting the demise of the USSR and political system preferences, and economic system preferences, and foreign policy orientations. And the relationships are in the predicted direction: those who regret the demise of the USSR are – in every case – more likely to favour the unreformed Soviet system, and less likely to favour Western-style democracy; more likely to favour a centrally planned economy, and less likely to favour the market; and more likely to believe that the former Soviet republics that are members of the CIS should form a unitary state.

Finally, did views of this kind have any implications for contemporary politics? Did communist nostalgia, in particular, make an observable difference to party allegiances, over and above the other factors that might also make a contribution? We set out the evidence in Table 2.7 in the form of a binary logistic regression in which we examine the impact of communist nostalgia – defined

Table 2.7 Predicting party vote by communist nostalgia, Russia and Ukraine, 2005/6

Party vote	*Russia*	*Ukraine*
Communist Party of the Russian Federation	1.5** (0.272)	
Liberal Democratic Party of Russia	0.671** (0.207)	
Rodina (Motherland)	0.146 (0.217)	
United Russia	−0.279* (0.111)	
Union of Right Forces (SPS)	−1.07** (0.312)	
Yabloko	−0.478 (0.300)	
Communist Party of Ukraine		2.06 ** (0.367)
Socialist Party of Ukraine		0.391 (0.228)
Party of the Regions		0.877** (0.123)
Bloc 'Our Ukraine'		−1.27** (0.177)
Bloc of Yulia Timoshenko		−1.05** (0.153)

Source: 2005 Russia and 2006 Ukraine surveys, binary logistical regression.
Notes: * = statistically significant at $p < 0.05$; ** = statistically significant at $p < 0.01$, both two-tailed; standard errors are in brackets. Party vote is predicted by regret for the demise of the USSR; controls are socio-economic characteristics as shown in Table 2.5. All variables, excluding age, are coded as 1 – denoting the characteristic, 0 = otherwise; 'age' takes single years.

as regret for the demise of the USSR – on party choice in the December 2003 Russian and March 2006 Ukrainian parliamentary elections, with socio-economic characteristics held constant. We find strong, consistent and statistically significant relationships in both cases. In Russia, all other things being equal, those who regretted the demise of the USSR were significantly more likely to vote Communist, and to support the Liberal Democrats, whose flamboyant but anti-communist leader had also called for a centralized state that occupied much more of the territory that had originally formed part of the Russian Empire. But it made a negative contribution to support for the Union of Right Forces and, somewhat less so, to support for the pro-Kremlin party United Russia. The contribution to the vote for Rodina, and against Yabloko, was in the expected direction but did not attain statistical significance.

We also find strong, consistent and statistically significant relationships between communist nostalgia and support or otherwise for the political parties that contested the March 2006 Ukrainian parliamentary election. The Communist Party, once again, drew strongly on the belief that it was a disaster that the USSR had come to an end, although its vote was very much less than in previous elections. So did the Party of the Regions, led by Viktor Yanukovich, which was the main winner of the election with 32 per cent of the vote and 186 of the 450 seats, and which campaigned strongly for a closer relationship with Russia and a greater degree of recognition for the Russian language. Communist nostalgia was also a powerful negative predictor of support for the Yulia Timoshenko bloc, led by the populist former prime minister, and for President Yushchenko's 'Our Ukraine' bloc, which were respectively the second and third most successful parties at the elections. Communist nostalgia, however, made no statistical difference to support for the Socialist Party of Ukraine, led by Oleksander Moroz, which took nearly 6 per cent of the parliamentary vote and joined the governing coalition that was finally established in August 2006.

Conclusion

Overall, we find that communist nostalgia matters. Most Russians (but not most Belarusians or Ukrainians) regret the demise of the USSR, without necessarily wishing to return to it. President Putin has himself described the collapse of the USSR as the 'greatest geopolitical catastrophe of the twentieth century',[22] and surveys have found a consistently positive view of the USSR in retrospect, and of a closer degree of integration in the future. Belarusians and Ukrainians are less concerned about the demise of the USSR (it was obviously incompatible with the independence they had obtained in 1991), and less likely to support the formation of a unitary state of CIS member countries, but they strongly supported a closer degree of cooperation; very few, in any case, thought the CIS should be dissolved. Generally, it was a 'more democratic Soviet system' that was the most strongly supported form of government across the three countries, but a broadly market-based economy had more support than a command economy of the traditional kind. This was a differentiated, not a simple view of the communist legacy.

But wherever the mass public offered support to the Soviet state and the economic and political principles on which it had been based, those who regretted the demise of the USSR were even more likely to do so. More than could be explained by random variation, they were more likely than other respondents to favour the restoration of a wholly Soviet system of government, more likely to favour a Soviet-type economy, and more likely (almost by definition) to support the formation of a unitary state on the basis of the CIS member countries. Regretting the demise of the USSR also made a strong contribution, all other things being equal, to the patterns of electoral support that were apparent at the 2003 Russian and 2006 Ukrainian parliamentary elections. Nostalgics were much more likely to support parties of the left, or at least those that favoured public ownership, a Soviet or at least 'more democratic Soviet' system of government, and a closer association among the former Soviet republics; they were much less likely to support the parties that favoured a 'civilized divorce', a wholly market economy and Western-style democracy.

'Communist nostalgia', at the same time, had to be disaggregated. There were very different views about the restoration of a unitary state in Russia and in Belarus and Ukraine, where it was incompatible with their newly acquired independence. There was support for a 'more democratic Soviet' system of government, but at the same time for the principles of the market economy. In the Baltic republics there were particularly low levels of nostalgia for the days of the USSR, but relatively high levels of support for a 'strong man' who would govern without much reference to elected institutions. Not many, in the post-communist or indeed in the late Soviet period, wanted a single party that exercised a political monopoly, or restrictions on what they could say. But there was a much larger constituency for full employment, low prices, comprehensive social welfare, and a state that took direct responsibility for economic management. In none of these three countries had there been a widely supported movement for the overthrow of Soviet rule; in each of them there was considerable support, in retrospect, for many of the principles on which it had been based; and attitudes of this kind had a substantial influence on the choices that were made when elections offered an opportunity to express a view about the future direction of national policy.

Appendix 2.1

Our 2005 Russian survey was conducted under the auspices of Russian Research. Fieldwork took place between 23 March and 20 April 2005. The number of respondents was 2000, selected according to the agency's normal sampling procedures; it was representative of the population aged 18 and over, using a multistage proportional method with a random route method of selecting households. Interviews were conducted face to face in respondents' homes. The sample was then weighted in accordance with sex, age and education in each region. The agency's standard procedures were employed to check the completion of questionnaires and the logical consistency of the data. Our 1993 survey was conducted by ROMIR between November 1993 and January 1994 ($n = 2141$) with the financial support of the Economic and Social Research Council under grant R233538; a full account appears in William L. Miller, Stephen White and Paul Heywood, *Values and Political Change in Postcommunist Europe* (Basingstoke: Macmillan and New York: St Martin's, 1998).

In Belarus, our 2006 survey was conducted by the Centre for Sociological and Political Research of the Belarusian State University between 5 and 19 June 2006, $n = 1000$, drawn from 57 different settlements. Respondents were interviewed face to face in their homes, and 12 per cent of interviews were checked by a second visit. The sample was designed on the basis of the 2005 Belarusian statistical yearbook, and then weighted by gender, age, education and place of residence. Our 2006 survey in Ukraine was conducted by Russian Research on similar principles between 24 April and 12 May 2006, $n = 1600$. There were 385 sampling points and 163 interviewers with an average number of interviews in each case of 10; 20 per cent of the interviews were randomly selected for verification. Our 2005 Russian survey has been deposited with the UK Data Archive, where the data files and documentation may be consulted; our 2006 surveys will be deposited in the same repository.

Notes

* The financial support of the Economic and Social Research Council under grant RES-000-23-0146 to Stephen White, Margot Light and Roy Allison is gratefully acknowledged, as is the support of the Nuffield Foundation under grant SGS/32823 to Stephen White and the research assistance of Julia Koresteleva.

1. *Izvestiya*, 23 August 1991, p. 1, and 12 November 1991, p. 1.
2. T. I. Zaslavskaya, *Sovremennoe rossiiskoe obshchestvo: Sotsial'nyi mekhanizm transformatsii* (Moscow: Delo, 2004), p. 193.
3. David Remnick, *Resurrection: the Struggle for a New Russia* (New York: Random House, 1997), p. 27.
4. Aleksandr Korzhakov, *Boris El'tsin: ot rassveta do zakata* (Moscow: Interbuk, 1997), p. 127.
5. Yuri Levada, 'Dvadtsat' let spustya: perestroika v obshchestvennom mnenii i v obshchestvennoi zhizni', *Vestnik obshchestvennogo mneniya*, 2 (2005) 8, 9, 11.
6. Mikhail Gorshkov and Vladimir Petukhov, 'Perestroika glazami rossiyan: 20 let spustya', in *Proryv k svobode: O perestroike dvadtsat' let spustya (kriticheskii analiz)* (Moscow: Al'pina Biznes Buks, 2005), p. 394.
7. Ibid., pp. 376, 380.
8. Chistian W. Haerpfer, *Democracy and Enlargement in Post-Communist Europe. The Democratisation of the General Public in Fifteen Central and East European Countries, 1991–1998* (London: Routledge, 2002), p. 9.
9. Ibid., p. 14.
10. Ibid., p. 17.
11. Ibid., p. 19.
12. Joakim Ekman and Jonas Linde, 'Communist Nostalgia and the Consolidation of Democracy in Central and Eastern Europe', *Journal of Communist Studies and Transition Politics*, 21, 3 (September 2005), 357.
13. Ibid., p. 358.
14. Ibid., pp. 359–60.
15. Ibid., p. 361.
16. Ibid., pp. 363–71.
17. Neil Munro, *Russia's Persistent Communist Legacy: Nostalgia, Reaction and Reactionary Expectations* (Aberdeen: Centre for the Study of Public Policy, University of Aberdeen, 2006), pp. 6–8.
18. Ibid., p. 24.
19. Sarah E. Mendelson and Theodore P. Gerber, 'Soviet Nostalgia: an Impediment to Russian Democratization', *Washington Quarterly*, 29, 1 (Winter 2005–6), 84–7.
20. Sarah E. Mendelson and Theodore P. Gerber, 'Failing the Stalin Test', *Foreign Affairs*, 85, 1 (January–February 2006), 2–8.
21. See James L. Gibson, 'Political and Economic Markets: Changes in the Connections between Attitudes toward Political Democracy and a Market Economy within the Mass Culture of Russia and Ukraine', *Journal of Politics*, 58, 4 (November 1996), 954–84.
22. *Rossiiskaya gazeta*, 26 April 2005, p. 4.

3
The Social Bases of Reform and Anti-reform in Russia and Ukraine

David Lane[1]

The transformation of state socialism is widely interpreted as a 'system transfer' involving the transition to capitalism and democracy. Alternatively, it is viewed as a revolution involving a comprehensive change of the social political and economic institutions and their personnel, of ideology and foreign relations. Writers advocating such different interpretations, however, share in common the view that the dominant movers of transformation are elites. Whereas an earlier generation of scholars theorized social change in terms of class and social revolution, by the end of the twentieth century elites and 'system change' have become units of analysis. This chapter considers empirically the social basis of the supporters and opponents of transformation in Russia and Ukraine; it is based mainly on public opinion surveys conducted by the author in the two countries. It is contended that though personal identity is defined in many ways, social class is a major form of identification and is a significant factor in the process of transformation.

Theories of 'system change' focus on the inherent instability of state socialism. The lack of markets and mechanisms for conflict resolution in a 'totalitarian' system leads to collapse when the coercive powers are removed.[2] In this paradigm, political actors, led by 'elites', manage consequent socio-economic change. There is no room for the role of classes promoting a revolution in property relations. The implicit assumption is that new elites replace the faulty institutions of state socialism with markets, private property and democratic institutions. From this point of view, domestic elite conflict, enabled by the weakness of the incumbent state leaders, leads to 'within system' challenges to the state system. Sometimes, though not always, popular support is courted to fortify ascendant elites against internal opposition. There occur 'liberation revolutions' removing constraints 'which fettered social development'. The implications here are clear: no significant *class* changes are necessary in the regime which follows.[3]

Elite analysis, however, is not a sufficient explanation of transformation. An elite, by definition, occupies the apex of very different social, political and economic domains. What interests do elites represent and why should they pursue systemic change? A major problem is to explain why the transforming political elites under, and after, state socialism have universally adopted the ideology and policy of markets, private property and competitive party democracy. As one writer on revolution and elites has put it, the objectives of ruling elite configurations are to maintain their 'organizational autonomy' and 'exploitative relationship'.[4] This does not tell us what policies they may adopt to do so, or why in the first place incumbents of power should transform their economic and political institutions. After all, the totalitarian perspective on power relations ensures complete control of organizational autonomy and an exploitative relationship of the ruling elite over the mass.

With important exceptions (China, Belarus), in the former state socialist societies, similar macro policies in the economy, polity and foreign affairs have been adopted. If elites are motivated '... to appropriate resources from non-elites ...[5]', why should they support the 'system transfer' of the uncertainty of an Anglo-American type of Western economic and political market institutions? Why not pursue a state-managed market system, leaving ownership in state corporations, as in China? A class-based approach to transformation, I claim, explains why such a move has occurred. The elite-led approaches do not explain why 'the elites' choose the policies that they do, nor do they tell us the sources of their social power (military, social, political, economic; internal or external to the society concerned). In the accounts of transformation, one has no indication of what social groups are likely to pursue and gain from, or oppose, a policy of marketization and privatization – common objectives of all the ruling elites of post-communist societies.

This reasoning also influences the analysis of political 'outcomes'. If the configuration of elite renewal is not thorough, systemic change may be imperfect and a 'transformation' does not occur. This is an argument which is often used in respect of countries such as Ukraine, Russia, Belarus and many of the central Asian former state socialist societies, dubbed as 'transition laggards'. The old regime continues in an attenuated form. The former ruling groups – popularly referred to as the *nomenklatura* – remain in power. In these countries, it is claimed, those supporting reform sought an end to an authoritarian and bureaucratic system, not a revolution. Capitalism was not introduced (or reintroduced) in Russia because of the continued presence of state ownership and the absence of a bourgeoisie and its preferred form of political system, competitive democracy. 'Reforms' were enacted which benefited the incumbent political elites, or factions of the elites. Policy, often orchestrated by Western interests as epitomized in the 'Orange' and other 'coloured' 'revolutions', is directed at the removal of one set of elites, usually dubbed as 'corrupt hangovers' by another set, usually defined as 'positive modernizers'.

What then of 'bottom-up' forces? Unlike classical theories of revolution, where societal actors (peasants, workers, nobility, bourgeoisie) provide the mass base and energy for a revolution from below, in the elite-led framework of system change, they either do not appear or are peripheral to the main elite players. The absence of any class analysis in these accounts may be partly explained by the decline of class analysis in scholarly activity in political science and sociology in the West. In his collection of essays *Identity and Social Change*, Joseph E. Davis points out that in the study of collective identity and political action, the analytical focus of 'group struggles' is on 'race, ethnicity, nationality, gender and sexuality'.[6] More traditional sources of group identity have shifted significantly in the 'postmodern' age from the 'social sphere' to the 'realm of culture'.[7] The commodification of culture 'destabilizes' the individual and leads to 'a disintegration of integrated, productivist roles as the subject becomes fragmented through new regimes of consumption and leisure'.[8] A paradigmatic shift has taken place in the analysis of social change: social class differences, determined by occupation and wealth, have been diminished and replaced by lifestyle distinctions formed by market-driven consumption. Social movements are amorphous bodies with a shifting focus and political parties lose their saliency. 'Class' analysis has become a politically incorrect five-letter word.

Though these writers do not explicitly refer to the transformation of state socialism, they have influenced those writing about it. Following the proclaimed decomposition of class with respect to advanced capitalism, Jan Pakulski and Malcolm Waters in *The Death of Class* deny its analytical role also in post-communist society. '...[P]ost-communist politics cannot be usefully analyzed using the class paradigm'.[9] As classes are irrelevant to the transformation project, then one would not expect attitudes and benefits to have a class basis. Moreover, like the postmodernist writers on identity, it is asserted that national, ethnic, gender and generational cleavages underpin political behaviour. Even writers such as Claus Offe and Valerie Bunce, who define the transformation as a revolution, do not recognize class forces either as causes or consequences. Nationalism, for Valerie Bunch, 'loomed large' in 'the departure of socialist dictatorships'.[10] But why should 'ethnic groups', gender associations or 'national groups' be motivated to change state socialism to capitalism? These accounts also are often lacking in empirical content and are either assertive or interpretive in style.[11] An understanding of the class system, however, is important as classes are a crucial component of a capitalist system providing it with a social ballast – as witnessed by the importance given to privatization in the transformation process.

Class interests and social identities

One might consider first the interests that the elites promote. It is my contention that the policies of privatization, marketization and the opening of the economies to the world market, have primed a capitalist system. They have also contributed to the formation of a polarized class system. The changes benefited disproportionately a new class based on ownership of assets, and were detrimental to those of the working classes whose only assets were labour power.

Geoffrey Evans and Colin Mills, on the basis of empirical research in Hungary and Poland in the early 1990s, show that class position (evidenced by occupation) 'is a marker for a wide range of inequalities of resources and conditions'.[12] On the basis of empirical survey studies in nine central and eastern European societies conducted in 1993/95, Evans found that members of the upper salatariat had the advantage of higher education which enabled them to benefit from the transition period. The working strata (manual and agricultural) had significantly higher levels of unemployment, much worse career prospects and very much lower incomes. His data also clearly indicate significant differences between the relative life chances of the manual and non-manual groups: the top social strata benefited from the changes but the two working-class strata were made relatively worse off.[13] Further evidence of the importance of class strata during the transformation in Poland is provided by the research of Kazimierz Slomczynski and Goldie Shabad[14] in the early 1990s. Their findings point to people in different class strata sharing common participation in organizations and political orientations. Even in the study of electoral behaviour, Szelenyi, Fodor and Hanley contend that 'during the first five years of post communism the significance of class ... *increased*',[15] a conclusion echoed by Mateju and Rehakova.[16]

The present work carries these results forward by considering not only the occupational background but also how the social identities of people are related to their perceptions of regime change. We study comparatively the social structure of Ukraine and Russia. Based on the results of public opinion polls conducted in the Russian Federation and Ukraine in 2005, we consider the formation of social identities in the post-communist period. The questions asked were designed to examine the extent to which the population had an 'objective' and conscious identification with a number of social groups and the extent to which such identification was linked to their political views and evaluation of the transformation process. We examine how people identified with different political positions and the extent to which these political positions were related to different types of identity: occupational, national, generational and gendered.

Two surveys were conducted: in Russia in April 2005, when 1600 people, aged 18 and over, were selected randomly from the population;[17] in Ukraine, a similar survey of 2015 people was conducted in September 2005. The respondents were questioned individually in their homes. The respondents were classified by occupation, age and gender, their area of residence, and their subjective social identity. These variables were then related to their political ideology and to their evaluation of the reform process, privatization and the introduction of a market economy. Identical questions were asked in Russia and Ukraine (occasionally adapted for Ukrainian conditions, for example with respect to nationality). The results of these questions were cross-tabulated. The results are outlined below: first, the social characteristics of the respondents, second, the analysis of different forms of identity; third, the relationship of social structural features to the market reforms.

Basic data: occupation and political identification

The respondents' current (or last) occupational status is utilized as an 'objective' definition of class position. Occupations were then grouped into seven categories: businessmen, managers (in private and public sector), specialists/intelligentsia, lower non-manuals, workers, peasants and students (a final residual category included those with no employment and non-response).[18] The distribution of respondents between occupational groups is shown in Table 3.1. The table illustrates the great similarity in the occupational distribution of the population in both states, with Ukraine having rather more in agriculture and relatively fewer workers and lower non-manuals than Russia.

The respondents were asked to place themselves in a political grouping on the basis of their ideological affinity. Respondents were asked to identify their own views with seven ideological alternatives, each being defined in turn: *communist* views (defined as the recognition of class interests, support for state ownership of the means of production, the state distribution of social welfare); *social democratic* (the state defending the social interests of the people under conditions of a market economic and private ownership); *agrarian* (stimulation and development of the agricultural sector), in Russia – *Russian nationalism* (supporting above all, the interests of the Russian nation [*narod*]), in Ukraine – *Ukrainian nationalism*; *liberal* (the strengthening of private property and the development of a market economy) and finally, a *regime of firm rule* (*tverdaya ruka*). As the answers were not mutually exclusive, people might have liberal economic views and require a 'strong leader' to effect them, more than one category could be chosen by each respondent.

In Russia, the 1600 respondents gave 2202 answers, and Ukraine 2015 respondents gave 2378 answers (including non-responses) as shown in Table 3.2. The responses show a remarkable similarity one to the other, the differences being only two or three percentage points between the various categories.

Table 3.1 Occupational background of respondents, Russia 2005 (%)

Occupational group (definitions below)	*Russia*	*Ukraine*
Businessmen	*4.7*	*4.2*
Managers – private and public	*1.5*	*2.2*
Specialists/intelligentsia	*19.5*	*20*
Lower non-manuals	*18.6*	*16.8*
Workers	*35.4*	*30.9*
Peasants (agricultural manual labourers)	*5.1*	*8.2*
Students	*7.3*	*6.7*
Other responses	*7.9*	*6*
Total *N* =	*1600*	*2015*

Table 3.2 Political orientations of Russian and Ukrainian population, 2005

Political identification	*Russia responses* N	*Russia % responses*	*Ukraine responses*	*Ukraine % responses* N
Communist views	268	12.1	343	14.4
Social democratic	621	31	770	32.4
Agrarian	332	15	299	12.6
Nationalists (Russia, Ukrainian)	225	10	246	10.3
Liberal	187	8.4	188	7.9
Regime of a 'hard hand'	345	15.6	442	18.6
None of these variants	224	10.17	90	3.8
Responses	2202	100	2378	100

The social background of political identification

The social composition of respondents is analysed under the six ideological headings. We consider in some detail the backgrounds of the communists, social democrats, nationalists and liberals and mention more briefly the major features of agrarian and also authoritarian views.

Communist views

Figure 3.1 shows the proportion in each occupational group of those with communist sympathies and compares Russia and Ukraine.

The pattern of identification is similar in both countries. As one moves down the social ladder, support for the communists increases. Students show a very low level of identification (some 5 per cent), specialists and intellectuals (labelled professionals) around 11 per cent, rather surprisingly perhaps, similar to businessmen and managers. At the other end of the scale, the largest occupational group holding communist views was composed of those working in agriculture – a third in Russia and 23 per cent in Ukraine, and around a fifth of the workers in both countries. The shortfall among the peasants in Ukraine is probably due to the nationality factor where the agricultural population in West Ukraine was attracted to the nationalists (discussed below).

As to the subjective identification of the respondent, we asked a number of questions about identification with seven preselected social groups: your generation, the Russian (in Ukraine, also Ukrainian) nation, businessmen, intelligentsia, workers, peasants and students. The respondents were invited to indicate with which group they had 'a lot in common' (*ochen' mnogo obshchego*), 'something in common' (*dovol'no mnogo obshchego*), 'not much in common', and 'nothing in common'.

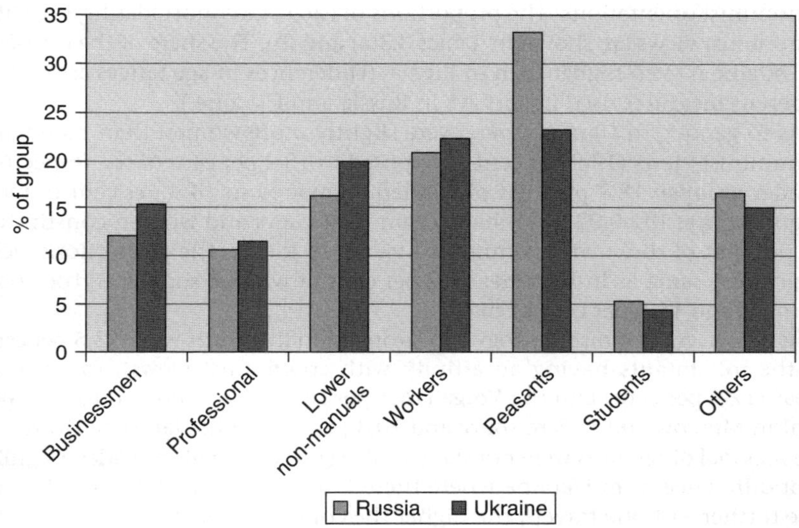

Figure 3.1 Occupation of people with communist political identification. Pearson chi-square significant at 0.001 for Russia and Ukraine

In Ukraine, the communists were composed of those who had a strong positive identification with the Russian nation: of the communists, 93 per cent had such identification – though, of course, many more had other political views. By nationality, 28 per cent of those self-defined as 'Russians' identified with the communists, but only half that number (14 per cent) among the much larger group of self-defined Ukrainians.

Considering the self-identification of working class by objective position, in Russia 89 per cent of workers by occupation had either a great deal or quite a lot in common with the working class. Of these, 79 per cent also identified with communist ideology. Conversely, of those respondents who felt they had little or nothing in common with the working class, 88.4 per cent had no affinity at all with communist ideology (significant at the 0.001 level). In Ukraine, there was a similar result; of those with communist views, 80 per cent had a positive identification with the working class and 72 per cent had a positive identification with the peasantry. At the other end of the scale, only 11 per cent of communists by inclination had a positive identification with businessmen. Hence both in terms of objective and subjective class position there was a close identification of the working class with the communists.

As noted above, students had a particularly low identification with the communists. This reflects significant differences between generations. As age rose, so dramatically did the identification with communist views. In the Russian survey, those in the over-55 age group accounted for over half of those with communist orientations. The proportions of each age cohort identifying with communist views are shown in Tables 3.3(a) and (b). The share of the over-50s in Ukraine is even higher than in Russia. (Differences in age ranges are due to different measures used in surveys in Russia and Ukraine.)

As to gender, in Ukraine there were slightly more women than men with communist views (17.9 per cent as opposed to 15.4 per cent of the respective gender groups); 18.7 per cent of women compared to 14.9 per cent of men (significant at the 0.02 level) had communist views and women constituted 60 per cent of those with communist views. In Russia, the proportions were almost the same as in Ukraine: 17.9 per cent of women supported the communists and 15.3 per cent of men.

In Russia, communist ideology was strongest in the north-west (23.5 per cent of the inhabitants having an affinity with communist views), the central areas (17.9 per cent) and the Volga (16.3 per cent); the figure fell to 14.9 per cent in Moscow and St Petersburg and 10.3 per cent in the far east). However, the regional differences were not statistically significant. This provides a significant difference from Ukraine where there is a clear regional differentiation. The further east one travels, the higher the communist support, as shown in Table 3.4. The eastern region accounts for 35 per cent of communist support and for over a quarter (27 per cent) of respondents; the western region, on the other hand, contains only 8 per cent of those with communist views and 7 per cent of the population in the region. The shortfall in the west is due to the prevalence of Ukrainian-speaking nationalists who drew support away from the communists.

Table 3.3 Age distribution of communist sentiments: Russia and Ukraine

(a) Russia

Age group	*18–24*	*25–39*	*40–54*	*Over 55*	*Total*
% in age group with communist views	6.0	9.1	16.0	29.9	16.8

N = 1332.
Significant at 0.001 level.

(b) Ukraine

Age group	*18–29*	*30–39*	*40–49*	*50–59*	*50–69*	*Over 70*	*Total*
% within age group with communist views	6.00	7.40	13.40	19.10	31.00	36.20	17.00

N = 1673.
Significant at 0.001 level.

We may confidently conclude that in both countries, using occupation as a proxy for class, the working class and peasantry provide a significant ballast to communist support. However, it overlaps with age: communism is associated with the older generation; there are regional differences: though slight in Russia, in Ukraine the regional overlaps with national differences, the Russian-speaking east being much more communist than the Ukrainian west.

Agrarians

As one might expect, the greatest support for 'agrarian' views came from those working in agriculture. In Ukraine 22 per cent of the occupational groups of 'peasants' and agricultural workers identified with agrarian views, followed by workers (15.4 per cent), lower white-collar workers (14.7 per cent), students (13.4 per cent), businessmen (12.8 per cent), managers and specialists (both at 11.4 per cent) (significant at the 0.04 level). There was a similar distribution in Russia where agricultural workers came to 23.5 per cent of the group, followed by 22.5 per cent of lower white-collar workers, 21.3 per cent of workers, 20.6 per cent of specialists and 18.4 per cent of businessmen and managers. Students, with just 10 per cent of the total, were significantly under-represented. In Russia, the spread between occupation and agrarian views was fairly even and not statistically significant.

Women are an important constituency in the agrarians' groups. In Russia, the spread between women and men was 59 to 41 per cent; 22 per cent of all women in the sample identified with the agrarians (significant at the 0.07 level). This is no doubt due to the higher proportion of women living in the countryside. In Ukraine, 16 per cent of women held 'agrarian' views, compared to 13.4 per cent of men.

As age increased, there was a tendency for an increase in the number of people with agrarian views, though in Ukraine the results were not statistically significant. (In Ukraine, in the 50–69 age group, 17.5 per cent supported 'agrarian' views.) The association with age was greater in Russia: those with

Table 3.4 Communist views by region: Ukraine

	Region					
	West	*West central*	*East central*	*South*	*East*	*Total*
N	28	54	52	89	120	343
Total with communist views	8.20	15.70	15.20	25.90	35.00	100.00
% respondents in region with communist views	7.30	11.20	15.90	23.10	27.30	17.00

agrarian views formed 14.7 per cent of the 18–24 age group, rising to 16.8, 21.7 and 26.5 per cent of the 25–39, 40–54 and 55+ age cohorts respectively (significant at the 0.001 level).

In Ukraine, respondents identifying with Ukrainian nationality (16 per cent of respondents) had a greater participation than those with Russian (11.5 per cent of respondents), as one would expect given the distribution of nationalities between occupational groups. There were also statistically significant differences between areas. The areas with the greatest density of Ukrainian-speaking people (west and west central) have the largest number of 'agrarians'.

In Russia there were also significant differences between regions: the north-west, central, far east and Urals providing support from just over a fifth to a third of the population. As might be expected, the cities of Moscow and St Petersburg had the lowest share of people with 'agrarian' views. These results were corroborated again when population density of areas is concerned: only 3 per cent of Moscow inhabitants supported agrarian views, compared to 40 per cent of people living in villages.

Socialist views

In both countries, the largest ideological group was composed of self-defined social democrats: in Ukraine 38 per cent of respondents and in Russia 38.7 per cent. There is a distinct distribution by occupational group: in Ukraine, of businessmen and managers 49.6 per cent ascribed to social democratic views, specialists and intellectuals 44.4 per cent, students, 36.6 per cent, whereas peasants (27.9 per cent) and workers (35 per cent) were the lowest. A similar picture is shown for Russia, though students formed the largest groups, followed by lower non-manuals and specialists and the intelligentsia. Workers and peasants had the lowest saturation (35.1 and 34.1 per cent respectively). Comprehensive data are shown in Table 3.5.

Women had more social democratic inclinations than men: in Russia, the proportions were 58 per cent compared to 41 per cent (significant at the 0.01 level). In Ukraine, however, the support was reversed; 40 per cent of men in the sample identified with social democratic views, compared to 36.7 per cent of women, though the difference is not statistically significant. In Ukraine there was also an insignificant difference between support by nationality (Ukrainian and Russian).

Age was important. As illustrated in Table 3.6, in Ukraine, the major support of the social democrats came from the 30–50 age group (averaging around 44 per cent of this group); support declined after the age of 60, falling to only 26 per cent of the over-70 age group. A similar tapering by age may be observed in Russia where younger people with leftist inclinations have moved from the communists to the social democrats.

By region, in Russia, the north-west (40 per cent), Volga (41 per cent) and Siberia (49.6 per cent) constituted the areas with highest concentrations; Moscow (36 per cent), far east (35.1 per cent), central (32.7 per cent) and

Table 3.5 Occupational background of social democrats

	Business and managers	*Specialists, intelligentsia*	*Lower non-manuals*	*Workers*	*Peasants, agricultural workers*	*Students*	*Others*	*Total*
Ukraine (*N* = 770) % of social democrats in this occupation group	49.6	44.40	38.10	35.00	27.90	36.6	41.30	38.3

Pearson chi-square significant at 0.001 level.

Russia (*N* = 621)								
% of social democrats in this occupation group	40.8	42.4	45	35.1	34.1	45.7	26.2	38.7

Pearson chi-square significant at 0.002 level.

Table 3.6 Social democrat ideology, by age group: Ukraine and Russia

Ukraine: Age group	*18–29*	*30–39*	*40–49*	*50–59*	*60–69*	*70+*	*Total*
% of social democrats in the relevant age group	38.80	44.30	44.00	38.50	32.30	26.50	38.20

Pearson chi-square significant at 0.001 level.

Russia: Age group	*18–24*	*25–29*	*40–54*	*55+*	*Total*
% of age group	44.5	44.0	37.3	32.6	38.8

Pearson chi-square significant at 0.001 level.

Urals (30.7 per cent) the lowest. An east–west division is also clear in Ukraine; as shown in Table 3.7, the further east one goes, the greater the affinity with social democratic views.

Social democracy is the most popular ideological orientation of people in Ukraine and Russia. However, there are significant differences between social groups. A much higher proportion of the higher occupational groups, of the younger population, support the social democrats. Women are slightly more sympathetic to social democracy than men.

Table 3.7 Social democratic ideology, by region: Ukraine

Region of Ukraine	*West*	*West central*	*East central*	*South*	*East*	*Average*
% of social democratic views in region	25.70	39.30	42.50	40.50	42.70	38.20

Pearson chi-square significant at 0.001 level.

National-patriotic views

As Russia is overwhelmingly populated by Russians, there is no significant national divide between ethnic groups, though there is hostility by Russians to national minorities, particularly from the southern parts of the former USSR. There is, however, a minority identification with Russian patriotic views: in this survey around 14 per cent acknowledged them. Russian patriots are fairly unequally divided between various social strata; the greatest difference is in terms of occupation. The greatest numbers are to be found among students (17.1 per cent of the group), followed by workers and lower non-manuals (16 per cent); peasants and agricultural workers had a very small participation (only 4.9 per cent) (see Table 3.8). There is no difference between the proportion of men or women in this group.

The situation in Ukraine is somewhat different as the nationality question is more pronounced. Self-identified 'Ukrainians' (rather than Russians) are the backbone of the Ukrainian nationalists. As shown in Table 3.8, the strongest supporters come from students (over a third of the group) followed by specialists and intelligentsia. This follows the general tendency of the middle classes to promote nationalist views. Lower non-manuals and workers provide the lowest levels of identification. In Ukraine only a small proportion of workers support the nationalists, though in Russia workers are the largest group after students. In Ukraine, workers are predominantly Russian and would not therefore support the Ukrainian nationalists, whereas in Russia, workers might be attracted to the nationalists as an alternative to the communists. There is no difference by sex – neither in Russia nor Ukraine.

One distinguishing factor is the very high density of young people. In the Ukrainian sample, students constituted 17.8 per cent of those who had nationalist views, though within the student category 31.3 per cent were nationalists. Those in the 18–29 age group made up 31 per cent of those with nationalist views: other age groups ranged from 10 per cent (over 70s) to 11.3 per cent (40–49 age group); 17 per cent of the 18–29 age group surveyed supported the Ukrainian nationalists. The relationship between age and nationalist views is significant at the 0.01 level. In Russia, age is less relevant: though rather more younger people are nationalists than older ones (in the 18–24 group, 16 per cent compared to 12.8 per cent for the over-55 age group), the difference

Table 3.8 Ukrainian nationalists and Russian patriots by occupational background

	Businessmen and managers	*Specialists and intelligentsia*	*Lower non-manuals*	*Workers*	*Agricultural workers*	*Students*	*Others*	*Total*
Ukraine N = 1663 Percentage within occupational group	11.6	13.6	8.8	9.8	11.6	31.3	10.50	12.30
Significant at 0.001 level.								
Russia N = 1374 Percentage within occupational group	14.3	11.9	15.8	16.0	4.9	17.1	10.2	14.1

Pearson chi-square significant at 0.06 level.

is not statistically significant. Clearly, in Ukraine the students had been mobilized in support of the nationalist movement – probably associated with the Orange Revolution which was largely a young people's affair.

One other significant variable (greater than 0.01) is that of the regional distribution – in both Russia and Ukraine. The far east, the central, Moscow and Petersburg areas were the strongest in support – Urals and Volga the lowest (see Table 3.9(a)).

In Ukraine, regional location is a major determinant of nationalist support. As noted in Table 3.9(b), 59 per cent of the nationalists in the sample were from the western provinces, accounting for 38 per cent of people in the sample in the western region.

The west-central area accounted for 20 per cent of supporters (10 per cent of the respondents in that area); the support fell to 13.8, 2.8 and 3.7 per cent in the east-central, south and eastern areas respectively. As a proportion of the population of the areas, the south and east had extremely small proportions of the population (1.8 and 2.0 per cent) sharing any sentiments in common with the nationalists. This points to a major division in the Ukraine between nationalists split on a regional basis and presents a qualitative contrast to Russia.

Supporters of reform (the 'liberals')

The 'liberals' are those who support a right-wing reform policy: private property and a market economy. As shown in Table 3.10, allegiance to reform policy was slightly stronger in Russia than Ukraine, though in neither was support very substantial (11.7 per cent compared to 9.7 per cent of the respective

Table 3.9(a) Russia: Russian patriots by area

Area	*Moscow and St Petersburg*	*North-west*	*Central*	*South*	*Volga*	*Urals*	*Siberia*	*Far east*	*Total* N = *1376*
Percentage of respondents with ideological affinity	18.0	18.6	19.1	11.2	9.7	8.0	12.5	20.5	14.0

Chi-square significant at 0.001 level.

Table 3.9(b) Regional affinity with Ukrainian nationalists

Region	*West*	*West-central*	*East-central*	*South*	*East*	*Total* N = *1770*
Regional distribution of people with Ukrainian nationalist views	59.30	20.30	13.80	2.80	3.70	100.00
% within each	38.40	10.30	10.40	1.80	2.00	12.20

Significant at 0.001 level.

populations). There is clear evidence of a polarization of social support. In Russia, nearly a third of the businessmen and managers in the sample (28.9 per cent), just under a quarter of students (24.1 per cent) and 18.3 per cent of specialists and managers were supporters. In Ukraine, the support of businessmen and managers was much lower in relative terms, coming after students. At the other end of the social scale, identity with reformist views was very low: in Russia only 3.7 per cent of agricultural workers, and 5.8 per cent of workers had any ideological affinity; the figures for Ukraine were 1.8 and 7.6 respectively. There is clear class identification with liberal views: the higher the social class, the higher the density of liberal attachment (Figure 3.2).

There is a tendency for men to have more 'liberal views' (in favour of private property and the market) than women: in Russia, 13.6 per cent of men in the sample supported this tendency compared to only 10.1 per cent of women (significant at the 0.03 level). In Ukraine, similarly, 10.4 per cent of men compared to 8.4 per cent of women identified with liberal views.

Age, in both Ukraine and Russia, was strongly correlated with right-wing views. As age increased, the frequency of liberal views declined considerably. In Russia, the 25–39 age group accounted for 39 per cent of the sample

Table 3.10 Occupational background of liberal support: Ukraine and Russia

Country	*Businessmen and managers*	*Professionals and intelligentsia*	*Lower non-Manuals*	*Workers*	*Peasants*	*Students*	*Other*	*Total*
Ukraine: Per cent of total within given occupation	14.9	13.40	8.80	7.60	1.80	18.50	6.70	*N* = 1713 9.70%
Russia: Per cent of total within given occupation	28.9	18.3	11.1	5.8	3.7	24.1	4	*N* = 1410 11.7%

Both sets of data (Russia and Ukraine): significant at 0.001 level.

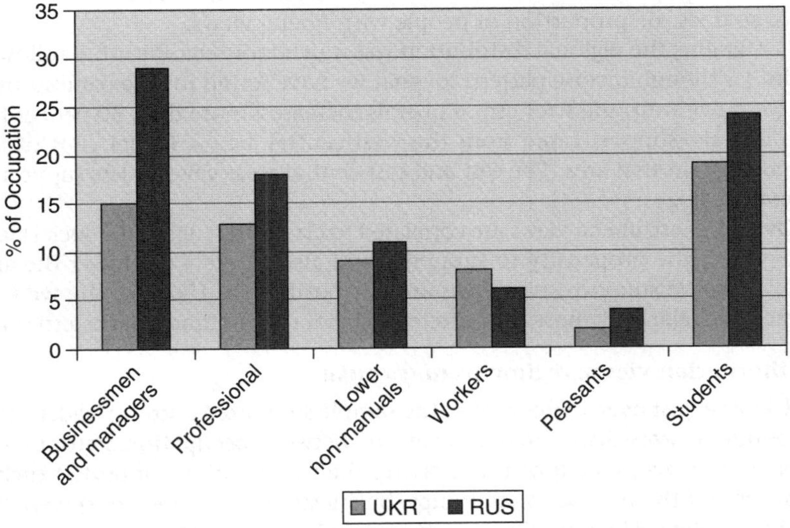

Figure 3.2 Liberal support: Russia and Ukraine

subscribing to liberal views (not shown in the table). Similarly, in Ukraine, age was a crucial variable. Of the sample subscribing to a liberal ideology, 38.6 per cent were aged between 18 and 29, and constituted 16.3 per cent of the age group, whereas the 60-year-olds contributed 6.9 per cent of the constituency and the over-70s 2.6 per cent; of these age cohorts the former had

Table 3.11 Liberal views and density of population: Russia

	Moscow	*500+*	*100–500*	*10–100*	*Villages*	*Total N = 1412*
Percentage in area supporting liberal views	14.1	17.4	11.9	11.8	7.0	11.7%

Pearson chi-square significant at 0.001 level.

only 4.4 per cent in this group and the latter only 1.9 per cent. (In Ukraine and Russia, age and liberal views were significant at the 0.001 level.)

In Russia, areas with populations supporting liberal views were Moscow (16 per cent) and the far east (15.6 per cent), whereas the Volga region (10 per cent) and Siberia (7 per cent) had very much fewer. However, these differences were not statistically significant. In Russia, of greater significance is the size of population points. As noted in Table 3.11, as size of settlement falls, so does the proportion of people with liberal views.

In Ukraine, the regional distribution was much more significant. It followed a similar though reverse pattern to what we have found for the communists. As we move west, the strength of liberals increases; more than 30 per cent of the liberals' support came from the west-central area – 12 per cent of the population in that area. The east and east-central areas gave far less support to liberal ideology.

Overall, then, liberal views are correlated to class – the higher the social class, the greater the propensity to support – and also to age – the lower the age, the larger the support; rural areas are less positive; in Ukraine, the western areas have relatively more supporters of liberal reform than the eastern ones.

Authoritarian views: regime *tverdaya ruka*

In Ukraine, just over 18 per cent of the sample supported a strong leader. Such respondents were distributed fairly evenly between occupational groups. On average just over a fifth of those giving their occupation supported such a position. Of the occupational groups, businessmen (28.2 per cent) were the highest, followed by unskilled non-manuals (23.5 per cent), and workers (22.8 per cent); managers (13.6 per cent) and students (17.9 per cent) (differences were not statistically significant). In Ukraine, the distribution of views was not significant between men and women, between age groups, nor between regions or nationalities. Such views seem to be shared among all population groups.

In Russia, more men had authoritarian views than women – 26.7 per cent of the males, compared to 19.1 per cent of the women, significant at the 0.008 level. There was no significant difference by age group. With the exception of those working in agriculture, of whom only 5 per cent supported a regime of a 'strong hand', in all the other occupational groups between 21 and 25 per cent had an affinity with such a position. Possibly those in the countryside thought they would be the recipient of the effects of a hard hand, if it materialized. There were no significant differences by area.

Overall, there seems to be no social basis for those who might favour an authoritarian regime. Such views are shared by a significant minority, but spread evenly across the population of Ukraine and Russia.

Conclusions

This study does not substantiate the widely accepted views of the 'decline of class' as a form of social identification. People have many identities, social class being one of the most important of them. Moreover, there is a common pattern of class-linked ideological orientations in Russia and Ukraine. Occupational position, age and, to a lesser extent, gender, place and size of area of living are systematically linked to political ideology on a right–left basis. While there is generalized support for a 'market system', it is strongly infused with backing for state activity – giving social democratic ideas the most widespread support with respect to the reform process. 'Class matters': no other variable is found to be as consistently associated with ideological position as class. 'Left' views were subscribed to by the industrial and agricultural workers, especially women among them, and older people. The 'right' was constituted predominantly by the new entrepreneurial/management classes and students, and concentrated in the urban areas (especially Moscow and St Petersburg). The positive identification with the market by students is a remarkable indication of the link between aspiring members of the bourgeois classes and marketization. There is one main difference between Russia and Ukraine – a distinct regional bias of the western Ukraine towards patriotic ideology and more right-wing policies. This association, however, is compounded by a more peasant and rural population and a less industrial social structure.

The consequences of transformation have left a considerable part of the population, concentrated in the lower classes and sections of the previous socialist intelligentsia, with a feeling of loss and opposition to reform. In the former state socialist societies there have been rising levels of tension.[19] As dislike of the costs of reform is widespread, why has there been relatively little political opposition? Part of the answer lies in the objectives of protest and the articulation of an alternative strategy. There is little evidence of wide-scale popularly based oppositional class movements – as opposed to the developing associations of businessmen and entrepreneurs – in support of the market and privatization. Political parties are weak, with ineffective levels of support and small memberships. (Many protest movements, such as the 'coloured' revolutions, have been financed and sponsored by foreign interests – supporting movements for market reform and pluralist political organization.) The new managerial and business classes have a keen sense of class interest indicated by support for a market system, though there is considerable backing for state involvement – an indication of a lack of class confidence in the face of market uncertainties. Opposition has been directed at non-class actors: the state administration, authority figures and national identities have become a political focus for many from the middle classes, though surprisingly few from the working class in Russia. Paradoxically, perhaps, there is still a quite widespread belief, even by those who have suffered the consequences of reform, that liberal reforms could work, if only properly implemented.

Another explanation of the weakness of social movements of protest is to be found in the forms of intermediary groups constituting civil society – both before and following state socialism. The economic space has not been filled by autonomous capitalist entrepreneurs in any significant numbers. Though social networks in state socialism were far greater than recognized in much of the civil society literature,[20] they were to a considerable extent dependent on the state – either directly or indirectly. The communist opposition has inherited, and been weakened by, this legacy. The creation 'from the top' of civil society organizations, sponsored by the West in the post-communist period, has been relatively unsuccessful and civil society associations without foreign donor support have remained fragile. 'Civil society' organizations, moreover, have had a neo-conservative function of weakening state institutions and replacing them with charities, voluntary associations and privatized 'service providers'. They have become, in many instances, a component of a neo-liberal ideology, replacing the former welfare state. Despite the high formal membership of trade unions, they are largely de-ideologized and economistic in orientation. There is a defensive bourgeois class. Civil society networks can provide the ballast not only for stable democracies but also for political opposition, protest and change.[21] The weakness of civil society has prevented the rise of counter-elites and social movements by the dispossessed and others opposed to the introduction of the market and private property. There is clearly a potential for counter-revolution in the unstable social conditions of Ukraine and Russia. It is therefore leadership, organization and a counter-ideology to the reform programme which is lacking – not forms of class consciousness. The political stability of the post-socialist countries has been due to an elite consensus that has not only guided these countries to a market-type society, but has also neutralized ideological opposition.

Notes

1 This work is a product of my research project, The Transformation of State Socialism, supported by the Leverhulme Trust (Grant No. F/01 034/A).

2 State socialism had 'major systemic incompatibilities caused by the absence of both a market and a mechanism of conflict resolution ... Because institutional arrangements

deprive state socialism of the capacity to channel self-interested behaviour into socially beneficial performance and condition its survival on the base of direct coercion, the whole concept of a politico-economic order is fundamentally flawed.' J. Kornai, *From Socialism to Capitalism* (London: The Social Market Foundation, 1998), p. 40.

3 For Mau and Starodubrovskaya, 'class analysis ... is not applicable to revolution'. V. Mau and I. Starodubrovskaya, *The Challenge of Revolution* (Oxford: Oxford University Press, 2001), p. 332.

4 These are the two 'vital interests' for ruling elites according to Lachmann. R. Lachmann, 'Agents of Revolution' in J. Foran (ed.), *Theorising Revolutions* (New York and London: Routledge, 1997), p. 97, n. 2.

5 J. Foran (ed.), *Theorising Revolutions* (New York and London: Routledge, 1997), p. 97, n. 2.

6 J. E. Davis, 'Introduction: Social Change and the Problem of Identity', in J. E. Davis (ed.), *Identity and Social Change* (New Brunswick and London: Transaction Books, 2000), p. 4.

7 R. G. Dunn, 'Identity, Commodification, and Consumer Culture', in J. E. Davis (ed.), *Identity and Social Change* (New Brunswick and London: Transaction Books, 2000), p. 124.

8 Ibid., p. 115.

9 J. Pakulski and M. Waters, *The Death of Class* (London and Thousand Oaks: Sage, 1996), p. 147.

10 V. Bunce, *Subversive Institutions* (Cambridge: Cambridge University Press, 1999), p. 152. C. Offe, *Varieties of Transition* (Cambridge: Polity Press, 1996).

11 One notable exception here is the article by D. Harvey, 'The Work of Postmodernity: the Laboring Body in Global Space', in J. E. Davis (ed.), *Identity and Social Change* (New Brunswick and London: Transaction Books, 2000), pp. 27–52. His work, however, is critical of the postmodernist position.

12 G. Evans and C. Mills, 'Are there Classes in Post-Communist Societies? A New Approach to Identifying Class Structure', *Sociology*, 33, 1 (February 1999) 42.

13 G. Evans, 'Social Class and Interest Formation in Post-communist Societies', in D.J. Lee and B.S. Turner, *Conflicts about Class* (London: Longman and New York, 1996), p. 232.

14 K.M. Slomczynski and G. Shabad, 'Structural Determinants of Political Experience: a Refutation of the "Death of Class" Thesis', in K. Slomczynski, *Social Patterns of Being Political* (Warsaw: IFiS Publishers, 2000), pp. 201–3.

15 I. Szelenyi, E. Fodor and E. Hanley, 'Left Turn in PostCommunist Politics: Bringing Class Back in', *East European Politics and Societies*, 11, 1 (1997) 196. Italics in original.

16 P. Mateju and B. Rehakova, 'Turning Left or Class Realignment? Analysis of the Changing Relationship between Class and Party in the Czech Republic, 1992–96', *East European Politics and Societies,* 11, 3 (1997) 501–42. They conclude that the association between class and party increased during this period, p. 537.

17 The survey was conducted in 128 urban settlements and rural regions in 46 subjects of the Russian Federation. The total number of contacts was 2949.

18 Businessmen include *biznesmeny* (predpriminately) farmers having their own property. Managers include persons having responsibility for more than five persons, and higher-level civil servants. Specialists include professionals (*spetsialisty*) and those with non-manual work requiring specialist or higher education. Lower non-manuals (*sluzhashchie*) include those doing non-manual work with lower than specialist or higher education. Workers include those in mechanical physical labour

in industry, building and transport. Peasants include all those employed in agriculture. Students include those studying at institutions of learning.

19 Golovakha and Panina, for example, have shown the rising level of tension in Ukraine. E.I. Golovakha and N. Panina, 'Potentsial protesta Ukrainskogo obshchestva', *Sotsiologicheskie issledovaniya*, No. 10 (1999) 31–40.

20 See David Lane, 'Civil Society and the Imprint of State Socialism', *Participation of Civil Society in New Modes of Governance. The Case of the New Member States* (Forschungsstelle Osteuropa Bremen, Arbeitspapiere und Materialien, May 2005) 7–16.

21 Michael Mann considers nationalist and right-wing movements which, as mass movements, may also articulate popular grievances against dominant powers. Michael Mann, *The Dark Side of Democracy: Explaining Ethnic Cleansing* (Cambridge: Cambridge University Press, 2005), p. 21. Michael Mann, *Fascists* (Cambridge: Cambridge University Press, 2004), p. 170.

4

Social Forces and the Post-communist Transition: Why Labour Turns Right

David Ost

In the summer of 1994, I visited the small Polish manufacturing city of Starachowice. A city of some 60,000 residents, it boasted one large factory, the Star car plant, which had employed some 24,000 workers in the 1970s, down to 18,000 in 1989, and now, after several rounds of layoffs, early retirements and industrial restructuring, left only with some 5000 employees and more layoffs scheduled soon. There were 14,000 unemployed in the city, giving an unemployment rate of about 45 per cent, but this did not include the 6000 people whose unemployment benefits had already expired. Inside the plant I met with two Solidarity officials, the vice president of the car assembly plant and the president of the union at the parts division. (Like most other large manufacturing plants, this one had been broken down into several formally independent companies as a prelude to full-scale privatization, and each company now had – or, in some cases, did not have – its own trade unions.) When I asked them about the situation at the plant, they both complained about the unprecedented economic depression and then unleashed a torrent of angry words filled with attacks on 'the communists' and insisting that a 'right-wing' government must come and change things. Such comments were already familiar to me, but I decided to play dumb, and so when one of them next told me about his 'right-wing' views I interrupted to express surprise, noting that many people see trade unions themselves, in their very essence, as leftist institutions. He responded at once: 'As unionists, we *should* be leftists, yes. But after 45 years of oppression by red barons, we can't be. So you're right: we should be leftists, but we aren't.'

This tells us a great deal about some of the social forces that have been dominant in post-communist transformations. For what 'not being leftist' has meant is that labour's discontent with the shape of post-communist transition has been focused less on the nature of the market system that replaced the old one than on the remnants of the old one that allegedly prevent 'good' capitalism from emerging. This is the narrative that has helped keep labour quiescent and led to its great fragmentation, both in times of the initial post-communist depression (when some expected a social explosion) and in times of economic improvement (when some expected labour to demand a greater share of increased productivity). But even more, it is the narrative, or ideology, that has kept workers from being a force for a politically inclusive democracy, turning them instead into the electoral base for illiberal populism, such as which came to power in 2005 with the victory of the Kaczyński brothers' Law and Justice Party.

My argument is that it is the way labour is organized to fight against the injustices of markets that shapes a country's political system. In the West, liberal democracy became consolidated when socialist parties persuaded workers to channel their anger at inequalities into a political programme for greater economic redistribution. In post-communist Europe, where labour has tended to be wary of class discourses (understandably, due to the legacy of authoritarian state socialism), parties that explain economic inequalities as due to identity rather than class cleavages – the enemy being an ethnic, religious or ideological other – have had greater success. Thus the gains of illiberal populism, for when economic anger is directed personally at other citizens rather than institutionally against an unfair system, the political result is a polity that keeps seeking internal enemies and never has an interest in actually resolving the economic issues that get workers and other non-elites mad.

Questions of class are thus crucial to understanding the success or failure of democratic politics.[1] Transition studies have largely missed this point, leading most theorists to see democratization as a political process alone without looking at the class arrangements that underpin them. Yet historically, political democracy became consolidated only when wedded to policies that guarantee economic inclusion for workers as a class. Recent years have seen the publication of a good deal of serious work on the connection between class and the consolidation of democracy. Some of this literature notes the large contribution of labour to bringing about stable democratic outcomes. We learn, for example, that while the bourgeoisie fought for political rights for itself, the working class consistently fought for the extension of such rights.[2] Or that working-class mobilization was the key factor in winning social welfare inclusion, the other element necessary for embedding democracy in a given national society.[3] Other studies focus precisely on the question of inclusion. In his work on interwar Europe, Gregory Luebbert shows that there could be no political stability without the incorporation of the working class.[4] Elite theorists, he notes, may have railed against 'mass politics', but there was nothing to do about it; practical politicians had to act within the new context created by dynamic industrialization. And the political outcome would be determined by which party would be able to win over this newly mobilized working class, which party would be able to capture their anger. For Luebbert, a democratic system resulted only when workers were won over by liberals, or when workers organized themselves and then won over the agrarian middle class. Where liberals failed to win over workers, or workers failed to win over farmers, fascists were able to win the support of those who felt excluded and come to power themselves. Luebbert's account confirms the thesis of consistent working-class support for democracy. More important, he shows how any kind of political democracy, whether of the liberal or social democratic variants, requires the inclusion of labour as a condition of its existence, a conclusion that other research demonstrates to be valid in Latin America and elsewhere.[5] The result of all this work is that they get us to see labour inclusion not as a 'substantive' issue secondary to the survival of democracy, as Schmitter and O'Donnell have argued famously,[6] but as an indispensable aspect of political democracy. The key question for politics in the modern era is not whether workers will be included, but how, and on what grounds.

As the comments of the Starachowice unionists suggest, Polish labour has been incorporated into the system behind a right-wing political programme. How did this happen? How did labour in Poland, and to some extent elsewhere in the region, become a social force pushing for exclusion rather than inclusion?

Sources of labour weakness

In 1989, market reformers in Poland feared that the introduction of capitalism would spur the emergence of a militant labour movement. After all, market logic would mean attacks on labour, the introduction of unemployment, and tightening labour discipline. The desired creation and empowerment of a new propertied class would require the disempowerment of workers, and reformers widely feared an imminent 'social explosion'. But while attacks on labour proceeded apace, neither in Poland nor elsewhere in the region did labour offer a militant response. This was not because they were shell-shocked and disoriented, unable to come up with a response to such a frontal assault. In fact, the assault was not so 'frontal'. Precisely because the political elite was so afraid of a social explosion, it tried to mitigate the potential damage. The new market-oriented governments consulted with organized labour, and set up tripartite councils to symbolically include labour representatives. When they eliminated economic subsidies and drove firms to lay off workers, they ensured that this be done, at least initially, through attrition or advantageous new early retirement laws.

Union leaders were certainly not deluded about what was going on. No sweetening measures could hide the fact that a grand systemic transformation was under way and that the new elites wished to marginalize the power and authority of organized labour. The reason labour leaders did not oppose these developments, however, is that far from being militant representatives committed to defending 'the working class' against a 'new bourgeoisie', post-communist union leaders were every bit as reformist as the new governmental leaders. They supported privatization efforts, and often tried to accelerate them. They accepted that new managers would have to lay off many and tighten labour discipline on the rest. 'Employees will have to learn', wrote a leading Solidarity activist in Poland, just days after market reformers came to power, 'that their salaries are a function of the talents and capabilities of the managers, economists, and engineers, and that the general state of our factories depends on the level of the cadre governing the firm.'[7] They went along contentedly with symbolic tripartite councils, allowing market reformers the veneer of social approval that made their plans go smoother.[8] So accepting were union leaders of a new system opposed to organized labour that they often refrained from trying to organize unions even in foreign firms that expected them.

Why was labour so compliant? Three reasons stand out. First, post-communist unions tended to be pro-capitalist chiefly because they were anti-communist, and came to believe that the enemy of their enemy was their friend. This was particularly true in Poland, where opposition union movements emerged before 1989, fighting against 'communism'. But even in those countries where the old official unions stayed dominant, post-1989 leaders were anxious to dissociate themselves from the past, and proclaimed their support for new market principles. Post-communist Solidarity leaders embraced two central tenets: that private employers are better for workers than state employers are, and that unions had common interests with employers in getting rid of the excess workers of communist-era firms. (Most local unions were led by skilled workers who were frustrated with the old system's practice of using the firm to administer social benefits, such as employing most of a small town's inhabitants, thereby devaluing labour and keeping skilled workers from advancing.)[9]

Second, workers had little sense of their own interests. With no experience of life in a market economy, they did not know which policies would promote whose interests. Everyone could believe that market reforms were going to make their own lives better, since the changes were being vouched for by a trade union that represented virtually the entire population. Moreover, there were no other political forces on the scene arguing anything else. The former Communist Party advocated market reform as much as Solidarity did. Critics did emerge within Solidarity when economic conditions soon became tough. But they claimed that what was hurting workers was not pro-capitalist reforms but not *enough* pro-capitalist reforms. Jaroslaw and Lech Kaczyński pushed this line already in 1990 in their short-lived Centre Alliance Party. Market reform, they said, was not being carried out quickly enough, and the fact that former communists had become private owners meant that the capitalism that existed was not 'real' capitalism, as if the pedigree of the owners made a difference in the kinds of policies that would be pursued. (In fact, research on the topic shows that domestic owners regardless of past affiliations treated workers in similarly exploitive manners, with little patience for trade unions, and that foreign owners tended to be better employees, probably due to the latter's greater familiarity with unions and the fact that foreign-owned firms tended to be larger and more capital-intensive than domestic ones.)[10]

Finally, the nature of the former communist class structure kept workers from seeing themselves as a discrete group with their own particular interests. Instead, because the Party/state was the employer of all citizens, all citizens (with the exception of the *nomenklatura*) had common interests and a common enemy. Society was able to come together with the kind of unity impossible in class-based societies, and intellectuals were able plausibly to claim to represent workers. But while this means that classic anarchist warnings about intellectuals dominating workers' movements in order to pursue their own interests did not make sense during the communist period, it also means that workers' movements as such were particularly vulnerable after communism, when there would no longer be a common enemy or common employer uniting different social groups.

It is only *after* the communist era that class becomes important. Democratic market reformers, after all, explicitly sought to create a 'normal' class society, meaning the emergence of owners, professionals and workers, but with the latter lacking the veto power or social support they had enjoyed in the past. After 1989, in other words, class as a *dividing* factor finally became relevant, but because of Solidarity, workers were still accustomed to accepting the political and intellectual leadership of intellectuals. (As noted above, this was particularly true of local union leaders, who were themselves ambitious and supportive of market reform.) Market reform thus became a common project of the political and union elite, thus making post-communist industrial relations relatively easy to manage.

Unions thus became weak not because they were attacked by capitalism and not because they were mollified by capitalism. They became weak because union leaders largely agreed with the policies aimed at weakening them.

Trade unions in the post-communist era are thus different kinds of creatures than the trade unions most sociologists and industrial relations specialists are used to. Seemingly straightforward definitions about unions being organs for the defence of labour's interests in the workplace and the advancement of their interests in society at large do not work for post-communist society. That is what unions are when they are formed within capitalist society, when activists are taking risks simply by being involved in unions. But that is not what unions were about in the communist era, and since the activists largely remained the same, it is not what they were about in the post-communist era either.

The right's capture of labour anger

Discontent soon appeared, on the part of lesser-skilled workers who quickly emerged as the economic losers in the transformation. But here we have the key dilemma that has shaped so much of the post-communist era: the latter ushered in a great deal of class frustration, but because of the communist legacies discussed above it was not politically organized *as* class frustration. Instead, class anger became transformed by political entrepreneurs into nationalist, religious and ideological anger. These, of course, are the classic right-wing modes of organizing anger. When the other is defined according to ascriptive features, or according to cultural attributes the other can do nothing about, the only way to defeat that other is to eliminate from the community those with the 'wrong' features or attributes. Class cleavages, on the other hand, are conducive to democracy precisely because the other is identified on the basis of interests, not identity. Class conflicts lead to a more inclusive polity because they target their enemies on an abstract rather than concrete basis. Unlike nationalist, communitarian, religious, racial or ethnic antagonisms, which exclude whole categories of people from citizenship on the basis of attributes one can do nothing about, class-based antagonisms target only an abstract distributional arrangement as the problem. Thus they can be resolved by adjusting the economic system, rather than, say, by killing Jews, subjugating blacks or expelling Muslims from Bosnia. Class is the democratic cleavage because it offers economic anger an economic narrative. No pretending here that the anger derived from the work experience is 'really' caused by alien nations or peoples. Instead, class narratives say economic anger is caused by economic problems, and that the complaints can be redressed by changing economic rules. In this way, anger is met head-on and compromise becomes possible.

When market reform appeared to be in everyone's interests, the liberal group that dominated Solidarity also dominated the political scene unchallenged. When discontent appeared, so did new political entrepreneurs, seeking to garner the votes that would be looking for alternatives.

The Kaczyński brothers, Jaroslaw and Lech, were the first to recognize the opportunities. Long before they swept into political power in 2005, they emerged as the first challengers to the old Solidarity leadership. How did they do this? What is important here is not so much the particular political steps they took – such as promoting a 1990 presidential run by Lech Walesa, pushing a 'war at the top' that would break up Solidarity's former unity, and then forming one political organization after another until building the Law and Justice Party that would eventually propel them to power. Rather, what is key is the *ideological narrative* they developed. It was this that would have such a deep effect on the social forces that have emerged since.

An alternative Solidarity elite needed a narrative that could explain the economic problems without rejecting market reform as such. It soon found one – through the narrative of lustration. The dominant political narrative of Polish politics in 2006, it first emerged as a powerful one in 1992, during the five-month tenure of Prime Minister Jan Olszewski. A lawyer who had played a key role in drafting Solidarity's charter in 1980, and a close ally of the Kaczyński brothers, Olszewski came to power as leader of a weak coalition in a fragmented parliament, which explains his short tenure.

The heart of the lustration narrative is that good capitalism is endangered by bad communism, and that all of the country's ills result from lingering communist influence. Indeed, Olszewski claimed that Poland in 1992 was still a communist country, and that his government would be the first to do something about it. He drew special attention to the lingering old-boy party networks still running the banks and to the presence of communist-appointed government officials still holding middle-level positions in government ministries. With McCarthyite flourish, he charged that communist agents were present at all levels of power, economic and political. And they had to be identified, and purged, he said, because failure to do so left them and the country open to blackmail and sabotage.

The Olszewski government was the first to criticize shock therapy and the post-1989 economic reforms, but it never followed through on any of its criticisms. Though it came to power promising an end to the neo-liberal Balcerowicz Plan, it soon ended up reproducing it. It attacked the previous government for not listening to the increasingly frustrated Solidarity rank and file, and then soon did the same itself. It railed against IMF austerity measures, and then meekly agreed to all conditions. It apologized for the 'arrogance' of previous governments, but when teachers started protesting, the Minister of Education waved his cane and threatened legislation taking away their right to strike. Olszewski supported the free market but claimed that in Poland it did not exist: the market was run by communists, and it was these bad individuals that caused the economic hardships angering workers. This government was going to organize anger not through an economic critique but a political one. Prime Minister Olszewski, just like Prime Minister Kaczyński today, painted himself as the master 'de-communizer', and offered radical lustration as the grand solution to the problems people were facing.

For all the moral force of the lustration narrative, with its emphasis on justice and on punishment for crimes committed, morality always played a secondary role for Olszewski. He focused on economic themes instead, which explains the support he would get from labour. The main reason for de-communization, according to Olszewski, was not to punish past perpetrators but to defend workers by taking the economy out of the hands of those ruining and corrupting it. He offered a discourse that attacked the actually existing market economy in the name of an idealized one. 'The invisible hand [of the market]', Olszewski said famously, was 'simply the hand of the swindler plundering public funds from the state treasury.' The remark outraged liberals, who thought it would undermine support for the market economy. But it is better interpreted as an attempt to maintain *support* for the market in face of increasing opposition, by locating the desired 'real' market economy still in the future. Olszewski lauded free markets and privatization when they were 'done right'. By blaming communists for the hardships of capitalism in its primitive accumulation stage, the myth of 'real capitalism' could be preserved intact. In this way he could both mobilize class anger and channel it onto non-class targets. He aimed to turn the already burgeoning economic anger, against which the liberals were doing nothing, into anger directed at political enemies instead.

The strength of this approach stemmed from the fact that there was no other pro-market ideology able to attract voters. Market ideas were popular while market realities were not, and de-communization offered an explanation that allowed people to hold onto their pro-market beliefs and oppose market results. The 'Olszeviks' (rhymes with 'Bolsheviks'), as they were labelled by liberals, gained strength not because workers were susceptible to 'irrationality', which was the usual argument of liberals (and not just in eastern Europe – recall Lipset's famous thesis of 'working-class authoritarianism').[11] Rather, they gained because they presented a non-socialist ideology able to explain economic woes. Liberals were saying that transition was a difficult time and that workers would just have to suffer. Socialists were beginning to make their classic economic critique, but as a result of the communist experience, that narrative could not yet be heard. Political illiberals filled the gap: they offered a critique of the market while maintaining all market rules.

Why did liberals not try to fill this gap? Because they looked upon any challenge to market reform as a dangerous sign of populism that would undermine both democracy and the market. There is no room here to go into this at depth, but the liberals' position stemmed from the reinterpretation of democracy that they carried out in the 1980s. In the initial Solidarity period the left liberals who were dominant in the movement, symbolized by Adam Michnik, believed that democracy could only be brought about by great civic participation; thus their efforts on behalf of building a civil society to challenge the state. Soon after the crushing of Solidarity in 1981, however, they changed their tune – in part due to their understanding of the 1980–81 experience, and in part due to new Western trends, in particular the ebbing of social democracy in favour of neo-liberalism. In the mid-1980s they discovered property rights theory, published Hayek in the underground press, and came to a conclusion that it was not civic participation but private property that was the foundation for democracy.[12] In short, they kept this view into the post-communist period, and pursued it even though it meant that they would not appeal to economic 'losers' for their votes. In this way, they abandoned the very base that they had cultivated as leaders of Solidarity, and left the field open to the right. Liberals and social democrats everywhere have been losing out to the right in the era of globalization, but unlike in the West, east European liberals had not earlier secured the allegiance of workers in organized political parties. The result is that the right has been able to build stronger political parties, and to do so with strong working-class support.

As Jaroslaw Kaczyński once said, characterizing his plans of the early 1990s, 'For us, the crucial question was who would articulate and use politically the protest against all the painful aspects of the economic reform.'[13] The right succeeded both because it asked this question and tried to answer it. The left failed to shape post-communist social forces because it feared the question, feared protest, and put all its eggs into the chimerical basket of neo-liberal economic reform.

In other words, it was the over-reliance on economic liberalism that led to the triumph of political illiberalism. So insistent were liberals that economic liberalism, or the market economy, not be challenged that they ended up making sure that the ensuing challenge to the market be framed by concepts of the right rather than the left.

Organizing anger in post-communist eastern Europe

I begin by summarizing the Polish experience and the implications for democracy, and then look at how these same problems have affected politics in other east European post-communist societies.

The Polish elite after 1989, including Solidarity leaders, entered the new era convinced that labour was the new enemy. They expected to deal with a powerful class opponent fighting against the new capitalism, and so they tried to nip class opposition in the bud. They did so in a variety of ways. First, they introduced policies minimizing labour input in the workplace, such as a privatization law requiring abolition of employee councils, wage-tax breaks for privatized firms only, restrictions on issues open to union–management discussion, and a long delay before institutionalizing collective bargaining. Second, they set in motion a constant media barrage prescribing support, patience and acquiescence as the correct emotional response to the calamitous economic depression. News coverage of labour protests presented activists as irrational hotheads, while grievances directed at government policies were interpreted as grievances 'really' aimed at the old regime, which the present policies were finally dismantling. Finally, the new elite tried to nip class opposition by channelling it along other lines. Solidarity played the key role here. Unable to eliminate economic discontent, it turned itself into an organizer of that discontent, and from Lech Walesa through to his successor Marian Krzaklewski, systematically sought to direct it against communists, crypto-communists, liberals, non-believers, criminals and other assorted 'aliens'. Solidarity still hoped to maintain class unity – it did, after all, claim to speak for labour – but it sought to organize workers along other than class lines.

The paradox, of course, was that labour was not anti-capitalist at all. In survey after survey, not to mention inaction after inaction, rank-and-file workers as well as local union officials demonstrated their acceptance of market reform. All they wanted was to have some say in that reform, to be treated as rational actors who could legitimately have a different opinion (such as about the wage-tax or infant-industry protection) and be talked with rather than lectured to. But since any expression of misgiving was perceived as a sign of incipient class opposition, which itself was perceived as ruinous to reform, workers could not be heard. As liberals ignored them, an emergent right was able to capitalize. For with discontent treated as irrational and illiberal, it made sense to embrace the role, for only then could one escape being condescended to.[14] So egregiously did liberals fail the test of representing an increasingly disenfranchised working class that it fell to the former communists to be the chief defenders of liberal principles of tolerance. But while electoral victories by the ex-communist Democratic Left Alliance helped stem the advance of illiberalism, the communist-era legacy prevented the DLA from being a hegemonic party of labour, and in any case a rash of scandals during its most recent administration, from 2001 to 2005, left it fragmented, leading to the decisive victory of the Law and Justice Party, which quickly entered into a coalition with two extreme right-wing parties that have consistently denounced democratic procedures as a waste of time. Jaroslaw Kaczyński, the head of Law and Justice and, since July 2006, the Polish Prime Minister, frequently embraces the same extremist views, leading one observer to note astutely that while Kaczyński claims to support democracy and probably believes he does, his views of the opposition as a haven for 'liars', his belief that the judiciary should do as the state bids, and his insistence on politicizing virtually the entire civil service has little to do with principles of liberal democracy.[15] Kaczyński seems to believe in democracy pretty much the way Putin does.

The stifling of class politics in Poland, in other words, has ended up having profoundly illiberal and anti-democratic consequences. It has led not to the absence of economic anger, but to that anger being organized in illiberal ways, with profoundly dangerous implications for the future of liberal democracy.

Is this merely a story of Poland? Hardly. Other countries in eastern Europe have been struggling with the same issue of how new class anger comes to be politically expressed, and everywhere this has had profound political implications. Wherever we look, we see labour decimated by neo-liberal reforms and new elites anxious to stifle labour discontent, leading to weak trade unions, low class sensibilities, burgeoning class anger looking for ways to express itself, and a rise in illiberal politics.

In Czechoslovakia economic discontent became fuel for the break-up of the country, particularly in poorer Slovakia, where the nationalist Vladimir Meciar succeeded in the early 1990s by blaming Slovak economic troubles on Czech domination. When independence rendered the nationalist narrative moot, Meciar sought to deploy the base he had built to consolidate his own illiberal rule, and had a great deal of success. Throughout the 1990s, as Jonathan Stein writes, Meciar

> attracted significant working class support by channelling economic fear and frustration into nationalist resentment directed against 'anti-Slovak' influences: pro-federalists, the country's ethnic Hungarian minority, and

> liberal reformers portrayed as 'selling out' the nation's interests and assets to foreigners.[16]

An authoritarian rule sufficient to keep it long out of NATO and to jeopardize EU entry was the result.

Czech labour woes also needed outlets. Things were not so bad in the early 1990s, when a combination of relative union strength and shrewd government policy kept unemployment rates lower than anywhere else in the region. By the end of the decade, however, the Czech Republic's labour advantages had dissolved. The unions never sought to capitalize on their initial strength, relying on economic growth alone to help their members. It soon turned out, however, that that growth had been a mirage, sustained by a combination of foreign investment, cooked books and widespread corruption in the privatization process that enticed the foreign investment in the first place. When the bubble burst around 1997, unions were as weak as they were elsewhere in the region. That they had lost all their clout became clear after 1994, when the government stopped signing even the weak annual agreements it had earlier negotiated with the union federation and began governing as if unions did not exist.[17] With unions an increasingly inappropriate vehicle for the articulation of economic discontent, vulnerable workers, mobilized by right-wing politicians, resorted to a familiar practice of the weak: they began deploying their anger not against the wealthy and corrupt but against the poor and defenceless, as the erection of a city wall in 1999 to separate Roma from the rest of the population in one small, depressed mining city demonstrated.

Hungary has seen a similar weakening of the labour movement. Union density dropped from about 90 per cent in the 1980s to around 30 per cent in the early 1990s, and has continued to drop since. (Even in Poland, union membership is today estimated at about 14 per cent.) But even this overestimates the role unions play in Hungarian workplaces. According to most analysts, Hungarian unions are almost powerless. On the one hand, this is an inheritance from the late communist period, when extensive market reforms empowered managers, and gave workers the ability to make extra money in quasi-private firms where labour laws did not obtain. As Laszlo Bruszt wrote, 'Hungarian workers "arrived" [at 1989] with the highest number of market institutions and the weakest and most divided trade unions.'[18] After 1989, things got worse. Before unions had the chance to rebuild themselves, the country adopted the German system of works councils, which only undercut the influence of unions in the firms. The councils, however, are much weaker than in Germany, with managers not required even to discuss layoffs with them, or with the unions. Moreover, while the councils are supposed to guarantee employee representation even in non-unionized firms, in reality they often do not arise without unions being there to press for them. This combination of weak legacy and marginalizing policy has contributed to the dramatic weakness of labour in the workplace as manifested in widespread and flagrant disregard of work rules. Unions rarely contest these violations, but when they do, protest is usually ineffective because of government commitment not to alienate employers.

While Hungarian labour did move toward the Socialists (former communists) in the early 1990s, as a response to the deterioration of conditions after 1989, the Socialists' decidedly neo-liberal administration created new political problems: in what ways would economic anger be articulated now? The answer came in the form of a party that reinvented itself precisely for the purpose. The Alliance of Young Democrats, or Fidesz, had been a liberal party itself in the early 1990s, but its weak initial showing, together with astute observation of the collapse of other liberal parties in the region (Hungary's Free Democrats, the Czech Republic's Civic Democrats and Poland's Democratic Union/Freedom Union) led it to transform itself from a party of young radical-liberals into one of class and national anger. In its new approach it emphasized the defence of diaspora nationals, the eradication of 'communists', the implementation of Christian morality, and the protection of the rural dispossessed against the new elite. Fidesz opposed trade unions because of their institutional ties to the Socialist Party, but since, as in Poland, such ties did little for labour except provide administrative jobs to some union officials, Fidesz managed to pick up some labour votes, too. Fidesz had drawn the correct political lesson from the collapse of east Europe's liberals: parties had to organize anger, not eschew it. With this line it swept to power in 1998. After four years of Fidesz's politically illiberal rule, voters swung back to the Socialists in 2002. Fidesz then transformed itself into the voice against the EU, despite having negotiated most of the terms for Hungary's entry.

The most egregious example of economic anger finding dangerous, non-economic, non-class modes of articulation remains, of course, the former Yugoslavia. This country that exploded in paroxysms of blood and fury was one of the first to tread the path of market reform, and the consequences were among the deepest. Indeed, the key story for most of the 1980s was precisely this escalating economic crisis. In response to a rapidly increasing foreign debt, triggered by the system's underlying inefficiency as well as the Western recession (which led to a dramatic decline in hard currency repatriation by guestworkers), the government began harsh austerity measures already in 1982, when food subsidies were abandoned. Prices on essentials rose one-third the following year, and imports were drastically curtailed as the currency lost 90 per cent of its value. By the mid-1980s, inflation rose by more than 50 per cent each year, unemployment soared, and the entire economy was plagued by shortages.[19] Successive deals with the IMF only made the situation worse. And with democratic changes now taking hold, this became a political problem as much as an economic one. For with discontent mushrooming and elections imminent, the political issue concerned how that discontent would be expressed.

That the emerging economic anger did not get mobilized around class cleavages but only around ethnic ones was due both to structural and voluntarist-political factors. 'Class' was a particularly weak unifier in Yugoslavia due not only to factors common to east European communism, as discussed above, but also to specific institutional arrangements that encouraged ethnic mobilization instead.[20] In the early 1970s, in response to recent protests, Tito amended the constitution to move formal power from the federal to the republican level. This not only ensured the creation of strong ethnically based political organizations, but virtually guaranteed that future opposition to the government would be directed along divisive national lines rather than unifying civic ones.

This is what happened with the burgeoning economic anger of the late 1980s, particularly once the federal government sought to reassert itself with a sweeping economic reform programme. For now the powerful republic-based ethnic politicians found themselves threatened not just by economic discontent from below but by a reform project from above that challenged their authority. It was at this point that republican politicians moved into action, assiduously stoking the economic anger of the populace and, in order to save their own skins, inventing a new narrative that blamed these problems on *national* others, and thus not on an 'other' that federal reform could ameliorate. As V.P. Gagnon writes, in a rich empirical and theoretical argument, rival Yugoslav national elites consistently sought to 'provoke and create' threats from outside in order to protect their own power bases threatened by the proposed reforms. 'By defining the collective interest in non-economic (cultural or ethnic) terms', he writes, elites substituted a political fight that they could win for an economic conflict that put them in jeopardy. In this way, local actors converted economic anger into nationalist rage, leading to a vicious war and sabotaging chances for liberal democracy for years to come.[21]

Conclusions

All these examples show, unsurprisingly, that neo-liberal economic transformation sparks frustration and discontent, or what I call 'economic anger'. Liberals who believed that the anger could and should be held in abeyance were profoundly mistaken, and only ended up marginalizing themselves. For through its policies of commodifying benefits that communitarian societies, whether pre-modern or communist, provide as a matter of course, transition to a capitalist economy *necessarily* produces economic anger. The key question for politics is not to suppress anger – that is impossible – but how to organize it. The Western record with building stable democratic systems suggests that for liberal democracy to succeed, economic anger is best organized along class lines. For a system in which rights for all citizens are guaranteed and secure, workers need to accept a narrative that explains their anger as a product of economic class divisions, rather than of national, religious or racial divisions. Class, in other words, is the cleavage of democracy.

If I am right that it is the failure of social conflicts to be organized around economic cleavages that leads to illiberalism, then it follows that it is counterproductive for supporters of liberal democracy, whether in eastern Europe or elsewhere, to oppose class conflict. That democratically minded capitalists and pro-market reformers *ought* to support the mobilization of anger along class lines is one of the key lessons of the Polish experience. They should do so in order to avoid anger being mobilized around ascriptive or other non-negotiable cleavages that inexorably push society toward dangerous and irresolvable internal divisions.

The liberals got it wrong: it is not capitalism but the way capitalism is *challenged* that underpins democracy. By doing their best to make sure that frustration and anger with the economic system *not* be expressed as economic anger, they only made sure that discontent be expressed as something else. This led to a labour movement unsure of itself – 'we should be leftists, but we aren't' – and organized chiefly around illiberal cleavages. In the end, then, class politics is crucial for post-communist society. The success of an inclusive liberal democracy depends on the way emerging class anger becomes politically mobilized. Democracy becomes secure when workers and other non-elites are won over by parties seeking to organize discontent around a programme of economic redistribution rather than identity persecution. Until that happens, illiberal right-wing populism will likely continue to succeed.

Notes

1 This is discussed at greater length in my recent book, *The Defeat of Solidarity: Anger and Politics in Postcommunist Europe* (Ithaca: Cornell University Press, 2005).
2 See D. Rueschemeyer, E.H. Stephens and J. Stephens, *Capitalist Development and Democracy* (Chicago: University of Chicago Press, 1992); and R. Aminzade, *Class, Politics, and Early Industrial Capitalism: a Study of Mid-Nineteenth Century France* (Albany: SUNY Press, 1981).
3 A. Hicks, J. Misra and T. Nah Ng, 'The Programmatic Emergence of the Social Security State', *American Sociological Review*, 60 (June 1995).
4 G. Luebbert, *Liberalism, Fascism, or Social Democracy* (New York: Oxford University Press, 1991).
5 On Latin America, see R.B. Collier and D. Collier, *Shaping the Political Arena* (Princeton: Princeton University Press, 1991).
6 G. O'Donnell and P. Schmitter, *Transitions from Authoritarian Rule*, Vol. 4 (Baltimore: Johns Hopkins University Press, 1986).
7 W. Arkuszewski, 'Od gory do dolu', *Tygodnik Solidarnosc* (22 September, 1989).
8 D. Ost, 'Illusory Corporatism in Eastern Europe: Neoliberal Tripartism and Postcommunist Class Identities', *Politics and Society*, 28, 4 (December 1989), 503–30.
9 D. Ost. 'After Postcommunism: Legacies and the Future of Unions in Eastern Europe', in C. Phelan (ed.), *The Future of Organised Labour* (London: Peter Language, 2006); J. Kurczewski, *The Resurrection of Rights in Poland* (Oxford: Oxford University Press, 1993).

10 See D. Ost, *The Defeat of Solidarity* (Ithaca: Cornell University Press, 1995); J. Gardawski et al., *Rozpad Bastionu?: Zwiazki Zawodowe w Gospodarce Prywatyzowanej* (Warsaw: Institute of Public Affairs, 1999); and D. Bohle and B. Greskovits, 'Capital, Labor, and the Prospects of the European Social Model in the East', Working Paper No. 58, Program on Central and Eastern European Working Paper Series (Cambridge: Harvard University, 2004).
11 S.M. Lipset, *Political Man* (New York: Doubleday, 1960).
12 See D. Ost, *Solidarity and the Politics of Anti-Politics* (Philadelphia: Temple University Press, 1990), pp. 165–9.
13 Quoted in T. Grabowski, 'The Party that Never Was: the Rise and Fall of the Solidarity Citizens' Committees in Poland', *East European Politics and Societies*, 10, 2 (Spring, 1996).
14 Eric Hobsbawm makes a similar point about the recent global successes of religious fundamentalists when he writes that '[t]heir major asset [is] probably an immunity to academic economics and the anti-state rhetoric of a liberalism identified with the free market'. See *The Age of Extremes: a History of the World, 1914–1991* (New York: Vintage, 1994), pp. 567–8. His point is that when the world around them affirms that the only rational policy is neo-liberal globalization, bringing much hardship and privation in its train, then it pays to feign irrationality, to refuse to enter into the discussion. They may not be able to solve the problems this way, as the economic record of Iran's Islamic Republic suggests, but such irrationality does get them a hearing, and may well be the road to power.
15 J. Zakowski, 'Rewolucja lut(d)owa', *Polityka* (20 February, 2006).
16 J. Stein, 'Neocorporatism in Slovakia: Formalizing Labor Weakness in a (Re)democratizing State', in S. Crowley and D. Ost (eds), *Workers after Workers' States: Labor and Politics in Postcommunist Eastern Europe* (Boulder: Rowman & Littlefield Press, 2001), pp. 59–60.
17 A. Pollert, 'Labor and Trade Unions in the Czech Republic, 1989–2000', in S. Crowley and D. Ost (eds), *Workers after Workers' States: Labor and Politics in Postcommunist Eastern Europe* (Boulder: Rowman & Littlefield Press, 2001).
18 L. Bruszt, 'Reforming Alliances: Labour, Management, and State Bureaucracy in Hungary's Economic Transition', *Acta Oeconomica*, 46, 3–4 (1994) 317. Such market opportunities helped make Hungarian workers more quiescent than in Poland, where the lack of individualistic strategies for advancement pushed energetic workers more into public activity. For more on this comparison, see M. Burawoy, *The Politics of Production* (London: Verso, 1985), pp. 199–200.
19 S. Woodward, *The Balkan Tragedy* (Washington: Brookings Institute, 1995).
20 V. Bunce, *Subversive Institutions* (Cambridge: Cambridge University Press, 1999).
21 V. P. Gagnon, Jr, 'Ethnic Nationalism and International Conflict: the Case of Serbia', *International Security*, 19, 3 (Winter, 1994–95) 130–66.

Part II

Outcomes of Transformation: Central and Eastern Europe

5
The European Union's Influence on the Development of Capitalism in Central Europe

*Philip Hanson**

For a number of nations, joining the European Union is part of the process of post-communist economic change. Eight ex-communist countries joined the EU in 2004. Two more joined in 2007. The purpose of this chapter is to shed light on the effects of the accession process on the evolution of those ex-communist economies that engage in it.

The economic impact of EU enlargement on the countries that accede is usually taken to be benign. And basic economic theory suggests some obvious reasons to expect economic gains. However, I am not going to try to put forward an overall assessment of the net effect of accession so far on the acceding states. The aim in this chapter is to examine one element of the EU's influence on accession states: its direct, explicitly negotiated influence on their economic institutions.

That influence is exerted along with macroeconomic, trade and investment influences. They will not be assessed here, but they form the setting for direct institutional influence, and should be briefly noted.

Entry into a large single market should provide opportunities of cost reduction for producers in the acceding countries. It will also sharpen competitive pressures to pursue process and product innovations. The prospect of entry should stimulate fixed investment in the accession countries by both domestic and foreign firms and individuals as perceived country risk is likely to be reduced by membership. There may be both trade creation and trade diversion (the latter away from countries outside the EU), but it is plausible that there may be net gains from trade in the classic sense. These effects do not come only after formal accession. They should begin to appear earlier, as preparations are made for accession, including EU financial assistance, and expectations of accession gather strength.

In the case of the central European countries, their trade was reoriented very rapidly away from the former USSR in the 1990s, well ahead of accession. This was partly because the EU reduced tariffs on their goods under the Europe agreements (ahead of their reducing tariffs on EU goods), and partly because the collapse of communist rule in what had been the Soviet bloc allowed the gravitational pull of the EU – reflecting its economic size and geographical distance – to exert itself where previously that influence had been partly blocked. Russian exports to central Europe and the Baltic states tended to become more concentrated on energy and raw materials, and the exports of these to former Comecon partners were not hampered – very broadly speaking – by the latter moving into the EU's common protective arrangements. Russian exports of steel and basic chemicals to central Europe were affected; in those two product groups, EU protectionism and Russian export capability intersect. Even so, it is probable that gains from trade creation will outweigh losses from trade diversion, so far as the accession countries are concerned.

In addition, one may perhaps expect net gains for the accession states from the adoption of certain EU institutions: EU competition policy; restrictions on state aid; possible improvements in state governance associated with the 'downloading' of the *acquis* (perhaps net benefits for regulatory quality, for example), and macroeconomic discipline required for post-accession adoption of the euro.

It could be that none of these effects is large, and some might even be negative. But the overall effect is likely to be favourable for new members. To put it simply: small economies that are in the neighbourhood of a very large single market will, other things being equal, be better off inside it than outside it. This view seems to be widely accepted by policy makers, and not just policy makers in the accession countries. After all, no established European market economy any longer tries to operate as an outsider. Switzerland and Norway may not be EU members but they have arrangements with the EU that provide most, if not quite all, of the benefits of membership.

In this chapter I shall focus on one channel of EU influence on the institutions of the 2004 ex-communist accession states: the requirement to adopt a certain set of laws, regulations and practices associated with the *acquis communautaire*, in order to become members. It is not obvious that this particular influence is necessarily benign. Small neighbouring economies joining the EU are entering an economic community whose growth has for some time been sluggish. The Union's eurozone core, in particular, is dominated by countries widely believed to need liberalizing reform. New entrants, or those negotiating entry, might well be adopting an economic regime that is not conducive to rapid growth in the future. It has indeed been argued by some commentators that the accession process was designed to steer the candidate countries towards a 'European' form of welfare corporatism.[1]

The questions to be addressed are these: does accession significantly shape the process of post-communist economic change? In so far as it does do so, does it produce a convergence on a set of institutions that is problematic for future economic performance? I shall argue that it is indeed, in a number of ways, significant, but that it has not – for better or worse – pushed the accession states towards a welfarist, continental European pattern of institutional arrangements. The evidence supports two generalizations. First, part of the accession process is to do with developing the state's capability to implement policies – of whatever kind.[2] Administrative effectiveness should not be specific to a particular version of capitalism. Second, in those chapters of the *acquis* that seem likely to have a bearing on business regulation and labour market regulation, and more generally on the business environment, accession requirements generally leave wide scope for institutional variation within an acceding country's economic institutions.

This is hardly surprising. The institutional variation among pre-2004 member states, and the variation in their medium-term economic performance, is great. I shall argue that, contrary to some predictions, accession has not led the new member states to adopt redistributive and corporatist arrangements.

In the next section I present some of the evidence about institutional variation among pre-2004 EU member states, 2004 accession states and (in less detail) the two 2007 accession countries, and relate it to the World Bank's Ease of Doing Business scores for these countries. In the section following that I review the accession process itself, concentrating on the cases of Hungary and Poland and on a small number of chapters of the *acquis*. The conclusions are about the links between the accession process and the current patchwork of 'varieties of capitalism' in the region.

The assessment presented here is based on interviews with expert informants listed in Appendix 5.1, as well as on documents and a modest amount of number-crunching.[3]

The business environment and EU status

There are now a large number of indicators available for comparing countries according to their institutions. In this section three such institutional indicators are used: the World Bank's Ease of Doing Business (EoDB) scores, the Kaufmann/World Bank measures of 'governance' and Transparency International's longer-established Corruption Perception Indices. All of these imply measurement along a single scale. To bring in the possible influence of different viable combinations of institutions I also use measurements by Knell and Srholec[4] of a country's position on a scale from liberal market arrangements to strategic coordination, and in what they call 'social cohesion' and I call 'redistribution'. First, a brief account of what the less familiar of these indicators measure, or purport to measure.

EoDB indicators include measures of the following: the speed, cost and number of procedures involved in starting a business; the difficulties of hiring and firing workers, the costs of firing workers and the rigidities in laws and regulations about employment and hours worked; the time, cost and number of procedures involved in registering property; the conditions for getting credit (including costs of creating collateral, legal rights and credit information); the protection of investors; the time, cost and number of procedures involved in enforcing contracts; and the time, cost and recovery rate (proportion of value retrievable) entailed in closing a business. What I have used here is the ranking (inverted in this exercise) of 155 countries on these indicators in total. For details of the scores see www.doingbusiness.org.

Governance scores are composed of scores on 'voice and accountability' (in relations between citizens and the state), political stability, government effectiveness, regulatory quality, rule of law and control of corruption. See http://info/worldbank.org/governance/.

The Knell–Srholec 'coordination' score is also a composite. It is made up of scores on 'social cohesion' (taken to be higher, the lower is income inequality and the higher are the top marginal rates of income and corporate taxation and the government consumption share of GDP),[5] labour market regulation (scores from the EoDB set of indicators) and business regulation (again, EoDB scores, plus the ratio of stock market capitalization to bank credit). Negative scores indicate the liberal half of the range; positive scores put a country on the 'strategic coordination' half of the scale. The contrast is akin to that made by Dore[6] between 'shareholder capitalism' and 'welfare capitalism'.

The 'social cohesion' scores, which are also scaled from negative (tending to minimize redistribution) to positive (tending to redistribute) are also listed separately in Table 5.1, where I have relabelled them 'redistribution' – a term that in my view begs fewer questions. The reason for listing redistribution scores separately from the coordination scores of which they are a part is that the other ingredients in a nation's Knell–Srholec coordination score are taken from the EoDB indicators. It makes no sense, therefore, to treat coordination as an independent variable influencing the business environment as measured by an EoDB score. The extent to which a country has redistributive arrangements, however, is a genuinely independent variable.

The data are in Table 5.1, where each variable is defined. They are for 2005 or for a year either side of 2005. The countries covered are 14 'established' EU countries (the pre-2004 EU15 excluding Luxembourg, on which some data were not available), the eight ex-communist countries that joined the EU in 2004, the two 2007 accession states (Bulgaria and Romania) and, for comparison, Japan, Russia and the US. As is explained in the notes to Table 5.1, I have tinkered with the scaling of some of the ready-made indicators to make for ease of manipulation.

There is a reasonably close correspondence between EoDB and governance (Gov): the simple correlation coefficient is 0.768. There is also a reasonably close relationship between governance and per capita GNI: $r = 0.785$.

These figures offer one way of tackling the question we are concerned with. What do they suggest about the EU accession process as a creator of an extended 'European' model? The first point to note is the considerable diversity on all indicators both within the 14 established EU states and within the accession states. This suggests that, despite the European Commission's best endeavours,

Table 5.1 Development level and some indicators of 'institutional quality', selected countries, around 2005

	EoDB	*Gov*	*pcGNI*	*Redistribn*	*ΔTI0105*	*Coordn*
Austria	123	65.1	79.9	4.1	9	3.8
Belgium	137	55	79.2	3.9	8	−3.4
Denmark	147	73.3	79.6	1.6	0	−1.6
Finland	142	76.5	74.8	1.6	−3	−5.4
France	111	45.8	74	4.5	8	8
Germany	136	56.9	70.7	2.4	8	4.8
Greece	75	28.9	55.8	1.4	1	11.6
Ireland	144	59.1	82.7	−1	−1	−5.8
Italy	85	28.8	70.4	2.5	−5	4.5
Netherlands	131	67.8	78.8	5	−2	2.7
Portugal	113	45.5	48.3	1.1	2	6.5
Spain	125	44.7	62.2	2.9	0	4.7
Sweden	141	69.4	75	5.6	2	0.9
UK	146	62.5	78.9	1.4	3	−5.8
Czech Republic	114	29.7	46.3	2.4	4	4.4
Estonia	139	42.5	34.2	−4.4	8	−5.7
Hungary	103	36.1	39.7	−1.8	−3	−3.3
Latvia	129	28.3	29.7	−1.8	8	0.6
Lithuania	140	30.9	31.9	−1.3	0	−3.8
Poland	101	21.7	32	−0.6	−7	−1.8
Slovakia	118	29.7	36.4	−0.4	6	−2.8
Slovenia	92	39.5	52.3	3	9	6.3
Bulgaria	93	8.3	19.2	−1.8	1	−0.8
Romania	77	−0.3	20.9	−2	2	4
Japan	145	45.3	75.1	1	2	−1.5
Russia	76	−25.3	32.4	−4.5	1	−9.6
USA	152	54.1	100	−1.3	0	−8.3

Notes: EoDB = country ranking on 'ease of doing business', out of 15 countries, with scores reversed from those published (here 155 = easiest, not 1); measures for 2006.

Gov = sum of governance scores (voice and accountability, political stability, effectiveness of government, regulatory quality, rule of law, control of corruption), converted into % of maximum possible score; possible range from +100 to −100. Refers to 2004.

pcGNI = per capita gross national income in international dollars at purchasing power parity, 2004, US = 100.

ΔTI0105 = percentage point change in Transparency International's Corruption Perception Index, 2001–5.

Coordn = score (based on multiple indicators) on strategic coordination versus competition; + tending towards coordination; − tending towards competition.

Redistribn = the Knell–Srholec 'social cohesion' score; see the text.

Sources: www.doingbusiness.org/EconomyRankings;
http://info.worldbank.org/governance/kkz2004/tables.asp/year_report.asp?yearid=1
World Bank, *World Development Indicators 2006*;
www.transparency.org/cpi/2005/cpi2005.en.html; M. Knell and M. Srholec, 'Emerging Varieties of Capitalism in Central and Eastern Europe', in D. Lane and M. Myant (eds), *Varieties of Capitalism in Post-Communist Countries* (Basingstoke: Palgrave Macmillan, 2007).

institutional convergence is not a feature of EU membership. More precisely, convergence towards either continental or Anglo-Saxon ways of doing things is not being enforced. It is true that there has been more pressure on new members to conform to a range of requirements beyond the *acquis* than there is on established members who are already inside the club. But the variability among the ten accession states does not suggest that institutional convergence in our sense was being enforced on them, either.

What might any of this have to do with prospective economic performance? The EoDB score should be a guide to a nation's adaptability and therefore to its medium-term economic prospects. It is therefore treated here as denoting a country's economic prospects *insofar as those prospects are determined by institutional arrangements*. Other influences, such as domestic macroeconomic management or the prices of main export commodities, could also influence the outcomes, but we are not concerned with those here.

EU states are not closely grouped on their EoDB rankings. It is striking that the EoDB ranking for Greece is little more than half that for Denmark or the UK, and below that of any of the accession states, while the EoDB score for Italy is also below those for all the accession states except Romania.

It appears that high coordination is not necessarily a barrier to a high EoDB ranking: Austria, Germany, the Netherlands, Spain and Sweden all come out looking more or less 'coordinated' but have very respectable EoDB scores.

It might be accounted a success for the EU accession process that EoDB rankings for the accession states look rather good, in light of their modest per capita national income levels. That is less obviously the case with their governance scores. But it is also striking that most of the eight 2004 accession states (five out of eight) have coordination indices suggesting they are towards the competitive (Anglo-Saxon) end of the spectrum, while the majority of the established EU countries (9 out of 14) are towards the coordinated end. That suggests that reference to the *acquis communautaire* as a benchmark for accession did not have the result – somewhat surprisingly – of bringing the newcomers close to a predominant EU variety of capitalism.

It appears that the routes to a favourable business climate are not necessarily the same for established and new member states of the EU. This certainly looks to be the case if we try to account statistically for the variance, across our 27 countries, in their EoDB scores. Using the Knell–Srholec 'coordination' score as an explanatory variable is a non-starter: two out of the three elements in that score come from the EoDB indicators. And it appears from some trial OLS regressions that statistically the Transparency International indicators do not add significantly to an explanation of variance in EoDB scores.

If we drop from the 'coordination' index all the indicators that are shared with the EoDB measure, and use instead just the Knell–Srholec 'social cohesion' or 'redistribution' measure, and if we also drop the statistically uninformative Transparency International measures, we get the following OLS regression:

$$\text{EoDB} = 74.693 + 1.037\text{Gov}^{***} + 0.102\text{pcGNI} - 4.348\text{redistribn}^{***}$$

$$(8.420) \quad (5.427) \qquad (0.520) \qquad (-4.348)$$

Adjusted $R^2 = 0.690$; $F = 20.330$; $n = 27$; *** = significant at 1 per cent.

This suggests that both good governance and a low concern for income redistribution (low 'social cohesion' scores) are, separately, favourable for business, and that development level is not a significant factor when adjusted for those two.

The striking observation about the emerging new Europe is that Bulgaria, Romania and the 2004 accession eight except for the Czech Republic and Slovenia are on the 'liberal', non-redistributive end of the redistribution scale, while all the established EU14 countries covered in Table 5.1 except for Ireland are on the 'redistributive' side of the dividing line.

The following conjecture seems reasonable. Good governance is developed, if it is developed at all, over long periods of time and is generally more evident in richer countries. It is therefore broadly the case that governance is quite strong in western Europe (Greece and Italy being exceptions) and less strong in recently communist and poorer countries. It is also broadly the case that richer west European societies have arrangements that reflect a high value placed on reducing income inequalities. The results of that high value include comparatively mild inequality, comparatively high marginal tax rates and highish government spending (the Knell–Srholec 'social cohesion' indicators); these are not conducive in themselves to a business-friendly environment, but in most west European countries that is offset by good governance. The ex-communist countries are in no position to replicate this balance of influences. Arguably, the state and social institutions that support a more liberal, free-market economy place fewer demands on state capacity than those required to provide effective governance compatible with a good business environment in a more welfarist society.

Table 5.2 provides some of the group characteristics: no very great difference, on average, in the business environment between established and ex-communist new members of the EU; still quite a wide gap in governance, and clearly different (average) positions on redistribution or social cohesion. Bulgaria and Romania lag badly on both business environment and governance.

The change over time in corruption perception indices (ΔTI0105) is, on the face of it, encouraging so far as the effects of accession negotiations are concerned, but only mildly so: there was on average a somewhat greater

Table 5.2 Selected European countries by group: unweighted average scores on selected indicators, *c.*2005

	EoDB	*Gov*	*ΔTI0105*	*Redistribution*
Established EU14	125.4	55.7	2.14	2.6
Accession 8	117.0	32.3	3.13	−0.6
Bulgaria + Romania	85.5	4.0	1.50	−1.9

Source and definitions: See Table 5.1, and text above.

improvement in the countries that acceded in the period than among established EU members. That is presumably what should be expected if meeting accession conditions requires better control of corruption. The World Bank–EBRD Business Environment and Enterprise Performance Survey (BEEPS) broadly supports this from business survey responses. It shows corruption tending to become less of a problem between 2002 and 2005 in most of the accession countries, including Bulgaria and Romania. The exceptions are Estonia (a small increase from a low level), Hungary and the Czech Republic. This evidence is, however, inconclusive so far as the effects of EU conditionality are concerned, for most ex-communist countries show an improvement: 7 out of 10 accession countries do so, but so do 10 out of 16 non-candidates.[7]

It appears, then, that those ex-communist countries that have joined the EU have either preserved or improved their business environments (the EoDB indicator is new and we cannot track changes in it from any past measurements). At the same time, while their governance indicators remain more modest than those of established EU member states (albeit with some overlap), they have not apparently had to alter their institutions in ways that would move them from the free-market to the welfarist or redistributive parts of the spectrum.

How does that interpretation square with what can be said about the accession negotiation process?

The EU accession process and economic institutions

Joining the EU may, through the introduction of greater competition, the increase in cross-border movement of labour and other channels, indirectly affect the development of economic institutions in the new member state. Here, however, the focus is on what might be called deliberate Europeanization.[8] To join the EU a candidate country is formally required to meet a number of criteria. It must be a democracy in which the rule of law is observed and minorities are respected; it must have a 'functioning market economy' able to take on the responsibilities of single market membership (the 'Copenhagen' criteria, dating from 1993).

There is no way of knowing how democracy and the market would have developed in central Europe in the absence of any prospect of EU accession. Still, the presumption must be that the lure of EU membership tended to assist the cause of liberal reform. At all events, there have been economic recovery and considerable consolidation of the institutions of parliamentary democracy. Political parties – admittedly still rather fluid in several countries – have taken shape. There have been orderly transfers of power between rival political teams, through elections, in all these countries. Some early excesses in the treatment of minorities – notably, of Russian speakers in Estonia and Latvia – have been curbed.

One indication of the limits of EU conditionality, however, is the political and economic policy instability in the region in 2006. It looks as though, in the Visegrad countries (the Czech Republic, Hungary, Poland and Slovakia), political malaise followed accession. This malaise was linked in one way or another with legacies of communism. It was also linked with widespread unease about globalization – which is a worldwide, and not purely central European phenomenon – and that in turn was linked with ambivalence or outright antagonism towards Brussels. Two years after EU accession, the coincidence of political instability in these four countries suggested that nationalist and populist tendencies had perhaps been reined in earlier, so long as EU accession was in doubt.

In Poland the government led by the Kaczyński brothers appeals to the belief that the old communist-era *nomenklatura* still runs the economy, that corruption is rife and that Ministry of Foreign Affairs officials are 'too European'.

In the Czech Republic there has already been a lustration of communist-era informers and high officials, but it was at the time of writing impossible to form a government.

In Hungary Prime Minister Gyurcsany was in difficulties in 2006 because he admitted to systematic lying, particularly about economic policies. Lying about the economy was something communist officials used to do. Gyurcsany made a fortune in businesses that, critics said, relied on contacts made in the 1980s in the Communist Youth Alliance, so there were overtones of anti-communism in the demonstrations against his government – demonstrations that overlapped with the fiftieth anniversary of the 1956 uprising.

In Slovakia, a populist government led by a defector from the communist successor party replaced a government that had pursued EU-friendly reform over two terms of office.[9]

All four countries have difficulties containing public spending and budget deficits to meet their accession commitments to early adoption of the euro. In general, it is hard to avoid the impression that the accession process put the political class in central Europe under considerable pressure to put on a show of 'orderliness' and 'progress'. Once inside, everyone could relax. To say this is not to say that the process as a whole was a sham and EU conditionality altered nothing. It is simply that conditionality is unavoidably more powerful while accession is in doubt than it is later. Some turbulence after accession should not be surprising.

The main theme of this chapter, however, is the effect of EU accession, not on politics or even on macroeconomic policies, but on the development of economic institutions. So far as direct and deliberate EU influence on central European economic institutions is concerned, the main form it has taken is the requirement for the accession countries to adopt the *acquis communautaire* into their legislation and procedures, and show that they can implement it. The *acquis*, notoriously, runs to some 80,000 pages.

That looks like a massive institutional transplant. But the focus of the *acquis* is limited, its meaning is sometimes vague and its implementation in established member states is patchy. Also, the process of agreeing that a candidate country had successfully 'closed' a given chapter of the *acquis* was opaque. Often political considerations were more important in determining that a chapter had been closed than anything to do with the economic and legal substance of the chapter itself.

Heather Grabbe, in her study of the politics of 'Europeanisation through conditionality' in central and eastern Europe,[10] notes that national economic systems in the EU15 have remained diverse partly because 'the EU's key governance function is regulating social and political risk rather than resource redistribution'. In other words, the emphasis has been on arrangements that enable a single market to work, including some common minima in some fields of regulation. This is reflected in the varying 'density' (degree of detail) in different chapters of the *acquis*. In the European Commission's *Comprehensive Monitoring Reports* on candidate countries, wrapping up the formal monitoring of 'progress' ahead of accession, the number of pages devoted to agriculture is consistently twice the length of the average number of pages on other chapters; see for example the *Comprehensive Monitoring Reports* on Estonia, Hungary, Poland and Slovenia (all published in 2003). The next longest section is on justice and home affairs, where west European concerns about border controls loomed large.

Moreover, large parts of the *acquis* that might seem to bear on domestic organization of the economy and the rules of the domestic economic game bear in fact on conditions required for a single market to function. This obviously has some implications for the domestic economy, but it leaves a great deal of scope for institutional variation.

Thus, discussion in the *Comprehensive Monitoring Reports* (henceforth CMRs; see above) of the *acquis* chapter on the free movement of goods is chiefly about standardized product specifications, metrology, product safety and rules for public procurement.

Negotiation over chapter 2 (free movement of persons) focused on mutual recognition of professional qualifications and the administrative capacity needed to coordinate [the application of national] social security systems – where no transposition into national legislation is needed.[11] In other words, what is needed from a new entrant is an ability to cope with the transfer of people between different social security systems, rather than an ability to make the candidate nation's social security arrangements converge on those of any one existing member state.

The freedom to provide services (chapter 3) exemplifies the limitations of the *acquis* in a different way. The CMRs routinely note that an acceding state's legislation must not hamper the right of establishment of a foreign-based company or its freedom to provide services. But in 2006 the EU accepted, in the face of strenuous objections by some of the more welfarist members, that the host nation's rules for (e.g. healthcare) service providers must apply, rather than those of the provider's country of origin.

Broadly speaking, this pattern of limited coverage can be seen in all the chapters of the *acquis*. Some have perhaps more bearing on basic institutions than others. Thus chapter 5 on company law covers legislation on accounting and intellectual property rights and requires that courts enforce judgments in civil and commercial cases. Chapter 10 on taxation lays down some ground rules about definitions and principles of VAT and excise duties – but not on other taxes, so the flat personal income tax regimes in Estonia, Latvia, Lithuania and Slovakia, for example, were not in any way affected.

Chapter 13 on social policy and employment covers 'minimum standards' in labour law. These seem – to judge from the CMRs – to have been in practice mainly to do with non-discrimination and health and safety, but there has also been a concern to establish 'tripartite consultation' – which could perhaps have some practical consequences for the flexibility of the labour market. The Commission urged Poland to strengthen incentives for job creation,[12] but the country's distorted labour market and very low employment rate (about half the working age population in employment) were not among the 'serious concerns' listed at the end of the CMR.

Chapter 28, on financial control, and chapter 29, on financial and budgetary provision, have little to do with such topics as relational banking and the role of the stock market. They are chiefly concerned with principles of internal monitoring of public spending and arrangements to make contributions to, and handle payments from, the EU budget, respectively.

So far as regulation is concerned, a great deal is left to national authorities. The tendency in most spheres of regulation is for Brussels to require certain minima and leave room for a good deal of variation in national regulatory regimes. On banking supervision, the principal EU requirement is that it should be independent of the government (information from interviews). Brussels may have pushed for deposit insurance schemes prematurely, when leaving bank development more exclusively to the market would have been better (interviews), but a great deal of banking development is not being steered by Brussels.

EU listing rules on stock exchanges exist, but again set a floor rather than a common standard; London Stock Exchange listing requirements are more stringent, for example, than the EU prospectus rules.[13] Informants pointed out that joint regulation in some areas by two EU member states, where the sectors being regulated are closely intertwined through common ownership, has been discussed between them without any need to involve the European Commission. In general, as foreign investment grows in, say, insurance or banking, and the foreign-owned branch offices are subject to regulation in the country where the parent company is located, smaller countries are tending to lose regulatory reach to larger countries – and this is a process not in any direct sense to do with EU membership.[14]

In general, the role of the EU in regulation, so far, has been to set minimum standards rather than usurp the functions of national regulators. So far as 'variety of capitalism' classifications of capital markets are concerned, those expert informants who commented on the subject took it as given that the central European accession states have, and are likely for the foreseeable future to have, a bank-based system. Some of the stock markets in the region may be developing fast, but in general their capitalization is modest by international standards relative to GDP and to bank assets. The relative rates of development of banks and stock markets in the region are not something that Brussels is trying to influence.

One thing that emerged from interviews with experts who had been involved in, or were close to, the negotiations, was that influence from Western pressure groups was considerable. I was assured, for instance, that German and Austrian trade unions lobbied the Commission hard over free movement of labour, contributing to the eventual deal under which a number of established EU member states were not obliged to open up to workers from the new member states for several years after accession. Another account concerned toys and pharmaceuticals, where German and British companies, reportedly, lobbied hard over product standards. These are two instances where the outcome was not in the interest of people in the accession states. (On pharmaceuticals, in particular, see Peggy Watson's chapter in this volume.)

Governments of individual established member states, of course, also brought pressure to bear on the negotiations. Germany and France, I was told, both tried to press for personal and corporate tax rates to be raised in the candidate countries, and attempted to use cohesion funds (for regional assistance) as a bargaining tool. There is no sign that they had any success, but then attempts to minimize tax competition have failed among established member states, as well.

Poland appears in all accounts to be the accession candidate that bargained hardest and longest, with demands of its own that were unwelcome in Brussels. Thus, for example, according to my informants, Poland's objections to opening its land market immediately to foreign buyers led eventually to a trade-off over transition periods allowed for the Polish land market and for the free movement of labour from Poland and the other accession states. This was an exception to the normal practice of negotiating over each chapter as a self-contained exercise, not linked with other chapters.

In short, there is no question that real, and often hard, bargaining went on and that the outcomes were often important for the accession countries. What I am suggesting is that interview and monitoring report evidence shows that the negotiations did not focus on the fundamental institutions that characterize a particular national production regime. The accession negotiations over chapters of the *acquis*, insofar as they can be judged from the Commission's regular reports, the concluding CMRs on the candidate countries, and the responses of knowledgeable informants, did not cover, and were not meant to cover, the basic legislation and practice in labour and capital markets in the accession countries that define an economy as welfarist or free-market.

Haughton draws attention to variations over time in the power of EU conditionality.[15] It is, he suggests, greatest at the stage where a candidate nation is waiting to see whether it will be admitted to accession negotiations ('the decision phase'). Once those negotiations are embarked upon, both sets of negotiators know that if the talks do not lead to accession, the process has failed. Whatever the preferences may have been within, say, the French political elite, the Commission negotiators did not want the process to fail. The pressure on the applicants was somewhat reduced.

This view was endorsed by informants in the interviews. One view was that the prospect of accession tended to keep non-reformist governments more or less on track; reformist governments would have liberalized anyway, but the aim of joining the EU (a popular objective) limited the undoing of reformers' work by non-reformist successor governments. It is therefore reasonable to suppose that at least some market and political liberalization took place in candidate countries in the decade up to 2003 that might not have occurred had there been no prospect of joining the EU. This is an important distinction between the processes of post-communist change in those countries and in the CIS countries. In the latter, after all, there was little or no expectation in that period that EU membership would be on offer, and by and large the political class in CIS countries did not seek it.[16]

It would therefore be perverse to argue that economic institutions in countries seriously seeking accession were not affected in general by the accession process. I am not arguing that there was no effect, but rather that the effects there did not extend to pushing fundamental economic institutions in the candidate nations into some standard, European mould. The evidence is that the Baltic states, Poland, Hungary and Slovakia, at least, had evolved along a low-tax, low-redistribution, low-job-security track that left them on accession markedly more 'Anglo-Saxon' than almost all the established EU member states.

It has been claimed that the more general economic reform agenda contained in the Accession Partnership agreements (1998–2002) was neo-liberal because it emphasized privatization, financial liberalization and a reduction in state involvement in the economy.[17] This is, I think, a misreading of the situation. For a society emerging from communism, movement towards free markets and private ownership of capital was the only known direction of change if the old system was not to be preserved. The language may have been less statist than in some other EU discourse; but the prescriptions were not detailed enough to be labelled 'Anglo-Saxon'.

For example, the pace and scope of privatization – one of the most fundamental steps towards a 'functioning market economy' – were, in the view of east European expert informants, not treated by Brussels as matters of high priority requiring detailed negotiation (interviews). This is perhaps not surprising when one considers the large, continuing role of the state in some established EU member states: for example, the legally entrenched role of the *Länder* in German savings banks.[18]

One indicator of the scope left to individual candidate nations is the post-accession variation among them in the economic role of the state. The state sector in mid-2005, on EBRD estimates, accounted for 20 per cent of GDP in the Czech Republic, Estonia, Hungary and Slovakia, for 25 per cent in Lithuania and Poland, for 30 per cent in Latvia and for 35 per cent in Slovenia.[19] If they were all being enjoined to lower the role of the state in the economy, nobody was setting the ceiling very low.

There are two fundamental ways, nonetheless, in which accession probably did affect accession candidates' economic institutions. First, the 'downloading' of legislation from the *acquis* may have been a process of transplanting rules that covered only highly selected parts of the economic game, but those rules were taken from a community of established capitalist countries. It is reasonable to assume that much of this legislation, for example about intellectual property rights, enforcement of contracts in courts, business accounting and the administration of VAT, was useful.

Second, in the admittedly somewhat touchy-feely domain of improving executive and judicial capability, much that was done in the course of the accession process looks as though it should have been effective. The EU15 governments, and the Commission, had powerful reasons to ensure that the Union did not end up admitting basket cases. That meant doing their best to secure that public administration and the courts functioned tolerably well in the candidate states. Devices such as 'twinning' – putting EU member state and EC officials into key posts in the state machinery of candidate countries on long-term secondment – should have imparted know-how and codes of practice. So, too, should the whole process of detailed and lengthy negotiation; that also transmits west European approaches, and ways of tackling problems ('framing policies').[20]

It has to be said that interviews with expert informants in central Europe provided some grounds for scepticism about the EU contribution to developing the capability of the state. First, 'twinning' in practice often involved placing in the administrations of candidate countries, not experienced officials from western Europe – possibly because it was not in their career interests to serve for long in someone else's bureaucracy – but hired consultants, whose capacity to transfer solid administrative know-how might be doubted.

Second, some of the transfers to government offices – e.g. of high-tech equipment to employment offices – were expensive luxuries that, in the absence of knowledgeable application in local conditions, did not necessarily improve performance.

Third, the procedures for applying for EU grants (e.g. by schools or school districts in accession states) are such that large numbers of organizations are pressed into allocating a lot of resources into bidding for allocations that will in the event go to only a very small number of applicants.

Fourth, dealing with Brussels has led, it was suggested, to the creation of a kind of double bureaucracy in accession states. One part consists of English-speaking generalists whose key skill is their ability to conduct business with the Commission; the other part consists of people, often with useful technical skills that the Anglophone generalists lack, whose knowledge of English or inclination to use it is less, but who get on with 'the real work'.

I have no data that would justify even a sketchy attempt at measuring the balance of positive and negative effects in Brussels' efforts to strengthen state administrative capacity. I can say only that the question is open; a net positive effect cannot just be assumed.

Conclusions

The questions I began with were: does the accession process affect the development of economic institutions in candidate countries in significant ways? And, insofar as it does have significant institutional consequences, do they amount to the promotion of a specifically 'European' set of welfarist, redistributive arrangements that may be problematic for future economic performance? The answers are yes and no, respectively.

The EU15 states contain a considerable variety of capitalisms. Three of these countries – France, Greece and Italy – have business environments and governance that look, on the scorecard in Table 5.1, unhealthy. Others look robust, and these are not just the 'Anglo-Saxon' UK and Ireland but also the 'Nordic' Denmark, Finland and Sweden.[21]

It is therefore not surprising that even the European Commission, with its own centralizing capabilities, did not in the course of accession impose some clearly defined model on the candidate countries.[22] Consequently, it is also not surprising that considerable institutional variety is to be found among the accession countries.

That does not mean that the accession process did not alter institutions. It may have contributed to an improvement of 'institutional quality' in central-eastern Europe, though we lack the evidence that would allow us to be confident about this. The apparent improvement in economic institutions more generally in central Europe is one that Crafts and Kaiser found historically unusual.[23] They conjecture that it has to do with the incentives for change that stem from prospective EU membership.

That conjecture has not been rigorously tested here, but the evidence discussed in this chapter does seem to support it. There was almost certainly an autonomous push towards the market and democracy in these countries, and liberal reforms would have taken place even if the EU had not existed. The west European economy would have had a large gravitational pull even if it had not been the EU single market. Opening up to trade and making one's economy better able to trade with wealthier neighbours would have been an attractive policy aim even in the absence of all the paraphernalia of the EU.

But the lure of being inside, not outside, a large customs union and single market must add to the incentives to become more like the neighbours.[24] And the accession negotiations – perhaps partly through the emphasis on government and judicial capability and partly through the downloading of the *acquis* – seem likely to have helped. The *acquis* is indeed a collection of rules and procedures that comes under the broad heading of 'institutions'. But, so far as the economy is concerned, the *acquis* does not amount to a prescription for any particular kind of capitalist order.

Appendix 5.1 List of experts interviewed

In Warsaw and Budapest, 17–28 June 2006

Leszek Balcerowicz, Governor of the National Bank of Poland
Miklos Losoncz, GKI Research, Budapest
Peter Mihalyi, Director, Europe Ltd; *i.a.* former Deputy Finance Minister of Hungary
Jan Monkiewicz, chairman of KNUIFE (Polish regulatory body for insurance and pensions)
Ryszard Rapacki, Warsaw School of Economics

In Brussels, 24 July 2006

Heather Grabbe, European Commission

In Brussels, 18 August 2006

Slawomir Tokarski, European Commission; previously (*i.a.*) a member of Poland's accession negotiating team

Notes

*I am indebted to the British Academy for a Small Research Grant that enabled me to conduct interviews in Brussels, Budapest and Warsaw with experts with policy experience, for the purposes of the research described here. I am also indebted to the experts consulted, to Tim Haughton and Colin Lawson, and to David Lane and other CRASSH conference participants for comments and suggestions.

1 This is argued by E. Iankova, 'Capitalism by Design? Central and Eastern Europe's Accession to the European Union' (draft), [US] National Council for Eurasian and East European Research, Title VIII Program, Washington, DC, 2000. She presents the accession countries as displaying corporatist forms of organization. See David Ost's chapter for a persuasive account of the very weak position of organized labour in Poland and elsewhere. Tripartite negotiation of pay and of economic policy more broadly was a matter more of appearance than of reality.

2 Perhaps, however, the EU's focus on certain topics, such as agricultural support, has had the effect of transferring some skills specific to those particular policy topics.

3 I have applied the Chatham House rule to the information from interviewees. In some cases their position makes it unacceptable to attribute specific remarks to them by name. To encourage all of them to speak freely, I therefore undertook to cite all interview material as simply 'from interviews', without identifying particular informants.

4 For a full exposition, see M. Knell and M. Srholec, 'Emerging Varieties of Capitalism in Central and Eastern Europe', in D. Lane and M. Myant (eds), *Varieties of Capitalism in Post-Communist Countries* (Basingstoke: Palgrave Macmillan, 2007). They developed their measures for the sake of classifying 'production regimes' between liberal market systems and strategic coordination systems – the latter relying more, at both micro and macro levels, on cooperation, and less on pure competition. This distinction is fundamental to the varieties-of-capitalism analysis.

5 In the interviews, the expert informants pointed out some of the limitations of these indicators: for example, that government consumption expenditures were high relative to GDP in communist countries but were not necessarily composed of spending that had much to do with redistribution, and both the level (relative to GDP) and the composition of such spending had been politically difficult to change. It is also the case more broadly that these indicators may be made up of components that, taken individually, tell very different stories. For instance, the US has the OECD's second highest marginal rate of corporation tax (*The Economist*, 1 July (2006) 82) but overall emerges as non-redistributive in the Knell–Srholec measure. Nor are most of these indicators unambiguous in what they say about a society. A Gini coefficient may rise substantially, as in Japan in recent years, because of the ageing of the population, while the distribution of income from economic activity remains relatively even (*The Economist*, 17 June (2006) 67–8).

6 R. Dore, *Stockmarket Capitalism: Welfare Capitalism. Japan and Germany versus the Anglo-Saxons* (Oxford: Oxford University Press, 2000). His examples of 'welfare capitalism' are Germany and Japan.

7 J.H. Anderson and C.W. Gray, *Anticorruption in Transition 3: Who is Succeeding … and Why?* (Washington, DC: World Bank, 2006), p. 8. The difference between the two ratios (7/10 and 10/16) is nowhere near a respectable level of significance (chi-square test). What changed on the corruption front between 2002 and 2005, of course, sheds no light on the influence of the EU on any curbing of corruption between the early 1990s and 2002. The prospect of EU accession, and the preliminary exertion of EU conditionality and EU assistance in that period may well have had desirable effects, but we do not have earlier evidence from BEEPS.

8 I use the term 'Europeanization' here in the broad sense of becoming economically more like western Europe, not in the narrow sense of downloading EU rules and regulations. Heather Grabbe, in *The EU's Transformative Power. Europeanization through Conditionality in Central and Eastern Europe* (Basingstoke: Palgrave Macmillan, 2006), uses it in the latter sense.

9 For more detail and discussion see V. Sobell, 'Central Europe Unhinged', London: Daiwa Institute of Research Ltd, 2 October 2006.
10 Grabbe, *The EU's Transformative Power*, p. 42.
11 See e.g. European Commission, *Comprehensive Monitoring Report on Hungary* (Brussels: European Commission, 2003).
12 See European Commission, *Comprehensive Monitoring Report on Poland* (Brussels: European Commission, 2003), p. 41.
13 *Financial Times*, 24 June 2006, p. 19.
14 See J. Monkiewicz, 'Polish Financial Sector in the Transition Period: from National to Regional Perspective', draft, 2005.
15 T.J. Haughton, 'When does the EU Make a Difference? Conditionality and the Accession Process in Central and Eastern Europe', forthcoming in *The Political Studies Review*, 5 (2007).
16 More recent developments in Georgia and Ukraine mark a change in this respect. But even for those two countries in 2006 the prospect of EU membership was pretty remote.
17 Grabbe, *The EU's Transformative Power*, p. 24.
18 *The Economist*, 1 July 2006, p. 79.
19 EBRD, *Transition Report 2005*, London: 2005, Table 1.1.
20 Grabbe, *The EU's Transformative Power*, p. 63.
21 André Sapir, in 'Globalisation and the Reform of European Social Models', Brussels: Bruegel Policy Brief, 2005/1, makes the case that the Nordic countries of the EU15 – which on his classification of social models includes the Netherlands – are both efficient and equitable; the Anglo-Saxons are efficient but not equitable, and therefore not necessarily viable in the long run; the countries with a continental model (Austria, Belgium, France, Germany and Luxembourg) or a Mediterranean model (Greece, Italy, Portugal, Spain) are neither efficient nor equitable. Changing the 'European model', he argues, is therefore primarily a matter of making large institutional changes in countries with continental and Mediterranean models, but in a 'Nordic', not an Anglo-Saxon, direction. His proxy measure for efficiency is the employment rate and for equity the percentage in poverty.
22 Another consideration that was put to me was this: the Commission is made up of units that each work closely to a specific theme or field; there is no mechanism on the Commission side of the negotiating and monitoring process that enables anyone to draw all the threads together and consider an accession state's social and economic system as a whole.
23 N. Crafts and K. Kaiser, 'Long-term Growth Prospects in Transition Economies: a Reappraisal', *Structural Change and Economic Dynamics*, March (2004).
24 The lure of a large customs union on the borders of an economically small nation can be expressed another way: by the disadvantages of being outside its protective walls. Trade is, after all, highly sensitive to distance. Alternatives for the central European countries were not enticing, even if their peoples had been well-disposed towards their neighbours to the east. The economic size of their eastern neighbours – as market or as source of supply – was tiny compared with that of the EU. World Bank *World Development Indicators* figures for 2004 put the gross national income (in dollars at the exchange rate) of Russia plus Ukraine at about one-fourteenth of the sum of France, Germany, Italy and the UK.

6
The Outcomes of the Czech Economic Transformation*

Martin Myant

The basic elements of the transformation of a centrally planned into a market economy are generally taken to centre on price liberalization, a predominance of private ownership and opening to the world economy. On these criteria, the Czech transformation has been successful, creating the 'functioning market economy' required for EU accession in 2004. However, market economies differ among themselves in many important characteristics and vary widely in terms of levels of development and potential for growth. A powerful Czech self-image sets the country among the advanced nations of the world and a fully successful transformation should imply reclaiming a place within, or not far behind, that family. Set in that context the Czech economic transformation up to 2006 appeared as a qualified success. Elements of the transformation strategy had created barriers to the development of an economy based on domestically owned firms and left the country heavily dependent on foreign-owned firms and on a continuing flow of inward investment. This created a basis for renewed economic growth after 1999, but left uncertainties about the future.

The economic transformation

The most familiar indicator of a country's economic level is per capita GDP. This shows the Czech Republic some way behind the advanced countries of western Europe throughout the twentieth century. Per capita GDP was probably about 57 per cent of the average for EU members in 1990 when compared by purchasing power parity (PPP). Table 6.1 shows the changes in real GDP levels over the years since 1989.

This indicates periods in the Czech transformation. The transformation depression, similar to that in other central east European countries (CEECs), was precipitated by a combination of the collapse in exports to the Soviet bloc and sharp deflationary policies introduced in 1991. It was followed by accelerating growth, as new private firms emerged and as established enterprises reoriented their exports towards western Europe. The EU took 69 per cent of Czech exports in 1999, compared with 18 per cent for Czechoslovakia in 1989.

Table 6.1 Annual percentage growth rates in GDP, 1990–2005

1990	*1991*	*1992*	*1993*	*1994*	*1995*	*1996*	*1997*	*1998*	*1999*	*2000*
−2.0	−11.6	−0.5	0.1	2.2	5.9	4.2	−0.7	−1.1	1.2	3.9
2001	*2002*	*2003*	*2004*	*2005*						
2.6	1.5	3.2	4.7	6.0						

Note: The methodologies used for calculating constant prices differ for 1990, 1991–92 and 1993–2005.
Source: Calculated from *Statistical Yearbook of the Czech Republic, 2005* (Prague: Scientia) Table 1, and *Makroekonomické údaje* (Prague: Czech Statistical Office, 2006, www.czso.cz).

The downturn after 1997 was followed by a resumption of growth bringing per capita GDP from 64 per cent of the level of the 25 subsequent EU members in 2000 to 73 per cent in 2005, compared by PPP.[1] The catching-up process was actually faster during the renewed recovery period than GDP growth, owing to a favourable shift in the terms of trade.

Renewed depression in the late 1990s was caused by weak export competitiveness and rising import demand in the context of premature financial liberalization. A rising current account deficit, coinciding with problems in banks and enterprises referred to below, led to a fall in international confidence and a foreign currency crisis. The authorities responded with restrictions on demand and credit. The downturn precipitated a substantial change in the nature of the Czech transformation. The emphasis shifted away from large enterprises, inherited from the communist past, towards selling to foreign owners and encouraging inward direct investment.

This created the basis for accelerating growth from 1999 and for the first trade surplus in the Czech Republic's existence in 2005. The current account was still in deficit, but that, as indicated below, posed no immediate threat. The budget deficit passed the 3 per cent of GDP marker in 2000, as spending rose due to higher unemployment, rising costs of health care and pensions and the need to write off debts created by the transformation strategy of the 1990s, but fell back to 1.9 per cent of GDP in 2005. EU accession confirmed the generally successful outcome of the Czech transformation and the country was on course for acceptance into the European currency, although a higher budget deficit in 2006 pointed to some delay beyond the earlier target date of 2010.

Sources of competitiveness

This story of success needs to be balanced with a recognition of the Czech Republic's economic level and the potential that it gives for further development. The World Economic Forum's annual Growth Competitiveness Index summarizes the variety of economic and institutional factors that it believes contribute to growth.[2]

For leading countries, the 'core innovators', innovations and the technology environment counted for half the rankings. Other, less advanced, countries are allowed to rely more on technology developed elsewhere. The Czech Republic was well below the top group of countries, coming thirty-eighth in the 2005 rankings, close to other CEECs. However, it occupied an encouraging twenty-second place on the technology index, firmly ahead of all other CEECs.[3] This is somewhat flattering although, as indicated below, the Czech Republic does have a research base.

Pre-1989 Czechoslovakia occupied a dual position in terms of its trading relationships. It developed and sold complex finished products in the CMEA market, but could only compete on world markets with raw materials and semi-manufactures, selling more sophisticated finished products, such as cars, at very low prices, reflecting obsolete design and technology. Renewed growth saw a shift back towards motor vehicles and electronics. Thus the share of machinery and transport equipment (SITC 7) in total (Czechoslovak) exports declined from 37.7 per cent in 1990 to a low point of 25.4 per cent in 1992 before rising steadily to pass 50 per cent for the Czech Republic in 2003.

However, much of Czech competitive strength depended on low labour costs. Productivity in 2005, measured as GDP per person working, stood at 67 per cent of the average for the 25 EU members. Labour costs, compared by the official exchange rate, stood at only 20–25 per cent of the EU average.[4] Wages, the largest element in labour costs, were around half the level of those in Slovenia, about the same as those for Hungary and Poland and significantly above Slovakia (on 14 per cent) and other post-communist accession countries,[5] suggesting that the advantage bestowed by low wages could be challenged from countries to the Czech Republic's east.

Other important elements of a more lasting competitive strength were assembled by a Czech team from a range of sources using both 'hard' and 'soft' (survey-based) data.[6] Czech weaknesses relative to more advanced EU countries lay particularly in the institutional environment, the climate for innovation and the labour force. They pointed to a country that could be very acceptable to a certain kind of inward investor that was not interested in innovation activities with the Czech Republic, but that offered less chance for innovative, new Czech companies.

Weaknesses in the institutional environment included the low effectiveness of bankruptcy laws, poor protection of intellectual property and limited access to credits and risk capital, all areas that could hamper innovative domestic firms. The Czech Republic also scored very badly in Transparency International's indices of perceptions of corruption,[7] as did other CEECs. There were frequent Czech press reports of corrupt practices and of networks with links into high levels in government, but little sign of large-scale crime organizations capturing positions of political power.[8] It remains unclear how harmful this is to economic development, a point taken up below.

On the climate for innovation, the Czech Republic was well behind the EU's leaders (Sweden or Finland on most indicators), but not too far behind the EU average on some input indicators. There was government support for research, enterprises did conduct R&D, there was collaboration between firms and universities and there were qualified scientists and scientific publications. Gross domestic R&D spending in 2003 was 1.26 per cent of GDP, compared with an EU average of 1.92 per cent and a highest EU figure of 3.98 per cent for Sweden.[9] However, output measures pointed to a wider gap with 'core innovators' with very few high-tech patents registered in the EU and an uptake of risk capital that put the Czech Republic around the bottom of the EU league.

In relation to the labour force and skill levels, the Czech Republic scored particularly badly on higher education, with 12.3 per cent of the population aged 25 to 64 in 2004 having attended compared with an EU average of 21.9 per cent. No post-communist country was below the Czech level. There was some compensation as the Czech Republic stood out for the numbers with a middle level of education, possibly very relevant to a particular kind of inward investor. There may also be problems of definition between countries and comparability of quality. Nevertheless, state spending on education as a percentage of GDP was actually lower in 2002 than in 1995 and remained at 85 per cent of the EU average.

Alongside these indicators of a general environment, the road to an innovative economy must also depend on key actors. These include firms and financial institutions. Firms able to operate in a market environment could be created from scratch, by transformation of existing state-owned enterprises into private companies, by sales of existing enterprises to foreign companies, by new investment from foreign companies or, finally, by transforming enterprises under continuing state ownership. State-owned firms actually performed quite well during the 1990s, but few were left unprivatized by 2006.

The assumption behind much of the strategy of the early and mid 1990s was that domestic entrepreneurs, managers and engineers would rise to the challenge and bring the country growth and prosperity. As the following sections demonstrate, elements of the chosen strategy actually helped create barriers to the development of innovative, indigenous firms. The kind of market economy that emerged was heavily dependent on foreign multinational companies and its prospects therefore depended on the place of the Czech Republic within their strategies. The following sections outline how this came about.

Banks

The development of domestic businesses depended on adequate means of finance and this centred at first on banks inherited from the communist past which were partially privatized during the 1990s. Central planning had relied

Table 6.2 Credits and deposits as percentage of GDP

	Credits					*Deposits*	
	Total	*Government*	*Households*	*Enterprises*	*Of which, manufacturing*	*Total*	*Households*
1993–97	61.1		3.2	57.9	18.7	62.8	30.4
1998–2001	52.0	2.5	3.9	45.6	12.6	59.9	38.9
1999	54.9	0.8	5.5	48.6	14.1	58.8	38.3
2002–4	38.8	5.9	9.3	23.6	5.9	66.08	37.5

Source: Calculated from *Statistical Yearbook of the Czech Republic*, various years, Chapter 7.

heavily on credits to the enterprise sector which were more than balanced by household savings. Table 6.2 shows the broad indicators for identifiable periods for 1993 onwards. In the first period a high level of household saving effectively financed the enterprise sector, providing a volume of credit that was unusually high by CEEC standards. By contrast, in the UK deposits from, and credits to, households have tended to be roughly equal.

The behaviour and performance of Czech banks have been analysed elsewhere.[10] Thanks to the large deposit base, and under pressure from the government, banks lent to new firms and to newly privatized enterprises. It was impossible to assess risks accurately with so little experience in the new market environment and it was clear from very early on that much of the lending was unsound, such that 29.3 per cent of credits were classified in December 1996,[11] meaning in many cases that nothing was likely to be returned. Banks dramatically cut lending after 1997 and the volume of credit in the two periods shown in Table 6.2 after that year was close to normal levels for CEECs. Credits to government increased to cover budget deficits and the volume of credit to enterprises fell dramatically. The sharp drop for manufacturing is noteworthy in view of that sector's importance for export performance. Recovery for the banking sector was based on the restoration of full state control and sale to established foreign banks. Classified credits, with bad debt continuing from the past, fell back to 12 per cent of the total in December 2005.[12]

The figures in Table 6.2 suggest that a favourable starting point existed for financing economic transformation in the 1990s, and for investment to improve competitiveness, but the promising macroeconomic base was wasted. The foreign-owned banks were more cautious with credits to enterprises and the period left behind a burden on the state budget, following the financial rescue of banks before further sale, which added the equivalent of 1.5 per cent of GDP to state spending over the 2000–5 period.[13]

New small businesses

Starting from practically no legal base up to 1989, individual entrepreneurs quickly established themselves as a powerful force, especially in trade, repair, personal services and catering. Their growth can be followed from figures on registered businesses, which record the first steps towards becoming an entrepreneur rather than actual activities undertaken. Labour force survey statistics, available from late 1993, show those in business as the principal employment activity. The figures in Table 6.3 indicate rapid growth, reaching a share of the working population higher in 2004 than that in other CEECs and also above the 12.8 per cent in the UK.[14] Although entrepreneurs complained about bureaucratic barriers to starting up, a factor that harms the country's standing in competitiveness league tables, these results do not indicate a major problem.

Czech entrepreneurs included a wide range of types and income levels. Some did achieve high incomes – earnings from enterprise were a major factor spreading inequality – but household survey data[15] showed average per capita household incomes consistently below the national average (87 per cent in 1993 and 92 per cent in 2004). The category probably included 'forced' entrepreneurs, unable to find other employment, and 'lifestyle' entrepreneurs, seeking independence but displaying no eagerness to establish larger businesses. Those that did grow were frequently 'Kirznerian' rather than 'Schumpeterian' entrepreneurs, seeking opportunities within the market to trade to make a profit rather than introducing innovations in production.

Voucher privatization, the breaking of established forms of contacts and the opening of the economy all provided scope for quick profits for those with particular skills and knowledge. Probably the most successful of the few manufacturing firms that grew from next to nothing to significant size was Linet,

Table 6.3 Registered and active non-agricultural entrepreneurs as percentage of the civilian labour force

	Registered	*Active*	
		Without employees	*With employees*
1991	2.5		
1992	18.1		
1993	21.5	6.5	2.9
1997	24.7	8.2	4.1
2004	41.6	12.2	4.0

Source: Calculated from *Statistical Yearbook of the Czech Republic*, various years, Tables in Chapters 10, 12 and 21.

claiming to be the world's fifth largest manufacturer of hospital beds. The founder chose the product because it was simple and there were market openings. He emphasized continuous innovation, but insisted that this did not require sophisticated technology or external finance,[16] the areas in which the Czech business environment was particularly weak.

Privatization into Czech ownership

Privatization of big state-owned enterprises into domestic ownership proceeded by two voucher waves, completed in 1994, and by direct sales.[17] By the end of the 1990s most of these firms were in very serious trouble. The nominal change in ownership had done nothing to overcome weaknesses of backward technology, lack of access to world markets and poor management abilities in relation to the new market environment.

A number of features of the transformation strategy exacerbated enterprises' problems. Voucher privatization created uncertain and unstable ownership, diverted efforts into battles for control rather than into formulating business strategies and created scope for investment in share dealing and acquisitions that contributed nothing to the restructuring of production. Sales to favoured entrepreneurs gave authority to architects of overambitious expansion plans, often involving unsound acquisitions, while again failing to address the backwardness of inherited technology. Czech-owned companies struggled to find markets with exports of simpler components replacing the finished products they had sold within the protected CMEA market. Escalating financial difficulties, leading to paralysis of many enterprises and of banks, led the government after 1989 to bring key firms back under state control with the aim of selling them off to foreign companies.

Table 6.4 shows changes in ownership in industry from 1997, after the completion of voucher privatization. Domestic private ownership was consistently associated with below-average productivity (measured both by gross output and by value added) and the share of these enterprises in both output and employment fell from 1997, initially largely by returns to state ownership. Sale to foreign owners or continued majority state ownership were both associated with higher, and in relative terms rising, productivity. Both produced firms that avoided diverting efforts into battles for control and into takeovers and acquisitions while the typical foreign-owned company had the expertise, finance and focus to invest in modern equipment and produce for clearly defined outlets.[18]

Voucher privatization was also conceived as a launching pad for a stock market with substantial share dealing. Projects were approved to transfer shares from 3459 enterprises, out of a total of 3818 in 1991, although the proportion of shares exchanged for vouchers was very variable.[19] Share prices quickly fell below their nominal values, as individuals sold the shares they had acquired to foreign portfolio investors and to domestic companies fighting

Table 6.4 Percentage shares of different forms of ownership in industrial value added and employment, selected years

	Public		*Private, Czech-owned*		*Private, foreign-owned*	
	Value added	*Employment*	*Value added*	*Employment*	*Value added*	*Employment*
1997	16.6	9.9	70.7	81.3	12.7	8.8
1999	17.5	9.8	60.6	76.3	21.8	14.0
2003	7.0	2.8	52.8	69.4	40.3	27.7

Source: Calculated from *Statistical Yearbook of the Czech Republic*, 2001 and 2005, both Table 16-10.

for control over each other. The share price index reached a low point of 35 per cent of its March 1994 level in October 1997.[20]

The breadth of share trading declined rapidly after the chaotic early years. The number of quoted companies fell from a peak of 1716 in 1995 to 320 in 1997 and to 39 in 2005. Engineering, electronics and a number of other branches of industry, already weakly represented in 1999, had disappeared by 2005. Instead, 98.8 per cent of trading was accounted for by seven companies, all linked to state or foreign ownership.[21] The stock market had become an element of no real significance either for corporate governance or as a means for new and growing companies to raise finance. This further emphasized the dependence on inward investors as the source of innovative growth.

Voucher privatization has also been linked to the high level of perceived corruption with criticisms from the start that it would contribute to 'the origin of the Czechoslovak branch of the Cosa nostra'.[22] It can be added that there were also scandals associated with privatization by direct sales. In the absence of significant accumulated wealth before 1989, it was inevitable that some unorthodox means would be used to gain capital and this was implicitly tolerated through the mid 1990s. However, the voucher method contributed immensely to an environment in which individuals could acquire wealth rapidly from very unclear beginnings and in which it was often unclear who owned enterprises or how control was exercised. The effects of that on economic performance are difficult to gauge, as can be indicated from two examples.

The major coal-mining company MUS, partially privatized by vouchers, slipped under the control of the US investment company Appian in 1998. There were allegations that this was no more than a front for the management, using the company's own money, to buy themselves control. The accusations remained unproven, but resurfaced when the company sought participation in further privatizations in the energy sector up to 2004. The management was not obviously bad or incompetent, despite continuing lack of transparency over the company's ownership. However, suspicion of illegal activities helped to foster negative perceptions – both within and to a lesser extent outside the country – of Czech business and politics.

A more notorious case was the chemical firm Setuza, a company privatized by vouchers that could trace its origins back to a soap producer founded in 1848. It still had 1300 employees in 2006. It appears to have come under the control, albeit through an opaque web of contracts, of a highly controversial entrepreneur in 2000 (this followed the failure of the state to establish full control after the debt crisis of the late 1990s). He recounted requiring a 'security adviser' – 'if you want to be an entrepreneur from the top drawer, it is unfortunately impossible without these contacts' – with experience of such work from before 1989.[23] The man was killed by a presumed professional assassin in January 2006. This company was one of the few Czech ones still quoted on the stock exchange and potentially of great economic significance as the country's producer of fuel from rape seed. Lack of clarity over ownership this time led to controversy, negative publicity and delays in government decisions over handling the company's burden of past debt. Development as a Czech-owned company was thereby put on ice.

Inward direct investment

Sale of state-owned companies to foreign owners was favoured by a number of managements in companies that had been exporting into western Europe before 1989. Enterprises that were sold secured access to markets, new technology where appropriate and resulting expansion, often in employment as well as output. Gains in these last two could be enormous when the parent company transferred production from plants in western Europe.

An example was the Barum tyre manufacturer, tracing its origins to a spin-off from the Bat'a concern in 1924. It was bought by the German firm Continental in 1992. Reasonable proximity to the target market is advantageous for this kind of heavy and awkward product, and output grew from 1.75 million tyres in 1991 to 18.5 million in 2005, with more than 80 per cent exported, accounting for 1.4 per cent of total Czech exports. Employment remained at 4300, as in 1993.[24] This geographical shift in production would have been impossible had Barum remained under domestic ownership. A similar process, albeit rarely as dramatic, occurred with several other engineering and car-component companies.

The Škoda car manufacturer was sold to Volkswagen in 1991 on the basis of assurances that it would retain the established name and that there would be further substantial investment to allow for a doubling of output. There were doubts and conflicts in the following years when it appeared likely that Volkswagen would scale back its plans, but the promised expansion went ahead broadly as planned, raising car output from 184,000 in 1989 to pass 500,000 in 2006.

Sale to foreign owners met political resistance wherever there was any scope for fears that the new owner might be aiming to close down an awkward competitor, to downgrade facilities to an assembly function or when the firm's name was judged important to Czech national pride, making it part of the 'family silver'. Barum did not qualify partly because its problems were so clear: its management knew the western European market in which it was losing its position due to its inability to keep up with the R&D spending and technological advances from the world's leading companies. Experience had also demonstrated the impossibility of modernizing the Škoda car manufacturer without a foreign owner. Negotiations failed in many other engineering and vehicle companies, leaving the firms to struggle through privatization into domestic ownership. A more welcoming approach to foreign firms from the start, closer to the strategy followed in Hungary, would have led to a more rapid restructuring of major industrial enterprises, a faster rise in unemployment, but the possibility of a more secure future for at least parts of the country's industrial heritage.

After 1998, sale to foreign companies was seen by the government as effectively the only road to prosperity for established enterprises. However, the new buyers were generally not particularly convincing. Thus the giant Škoda-Plzeň engineering combine, with 45,000 employees in the 1980s and a possible deal with Siemens in 1992 that would have taken part of the company with 8000 employees, was reduced to 7000 employees by 2002 when it was sold to the Appian group, a company that, as indicated above, probably qualified only nominally as a foreign investor. Employment was 2900 in a greatly thinned-down operation at the end of 2006.

The switch to encouraging sales to foreigners coincided, from 1998, with a commitment to support inward investment on greenfield sites, including financial incentives and the preparation of industrial zones, following the introduction of similar incentives in Hungary and Poland. Greenfield investment grew as a share of FDI to reach roughly the same level as acquisitions by 1997, moving slightly ahead in most following years.[25] The activities of CzechInvest, the inward investment agency that supported manufacturing investment to the value of up to half the capital, show support over the period from April 1998 to May 2006 to 224 foreign companies proposing investment valued at Kč285 bn, creating 66,000 jobs. Assuming all these projects were implemented as promised, they would contribute the equivalent of 55 per cent of the stock of FDI in manufacturing at the end of 2004.[26]

Assessing FDI

Czech government assessments of the impact of FDI have been overwhelmingly positive. However, the long-term implications of this transformation need to be assessed carefully.[27] FDI can have various impacts on employment, GDP and the balance of payments. These will depend on both direct

Table 6.5 Key indicators of the Czech balance of payments as percentages of GDP

	1993–96	*1997*	*1998–99*	*2000–4*	*2005*
Current account	−3.0	−6.3	−2.3	−5.7	−2.1
Balance of incomes	−0.5	−1.4	−2.0	−4.3	−4.9
Financial account	9.7	1.9	5.0	8.3	4.7
Balance of direct investment	2.6	2.3	8.3	6.8	8.3

Note: The balance of incomes, part of the current account, includes, among other items, repatriation of profits by foreign-owned companies. The balance of direct investment, part of the financial account, includes investment by foreign companies in the Czech Republic and investment by Czech firms in other countries.
Source: Calculated from *Balance of Payments Time Series Data from 1993* (Prague: Czech National Bank, 2006, www.cnb.cz), and *Statistical Yearbook of the Czech Republic*, 2005, Table 1.

and indirect effects, the latter including any impact on technology transfer and job creation, or loss, beyond the investment itself. There may also be differences over time, with inward investors introducing an element of instability through their ability to leave and transfer production elsewhere. This implies a cyclical process: investors come, bringing immediate benefits to the balance of payments and employment, but gradually shift towards repatriating profits before finally ending their operations. Set in this context, there are substantial differences in the impacts on the Czech economy of different kinds of FDI. First, however, it is helpful to look at the immediate significance for the balance of payments.

Table 6.5 shows a division into four periods, with rough consistency of indicators within each and 2005 possibly marking the start to a fifth. The current account was in deficit throughout, with a trade deficit up to 2004. The balance on incomes moved steadily into deficit, reflecting the outflow of earnings to foreign owners. However, the financial account was always in surplus and the overall balance was positive in all periods apart from the crisis year of 1997.

Behind this lies an important change. The surplus on the financial account up to 1996 was due in large part to portfolio investment, with purchases of shares made available through voucher privatization, and to short-term finance, attracted by the country's then high interest rates. This was withdrawn to precipitate the foreign currency crisis of 1997. The following years saw the growth in inward direct investment covering the current account deficit. This brought little immediate danger of instability partly because the finance could not be withdrawn quickly and partly because the current account deficits included reinvested profits which, following the accepted IMF methodology, also appear as a positive figure under FDI, although no foreign exchange transaction takes place. The current account deficit therefore exaggerates the actual volume of financial flows.

Table 6.6 Breakdown of FDI by sector and by direct effect on the balance of payments

	Share of sector in total stock	*Per cent of FDI from reinvested profits*	*2004 balance as per cent of GDP*
All	100	25.1	−1.0
Manufacturing	40.1	30.3	−1.5
Motor vehicles	8.0	36.4	−0.8
Rubber products	2.7	66.2	−0.1
Electronics	4.9	19.1	–
Trade	12.9	10.4	0.2
Transport and communications	6.2	10.4	−0.1
Finance	16.5	46.3	−0.5
Property and business services	11.3	0.8	1.1
Other	13.0	24.7	1.1

Notes: Figures for balance show incomes allocated to the foreign company minus net further investment. Reinvested profits are ignored as they appear in both figures. Exports and imports are not included in these figures.
Sources: Calculated from ČNB, *Přímé zahraniční investice za rok 2004* (Prague: Czech National Bank, 2006, www.cnb.cz), pp. 18 and 47.

The figure for 2005 suggests a declining current account deficit, due to good performance in goods and services, but a continually increasing deficit on the income balance. This was still below the level for Hungary, which had been above 5 per cent of GDP since the mid 1990s, and well below Ireland's level of 17.2 per cent of GDP for 2002–4.[28] Nevertheless, the Czech Republic's level was well above that of other CEECs. Continuing external stability depended on further investment to counterbalance repatriated profits and on the impact of foreign-owned companies on other elements of the external balance.

Table 6.6 shows the rising importance of reinvested profits as a source of FDI, leading to a negative balance from FDI as a whole by 2004. The main culprit was manufacturing industry, especially motor vehicles and rubber products, meaning predominantly car tyres. Finance and transport were also negative while trade still showed a net surplus. These figures reflect to some extent annual fluctuations, with motor vehicle investment due to rise again because of two major new assembly plants, set to start production in the following years. The figures point to the limitations of dependence on inward investment as a source of growth, although that needs to be set in the context of the full effects of FDI outlined below.

Table 6.7 shows the contribution of enterprises with a foreign ownership share to employment, value added and exports and imports of both goods and services, providing a more complete overview of their direct effects on the economy. This confirms the strong positions in manufacturing and finance and

Table 6.7 Percentage shares of enterprises with a foreign ownership share in key economic aggregates, 2003

	Employment	*Value added*	*Exports*	*Imports*	*Balance*
All	14.9	19.0	28.4	26.7	1.8
Manufacturing	29.0	37.8	25.7	16.8	9.0
Trade	17.1	14.3	1.1	6.3	−5.2
Transport and telecommunications	5.0	12.8	0.6	2.0	−1.4
Finance	79.0	87.8	0.3	0.4	−0.2
Property and business services	8.7	7.9	0.3	0.4	−0.1
Others	4.5	7.6	0.5	0.8	−0.3

Notes: Employment is a percentage of total civilian employment in that sector. Value added is a percentage of gross value added from national income accounts. Exports and imports and balance include goods and services and are percentages of GDP.
Sources: Calculated from *Přímé*, pp. 60, and *Statistical Yearbook of the Czech Republic* 2005, Tables 1 and 5–4.

to a lesser extent in trade. Productivity was consistently above the average for all sectors. However, the foreign trade figures indicate a relatively small overall surplus, due almost entirely to the strong showing from manufacturing which more than cancels out the negative balance for this sector shown in Table 6.6. The other sectors contributed negatively to the trade balance. They may have had other positive benefits. Thus, for example, foreign ownership of banks assured stability to the sector, an essential precondition for a functioning market economy.

Within manufacturing the indirect impact on the domestic economy varies between branches and forms of investment. It is lower, in terms of use of domestic components or transfer of technology and expertise to other firms, for greenfield investment rather than acquisitions. It is particularly low for electronics assembly firms. The US firm Flextronics invested in Brno, benefiting from various forms of government help and employing 2400 in 2002. It then announced the plant's closure and transferred production to Hungary. The wider impact on the local economy was negligible.[29] Similarly, Philips started production of television screens in a newly built factory in September 2001 and increased employment to 1300. It announced its withdrawal in January 2006, as demand shifted towards flat screens, leaving open the fate of the Kč1.3 bn ($55 m.) that had been received in state support.

It can be added that a strong representation in sectors requiring a high knowledge input has been used as an indicator of a country's level of innovation activity. The Czech Republic seems to do well here with 13.5 per cent of exports from such sectors, meaning primarily electronics, in 2004.[30] However, employment was overwhelmingly in relatively low-level activities, and figures for R&D spending in this sector show that it fell below the average for Czech manufacturing industry as a whole.[31]

Much of the investment in industrial zones, 95 of which were created between 1998 and 2005 with support from CzechInvest, was based on relatively small branch plants of multinational companies making very specific components and requiring labour of a low general skill level. In these cases the impact of FDI was fairly precisely measured by the jobs directly created, estimated at 50,000 in all zones by 2005,[32] and by the impact on the balance of payments.

The diversity of forms and impacts of inward investment makes further generalizations dangerous. Thus, for example, although some investors required employees with relatively low skill levels, the jobs lost from the past also included above all those with a low skill content. The trend in the economy as a whole was towards higher-quality services and public sector employment associated with a more qualified labour force. Within manufacturing those multinational companies with major operations often brought new skills, but it is noticeable that skill shortages were rarely mentioned as a general problem. Inward investors often seemed to have taken advantage of, and to have been satisfied with, the basic skill levels that already existed. There may have been some loss of R&D capacity, notably in electronics, but its level in the past was inadequate for the production of internationally competitive products.

Motor vehicles

If there is a clearly and unambiguously positive story to be told in manufacturing then it should be in the motor-vehicle sector. This was crucial to the country's economic prosperity and 90 per cent of its output came from foreign-owned firms by 1999.[33] Displacement of jobs from domestic firms, or transfer of technology and expertise to domestic firms, were therefore largely irrelevant. In fact, apart from a very few with a strong tradition in a particular component, domestically owned firms frequently sought out a foreign partner that could assure access to markets.[34]

This is not considered a high-tech industry, but spending on R&D stood at 12.5 per cent of output over the 1997–2001 period, a figure well above the manufacturing average and not far below Japan's level of 13.7 per cent.[35] The figure was higher for foreign-owned firms, but still around 9 per cent for the remaining domestically owned firms. However, internationally comparable figures suggest labour productivity levels in domestic and foreign-owned firms in the passenger-car sector at 12.5 and 30 per cent respectively of the OECD average in 2001.[36] Even allowing for relative price levels, that suggests a substantial gap that requires an explanation both of its causes and of its implications. The point is taken up at the end of the section.

The motor-vehicle industry inherited from the past included finished passenger cars, buses and lorries and the necessary components. None were fully competitive in world markets. Škoda's takeover by Volkswagen was accompanied by a transformation of component manufacturers, frequently based on foreign takeovers. Škoda cars gradually took more common Volkswagen components, but domestic inputs were still contributing over 60 per cent of output value after 2000.[37] Moreover, many Czech component manufacturers increased their exports both into the Volkswagen combine and to other multinational car manufacturers. They were joined by greenfield investors, exploiting the Czech Republic's low labour costs and geographical location.

Thus, strong traditions helped give the Czech Republic a lead over other CEECs in this sector, reflected in its ability to achieve a trade surplus on vehicles and components together by 1993, a status matched first by Hungary and then by Slovakia towards the end of the decade.[38] That in turn provided a basis for attracting two further major assembly plants which, along with expansion by Volkswagen, were expected to raise total vehicle output to over 1 million by 2010.[39] However, the comparative figures set out in Table 6.8 also demonstrate the extent to which other CEECs made up ground. Particularly Slovakia's rapid appearance as an exporter of finished cars, while maintaining balance within a high volume of trade in components, suggests that past traditions were important only for a limited period.

The future of the Czech motor-vehicle sector depended on the strategies of major investors, particularly Volkswagen. This evolved in the mid 1990s into using Škoda to produce high-quality vehicles – using some parts and design elements in common with other Volkswagen cars – that were then sold at

Table 6.8 Share in total exports and imports of passenger cars and components, selected countries, 2003

	SITC category	*Exports*	*Imports*	*Balance/exports*
Czech Republic	713	1.19	1.43	−0.24
	781	7.16	2.85	4.31
	784	7.00	4.26	2.74
Slovakia	713	0	2.86	
	781	18.34	3.18	15.16
	784	8.72	8.81	−0.15
Hungary	713	0.71	4.73	4.73
	781	3.52	4.00	−0.48
	784	3.75	2.82	0.93
Germany	713	1.78	1.34	0.44
	781	12.22	4.38	7.84
	784	3.43	2.16	1.27

Note: SITC 713, 781 and 784 are internal combustion piston engines, passenger cars and motor vehicles parts and accessories respectively.
Source: Calculated from United Nations, *International Trade Statistics Yearbook*, Vol. 1 (New York, 2004).

prices below those with the Volkswagen name. This opened (or retained) a lower-income market without reducing prices, or harming the more expensive image, of cars with the Volkswagen name.[40] R&D activities were retained at Škoda, building on past traditions and taking advantage of lower labour costs. This made sense as long as the parent company's strategy involved using its Czech subsidiary to produce distinct models. That option was vigorously supported from the Czech side, but need not be a permanent feature of Volkswagen's strategy.

As indicated in Table 6.8, car exports in 2003 were very important to the Czech Republic, but they still did not play as large a role as in Germany's exports. Slovakia had overtaken both and developed a substantial component capacity, albeit also with the need for substantial imports. Thus, in terms of volume alone, the Czech motor industry could be caught by other emerging exporters.

Moreover, the Czech motor industry suffered from the low price of its exports. The kilogram price for finished cars, a rough indicator of product quality or sophistication, was 40 per cent of the German level in 1993, when Škoda was still producing models designed before 1989. It had risen only to 57 per cent of the German level by 2003. This difference need not reflect substantial differences in labour skills or capital investment. Small, cheap cars are not much easier to make than bigger, expensive cars, but they are sold at significantly lower prices, leading to lower productivity in terms of the value of output per employee. The division of labour within the Volkswagen group, to be followed in effect by other incoming car manufacturers, therefore explains at least part of the apparently low productivity in the Czech motor industry. This implies a limit to the scope for catching up with the most advanced EU countries, even for the most successful part of Czech manufacturing. It can be added that the kilogram prices of Slovak and Hungarian exports in 2003 stood at 76 and 97 per cent of the German level respectively. This suggests a possible cost of the Czech heritage of small, cheap cars carrying the Škoda name while multinational companies have chosen to produce more expensive vehicles in other countries.

Conclusion

The transformation from a centrally planned economy can have a variety of different outcomes. It some cases it appears to have led to chaos and instability. The Czech Republic appears to have followed a more successful path, creating a functioning market economy with prospects for further growth. Several indicators point to a marked improvement, with accelerating growth, a trade surplus and a decline in the budget deficit, at least up to 2005. The roots of this success lie in the base left from the past, in particular in the strong motor-vehicle industry, skill levels that are attractive to a certain kind of inward investor and a favourable geographical location for exploiting the benefits of EU membership. Government policies of encouraging foreign ownership, pursued cautiously and somewhat sporadically before 1998 and enthusiastically in subsequent years, have also been important.

Reservations relate to a limited scope for autonomous development of Czech firms and to a heavy dependence on foreign ownership of those parts of the economy that are crucial to future success. The chosen forms of privatization, particularly the voucher method, and the encouragement of unsound lending by banks left weaknesses in the finance sector, indicated by the subsequently low level of credit and the small role for the stock market, which created unfavourable conditions for the growth of innovative, domestically owned firms.

Foreign-owned companies filled this gap, but dependence on inward investors carried dangers of instability from the cyclical nature of many multinational companies' inward-investment activities. The dangers were apparent by 2004 in balance of payments figures, but a continuing inflow of investment and good export performance from foreign-owned companies in manufacturing could be expected to ensure continued net benefits for some time to come. However, dependence on foreign-owned companies may also set limits to the economic level that can be achieved. The kinds of products they choose to manufacture, either less sophisticated or cheaper than those made in the most advanced countries, point to a lasting trap of productivity, and hence incomes, below the levels of the richest EU countries.

In short, by 2006 the Czech economy had been successfully transformed into a reasonably strong market economy, well up among middle-income countries. The basis had not been laid for a place among the world's 'core innovators'.

Notes

*An earlier version of this chapter appeared as 'Economic Transformation in the Czech Republic – a Qualified Success', *Europe-Asia Studies*, 59 (3).

The author would also like to thank Martin Srholec of the Centre for Technology, Innovation and Culture, University of Oslo for helpful comments and advice on an earlier draft.

1 V. Spěváček, R. Vintrová, M. Hájek and V. Žd,arek, 'Růst, stabilita a konvergence české ekonomiky v letech 1996–2005' (Prague: Centrum ekonomických studií VŠEM, Working Paper No. 11, 2005), p. 52.
2 World Economic Forum, *Global Competitiveness Report 2005–2006* (Basingstoke: Palgrave Macmillan, 2005).
3 Ibid., p. xviii.
4 Spěváček et al., 'Růst', p. 57.
5 Ibid., p. 63.
6 A. Kadeřábková et al., *Ročenka konkurenceschopnosti České republiky 2005* (Prague: Linde, 2005).
7 *Annual Report 2004* (Berlin: Transparency International, www.transparency.org).
8 For evidence and a recent discussion, see B. Dančák, V. Hloušek and V. Šimíček (eds), *Korupce: Projevy a potírání v České republice a Evropské unii* (Brno: Masarykova univerzita Mezinárodní politologický ústav, 2006).

9 Kadeřábková et al., *Ročenka,* p. 83.
10 M. Myant, *The Rise and Fall of Czech Capitalism: Economic Development in the Czech Republic since 1989* (Cheltenham: Edward Elgar, 2003), Chapter 8.
11 *Initial Capital, Capital Adequacy and Classified Credits as of 31 December 1997* (Prague: Czech National Bank, 1998, www.cnb.cz).
12 *Basic Indicators of the Banking Sector* (Prague: Czech National Bank, 2006, www.cnb.cz).
13 Calculated from *Macroeconomic Forecast* (Prague: Ministry of Finance of the Czech Republic, 2006, www.mfcr.cz).
14 Figures are in *Labour Force Statistics 1984–2004* (Paris: OECD, 2005).
15 Annually in Table 9.3 of *Statistical Yearbook of the Czech Republic.*
16 Z. Fiala and P. Korbel, 'Proč uspěl Zbyněk Frolík?' *Ekonom,* No.12 (2006) 14–21.
17 For an account of Czech privatization, see Myant, *The Rise,* Chapter 7.
18 Myant, *The Rise,* Chapter 9.
19 *Statistical Yearbook, 1997,* pp. 510 and 514.
20 *Statistical Yearbook, 1999,* p. 215.
21 Calculated from *Ročenka 2005* (Prague: Prague Stock Exchange, 2006, www.pse.cz), p. 37.
22 M. Zeman, *Hospodářské noviny,* 27 February 1992.
23 Z. Fiala and E. Szirmai, 'Jak to dělá Pitr,' *Ekonom,* No. 10 (2006) 30–3.
24 Basic information is from the company's website at www.conti-online.com.
25 M. Srholec, *Přímé zahraniční investice v České republice: Teorie a praxe v mezinárodním srovnání* (Prague: Linde, 2004), p. 33.
26 Calculated from *Investment Incentives: Manufacturing* (Prague: CzechInvest, 2006, www.czechinvest.org), and Srholec, *Přímé,* p. 19.
27 The most comprehensive attempt is Srholec, *Přímé.*
28 Calculated from *International Financial Statistics Yearbook* (Washington, DC: International Monetary Fund, 2005).
29 Srholec, *Přímé,* p. 152.
30 Kadeřábková, *Ročenka,* p. 107.
31 Srholec, *Přímé,* p. 93.
32 *Hospodářské noviny,* 14 April 2006.
33 Srholec, *Přímé,* p. 29.
34 Myant, *The Rise,* Chapter 9.
35 Srholec, *Přímé,* p. 93.
36 Ibid., p. 91.
37 Myant, *The Rise,* p. 257.
38 Ibid., p. 254.
39 *Hospodářské noviny,* 6 May 2006.
40 M. Myant, 'Inward Investment and Structural Transformation', in A. Lorentzen, M. Laky and B. Widmaier (eds), *Institutional Change and Industrial Development in Central and Eastern Europe* (Aldershot: Ashgate, 1999), pp. 61–84.

7

The Integration of the GDR into the Federal Republic: Challenges and Constraints

Rudi Schmidt

Societies are fundamentally shaped by institutional structures, norms and values guiding action and actors. It is assumed that in democratic societies these three levels should tend more or less toward harmony (coinciding correspondence) and that these societies draw their dynamic from the unequal development of these levels. The specific tensions and challenges, which resulted from the transformation after 1989, were due to the fact that a rapid and often radical institutional conversion met hesitation to adapt on the part of the citizens. This hesitation was often reinforced by the fact that the institutions did not hold what was promised or that, for example, the norms of the competitive exchange society collided with the internalized values of the old (state socialist) society.

A further feature specific to the transformation in mid-eastern European states is that the transformation took or is taking place at an unequal pace within the different societal spheres. For example, the transformation of the economy may advance faster than that of the political system or vice versa. This unequal pace of transformation has resulted in enduring problems to date. In Germany, the transformation took place at all levels at the same time (holistic model),[1] and the delayed adaptation of the new institutions and norms by the actors of the transitional society (former GDR or New *Bundesländer* [New German States]) posed a specific problem. This actor–institution discrepancy has to date constituted the structural core of the perceived shortcomings in East Germany and of the enduring dissatisfaction. This discrepancy becomes manifest in the results of the transformation, especially in the performance of the market economy, which is considered inadequate, in particular with respect to the insufficient integration of job seekers into the labour market. The mode and extent of, and the reasons given for, the widely voiced dissatisfaction of a majority of the East German population with the course and the results of the transformation process may be a problem specific to East Germany.

I have discussed the economic problems of the German transformation process in detail elsewhere.[2] In this context, I will only briefly touch on them. In this chapter, the primary focus will be on the differences East German actors show in handling the common institutions and on socio-psychological problems expressed in the different political and social orientations of West and East Germans.

Even though the population in the New *Bundesländer* (New German States) commands a lower household income (approximately 80 per cent of the West German average) and has to make do with lower wages (approximately 70 per cent), it consumes more than the value created. Therefore, the New *Bundesländer* are subsidized by West German transfers amounting to approximately €130 billion a year or 4 per cent of the gross domestic product (GDP). The reasons lie in the shrinkage course pursued during privatization, accompanied by deindustrialization, suboptimal company sizes, a too low network density of industrial enterprises and industry-related service providers, etc., from which the East German economy has not recovered to date. The economic weakness finds its expression in the low per capita gross national product, a low volume of employment, along with unemployment twice as high as in the West, and low productivity. The economic growth rates, too, are stagnant and, in part, lie below those of West Germany. A closing of the gap, the precondition for the equalization (of living conditions) so longed for by the East, will not be achieved in the foreseeable future.

The situation is aggravated by demographic problems. At 1.34 per cent Germany has one of the lowest rates of reproduction among the European countries. In East Germany, however, the rate is even lower. In two to three years this drop-off in births will make itself felt. From 1991 to 1993, in the course of the mass layoffs, the birth rate dropped to a record low of just one-third of the long-time average of East Germany. Many young people are still migrating to the West due to the fact that they cannot find apprenticeship training positions in the East. However, East German enterprises will soon experience a lack of young people to replace or expand their workforce. This could also lead to the reversal of manufacturing industry's favourable development – the only economic sector with above-average growth rates. Death surplus and migration add up to a population loss of 2.2 million people (from 16.7 million down to 14.5 million) from mid 1989 to 2005. This trend has, in fact, levelled off but still holds on. This, too, negatively affects economic capacity; retail and services, for example, are immediately affected.

A 'mezzogiornization',[3] which has always been warned against[4] has nevertheless not (yet) occurred. Thanks to the enormous monetary transfer of gross €1.3 trillion (between 1991 and 2004) the East has an excellent infrastructure, renovated cities, well-developed universities and modern companies. Yet, the East continues to be the poor relative of the republic. Their own tax revenue covers only 40–45 per cent of the New German States' budgets. The remaining part is financed by transfers from the West or on credit. And this budget situation will deteriorate further since many regions in East Germany will lose eligibility for aid from the EU structural fund, due to the mid-eastern

European states' admission into the EU, and the special allocations out of Germany's federal budget are also scheduled to cease in 2020. Hence, assistance for economic and structural development for East Germany is already being shifted from an all-encompassing to a selective mode. The new approach envisions development nuclei which are to receive priority assistance. Their endogenous growth dynamic is expected to spread to the environment, thus furthering the development of strong clusters of industry, services and science characteristic of the West and South German economic centres. Dresden (IT sector), Chemnitz/Zwickau (automobile industry), and Jena (opto-electronics) are mentioned most in this context. It remains to be seen whether this will be successful, since the competition for locating businesses is fierce and has long since been internationalized.

Initially, the thesis of 'catch-up modernization', based on modernization or differentiation theory, dominated theoretical explanations of system breakdown and the problems of transformation societies.[5] At least in the German case, this thesis has been pushed aside as being too coarse and has been replaced by more empirically oriented approaches of inductive theory-building drawing on action theories. However, with a few exceptions, social scientific interest in the East German transformation process has waned considerably. This has also been due to the fact that, in the East German case, along with the one-to-one adoption of the West German institutions and value system, scientific curiosity dwindled rapidly once the initial surprise effect wore off; since the destination had been determined, the path leading there did not appear to hold any more surprises.

In the meantime, the scientific focus has shifted to institution–actor relations, to intermediate organizations and collective actors, to the role of elites, etc., that is, to meso- and microsociological issues. In this respect, in particular, the collaborative research centre 580 of the universities of Halle and Jena, 'Social Developments after the Change of Regimes – Discontinuity, Tradition, Structural Formation', must be mentioned, with the focal points 'elites', 'labour markets' and 'social sector' with 15 research projects, financed for 11 years by the Deutsche Forschungsgemeinschaft (German Research Foundation).[6]

The transfer of institutions is only efficient in cases where the informal practices of dealing with them, the contextual knowledge socially framing them, and the tacit knowledge the functional elites draw upon to steer them, are transferred as well. This knowledge is bound up with actors. For this reason, in the course of the East German transformation process, there was an interest in sending along actors familiar with the institutions at least for a transition period. Because of this, West German officials and functionaries were found at the top of government agencies, courts, as well as associations during the first one to two years. Within the enterprises sold to western investors, managers familiar with the capitalist market economy also took charge. The only exception were the newly founded political parties.

Within the practice of institution–actor transfer different patterns can be distinguished. The highest degree of continuity prevailed among those institutions which survived essentially unchanged, mainly those providing for citizens' basic needs, such as hospitals, schools, kindergartens, local government, etc. They were either, with regard to their function, considered to be indifferent to the systemic context in which they are embedded, or their basic structures were left untouched due to the lack of feasible alternatives. The latter applied, for example, in the case of schools which will be compared to unions in the following.

The teachers in East German schools were considered to be system-oriented and loyal to the party – almost all of them were members of the SED (Socialist Unity Party of Germany). Now, they were expected to teach social studies and history according to new curricula that were supposed to abandon established concepts of an enemy and educate pupils toward being responsible citizens who have their own point of view, individual judgement, capacity for discourse and conflict, and show tolerance and civil courage. That had to go awry. Most of them were not prepared to go beyond paying lip service. Knowledgeable observers consider this to be a generational problem. The results were noticeable at the universities as well. East German students were mostly to a larger degree apolitical, oriented toward conformity, and more focused on the successful completion of studies. Just recently this difference has started to level off.

Reorganizing the unions was a different case.[7] The East German FDGB (Free German Trade Union Federation) with its individual unions was a dependent party appendix (with mandatory membership) and became obsolete after the transition. It disbanded in 1990. The West German DGB unions were indeed interested in the East German union members, but not in taking over the paid functionaries. Depending on the significance of either ideological concerns or financial interests, different paths were taken. IG Metall (union of metalworkers) newly built up its organization in the East. IG Chemie (union of chemical workers) took over parts of the respective organization and its officials.[8] IG Metall made sure that experienced West German officials were appointed to all important positions, down to the regional office directors; the West German officials were flanked by East German deputies. This was done to assure uniformity in handling the collective labour agreements in East and West, on the one hand, and to avoid mistaken appointments of politically and morally discredited FDGB officials in the course of rapid organization-building, which might have undermined the still weak membership ties, on the other.

This process of organization-building was successful. However, the unions faced two problems from the beginning: excessive expectations and the radical shrinkage regimen in the course of privatization. According to the East German citizen's dichotomic world view – a 'those up there and us down here' perspective – the FDGB represented the state, that is, the social security and full employment typical of state-socialist countries. In contrast, western unions are member-dependent organizations to represent and fight for member interests vis-à-vis business. Their ability to prevail depends considerably on the mobilization of their resources (members and their voluntary contributions). None of the unions were able to provide for the most important interest of every single member: to safeguard one's job. Therefore, the disappointment of union members increased along with the mass layoffs that started in 1991 – many left the unions. The basic insight that a union can only be as strong as its members make it is far more widespread in the West and has only very slowly gained ground in the East. To date, East German members show more reserve. They are less willing to take on an honorary post (for example, as a shop steward) and, generally, are more reserved toward the emancipatory agenda, according to which the West German unions still conceive of themselves as democratizers of capitalism. In 2003, large parts of the East German workforce refused to follow IG Metall when calling a strike to introduce the 35-hour work week, which has been in effect in the West. They rather followed the reasoning of business representatives, who claimed that perpetuating the cost advantage resulting from the 38-hour work week would allow jobs to be saved, than the argumentation to the contrary put forward by IG Metall. The strike failed – with long-term negative effects for the union.

The collective actor union conceives of itself as an institution to protect the interests of wage-dependent employees for all of Germany. Behind the strategy of equalizing wages and working hours lay IG Metall's intention to protect western companies and, accordingly, its western members against 'dirty competition' from the East. There was belief that, by this means, the union would be able to present itself to its East German members as the champion of an increase in living standards and the equalization of wages at the western level. Achieving equality continues to be an important motive within the aspirations of East German employees shaped by ideas of equity. However, as far as actual interest-oriented action is concerned, this generalized expectation structure is relativized or interfered with by a competition-minded regional awareness. The calculation is this: if it serves to protect my job, I am willing to make compromises in terms of working hours and wages in order to preserve the cost advantage vis-à-vis the West.

Regional differences also exist regarding the self-conception of the works councils and in dealing with labour law. Within the sphere of interest-oriented action at the company level dominated by power relations, labour rights as well as the Works Constitution Act are not legal goods automatically in effect. Rather, they have to be deliberately called upon by the employees and their representatives; at times, this may require conflict. In East Germany, this was a long learning process, explicable against the background of the GDR experience, whereby the state and the party apparatus, which were virtually identical, were the only immediately effective powers.

The fact that legal norms within the sphere of the capitalist economy are power-based and, at the same time, subject to negotiation, was knowledge that actors first had to acquire. The same was true for the far more essential insight that, after the transition, there was not just the duality of state and individuals or workers; rather, an intermediate sphere, in which partially autonomous groups play an important role in mediating the relation between individuals and the state, had complemented this duality.

Works councils are formed in accordance with the Works Constitution Act and thus according to law enacted by the state. The works council members may be, but do not have to be, union members as well; mostly they are. Since the works councils, at the same time, have to monitor compliance with the norms of the labour contract, the workforce, in fact, perceives their members as in-house union representatives. West German works council members also generally accept this role – in the East this is much less so. The East German works councils take much the same stance toward the unions as the members do: they are more passive and more reserved. Their interest-oriented action is more moderate than in the West and they show an especially pronounced understanding of the constraints facing the company. This is also the case regarding the exercise of costly rights and duties arising from the Works Constitution Act – indeed, not just in case of the works council members' right to be released from normal working duties (in enterprises larger than 200 employees) or to training during working hours, but regarding their obligation to hold quarterly works meetings as well. Only a minority of works councils takes this requirement seriously. Most of them settle for one to two meetings a year without attempting to get anything in exchange for the concession, as is commonly done in West Germany.

As a comprehensive interest organization, reaching beyond the single company, unions have to be bent on establishing norms for and standardizing labour relations. This is the precondition for regional or industry-wide collective agreements which take the burden from the works councils. However, focusing on the individual company and the lax handling of the labour contract, as is typical in East Germany, promote a distanced relationship between works councils and the unions.[9]

In this respect, too, special conditions prevail in the New *Bundesländer*, inasmuch as – with the exception of branches of western corporations – there are only a few large companies that are fully integrated into the capital market. The bulk of companies are small and medium sole-owner businesses or partnerships. However, it can be observed that at least a part of these entrepreneurs take advantage of the general climate of uncertainty in order to push their own rationalization strategies through, and, in doing so, further constrain the scope of the works councils. However, in one respect both East German business leaders and works councils agree, that is, with regard to the attempt at maintaining a productive balance between preserving a competitive cost advantage on the market and the insight that keeping good people at East German companies requires adequate market-oriented wages. On the other hand, for most East German works councils the demand for equal living conditions and equal income or equal industry-wide wages throughout Germany has low priority. For this reason, the frequently spread thesis of the East being the deregulation laboratory for West German reduction strategies is far from reality. Rather, an elevator effect is more likely. Reductions in the West will entail reductions in the East, accordingly; East German companies do not want to lose this competitive edge. While most East German works councils do not welcome this policy, they do at least accept it.

Works councils and unions are examples of a specific interpretation of societal institutions, which function differently in East Germany irrespective of their common basic normative and organizational structure. The actors shaping them define their interests differently from those actors who set the initial context from which the institutions were taken. This can be demonstrated in the case of business associations[10] or institutions from other societal spheres just as well.

The attitudes or political opinions of individuals, as expressed in elections and surveys or in face-to-face encounters, are, for the most part, more visible or can be experienced immediately. That quickly became apparent as early as 1990. While cheering each other in euphoric ardour for the regained German unification just a little while before, West German visitors to the now accessible part of the country quickly became aware of how alien the country and the people had become to them in the course of 45 years of separation and system competition. According to many travel reports at the time, West Germans, in the meantime, felt more at home in neighbouring countries than in the other part of their own country. And still, in the year 2000, a quarter of West as well as East Germans said, 'the citizens of the other part of Germany are in many respects stranger to me than the citizens of other countries'.[11]

While the inhabitants of the Federal Republic of Germany had so far perceived themselves as 'Germans', they now experienced being called 'West Germans' or, in short and in a familial and mocking manner, 'Wessis'. Conversely, the token 'Ossis' was assigned to East Germans. Along with the difficulties encountered in the course of the unification process, especially in regard to the economy, the need to distance one from the other grew on both sides. Especially in East Germany, there has been a strong mood swing; one could almost speak of a reactive collective identity formation. Katja Neller calls it 'retrospective GDR identity' (*retrospektive DDR-Identität*).[12] In 1990, 79 per cent of East Germans declared to feel positively attached to the new collectively shared nation when asked about their identification with unified Germany and her citizens. In 1993, this value had decreased to 53 per cent. Almost simultaneously, nostalgic reversion to the country of origin had increased. While, in 1991, 41 per cent of the East Germans asked claimed that they felt aligned with the former GDR and her citizens, in 1993, this value had increased to 65 per cent.[13]

How can this rapid loss of confidence in the new nation be explained? The first years following unification were, at the same time, years of the rapid and radical conversion of the state-socialist combines to privatized companies, accompanied by massive layoffs. The resulting consequences were further aggravated by the structural crisis of industry from 1991 to 1993. From 1989 to 1993, 3 million jobs were lost in the GDR and the New *Bundesländer*. The most severe decline was recorded by manufacturing industry (down to one-third of the level of 1989) and agriculture (down to a quarter of the level of 1989).[14]

The most massive layoffs took place from 1990 to 1992. Starting in 1994, the labour market balance recovered somewhat. Employment in the service sector and the construction industry, in the latter case stimulated by tax policy, temporarily exceeded the number of layoffs throughout the remaining economy.[15] The development then stagnated; from 1999 on, the number of gainfully employed persons has been decreasing slowly but continuously, also due to demographic factors.[16]

The special drama of events during the initial years following the transition is evident. It is, indeed, appropriate to speak of a shocking experience. 'About a third of the GDR citizens still gainfully employed in 1990 were no longer working in 1993.'[17] They were either unemployed or had retired early. By 1993, one-third were no longer working at the occupation they had been trained for, a circumstance rarely due to career advancement. And, at this time, just under a third were still employed at the same place.[18]

In my judgement, the East German appraisal of the transformation process and the basic attitudes toward the political and economic institutions were established during that time. The civil rights activist Friedrich Schorlemer, at the time, spoke of 'a kind of depression due to demand overload' and 'uncertainty regarding the future' affecting many East Germans.[19] This mood swing had far-reaching consequences. There was a feeling of being the object of others' decisions and of being sacrificed for the sake of abstract market logic. This traumatic experience of the radical loss of employment, in a society in which full employment had been essential, has shaped the mental digestion of the transformation during the last 15 years. The collective expectation was generally that if capitalist business leaders fail the state has to act on their behalf. This was expected all the more since the separation between economic and political spheres, constitutive of market economies, contradicted their hitherto existing experiences. The East Germans had learned that the political authorities were universally responsible. Why should the western state not have the same power to act? It did not have this power and, moreover, it had surrendered authority to the EU as a result of the Maastricht agreement; the neo-liberal interpretation dominant at this level made a state-interventionist structural and industrial policy even more difficult.

The shock, triggered by the drastic consequences of transformation, reactivated the basic étatistic–egalitarian orientation of East Germans, which, being a part of the socialist heritage of the GDR, may have initially receded.[20]

There are many indicators of this, but the most distinctive ones are the differences in party preferences and in voting behaviour. Accordingly, the PDS (Party of Democratic Socialism) as the successor of the communist SED (Socialist Unity Party) drew only 11 per cent of the East German vote in 1990, whereas it almost doubled its share of the vote reaching 20 per cent in 1994.[21] The rise has been even more significant in East German regional elections. While the PDS had, for example, only acquired 13.4 per cent of the vote at the elections to the Brandenburg Parliament in 1990, its share of the vote had risen continuously to 27.9 per cent by 2004; this makes it the second strongest party behind the SPD (Social Democratic Party of Germany). The PDS is similarly strong in other East German states.[22]

The strong increase in the vote from 1990 to 1994 could also be interpreted as a situational reaction. However, the PDS has consolidated itself as an option and has overcome being simply a protest party. When Chancellor Gerhard Schroeder, after 2002, proposed restructuring and dismantling the welfare state in the 'Agenda 2010' and a severe cut followed in the course of the 'Hartz IV' labour market reform, a left oppositional movement began to form in East and West. In the West, it operated under the name 'Election Alternative Social Justice' (Wahlalternative Soziale Gerechtigkeit). In the East, the movement stayed weak, just like, on the other side, the PDS in the West. For the election to the Bundestag (German Parliament) in 2005 the WASG (Election Alternative Social Justice) formed an alliance with the PDS that received 25 per cent of the East German vote. In the West, at just under 5 per cent, it received the highest vote of any party left of the SPD since 1949. Whether this will lead to a fifth party, permanently represented in the parliaments, establishing itself within the solidified party system of the West, for the time being remains to be seen.

When measured by the promises and expectations engendered at the outset of the transformation of the state socialist society in Germany in 1990, as well as by the tremendous amount of resources committed, the transformation can be viewed as a failure. In the meantime, hopes that the East could be helped to reach the economic prosperity of the West in the foreseeable future have waned in both parts of the country. Instead of continuing to demand equal living conditions, East German politicians, too, have begun to acquaint their citizens with lingering structural differences. Just as there has been an economic North–South gap in West Germany for a long time, there will continue to be an East–West gap as well. Economic and fiscal policies are starting to abandon all-encompassing assistance and are beginning to target scarcer resources on the promotion of economic growth nuclei with regional dissemination effects. It is accepted that remote rural areas will be further vacated, due to a lack of future opportunities, and that only residual infrastructure will be provided for the immobile elderly population.

But perhaps whole new perspectives of development will, indeed, arise from the East: the first Stettiners, having been invited by mayors and housing companies, have moved into vacant apartments in German villages and small towns on the west side of the Oder. The tight housing market and the price development in Stettin turn this into a favourably priced opportunity; perhaps more Poles will follow. The story has an ironic punchline: 60 years after displacing Germans from the former East German regions, Poles are being invited to settle on German territory, voluntarily left behind by Germans heading west.

Conclusion

Recapitulating East German experiences in the light of the former state socialist countries' transformation processes, one may conclude that the complete transfer of an established democracy's time-tested institutional arrangements has proven advantageous. The New *Bundesländer* show a higher degree of political stability than Poland or Hungary. In addition, the institution and resource transfer has resulted in a well-developed modern infrastructure, which, then again, has not yet offset the destructive consequences of radically exposing the East German economy to capitalist markets. The East German economy's performance still markedly lags behind that of West Germany. The tremendous financial transfer, two-thirds of which is spent on consumption, has also dampened West German economic growth.

The balance drawn from a subjective standpoint turns out to be just as ambivalent as one based on an objective view: a large minority of East Germans are still dissatisfied, even though their average income and standard of living are higher than is the case in the other mid-eastern European countries; this circumstance is expressed in surveys as well as in voting behaviour and in their readiness to organize. This can be interpreted in two ways: as the result of disappointed expectations and unrealistic aspirations as well as a structural problem resulting from an institution transfer beyond their control.

The efficacy of institutions relies on functional knowledge bound to the actors; it is thus essential to transfer this actor-bound knowledge along with the institutions. However, in doing so, there is a disadvantage: proxy action by foreign actors curbs the adaptation process within the recipient society, furthering alienation and passivity. The East German case, too, even in the light of its almost ideal conditions for institution transfer, supports the insight that there is neither an 'ideal path of transformation' nor a 'laboratory-confirmed solution' for nation-building, pursued to no avail in Iraq since 2003 based on misjudging actual preconditions and drawing on misconceived parallels.

Notes

1 See H. Wiesenthal, 'Die Krise holistischer Politikansätze und das Projekt der gesteuerten Systemtransformation', *Berliner Journal für Soziologie,* V, 4 (1995) 515–32.

2 R. Schmidt, 'Eastern Germany's Incorporation into the Federal Republic', in D. Lane and M. Myant (eds), *Varieties of Capitalism in Post-Communist Countries* (Basingstoke: Palgrave Macmillan, 2007). For more economic and social data see G.A. Ritter,

Der Preis der deutschen Einheit. Die Wiedervereinigung und die Krise des Sozialstaats (Munich: C.H. Beck, 2006). See also R. Pohl, 'The Macroeconomics of Transformation: the Case of East Germany', Diskussionspapiere 109 (Halle: Institut für Wirtschaftsforschung, 1999). Some economic aspects at the beginning of transformation are discussed by Jan Jeffries, 'East Germany: German Economic and Monetary Union', in J. Jeffries, *Socialist Economies and the Transition to the Market. A Guide* (London and New York: Routledge, 1993), pp. 393–420.

3 This term is derived from the southern Italian region the 'Mezzogiorno' and has been coined to denote the persistence of an economic, social and cultural divide. In Italy, this cleavage between a rich North and a poor South could not be bridged, irrespective of tremendous resource transfers throughout the decades following the Second World War.

4 A. J. Hughes Hallet and Y. Ma, 'East Germany, West Germany, and their Mezzogiorno Problem: a Parable for European Economic Integration', *Economic Journal,* 103, 417 (1993) 416–28. A. Boltho, W. Carlin and P. Scaramozzino, 'Will East Germany Become a New Mezzogiorno?' WZB Discussion Paper FS I 95-307 (Wissenschaftszentrum Berlin, 1995).

5 In Germany mainly proposed by Wolfgang Zapf (W. Zapf, 'Modernisierung und Modernisierungstheorien', in W. Zapf (ed.), *Die Modernisierung moderner Gesellschaften.* Verh. des 25. Deutschen Soziologentages in Frankfurt am Main 1990 (Frankfurt/New York: Campus, 1991) pp. 23–39 and W. Zapf, 'Die Transformation in der ehemaligen DDR und die soziologische Theorie der Modernisierung', WZB Discussion Papers (Wissenschaftszentrum Berlin, 1992), pp. 92–104. With respect to its explanatory potential as well as its potential for normatively shaping the transformation process, modernization theory was early on subjected to criticism, e.g. by D. Stark (D. Stark, 'Path Dependence and Privatization Strategies in East Central Europe', *East European Politics and Societies,* 6, 1 (1992) 17–54 and D. Stark, 'Rekombiniertes Eigentum im osteuropäischen Kapitalismus', *PROKLA. Zeitschrift für kritische Sozialwissenschaft,* 24, 94 (1994) 127–42. See also K. Müller, 'Der osteuropäische Wandel und die deutsch– deutsche Transformation. Zum Revisionsbedarf modernisierungstheoretischer Begründungen', in R. Schmidt and B. Lutz (eds), *Chancen und Risiken der materiellen Restrukturierung in Ostdeutschland* (Berlin: Akademie Verlag, 1995), pp. 1–42.

6 See www.sfb580.uni-jena.de

7 For more details see R. Schmidt, 'The Rebuilding of Industrial Relations in Eastern Germany', in W. Müller-Jentsch and H. Weitbrecht (eds), *The Changing Contours of German Industrial Relations* (Munich/Mehring: Hampp, 2003), pp. 81–102. For the first period see also R. Hyman, 'Institutional Transfer: Industrial Relations in Eastern Germany', *Work, Employment and Society,* X, 4 (1996) and L. Turner, *Fighting for Partnership. Labor and Politics in Unified Germany* (Ithaca and London: Cornell University Press, 1998).

8 See I. Artus, 'Die Etablierung der Gewerkschaften', in J. Bergmann and R. Schmidt (eds), *Industrielle Beziehungen. Institutionalisierung und Praxis unter Krisenbedingungen* (Opladen: Leske und Budrich, 1996), pp. 21–48.

9 A survey of the East German metal industry, conducted by the Institute of Sociology at the University of Jena in 2001, showed that the companies bound by a labour contract, too, in part deviate from the agreement, namely with regard to working time and pay – up to now, this could not have been imagined in the West (see R. Hinke, S. Röbenack and R. Schmidt, *Diesseits und jenseits des Tarifvertrags. Die Gestaltung der Lohn- und Leistungsbedingungen in der ostdeutschen Metall- und Elektroindustrie,* Arbeitsheft der Otto-Brenner-Stiftung 30 (Berlin/Jena, 2002) and

R. Schmidt, S. Röbenack and R. Hinke, 'Prekarisierung des kollektiven Tarifsystems am Beispiel der ostdeutschen Metallindustrie', *Industrielle Beziehungen,* 10 (2003) 220–49). This means that the norms established by IG Metall by means of collective agreement are losing their actual formative potential.

10 See W. Schroeder, *Das Modell Deutschland auf dem Prüfstand. Zur Entwicklung der industriellen Beziehungen in Ostdeutschland (1990–2000)* (Wiesbaden: Westdeutscher Verlag, 2000) and I. Artus, *Krise des deutschen Tarifsystems. Die Erosion des Flächentarifvertrags in Ost und West* (Wiesbaden: Westdeutscher Verlag, 2003).

11 K. Neller, 'Getrennt vereint? Ost-West-Identitäten, Stereotypen und Fremdheitsgefühle nach 15 Jahren deutscher Einheit', in J.W. Falter, O.W. Gabriel, H. Rattinger and H. Schoen (eds), *Sind wir ein Volk? Ost- und Westdeutschland im Vergleich* (Munich: C.H. Beck, 2006), pp. 13–36, here p. 31.

12 Ibid., p. 13.

13 Ibid., p. 22.

14 B. Lutz and H. Grünert, 'Der Zerfall der Beschäftigungsstrukturen der DDR', in B. Lutz, H.M. Nickel, R. Schmidt and A. Sorge (eds), *Arbeit, Arbeitsmarkt und Betriebe,* Berichte der Kommission für die Erforschung des sozialen und politischen Wandels in den neuen Bundesländern, Vol. I (Opladen: Leske und Budrich, 1996), pp. 69–120, here pp. 79 ff.

15 R. Schmidt (ed.), *Reorganisierung und Modernisierung der industriellen Produktion* (Opladen: Leske und Budrich, 1996), p. 216.

16 DIW (Deutsches Institut für Wirtschaftsforschung Berlin), *Zweiter Fortschrittsbericht wirtschaftswissenschaftlicher Institute über die wirtschaftliche Entwicklung in Ostdeutschland,* 70, No. 47 (Berlin, 2003).

17 Lutz and Grünert, 'Der Zerfall', p. 79.

18 Ibid. Early on Stanley Fisher drew the following conclusion: 'The obvious lesson from the East German case is that the formerly socialist economies cannot provide much employment at the wage levels of Western Europe' (S. Fisher, 'Socialist Economic Reform: Lessons of the First Three Years', *American Economic Review,* 83, 2 (1993), pp. 390 ff, here p. 392. See also Pohl, 'Macroeconomics'.

19 F. Schorlemer, *Freiheit als Einsicht. Bausteine für die Einheit* (Munich: Knaur, 1993), p. 29.

20 It is pointless discussing the significance of the socialization hypothesis as opposed to the situation hypothesis. In this respect I agree with the interpretation by R. Kollmorgen, who assumes situational activation of prior identity formation (R. Kollmorgen, *Ostdeutschland. Beobachtung einer Übergangs- und Teilgesellschaft* (Wiesbaden: VS-Verlag, 2005), pp. 171 ff.

21 In West Germany the PDS stayed marginalized at 1 per cent.

22 In this respect cf. H. Schoen and R. Abold, 'Zwei Wählerschaften in einem Land? Wahlverhalten im vereinigten Deutschland', in Falter et al.; *Sind wir ein Volk?,* pp. 128–57.

8
The Russian Transformation: a New Form of Etacratism?

Ovsey Shkaratan

There are two major approaches to the interpretation and understanding of transformation processes. First, according to a Eurocentric approach, these processes develop in a single line with the inner logics of the one-way unitary transition from non-market economy to market economy. Hegel's scheme of a 'step-type' development of history towards a single ideal for all mankind has influenced the denial of multilinearity in the development of particular societies by both Marxists and liberals. It also suggests development without alternatives. At the same time countries and nations are allocated to different 'echelons' (at different stages) of movement towards a single ideal – towards a universal Western democracy and liberal capitalism. Linear understanding of human development evolved in a classical theory of modernization epitomized in the work of W.W. Rostow and Talcott Parsons.

Second, this approach is contrasted with the idea of deep civilization differences between nations which carry out the transformation and influence the path of development. From this viewpoint, each type of civilization attempts to apply the achievements of science and technology, proceeding from its own views about the contents of real and potential wealth, its own criteria of economic growth and social development, economic interests and features of social development inherent in them. Writers such as Samuel Huntington consider that, for the first time in history, modernization is separated from 'westernization'. The distribution of Western ideals and norms does not result either in the occurrence of a universal civilization, or in the westernization of the non-Western societies. Non-Western civilizations again maintain the value of their cultures.[1]

In reality, the transformation processes in the countries of European and Eurasian areas proceed in a multilinear way. In the modern world coexistence of several main civilizations with distinct institutional, axiological and behavioural features takes place. These civilizations are connected by dominating religious systems. As applied to central European, southern European and Eurasian areas (post-communist countries, which are in the process of transformation) – these religious systems are Catholicism, Protestantism, Orthodoxy,

Islam. Liberal reforms in European and Eurasian post-communist countries originate from the same principles, the same universal methods: voluntary opening of national economies to the outer world, liberalization of prices, macroeconomic stabilization on the basis of strict monetary policy and privatization of the state property. However, the consequences of the same economic strategy have had different effects on the development path of countries. After a rather short period of time the success in economic growth and establishment of liberal democracy became evident and convincing in the countries of European cultural tradition, countries of western Christianity, countries with centuries-old tradition of private property and with some experience of civil relationships and a rule-of-law state – Czech Republic, Slovenia, Poland, Hungary, Slovakia.

At the same time eastern Christian societies (Russia, Ukraine, Bulgaria, Romania, Georgia), which began to transform their economies to the competitive market during the 1980s–1990s, found themselves in a much worse situation. As noted in Chapter 1 of this book, initially economic growth declined considerably in countries such as Russia and Ukraine, as did the level of investment.

The nature of the 'real socialist system' and its historical roots

By the beginning of the 1990s Russian scholars were making attempts to discover the nature of the societal system which was about to disappear (as it seemed at that time). I outlined the concept which viewed such societies as etacratic (or statist). This system was formed at the beginning of the 1930s and had remained intact until 1990.[2]

A specific social, economic and political system, which was neither capitalist nor socialist, emerged in the USSR and later it was spread to other countries. This system may be called etacratic according to its specific and steadily reproduced features (literally – power of the state – from French and Greek). Etacratism is not a series of deformations and deviations from some exemplary model of capitalism or socialism, it is a parallel branch of the historical development of contemporary industrial society with its own rules of functioning and development.

Etacratism can be viewed both as an independent social and economic system in a civilization dichotomy of 'West–East' and as one of the forms of modernization (industrialization) of the countries of the non-European cultural area. The fundamental principles of etacratic society are the following: the predominance of 'power-property' type relations; predominance of state property; economic activity regulated by the state (with the exception of the shadow economy); the predominance of centralized distribution; hierarchy-type estate and strata differentiation, in which positions of individuals and social groups are determined by their position in the power structure and are fixed in formal ranks and corresponding privileges; the predominance of bureaucracy, which forms etacracy and gains control over state property; social mobility organized from above which promotes people most loyal to the system: the absence of civil society, rule of law and, correspondingly, the presence of a partocracy system.

The predominance of power-ownership relations means that property relationships are not expressed in the opposition 'owner–non-owner', but in the continuum, reflecting the degree of appropriation depending on position in the power hierarchy, which determined social status and privileges. It was the power and the privileges it gave, which opened to the individual and his heirs more favourable access to knowledge and material well-being.

Social selection, which replaced spontaneous social mobility, had a devastating effect on the middle strata, and especially the intelligentsia. The Soviet system could have been built only through the social potential of marginal groups of the population. It is typical that in 1965–84, i.e. in the period of rapid development of electronic, nuclear, space, bioengineering and other supertechnologies, among the members of the Politburo of the Central Committee of the CPSU there predominated people who came from families of poor peasants and unskilled workers (70.5 per cent), 13.1 per cent were born in the families of unskilled white-collar workers, and only 8.5 per cent were born in the families of skilled workers, 8 per cent in the families of skilled non-manual workers).[3]

The concept of etacratism is supported by writers such as M. Castells:

> In the twentieth century we have lived, essentially, with two predominant modes of production: capitalism and statism ... Under statism the control of surplus is external to the economic sphere: it lies in the hands of the power-holders in the state: let us call them apparatchiki or ling-dao. Capitalism is oriented toward profit-maximizing, that is, toward increasing the amount of surplus appropriated by capital on the basis of the private control over the means of production and circulation. Statism is oriented toward power-maximizing, that is, toward increasing the military and ideological capacity of the political apparatus for imposing its goals on a greater number of subjects and at deeper levels of their consciousness.[4]

Bertrand Russell, M. Djillas and many others paid attention to the similarity of the backbone features of the so-called Soviet socialism and the system, which was called by K. Marx the 'Asiatic mode of production', and which contemporary Russian researchers prefer to call 'the state mode of production' or Eastern despotism.[5]

Russian authors attempted to explain the similarity in the history of the country; they write that in pre-revolutionary Russia there existed either the Asiatic mode of production itself or feudalism with elements of Eastern despotism. Anyhow there existed a developed institution of power-property.[6] O.E. Bessonova has put forward an institutional conception, according to which the economy of Russia had been a distributive system from the ninth to the twentieth centuries, and economic evolution of the country went in line with the evolution of the institutions of a distributive economy. The Soviet epoch (1920–80) is assigned by Bessonova to the next stage of predominance of a distributive economy.[7] It is obvious that the economy of distribution is no more than one of the subtypes of the state mode of production.

In this context one can regard the Bolshevik revolution as an organic roll-back of the country to the peculiar features of the Russian societal system which had evolved over a long historical process. For Russia communism was historically a logical stage of its development. The collapse of the communist system signified the beginning of a new stage of evolution of specific Eurasian civilization.[8] The historical roots of the contemporary Russian order lie in the long centuries of the country's history – Eurasian Orthodox civilization which ignored the private property institutions, the market, law-based state and civil society. Until the middle of the thirteenth century, i.e. in pre-Mongolian Russia, power was distributed among four sides of a square: prince–Veche–boyars–Church, and on the whole the situation was similar to European feudal society. The Golden Horde system brought Asiatic despotism, Asiatic (state) mode of production, and the flabby classless structure of society without private property, without social groups of proprietors. It was the Golden Horde which brought the following principle to Russia: 'Power is everything, population is nothing.'[9] From the thirteenth century until now, except for short historical periods, there has been no society beyond power in Russia, there are only people – faceless, a dumb community, deprived of civil rights.

Let me draw attention to such an important development factor as property relations. Since the coming of the Golden Horde, an individual could not really own property, he could only wield it. The supreme owner and power was the state, which existed as a typical despotism, where almost everyone was enslaved. Only by the end of the eighteenth century were the first laws introduced which assigned land and other property to the nobility. Even on the eve of the October revolution most land in Russia belonged not to single peasants but to rural communities, and all their members used this land on equal terms; for the majority of the Russians private property was not a tradition. In other words, Russia did not follow the path from traditional to feudal and then to capitalist society, unlike the countries of the European civilization area. As for socialism, which was brought from the West, it was transformed into the paradigm of traditional peasant views of the proper life.[10] That is why in Russia (unlike European countries) bolshevism had considerable social support.

Russia as a core of Soviet-type societies. The obstacles for capitalist and democratic development

After the fall of the USSR, economic reforms in Russia, the Baltic countries and all across central and eastern Europe started under the 'back to Europe' slogan. At first sight, the reforms were initially the same, as were the advisers, but the results turned out differently. The uncomfortable result of the transformations for the former Soviet republics was a consequence of a complex interlacement of historical factors, sociopolitical situation and unfavourable external actions. I would define four major factors.

First, there is a very important distinction between the former Soviet republics and the countries of central and eastern Europe (CEE) in that the latter had a shorter history under 'real socialism' – with a whole generation difference. The older generations of these people retained market economy skills and skills for civil self-organization. Their younger generations had a lot more freedom to go abroad in order to adopt these skills. In many countries of CEE private property for land and small businesses persisted, and the first steps towards liberalization of the economy had already been taken in 'socialist' regimes. In a socio-economic sense CEE was always ready for reforms, while there was absolutely no socio-economic ground for such transformation in Russia.

Secondly, liberal reforms in the countries of CEE were supported by a consolidated and ready-made society guided by national counter-elites, which for many years had opposed the Soviet regime. The same reforms in Russia were proclaimed to be in the interests of non-existing groups of population; the reformers were not able, and ruling groups never wanted, to achieve the primary goals of the democratic movement. Neither Russian democrats, who took part in the first parliamentary scrambles, nor young academic scholars, who knew the principles of a capitalist economy according to the Western literature, were prepared to apply their ideas in real situations. It was not by chance that the ruling positions in the process of decision-taking were soon to be grasped by an agile part of the Soviet *nomenklatura* headed by Yeltsin and Chernomyrdin. In Russia it was only the Soviet *nomenklatura* which had both class consciousness and class identity. That is why in Russia and most of the CIS countries, power was seized by young *nomenklatura* leaders.

Thirdly, the population's readiness to participate in the complicated transition to a market economy and civil society imposed a number of specific requirements on the individuality and creativity of its actors. Analysis shows that the significant empirical indicator is degree of urbanization. Quick urban population growth, dramatic collisions, which develop through invasive isolation of yesterday's peasantry, and the domination of pathological urban processes have all led to the marginalization of the typical Russian city from the people, who 'gave up' their traditional culture without accepting modern urban culture. The author's analysis shows that *the proportion of transforming actors across the whole country was still quite small*. This was then proved by the following events beginning with the democratic meetings of the end of the 1980s. The scale of these events was incomparable to the same processes in the Baltic states and CEE.[11]

What followed at the beginning of the 1990s reduced the quantity of potential actors. The matter is that a majority of the most advanced urbanites, the intellectual forces of the country, was concentrated in the military industrial complex (MIC). The number of employees in defence research institutes and engineering departments was around 1.8 million people. In addition, it was military engineers who worked in these industries. They made up the core of the democratic movements in 1986–92. They were the most active supporters of a market economy, a law-based state, demilitarization of the country and westernization. Russia's demilitarization resulted in the collapse of the economic backbone and de-urbanization. A large number of the most educated citizens from the MIC have emigrated.[12]

The MIC in today's Russia has been replaced by an economy of natural resources extraction. But here is a different quality of worker. These are 'peasant workers', in the terms of Polish sociologists. That is how Russian demilitarization shifted the country's economy to make it an extracting periphery of the world system with the relevant quality of human resources. Thus by virtue of the structural economic specifics of pre-reform Russia the deterioration of the MIC has led to the deterioration of the democracy-oriented and active part of the Russian population.

Finally, and most important, the system of quasi-socialistic countries had its core, semi-periphery and periphery. The core is the predominance of 'pure forms' of etacratism (or statism). The periphery is the combination of the sharp weakening of the characteristics of etacratism, imposed by the armed forces of the etacratic USSR, with the economic institutes, values and social norms, peculiar to the West. We refer to the core as most of the republics of the former USSR; to the semi-periphery as Bulgaria, Romania, Serbia, Ukraine, etc.; to the periphery as Poland, Hungary, Czech Republic, Lithuania, Latvia, Estonia and some other countries.

The geographic area of socialist 'coverage' coincides with the region of secondary peasants' enslavement in the west of this area (Prussia, Poland, Hungary, etc.) and the regions which had not known steady private property institutions, the market, a lawful state, a civil society with the predominance of the state mode of production, with a lack of significant private property relations and the predominance of relations of the 'power-property' type. There are no classes, no civil relationships in these societies. Here lies the fourth latent difference between Russia and its western neighbours: 'we' were the core and 'they' were the periphery of the geographical system of pseudo-socialism.

The idea of considering the system of the state socialist countries as consisting of core, semi-periphery and periphery, is expressed here as a theoretical framework which demands considerable further development and argumentation.

It is characteristic that most of the CEE countries were forced into etacratism by the USSR. Thereby the toughest resistance to this system was observed in countries with stronger ties to a market economy and democratic institutions. All of them belonged to Catholic and Protestant cultures. At the same time etacratism flourished in other historical entities – in Russia and China, Vietnam and Mongolia, which proves the logic of its emergence.

Societal system of post-Soviet Russia

Most academic papers consider post-Soviet Russia to be a form of capitalist development, though usually with a negative assessment. Stefan Hedlund considers it to be, as aptly summarized by the title of his book, *Russia's 'Market' Economy: a Bad Case of Predatory Capitalism*;[13] M. Castells described the 10 years of constant reforming in Russia as an 'infinite transition from surrealistic socialism to unrealistic capitalism';[14] Marshall I. Goldman published a book with another apt name *The Piratization of Russia* (Russian edition in 2005). The comparative analysis of data gathered in the Czech Republic, Poland and China makes him conclude that the tragic Russian experiment with the country and its people is a unique one. But he does not question capitalist development in Russia even in its bad design.[15] David Lane's assessment, referring to the late 1990s, takes a rather different position and was later proved correct by the events of the 2000s. He wrote: '... *Capitalism as an economic system which regularly supports capital accumulation has not been established* ... Personal networks of communication on an industrial, regional and bureaucratic basis determine profits and performance to a much greater degree than market activity.'[16] Moreover, I would contend that contemporary Russia forms an entity with a specific institutional structure and system of values, derived from a specific civilization (Eurasian) and which are significantly distinct from the European (Atlantic) model.

In the times when the system flourished under Stalin, the *nomenklatura* possessed the power because it controlled the state, which, in its turn possessed almost all the property of the country. However, this property was not individually private, it was collectively private. As soon as the repressive regime ceased to press down on etacracy, as soon as the ruling strata received guarantees of personal and property safety and so on, the problem of property came to a head. Personal accumulation began. Many representatives of *nomenklatura* and shadow entrepreneurs became the owners of primary capital, which began to form from the middle of the 1950s.

However in 1953–85 the change of the system of state property management was of key significance in these initial processes. A strict hierarchical command system of economic management from a single centre was step by step replaced by an administrative (bureaucratic) market, a rather peculiar system of economic relations, which is reasonably called the 'economy of agreements'; it is a complicated bureaucratic market, built on exchange trade, carried out by both the authority and individuals. In contrast to ordinary money markets of goods and services, at this market there takes place not only the exchange of wealth but the exchange of power, breaking rules (when necessary), securing prestige. The concept of the administrative market in late Soviet Russia was developed by Russian authors Najshul and Kordonsky.[17]

In 1988–91 the hidden processes of the former period became clear. The overt *nomenklatura* privatization began. It was the social meaning of

Ryzhkov–Gorbachev reforms. State property was then under 'full economic control' of the corresponding officials. It was a secret privatization which was not followed by the change of legal property status. Corporate ownership turned into the corporate individual. As a result there emerged a *nomenklatura* pseudo-capitalism in its highly beneficial variant – a pseudo-state form of private capital. The commercial activity of *nomenklatura* began in 1987 after the introduction of a special decree of the Central Committee about Komsomol participation in the market economy. The second person of the party, E.K. Ligachev, headed the coordination committee of this movement. They started creating various commercial centres, which were in fact controlled by higher officials. These organizations paid practically no taxes, they bought foreign currency at the state bank at ridiculous official rates (0.56 ruble for 1 dollar) and sold it immediately at commercial rates (from 20 to 150 rubles for 1 dollar). They had access to all the state supplies of raw materials and manufactured goods, which they sold abroad in huge volumes. And moreover, all these 'right' people were fully protected by law enforcement offices. A good example of successful involvement of the 'pioneers' of this movement was the financial empire 'Menatep' (under the leadership of M. Khodorkovsky).

When Yeltsin's government came to power, it did not create a new state system separated from property, but rather reorganized the old system. That is why former authority structures and people were integrated into new institutional units. Privatization that followed after 1992 transformed the same *nomenklatura* property into various mixed semi-state forms and thus assigned it even more safely to *nomenklatura*, hiding it from the claims of other social groups. As a result both power and property remained in the hands of the former masters of Russia.

First of all state officials privatized the economic infrastructure, i.e. the management of industry, bank system and distribution system. It was a stage of latent (pure *nomenklatura*) privatization. Commercial *nomenklatura* banks were created out of state banks, they received the status of authorized dealers and carried out the most profitable transactions. State organizations had their bank accounts there. Usually these banks were created either with the assistance of the Party ('Incombank', 'Menatep') or under the aegis of government structures (international financial company, ONEKSIMbank) as far back as the end of the 1980s.

Privatization of the Soviet distribution system involved the replacement of former state institutions (*gossnabs* and *gosstorgs*) with 'Komsomol' exchanges (the Moscow commodity exchange, Moscow central stock exchange and others), a great number of firms and business joint ventures. Concerns were created in place of ministries. The most well-known examples are the Gazprom concern, headed by V. Chernomyrdin, the 'Norilsk Nikel' concern and the large company 'Almaz Rossii'. For some short time they existed formally in the form of state companies, but quite quickly they were reorganized into partly or predominantly privatized ones, and real control remained in the hands of state officials. As a result financial and administrative structures were appropriated, boosting the concentration of financial capital.

The origin of the new Russian upper stratum of proprietors has in many respects determined the features of their consciousness and behaviour. Certainly they were not normal economic agents acting in a market competitive environment. They were quasi-capitalists – direct continuation of *nomenklatura* actors of an administrative market.

The beginning of open privatization (since 1992) suggested a change in property relations without (in the majority of cases) changing the proprietors. In principle one may have expected that directors, ministry and other officials would personally initiate the transition from a pseudo-state form of property to really private property and market property redistribution. However, the process went predominantly in a different direction. There is so far no system of developed private property separate from the state. The goal of the *nomenklatura* stayed unchanged during the whole post-Soviet period – to preserve the relations of 'no man's property' in order to use its incomes as private property incomes without being responsible for it.

The ideological basis of economic reforms was neo-liberalism and its supporters, particularly American experts, were invited to work in Gaidar and Chernomyrdin's government. In particular, they played a key role in the activity of the government connected with privatization. For example, by order of the chairman of the State Property Committee of the Russian Federation A.G. Chubais dated 31 July 1992, 'The Department of Technical Help and Examination' had been created which consisted of American economists and was led by Jonathan Hay. This department was engaged in accumulation and processing data about the economic complex of Russia in consultation with Russian reformers.[18]

The real priority of the new post-Soviet regime was the policy of concentration of national resources in the hands of a minority. Rapid privatization played a crucial role in this, which practically gave away for free the vast state property to the ruling *nomenklatura* and, first of all, to those who were close to the president. This privatization consisted of two main stages – voucher stage and the stage of deposit auctions. These were deliberate actions aimed at the formation of non-competitive, policy-forming large-scale business with comprador orientation.

At the first stage of mass privatization in 1992–93, under the direction of A. Chubais, 500 of the largest enterprises with a value of not less than 200 billion dollars were sold for 7.2 billion dollars.[19] And it was only the beginning. The stocks of oil companies were sold through six deposit auctions (1995–97) for a price 18–26 times lower than their actual market price. Just as an example, the market value of 'Yukos' at 1 August 1997 equalled 6.2 billion dollars while its shareholdings were sold for 353 million dollars. The situation with 'Lukoil' was a similar one – a 15.8 billion dollar selling price and

700 million dollars in market price correspondingly. 'Norilsk nikel', which was taken over by the 'Interros' company for a sum somewhat less than 300 million dollars, was insured by Western insurance companies for 30 billion dollars, i.e. a 100 times higher evaluation.[20]

Between 1992 and 1999 more than 133,000 enterprises and economic units were privatized for which Russia received 9.25 billion dollars, that is 69,500 dollars each. There was far more property privatized in Russia in 1990–98 than in other countries, though it was only twentieth among them according to revenue from privatization with its per capita value of just 54.6 dollars.[21] Judging the phenomenon of accelerated privatization in Russia, a prominent Polish economist, G. Kolodko, emphasized that

> ... the primary aim of those who benefit from the accelerated privatization lies neither in the improvement of corporate management, strengthening of financial balance nor the increase in living standards of the population, but in purchasing of valuable assets much below real value. It is a strange situation: the convinced supporters of the free market agitate for the accelerated sale of state property at well below market clearing prices.[22]

Together with many other analysts it is thus necessary to consider the distinction between the formal legality of privatization and its legitimacy. The legality has been provided by laws and decrees of the president. The legitimacy depends on traditions, values and laws which have settled in a society. Meanwhile, the data from the all-Russian polls still show that a majority of Russians reject the legitimacy of privatization. According to VTSIOM (headed by Yu. Levada) 37 per cent of the respondents in 2003 and 43 per cent in 2005 support nationalization of privatized companies; and 31 and 32 per cent agreed that nationalization should be carried out if companies had been privatized illegitimately.[23]

The growing concentration of power and property in the same hands prevented the formation of a civilized market economy and led to corruption, economic stagnation and impoverishment of the population. Over all the post-Soviet years the authority allowed some businessmen to prosper, while others could be put out of business, humiliated, eliminated if not physically then socially, with no regard for laws and moral norms. In Russia the oligarchs were appointed. Nobody became an oligarch following civilized competitive struggle. The young age of some representatives of oligarchy should not mislead: the *nomenklatura* exchanged power for property, they did not always personally participate in commercial adventures. For most risky businesses they selected people from the 'party reserve' – the Komsomol, who operated with state money. That is why one can hardly meet former party secretaries among them. They were people of a different generation – active Komsomol functionaries, lower officials of middle rank. In 1995–2006 corruption became a steady system of relations between officials and the businessman. The most typical feature of the interaction between entrepreneurs and officials since the end of the 1990s to the present (2007) – in contrast to the unstable situation of 1992–94 – is that these relations acquired a long-term character. Special 'contract relations' were formed, going beyond the mere exchange of services between official and businessman. They rather mean mutual strategic and tactical support within the framework of long-term cooperation, in which a particular official begins to act as a business partner of a particular businessman.[24]

Another privileged group of society besides big property owners comprises Russian officialdom, the direct continuation of the Soviet *nomenklatura*, which preserved and strengthened its position. The number of officials in the country is striking – 1.34 million people (excluding the so-called *siloviki*).[25] The data of a study of the Russian elite organized by the author in 1993 are very suggestive. In the administrative elite 60.1 per cent preserved the status they had before August 1991; 27.2 per cent improved it; and only 12.7 per cent went down.[26] In 1994–2000s the role of the 'old' personnel on the federal level has been substantially increased, naturally with regard to demographic changes. The growth of the influence of the representatives of special services, the very core of the Soviet *nomenklatura*, appears quite organic. According to the estimations of O.V. Kryshtanovskaya, over 6000 representatives of security services occupied the highest official posts in July 2003.[27] The share of the military and representatives of special services in authorities reached 25.1 per cent in 2002 as opposed to 11.2 per cent in 1993. At the same time the share of people with an academic degree in leading positions has decreased over the same ten years from 52.2 per cent to 21.0 per cent. We must add that a considerable number of neophytes in the political upper class belong to the families which used to form the elite groups of the former power hierarchy.

It is well known that social privileges – an organic part of etacratic system – inevitably become part of the social policy of this system. Non-market distribution of a considerable part of resources controlled by the state in the form of goods and services rendered to the upper and middle-level officials has even grown since Soviet times, which proves that such a social system is not bourgeois-democratic but rather post-etacratic. What is owned by the administrative department of the president considerably exceeded the property of the administrative department of the Central Committee of the CPSU.[28] Here are just a few examples. The provision of pensions to the majority of the population still holds; pensions of officials were assigned without any public discussion and came to 75 per cent of their salary, and in some cases officials can even receive pensions before reaching the age of 60. In 2004 a particular pension system for officials was developed and legalized. The state has been obliged to spend about 1.5 billion dollars annually to maintain their personal cars.

The deputy of the State Duma, Mr Mitrofanov, informed the parliament in February 2005 that general expenses for maintaining one state deputy would amount to no less than 50,000 dollars per month.[29] In recent state budgets the expenses for maintaining government officials have been steadily increasing. They were raised by another 50 per cent in the federal budget of 2007. Now add to that the information repeatedly mentioned in the mass media about flats transferred to higher officials as private property, the cost of which goes up to 300,000–500,000 dollars.

But the income of officials is not limited to goods received legally from the government. According to data of the 'Indem' foundation (president G.A. Satarov), 100 per cent of state structures are infected by corruption. According to the data from the first stage of the survey (2001), officials receive around 30 billion dollars in bribes annually. Vacant state posts are often displayed for sale. Prices vary from 500,000 dollars (for the seat of deputy minister) to several million dollars (for the seat of vice prime minister). According to the data from the second stage of the survey (spring 2005), the volume of the corruption market has grown almost 10 times, exceeding 300 billion dollars. In 2005 the general volume of corruption income exceeded the federal budget income almost 2.66 times.[30]

If we take a look at legislative and standard Acts, it may become obvious that there exist all necessary prerequisites for effective business activity. It is even noted in the Constitution of the Russian Federation: 'each person possesses a right to use his abilities and property in business and other economic activities which are not forbidden by the law'. It is then clearly stated in the Civil Code of the Russian Federation. But formal institutions and real practices stay in sharp conflict.[31] The majority of businessmen believe that in litigation it makes a lot more sense to apply to anybody except state judicial bodies. They assume it is useless to apply to arbitrage. It is impossible to settle litigation without the use of force. Even illegal law enforcement agencies recede into the background. The winner is always the person who supports better relations with state structures – the court, the militia, the office of public prosecutor – which act outside the law. The situation is particularly bad in the provinces. Only big property owners, federal and interregional oligarchs are protected by informal practices through direct relations with the government and the administration of the president.

To conclude, the existing relations of authorities and business, where business acts as a social subject depending on, and manipulated by, authority, are an organic feature of the contemporary societal system in Russia as a late-etacratic system.

Privatized property in Russia since it has appeared was not in a strict sense private. It is an absolutely different type of property. Real private property is productive and creative in character. Not only the appropriation, but also the production of property is private. The norm is the predominance of production over appropriation. In post-Soviet Russia the private principle applies mainly to appropriation, while it does not include production. By appropriating property the owners who privatize acquire something they have not actually created: it includes capital assets accumulated by former generations, natural resources and budget funds. It is no coincidence that it was practically impossible for our oligarchs to protect their property from state despotism; it was in principle no man's property as in Soviet times. Here is another important feature. In contrast to real private property, which is broadly spread among the population in capitalist societies, in Russia, privatized property is spread among a narrow set of people. It is almost an estate privilege of a ruling stratum. The holding back of small and middle-size business, the permanent neglect of the rights of professionals to intellectual property, the lack of legal protection of labour – workers' primary property – are not just random facts. These are not faults of state policy, but an organic feature of an economic system which is liberal in form and statist in content with limited independence of private businessmen.

Preservation of etacratic relations is reflected in the most obvious way in the functioning of the property institutions, where 'power-property' relations most important for this type of society were shown in a new light. In the years of Putin's presidency new dominating property patterns were finally shaped which marked the new stage in development of the so-called 'privatized property' and 'power-property' relations. They were represented by the emergence of companies with predominantly state assets with minor shareholders. It is a so-called 'state–private partnership'. The availability of private capital (which is often symbolic) is used by those corporations for manipulating enormous assets costing tens and hundreds of billion dollars without any feasible control of the formal owner – the Russian people represented by parliament or even governmental authorities. Total control over the prevalent part of the national wealth (in other words, its appropriation) lies in the hands of government officials and their executive directors – managers of these corporations.[32]

The nature of the developing societal system showed itself in the changing policy towards professionals – a potential core of the new middle class. During Putin's period and the economic growth the resources of both state and society were increasing. Since 2000 there appeared a steady tendency in state policy towards a Soviet tradition of close interaction between the elite and weak social groups to the detriment of the social interests of the middle strata. Additional resources were partly used to stabilize and improve the position of the lower groups.

Regarding the professionals, the increase in their wages and family income was miserable compared to the losses which they had been suffering during the previous years. Their losses over the years of reforms meant a substantial reduction of resources necessary for the reproduction of the social status of their families (for the continuing of professional education, better education for children, health care, improvement and, in many cases, preservation of the level of housing provision, etc.). The professionals became more vulnerable after the acceptance of the new Labour Code. The professionals' salaries in Moscow vary from 200 to 1000 dollars per month, and in St Petersburg and Nizhni Novgorod from 150 to 300 dollars. There is no need to say that in other, less successful cities the situation is much worse. For example, in Tver (December 2005) from 100 to 150 dollars.

Conclusion

The collapse of the communist system in Russia has resulted in a new stage of particular Eurasian civilization, which is essentially different from the European (Atlantic) model in institutional structure and the system of values. Analysis of post-Soviet Russian development proves the soundness of the path dependency theory. The essence of the path dependency theory is that preconditions of successful transition and development differ between countries and periods of time – which emphasizes the role of history on the one hand and culture on the other. Therefore, Russia's case has demonstrated that there exists no general theory of transition (or transformation), for there is no universal post-communism.

It is very important to analyse possible tendencies of the formation of the information-based economy along with the preservation of archaic social and political 'cover'. The appropriation of progressive technical–economic and cultural–domestic borrowings from the West along with the conservation of institutional and value-normative structures had been repeatedly observed in the history of Russia since the reforms of Peter I. In other words, it is a question of tendencies of etacratic restoration (or reproduction of etacratism) observed in contemporary Russia and the elements of such processes in other countries of the area under consideration.

Such tendencies are the form of adoption of an alternative set of values and principles of existence with respect to the developing global economy and democratic world community. Countries which develop innovation-based economies with preserving etacratic social institutions inevitably challenge optimistic perspectives of the information epoch and humanity. The question that remains is whether there is any way out from this situation in Russia, are there any social forces capable of changing this situation and bringing Russia to the path leading to a information-based market economy and democracy?

Notes

1 S.P. Huntington, *The Clash of Civilizations and the Remaking of World Order* (New York: Simon and Schuster, 1996).

2 V. Radaev and O. Shkaratan, 'Vlast' i sobstvennost',' *SOTSIS*, 1 (1991); V. Radaev and O. Shkaratan, 'Power and Property – Evidence from the Soviet Experience', *International Sociology*, 3 (1992); O. Shkaratan, 'Ot etakratizma k grajdanskomu obshchestvu', *Rabochii klass i sovremenni'i mir*, 3 (1990); O. Shkaratan, 'The Old and the New Masters of Russia. From Power Relations to Proprietary Relations', *Sociological Research*, New York, 5 (1992).

3 'Sostav rukovodyashchikh organov central'nogo komiteta partii – politburo (prezidiuma), orgburo, sekretariata CK. 1919 – 1990gg.', *Izvestiya CSK KPSS*, 7 (1990) 69–136.
4 M. Castells, *The Information Age: Economy, Society and Culture*. Vol. I. *The Rise of Network Society* (Oxford: Blackwell Publishers, 1997), p. 16.
5 L. Vasiljev, *Istoriya Vostoka. V.1 (Vvodnaya chast'. Sutchnost' problematiki)* (Moscow: Vi'sshaya shkola, 1994).
6 R. Nureev, 'Social'nie sub"ekti' postsovetskoi Rossii: istoriya i sovremennost", *Mir Rossii*, 3 (2001) 8.
7 O. Bessonova, *Razdatok: institutsionalnaya teoriya khozyaystvennogo razvitiya Rossii* (Novosibirsk: The Siberian Branch of the Russian Academy of Science, 1999).
8 V. Pastuhov, *Tri vremeni Rossii: Obshchestvo i gosudarstvo v proshlom – nastoyatchem – budushchem* (Moscow: POLIS–RSSPAN, 1994), p. 7.
9 U. Pivovarov and, A. Fursov, *Russkaya vlast', russkaya sistema, russkaya istoriya/Krasnie holmi'* (Moscow: 'Gorodskaya Sobstvennost', Publishing House, 1999), p. 190.
10 B. Mironov, *Social'naya istoriya Rossii perioda imperii. XVIII–nachalo XX v: Genezis lichnosti, demokraticheskoi sem'i, grajdanskogo obshchestva pravovogo gosudarstva*, Vols 1 and 2, 2nd edn (St Petersburg: Dmitriy Bulavin, 2000), p. 344.
11 O. Shkaratan, 'Paradoksi sovetskoi urbanizatsiyi', in O.I. Shkaratan (ed.), *Syud'bi sovremennogo goroda* (Moscow: ISRAS, 1990).
12 O. Shkaratan and J. Fontanel, 'Convertion and Personnel in the Russian Military-Industrial-Complex', *Defense and Peace Economics,* 8 (1998).
13 S. Hedlund, *Russia's 'Market' Economy: a Bad Case of Predatory Capitalism* (London: UCL Press, 1999).
14 M. Castells and E. Kiselyova, 'Rossiya i setevoe obtchestvo', *Mir Rossii*, 1 (2000) 46.
15 M. Goldman, *The Piratization of Russia: Russian Reform Goes Awry* (New York: Routledge, 2003).
16 Italics added. D. Lane, 'Preobrazovanie gosudarstvennogo sotsializma v Rossii: ot "khaoticheskoi" ekonomiki k kooperativnomu kapitalizmu, koordiniruemomu gosudarstvom?', *Mir Rossii*, 1 (2000), 15–16.
17 V. Najshul', *Vi'sshaya i poslednyaya stadiya socializma/Pogrujenie v tryasinu* (Moscow: Progress, 1991); S. Kordonsky, *Ri'nki vlasti: Administrativni'e ri'nki SSSR i Rossii* (Moscow: OGI, 2000).
18 D. Saks, *Rinochnaya ekonomika i Rossiya*. Translated from English (Moscow: Ekonomika, 1994) (http://ru.wikipedia.org/).
19 V. Polevanov, *Tehnologiya velikogo obmana* (Moscow, 1995), p. 50.
20 P. Khlebnikov, *Krestni'i otets Kremlya Boris Berezovskii ili Istoriya razgrableniya Rossii.* Translated from English (Moscow: 'Detectiv-Press', 2001), pp. 196–210.
21 I. Ustinov, 'Privatizatsiya po-rossiiski', *Politekonomiya,* 11 (26 June 2001) (http://politeconomy.ng.ru).
22 G. Kolodko, *Ot shoka k terapii. Politicheskaya ekonomiya postsocialisticheskikh preobrazovanii*. Translated from English (Moscow: 'Journal Expert' Joint-Stock Company, 2000), p. 199.
23 *Obschestvennoe mneniye – 2005* (Moscow: Levada-Centre, 2005), p. 97.
24 V. Radaev, *Formirovanie novi'kh rossiiskikh ri'nkov: tranzaktsionni'e izderjki, formi' kontrolya i delovaya etika* (Moscow: Centr politicheskih tehnologii, 1998).
25 V. Gimpel'son, *Chislennost' i sostav rossiiskoi burokratii: mejdu sovetskoi nomenklaturoi i gosslujboi grajdanskogo obtchestva* (Moscow: SU-HSE, 2002).
26 'Politicheskaya elita Rossii' (cycle of articles), *Mir Rossii*, 3–4 (1995).

27 O. Kryshtanovskaya, *Transformatsiya rossiyskoy eliti* (Moscow: Published by A.V. Solovyov, 2004).
28 B. Vishnevski, 'Pyatiy vid sobstvennosti: presidentskaya', *Novaya Gazeta*, 63 (21 August 2006).
29 *Moskovskie novosti* (25 February–3 March 2005), 10.
30 'Diagnostika rossiiskoi korruptsii 2005', *Predvaritel'ni'e rezul'tati' proekta Fonda INDEM* (2005) (http://www.indem.ru).
31 Here I rely on the interview data gathered by my students in 2003–December 2005 in Moscow, Saint-Petersburg, Nizhny Novgorod, Tver and Perm (I. Ivanov, G. Tumatova, S. Inyassevski), where they evaluate the corresponding business environment as non-stimulating.
32 A. Illarionov, 'Pobeda GChP [Gosudarstvenno-Chastnoe Partnerstvo]', *Novaya Gazeta*, 57 (31 July–02 August 2006), 16–17.

Part III

Consolidation of New Regimes: the Problem of Inequality

9

Effects of Transformation on Inequality in Russia

Nick Manning

Most observers agree that there has been a dramatic increase in inequality in Russia, and that inequality matters. But there are many arguments as to why it is significant. The key question concerns the effect of the transformation of Russia on inequality and poverty. Marshall[1] once characterized (and celebrated) the hyphenated society of democratic-welfare-capitalism as the ideal mechanism for managing the transition from pre-industrial to post-industrial society. This was to be accomplished by the political control of a capitalist economy. Inequality would grow, but the poor would be helped and enabled to retain their place in society. The traditional view was that it is economic growth that matters, particularly in relation to poverty reduction, and that a period of inequality within a country was a price to be paid for moving from an agricultural economy to a developed economy, epitomized in the Kuznets 'curve'.[2] In the Russian case, the process of transformation into a capitalist economy was expected to generate inequality, but the simultaneous evolution of democracy would, it was hoped, enable citizens to vote for enough welfare support to contain the impact of the transformation on those at the bottom.

In more recent times, it has become accepted that there are 'varieties of capitalism'[3] and that successful connections between a polity and an economy can come in various ways. Mid-twentieth-century optimism is no longer justified. Inequality does not seem to have moderated in Latin America, and appears to have grown around the world, and particularly in the post-transition years for central and eastern European countries. Economic growth has not delivered reductions in inequality, and consequently inequality has itself come to be scrutinized for its consequences. In a major reversal of the traditional view, there is now concern that inequality itself may hamper economic growth.[4] Possible reasons cited for slower economic growth in more unequal societies include inefficient access to land and capital for economic development, the inability to adapt quickly to increasingly volatile global economic change, the erosion of social capital in civil society, the growth of crime and violence, and poorer health status for the population as a whole.[5]

In the long view, global inequality has shifted from within-country differences in the nineteenth century, to between-country differences, which now account for around 70 per cent of global inequality.[6] To that extent, inequality within Russia is only part of the story since there has been a clear divergence of per capita incomes between the transition countries since 1990, with those in central Europe and some of the Baltic states moving closer to western Europe than the CIS countries.[7]

What is the pattern of inequality in Russia?

A cursory examination of published data on poverty and inequality in Russia reveals a large and striking variation in the reported levels. Poverty estimates vary between around 20 and 40 per cent, and the Gini measure of inequality varies between around 0.35 and 0.5. The key difference between these reported levels of inequality is whether they refer to income (usually measured through wage levels) or consumption. It is now well established that consumption is only partly driven by wage levels. No more than 50 per cent of the population are likely to be in employment, and Mroz, Henderson and Popkin[8] report that wages account for slightly less than 50 per cent of Russian household money incomes. Other kinds of money income might include pensions, rents, dividends, interest, capital sales, intra-household transfers, and so on. The alternative is to measure consumption. Again there are problems. Individuals will be sharing consumption in households in various ways, and will also be sharing consumption through non-money services such as education, health care, housing utilities, and so on. For example, Mitra and Yemtsov[9] show that the 2003 Gini coefficient for Russia moves down from 0.45 to 0.35 if housing consumption (rent, utilities, etc.) is included alongside money expenditures.

Russian data sources for these measures are limited. Most of the literature relies on two sources: the Russian Longitudinal Monitoring Survey (4700 households) and the Goskomstat Household Budget Survey (49,000 households). The particular significance of these over other surveys is that they are repeat measures stretching back to the early 1990s, and can show general changes over time. The former has generally measured a wider range of household income and consumption than the latter. There is an acknowledged difference in the results from these two surveys, with the former suggesting, for example, a rapid rise in inequality in the mid-1990s, while the latter showed the opposite.[10] This is caused by the different sample sizes, different regional coverage, and differences in the way in which intra-household consumption sharing is estimated (technically, per capita needs are deflated on the assumption that utilities can be shared, children consume less, and so on). Both surveys suffer from under-reporting of non-waged income (informal economic activity), of non-money income (e.g. barter), and poor representation of and under-reporting by rich households.

The two main indices of inequality are the Gini coefficient and Theil's 'entropy' index.[11] As an overall measure, the Gini has intuitive appeal, since it is a Lorenz curve of the cumulative distribution of income which varies between zero (perfect equality) and one (perfect inequality). It is very commonly cited in reports by international organizations to show how different countries are moving in relation to inequality (e.g. Russia moving from around 0.3 to around 0.45 in the 1990s), or how different groups of countries move together (e.g. Scandinavia holding at around 0.25 over the same period). Total global per capita inequality is currently around an all-time high of 0.65, since the differences between countries have grown in comparison to differences within countries.[12]

To establish the causes of inequality requires a process of inequality 'decomposition', which shows how much different groups or regions in a population are contributing to the overall inequality. There are technical problems with using the Gini for this, and generally the alternative, Theil's 'entropy' index, is commonly used. This is a measure of the probability of a unit of income coming from a particular individual. As with the Gini, zero indicates perfect equality, but the upper limit varies with the population size, and thus any specific figure means very little out of context. But it is good for decomposing inequality between population groups or regions.

Bearing in mind these caveats, what is the overall picture of inequality in Russia? The general picture is of a rapid rise in inequality from early 1992 after the liberalization of prices and collapse in production. Subsequently a moderation of this rise, and indeed a slight reduction of inequality, has appeared with the resumption of steady economic growth since 2001 (see Figure 9.1).

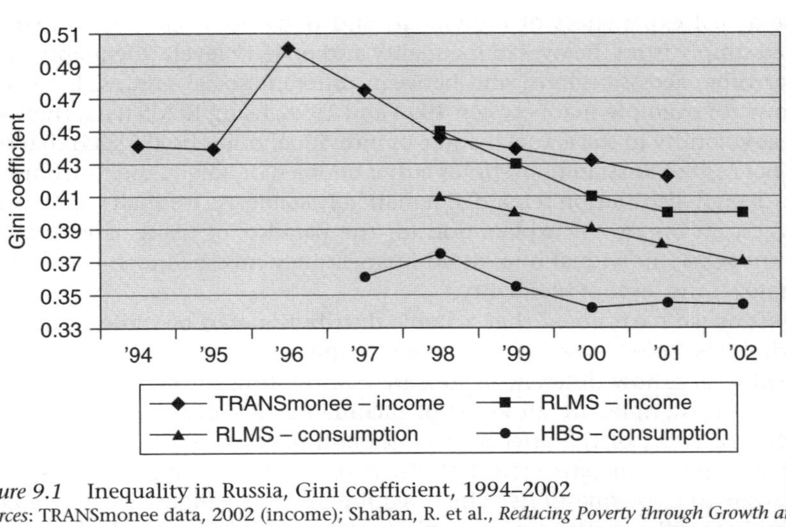

Figure 9.1 Inequality in Russia, Gini coefficient, 1994–2002
Sources: TRANSmonee data, 2002 (income); Shaban, R. et al., *Reducing Poverty through Growth and Social Policy in Russia* (Washington: World Bank, 2006), for RLMS data ('real' income); RLMS data ('real' consumption); Goskomstat HBS data ('real' consumption)

Table 9.1 Inequality in Russia and other countries, Gini coefficient, mid-1990s

Brazil	1996	0.571
Mexico	1995	0.494
Argentina	1996	0.442
USA	1997	0.372
Canada	1998	0.305
Germany	1994	0.261
Russia	1995	0.447

Source: T. Smeeding, 'Globalisation, Inequality and the Rich Countries of the G-20: Evidence from the Luxembourg Income Study (LIS)', Center for Policy Research Working Papers, No. 48 (New York: Syracuse University, 2002).

We can set this pattern in context through Luxembourg Income Study data. This uses income rather than consumption, money rather than non-money items, and households rather than individuals. Smeeding[13] shows that in the mid-1990s, a point of particular economic difficulty for the transition in Russia, Russia's Gini was typically Latin American rather than European or North American in size (Table 9.1).

How can this inequality be decomposed into different component contributions?

The actual experiences of individuals and households cannot be extrapolated simply from the overall inequality and poverty levels. Inequality varies over time, across regions, and between different social groups. Janovich[14] shows for example that between 1994 and 1998, using RLMS data, there was great volatility in the actual income of individual households, such that over 60 per cent of Russian households either doubled or halved their income. Yet the overall distribution remained remarkably stable. As we shall see, this may suggest an important explanation for the paradox of rising satisfaction in recent years: individual household finances may now be much more stable, whatever the level of inequality.

Just as we have noted that a stable distribution can be quite compatible with households experiencing rapid changes, so we need to check out whether and how different factors are contributing to the overall distribution. For example, are all kinds of income equally distributed? What has been the effect of the arrears in wages and benefits typical of the 1990s? What is the comparative effect of distribution within and between regions? Answers to these questions, which require us to decompose the overall distribution, will suggest some possible explanation of the overall changes we have seen.

Table 9.2 Decomposition of income inequality by sources before and after the transition by country groupings in central and eastern Europe

Region	*Wages*		*Non-wage private income*		*Pensions*		*Other social transfers*		*Total*	
	Pre-	*After-*	*Pre-*	*After-*	*Pre-*	*After-*	*Pre-*	*After-*	***Pre-***	***After-***
Shares of incomes (%)										
CEE	60	50	20	24	17	21	5	7	**100**	**100**
CIS Middle I	78	53	9	23	8	18	5	6	**100**	**100**
CIS Low I	50	20	30	70	10	5	10	5	**100**	**100**
Concentration coefficients (×100)										
CEE	23	32	31	31	16	23	−8	−12	**22.3***	**27.4***
CIS Middle I	25	52	17	43	0	20	0	11	**21.0***	**41.7***
CIS Low I	30	55	30	50	−5	5	0	−5	**23.5***	**46.0***
Contribution to inequality (%)										
CEE	62	58	28	27	12	18	−2	−3	**100**	**100**
CIS Middle I	93	66	7	24	0	9	0	2	**100**	**100**
CIS Low I	64	24	38	76	−2	1	0	−1	**100**	**100**
Contribution to change of inequality (in points of Gini)										
CEE		+2.2		+1.2		+2.1		−0.4		**+5.1***
CIS Middle I		+8.0		+8.4		+3.6		+0.7		**+20.7***
CIS Low I		−4.0		+26.0		+0.8		−0.3		**+22.5***

* Gini indices, or change in Gini points.
CEE: Czech Republic, Estonia, Hungary, Latvia, Lithuania, Poland, Slovenia.
CIS Middle I: Belarus, Russia, Ukraine.
CIS Low I: Armenia, Azerbaijan, Georgia, Kyrgyzstan, Moldova.
Source: Mitra and Yemtsov,[9] pp. 40–1.

As we have observed, wages account for around half of household income. Inequality in wages is thus the first place to look for an explanation of income inequality. Mitra and Yemtsov show in Table 9.2 [15] that in Russia (CIS Middle I) the big shift upwards in inequality in the initial transition years was the result of the growing impact of three things: wages, non-wage private income, and pensions. Although wages are a falling share of overall income (from 78 to 53 per cent for CIS Middle I) their rise in inequality, from 22 to 52 Gini points, is dramatic, such that they provide a large proportion of the rise in inequality for Russia, seen in the penultimate row at 8.0 per cent. A second dramatic shift is the rise of non-wage income in the overall 'share of income' (from 9 to 23 per cent for CIS Middle I), combined with the rise of inequality ('concentration coefficients') from 17 to 43 for non-wage income, resulting in non-wage income providing the biggest proportion of the rise in inequality for Russia, seen in the penultimate row at 8.4 per cent.

Table 9.3 Decomposition of wage inequality by factors of earnings (%), measured by variance of monthly wages

	Poland 1995		*Hungary 1997*		*Russia 1996*		*Russia 2001*	
	% Total variance	*Explained variance*	*% Total variance*	*Explained variance*	*% Total variance*	*Explained variance*	*% Total variance*	*Explained variance*
Education	11.5	43.9	25.9	61.7	2.7	8.1	3.5	11.9
Job experience	3.8	11.6	2.1	5.0	1.5	4.6	0.2	0.7
Gender	6.8	20.5	3.8	9.1	6.5	20.0	4.9	16.7
Ownership (private/public)	−0.6	−1.9	0.0	0.0	1.0	3.0	3.4	11.6
Sector	8.7	26.3	4.8	11.3	7.5	23.0	5.7	9.4
Location	2.9	8.6	5.5	13.1	13.5	41.3	11.7	39.8
Unexplained	66.9		57.9		67.3		70.6	
Total	100.0		100.0		100.0		100.0	

Source: Mitra and Yemtsov,[9] Table 13.

There are two processes here: changes in distribution within each group, and movement of people between each group. The dramatic increase in the contribution of the non-wage private sector to inequality was a result of both growing numbers joining this sector (the 'hollowing out of the middle class' – Milanovic[16]), and the increasing inequality within this sector also.

Nevertheless since wages also influence pensions, wages are the key contributor to inequality. How can we decompose this single key item a bit further? Four factors appear in much of the literature (e.g. Mitra and Yemtsov[17]). The first is growth of payment arrears, which was a big issue in the 1990s. The peak was in November 1998, when two-thirds of workers were owed back pay, and actually paid wages showed a very high Gini of 0.58. By 2004 arrears were down to 15 per cent of workers, and the pay Gini had also fallen to 0.44. A second factor is the very low minimum wage set in Russia. At 10 per cent of the average it is a long way out of line with the rest of central and eastern Europe where it averages 40 per cent. Turning to the top of the distribution, as has already been mentioned sectoral differences, especially the public/private sector, have been important for delivering high wages. The premium for private sector wages was probably enough to double them over public sector wages for the early 1990s, falling to around 30 per cent higher towards the end of the decade. Finally, there has been great regional differentiation in wages, which almost tripled between 1995 and 2003, and is explored in more detail below.

Turning to analysis of some of the less prominent factors, we find varied effects reported in the literature. For example, Mitra and Yemtsov[18] show that in comparison with Poland and Hungary, gender in Russia is important, but education less so, as we can see from Table 9.3[19] reproduced from their paper.

Table 9.4 Proportionate contributions of household characteristics to income inequality in Russia, 1994–2000

	sj				% R^2			
	1994	*1996*	*1998*	*2000*	*1994*	*1996*	*1998*	*2000*
Sex of household head	1.5	0.8	0.5	**1.2**	6	3	2	**6**
Age of household head	1.2	0.6	0.5	0.2	5	2	2	1
Education of household head	3.4	2.9	3.2	**3.8**	13	11	15	**19**
Household composition	0.1	0.1	0.3	0.2	0	0	1	1
Earnings status of household	11.9	16	13.8	10.5	45	59	63	**52**
Employment status of household head	1.4	0.9	0.4	1.2	5	3	2	6
Region	5.6	4.9	2.7	2.1	21	18	12	10
Type of settlement	1.3	0.9	0.6	0.9	5	3	3	4
R^2	**26**	**27**	**22**	**20**	**100**	**100**	**100**	**100**

Notes: sj is the actual contribution of each variable to income inequality (all of which together explain about a quarter), whereas % R^2 is the contribution of each variable to the overall amount of income inequality explained within the model.
Source: Kislitsyna,[4] Table 8.

By contrast, Kislitsyna[20] finds education rather more important than gender: in 2000, sex accounted for 1.2 per cent of inequality, and education 3.8 per cent (Table 9.4). These amounted respectively to 6 and 19 per cent of all the inequality she explained in her analysis, which in comparison to earnings, at 52 per cent, were still minor themes (relevant figures in bold).

Popova[21] confirms that decomposing inequality by gender shows that 95 per cent of inequality remains within the gender groups and only 5 per cent arises from differences between them. Indeed this seems to be true of a whole variety of factors that have been used for decomposition, nicely illustrated in Kislitsyna.[22] (See Table 9.5.) What this table shows is that although there is some inequality between groups (e.g. between men and women, young and old, or employed and unemployed) most inequality is within groups (e.g. within men or within women, etc.), although by the year 2000, earnings and employment status are clearly beginning to create growing between-group effects.

Turning to the regional factor, most studies report that this has generated considerable inequality, and is the biggest effect alongside the private/public sector distinction. To be clear this is between-region differences: within-region differences include all the already mentioned factors such as wages arrears and the growth of the private sector. Yemtsov[23] shows from the Goskomstat Household Budget Survey that a third of overall inequality can be attributed to this between-region differentiation. Tikhonova and Manning[24] show that poverty rates measured through income vary substantially between a metropolitan city such as Moscow, and an agricultural (Voronezh – black earth) or peripheral (Vladikavkaz – northern Caucasus) region (Table 9.6).

Table 9.5 Within-group and between-group Inequality, 1994–2000

Subgroup partition	*Year*	I_0	*Components*		$\%I_0$	
			Within	*Between*	*Within*	*Between*
Sex of household head	1994	0.389	0.385	0.004	99.0	1.0
	1996	1.217	1.215	0.002	99.8	0.2
	1998	0.611	0.610	0.001	99.9	0.1
	2000	0.319	0.316	0.003	99.0	1.0
Age of household head	1994	0.389	0.381	0.008	97.8	2.2
	1996	1.217	1.205	0.012	99.0	1.0
	1998	0.611	0.605	0.005	99.1	0.9
	2000	0.319	0.312	0.007	97.7	2.3
Education of household head	1994	0.389	0.375	0.014	96.4	3.6
	1996	1.217	1.197	0.020	98.4	1.6
	1998	0.611	0.598	0.013	97.9	2.1
	2000	0.319	0.307	0.012	96.3	3.7
Household composition	1994	0.389	0.389	0.000	99.9	0.1
	1996	1.217	1.215	0.002	99.9	0.1
	1998	0.611	0.610	0.001	99.8	0.2
	2000	0.319	0.319	0.000	99.9	0.1
Earnings status of household	1994	0.389	0.363	0.026	93.2	6.8
	1996	1.217	1.160	0.057	95.3	4.7
	1998	0.611	0.578	0.033	94.6	5.4
	2000	0.319	0.295	0.024	92.5	7.5
Employment status of household head	1994	0.389	0.369	0.020	94.9	5.1
	1996	1.217	1.192	0.025	98.0	2.0
	1998	0.611	0.592	0.019	97.0	3.0
	2000	0.319	0.302	0.017	94.8	5.2
Region	1994	0.389	0.375	0.014	96.4	3.6
	1996	1.217	1.199	0.018	98.5	1.5
	1998	0.611	0.604	0.007	98.8	1.2
	2000	0.319	0.314	0.005	98.5	1.5
Type of settlement	1994	0.389	0.379	0.010	97.4	2.6
	1996	1.217	1.202	0.014	98.8	1.2
	1998	0.611	0.604	0.006	99.0	1.0
	2000	0.319	0.314	0.005	98.3	1.7

Notes: I_0 is a measure of inequality using Theil's 'entropy' index, a measure of the probability of a unit of income coming from a particular individual. As with the Gini, zero indicates perfect equality, but the upper limit varies with the population size. $\%I_0$ is the per cent of I_0 explained.
Source: Kislitsyna,[4] Table 6.

The *poor* were those who had no more than 50 per cent of the regional median income; the *badly off* were those whose incomes were over 50 per cent but lower than the regional median; the *averagely well-off* were those who had incomes within the range of one to two times the regional median; while the *prosperous* were those whose incomes were more than twice the

Table 9.6 Incomes of Russian families (%)

Income level	*In regions studied in depth*			*Average across Russia*
	Moscow	*Central black earth*	*Northern Caucasus (Vladikavkaz)*	
Poor	12.4	24.0	23.2	18.6
Badly off	32.7	32.0	37.0	35.1
Averagely well-off	34.5	38.0	27.5	33.9
Prosperous	20.4	6.0	12.3	12.4
Total	100	100	100	100

Source: RIISNP Pan-Russian Representative Survey, October 2000, $n = 1751$.

regional median. This Pan-Russian Survey shows higher rates of poverty in Vladikavkaz and Voronezh than in Moscow.

It is sometimes suggested that federalism and weak regional policies are to blame for large regional effects, but in a detailed analysis of a range of data, Bradshaw and Vartapetov[25] show that it is incomes that are the real basis for growing divergence and that the distribution of social consumption (e.g. health and education) and infrastructure such as roads are in fact much more stable and egalitarian. Fedorov[26] reaches a similar conclusion, showing that the extent of a region's trade export contribution is the most dominant factor contributing to regional inequality.

The other end of the distribution

Inequality in Russia is also a product of the rapid concentration of wealth that occurred from the early 1990s. There has been a rapidly growing group of very wealthy Russians, but a relatively small development of a prosperous middle class.

Wealth was accumulated in several ways. Access to control over resources under perestroika by *nomenklatura* officials, such as industrial, trade or senior government bureaucrats, enabled a smooth move for these individuals and members of their families to market relations in the early 1990s. Industrial directors and managers similarly were able to trade resources from their factories or raw materials sectors on to the rapidly emerging market. This transfer of political and organizational power into wealth was aided by a voucher privatization process that enabled pre-existing groups to gain control of many assets, or in the case of the gas and oil industry, to sell off underpriced resources in the world market without any formal privatization. In addition the market enabled black/grey marketers and speculators that had emerged in the late 1980s to enter the market openly, alongside a small number of self-made entrepreneurs that had been allowed to operate cooperatives and build businesses under perestroika.

Alongside this emergence of new wealth at the top, there has been a much weaker development of a prosperous middle class. In comparison with western Europe, Russia has not yet enabled well-paid professionals and family businesses to flourish. Professional salaries have remained low, and the barriers to small business development have proved formidable – a poorly functioning banking system, limited property assets, and cumbersome government regulation, as well as active discouragement by small networks of wealthy business owners who are able to discourage new market entrants.[27]

This combination of a very wealthy elite, and a small and weak middle class, has reinforced the level of inequality generated among the broad mass of the population.

The experience of inequality and poverty

A further aspect of inequality to consider is how it is perceived by individuals and households. Since Russian inequality grew rapidly in the 1990s but then subsequently moderated, we might reasonably expect this to be reflected in public opinion. With the reduction in incomes and the growth in inequality up to the mid-1990s in Russia, surveys at the time captured popular dissatisfaction with the poorer circumstances in which most households found themselves. There was widespread distrust of the political system, and a widespread judgement that the previous era was better than the new one.[28] However in recent years there has been a substantial shift. Life satisfaction has doubled since the mid-1990s,[29] and there has been a marked rise in subjective measures of welfare and personal power.[30] Economic satisfaction about family financial circumstances has rapidly improved.[31]

However, the moderation in inequality and the jump in subjective satisfaction are not strongly related in the data. Although income level is the most significant factor associated with satisfaction change, Fritjers et al.[32] found that it only accounted for about 10 per cent of the change. Similarly Lokshin and Ravallion[33] found that income inequality was only weakly related to the growth of 'subjectively perceived power and welfare'. It may be that the link between satisfaction and the moderation of inequality comes less from the individual's personal evaluation of their place on the income distribution, than their general attitude towards inequality, since general attitudes in favour of equality in central and eastern European countries, and especially Russia, remain strong, and markedly stronger than in western Europe.[34]

In view of the volatility of household incomes reported by Janovich,[35] the impact of inequality and poverty on the lives of households and individuals is best captured through in-depth interviews. Echoing the problems of measuring inequality through either income or consumption, poverty studies have also struggled to identify an agreed cross-national definition. The current consensus is that poverty should be measured in terms of the extent to which households are deprived of particular goods and services (for example, food, clothing, housing, medical care) which other households have judged in a survey as unacceptably low, and which the survey respondents feel indicate a threshold below which a household is in poverty. This approach was pioneered by Mack and Lansley[36] in the UK, and has been used for Russia by Macauley et al.[37] and Manning and Tikhonova.[38]

Manning and Tikhonova[39] used qualitative interviews with 105 households containing 440 individuals in Moscow, Voronezh and Vladikavkaz to identify 26 indicators of deprivation (IODs) (e.g. cannot afford food, clothes, medicines), which were used as the basis for generating four deprivation bands (pp. 69–70):

- *Band IV deprivation – indigence* (16 + out of 26 IODs) when there are not enough resources for normal food or consumer durables such as a TV or fridge.
- *Band III deprivation – severe need (poverty)* (13/26 IODs) when there are further deprivations related to the quality of food and to lack of clothing and shoes; there is difficulty purchasing vital medicines and medical appliances; there are limited possibilities of inviting people round or visiting.
- *Band II deprivation – constrained circumstances (being badly off)* (7/26 IODs) when there are insufficient means to buy presents, newspapers, magazines and books; the family cannot afford a washing machine, or to visit relatives who live at a distance; they cannot afford fee-paying medical services.
- *Band I deprivation – borderline* (5 or fewer IODs) is characterized by living standards that are close to the average, generally accepted in Russian society. These families need better housing conditions; they have cut back on up-to-date consumer durables, family holidays and entertainment.

After 12 months 99 of the 105 households were reinterviewed, and the distribution of households between the deprivation groups for the two dates is given in Table 9.7 (in the left-hand column are the initial bands for 1999, and the table shows their subsequent movement in 2000). There are two patterns to be noted from this table. The first is that in all four categories, the majority remain where they were 12 months earlier (numbers in bold in the table), but that there is relatively more stability for the best- and worst-off households: the indigent (band IV) tend to stay indigent, and the borderline (band I) tends to stay borderline. The second point is that, of those that move between categories, there is a general movement up out of deeper poverty (the indigent and poor) compared with the drift down into poverty from those only badly off or borderline.

Within this sample there are 19 households that have been tracked longitudinally in four interviews between two projects since 1996, and give some idea of the experiences of households over the critical period before and after 1998

Table 9.7 Change in living standards in Moscow, Voronezh and Vladikavkaz, 1999–2000 (% in each band/city, and *n*)

	Year 2000															
	Moscow				*Voronezh*				*Vladikavkaz*				*Total*			
Bands	***IV***	***III***	***II***	***I***	***IV***	***III***	***II***	***I***	***IV***	***III***	***II***	***I***	***IV***	***III***	***II***	***I***
1999																
IV %	100	0	0	0	100	0	0	0	50	50	0	0	**63**	37	0	0
n	1	0	0	0	3	0	0	0	6	6	0	0	**10**	6	0	0
III %	9	55	27	9	20	60	20	0	0	70	30	0	10	**61**	26	3
n	1	6	3	1	2	6	2	0	0	7	3	0	3	**19**	8	1
II %	0	15	62	23	0	18	82	0	11	26	42	21	5	21	**58**	16
n	0	2	8	3	0	2	9	0	2	5	8	4	2	9	**25**	7
I %	0	0	0	100	0	0	0	100	0	0	20	80	0	0	11	**89**
n	0	0	0	2	0	0	0	2	0	0	1	4	0	0	1	**8**

Source: N. Manning and N. Tikhonova, *Poverty and Social Exclusion in the New Russia* (Aldershot: Ashgate, 2004), p. 216.

when the rouble collapsed and poverty rates jumped. Here is an example of two households, one sinking further into poverty, and the other climbing out:[40]

- *Household 18* – This household was among the most underprivileged in the whole sample: it consisted of a lone mother with a large number of children, and was made up entirely of women. Our respondent, Tat'yana (d.o.b. 1963), and her three daughters (born 1981, 1988 and 1992) were later joined by Tat'yana's aunt (d.o.b. 1925), who was the official tenant of the flat where they all lived (allocated through her former employer, an aircraft factory). Throughout the whole period of observation, the head of the family worked as a cleaner in another block of flats owned by the same factory. She joined our 1996 sample as someone who had found work after a period of registered unemployment (she had first worked in the factory canteen). Although Tat'yana had secure employment throughout the period of observation, she received a low wage: she was trapped in this dead-end job partly because she wanted to ensure she got the tenancy of the flat after her aunt's death.

  In a material sense, the family was going downhill, and over the period of observation, they fell from poverty into profound indigence. The household went without meat products, could not buy clothes, even for the children, or give them money to buy food at school; they had no television and could not afford to invite guests round, let alone carry out the repairs that that their small two-room flat desperately needed, or buy the simplest furniture.

  Tat'yana associated her increasingly difficult position, firstly, with alcoholism ('If everyone who can work didn't drink, it would be easier. Both my ex-husbands went downhill that way, and I've done so too, because of them'), and secondly with her large number of dependants:

> I view my family as poor, and when you ask for help, even for child benefits, they say something crude like: 'why did you have so many kids?' So we just have to toil on ... A woman on her own with children has to bring them up, shoe them, clothe them, feed them.

- *Household 2* – Throughout the whole period of observation, this Moscow household consisted of one young woman (d.o.b. 1965), who came from a family of doctors and she, herself, had higher education in medicine. Like the previous household, she was a typical example of the 'new poor'. Nataliya was typically representative of an active, energetic disposition towards life.

  Before the reforms, Nataliya had lived in Voronezh (our provincial survey city), but in the early 1990s she moved to Moscow and began her own small business there, selling souvenirs to foreign tourists. After her unregistered trade was forcibly brought to an end in 1993–94, she gradually began to slide into deep poverty. She could not register as unemployed, since she had no official residence permit for Moscow; thus, she was an example of a de facto unemployed person who had no possibility of obtaining official unemployed status – a situation typical of Moscow.

  After the failure of her small business, Nataliya lived on her savings for some time, but these rapidly ran out, since she had to rent a flat at market price – a problem which the previous household did not have, since they were native Muscovites and their rent was notional. Although the flat she rented was the cheapest available, without furniture or a telephone, it was still fairly expensive. Over almost five years, Nataliya slowly reduced her needs, working only from time to time (if her former friends and colleagues trading on Arbat Street asked her to) and stretching her remaining money just to pay for the flat. Once a month, she received a parcel from her mother in Voronezh, containing food – generally potatoes, cabbage and beetroot and, sometimes, cooked rissoles – which she lived on for a long time. In 1996, when she joined our first survey as a de facto unemployed person, and in 1997, she was very highly deprived. In fact, throughout that period, Nataliya lived practically at the level of indigence.

  Her situation was aggravated by serious depression resulting from lack of success in her personal life, and it was this that actually prevented her from going back to regular work. Some time in 1998, Nataliya attended meetings of a pseudo-religious cult, which, she claimed, helped her a lot in regaining her psychological stability. After this, she asked an old friend, who also came from Voronezh and had her own tourist business in Moscow, to lend her money, to train first as a masseuse and then as a homeopath. Having received this money, she was putting these plans into effect. As a result, both initial direct help with food from her relations and, more importantly, later substantial financial assistance from friends (to train in a field for which there is demand on the Moscow labour market) allowed her to overcome a difficult period in her life successfully. Thus, Nataliya's case was a clear example of the significance not only of particular personality traits, but also of social network resources, in helping people to get out of poverty.

As a result, at the time of the 1999–2000 surveys, Nataliya was self-employed as a masseuse in private practice, charging $10 per session, which was a fairly high rate for Moscow. Because of her increasingly difficult material circumstances and the need to pay off her debts, Nataliya was working practically every day of the week. As a result, in 1999, she had already risen to 'badly off' on to the Material Deprivation Index, and by 2000 she was 'averagely well-off'. She continued to rent the same cheap flat (although she was doing repairs there and had obtained a cell phone, since having no telephone in the flat had made her work impossible) and to economize on literally everything, even going without new clothes – but she was doing this with the aim of having a flat of her own after some time.

An advantage of qualitative data is that it can show that poverty and the various degrees of qualitative deprivation have their own specific features in different regional and ethnic communities. Manning and Tikhonova[41] report that a distinct feature of extreme deprivation in north Ossetia (Vladikavkaz) was the state of housing: cramped, overcrowded and impossible to maintain in good repair. In the northern Caucasus, another fairly important criterion of poverty – a marker of having 'crossed the threshold' – related to traditions of ritual and ceremony: someone who cannot afford to organize these when they have a duty to do so is often considered indigent. Lack of money for meat, household appliances or – especially – holidays was perceived in the Vladikavkaz community as less painful than in Moscow and Voronezh: although these instances provided evidence of being in need, they were not markers of extreme poverty. If members of the Russian population of north Ossetia, surrounded by people of a different nationality, could rarely afford to visit relatives living at a distance, this implied that the family's standard of living was extremely low; in contrast, this type of deprivation was less significant for Ossetian families in Vladikavkaz.

Voronezh respondents felt restrictions on clothing much more keenly than they did problems with food or lack of certain household appliances. More significant in Voronezh communities were social contacts with friends and neighbours – a sense of being part of a community. Those who could not invite guests or visit others, because of poverty, were seen as excluded from the local community, and thus as extremely deprived.

Perceptions of need in Moscow related more clearly to issues of social participation and the corresponding quality of life: Muscovites often classed as 'poor' those who could not afford fee-paying leisure, medicine or education for themselves or their children. Muscovites were much more keenly aware of lack of money for high-quality foods (fresh meat, vitamins, delicatessen foods) and restrictions on buying newspapers, books and magazines: this obviously related to the respondents' perception that the higher standard of living enjoyed by most of the capital's population – by comparison with residents of the other regions we studied – was normal and generally accepted.

It has been widely argued that informal mutual assistance has been a significant factor for households to overcome the difficult circumstances of economic transition.[42] Does this survival strategy also apply to poor households? Unfortunately, there are few data on the social contacts of households. We know little about the functions of social networks and how they change according to household situation; about the nature and conditions of the chief kinds of mutual exchange; above all, about how changes in the living standards of various kinds of family are reflected in changes in the structure and types of help they receive. Manning and Tikhonova[43] examined three kinds of support network:

1. Simple instrumental (household) help: support with everyday activities – running the house, looking after family members, sympathetic support, etc. – and simple resourcing support: resources in kind, such as foodstuffs and other items, including home-grown food;
2. Financial assistance: direct cash support from others in the family's social networks;
3. Complex instrumental/material/informational support: deploying social capital (exchange of services, recommendations and connections), not just cash or resources in kind; getting jobs, extra work, educational advice or training opportunities; help with repairs, building work, transport, organizing expensive events and ceremonies.

Although half of the households received some kind of support from social networks, when the poorest families got help from social networks, it was primarily in the form of simple household or material support: their involvement in the exchange of social capital was substantially lower than that of better-off families. Thus the poor had less access to social capital – which is the most important aspect of social support and precisely the one that actively helps to overcome difficulties. Rusinova and Brown[44] echoed these findings in a study of the way in which 32 rich and poor individuals gained access to medical care in St Petersburg in 1999. Those with higher social status were adept at using their networks, knowledge and, where necessary, money to gain the most from the medical care system. These resources were simply unavailable to poor families, who as a result consumed noticeably less health care as a consequence.

Conclusion

The data on inequality and poverty show clearly how the transformation of both the Russian economy and the Russian polity has not resulted in the harmonious development of what T.H. Marshall characterized as the hyphenated society of democratic-welfare-capitalism.[45] In this view inequality would grow, but the poor would be helped and enabled to retain their place in society. There seems little evidence of this being accomplished in Russia.

Inequality grew rapidly in the 1990s in Russia. There are a variety of ways in which this has been measured, but the trend over time comes through clearly. In the five years to 2000, the rate of growth of inequality has slowed and reversed. The significance of this pattern varies. For macroeconomic issues, there is the question of whether inequality hampers economic growth – now becoming a new orthodoxy in some economic circles. However, this probably depends on whether Russian economic growth is widely embedded, or, as is more likely the case, it is driven by export-oriented raw materials sectors. These are likely to be far less sensitive to domestic inequality than the manufacturing sectors of the Asian 'miracle' in the 1990s.

The causes of inequality are relatively clear. Those who moved into the private employment sector benefited from a marked premium, as did those who were able to develop private non-wage economic activities. Those who remained in traditional employment, either manufacturing or services, suffered from wage arrears and pay restraint in the face of inflation that undermined the old egalitarian distribution. In contrast to central European societies, the returns to education have not been strong in Russia, nor are gender effects pronounced. Some of these effects have been ameliorated in recent years – especially the reduction in wage arrears. On the other hand, regional inequalities have not reduced, and the impact of capital cities (especially the Moscow effect), and export-oriented raw materials regions, remains substantial. However, the ability of survey techniques to capture the upper end of the income and wealth distribution has been limited and we cannot find a clear picture of the rich from this general work on inequality.

While inequality may not get in the way of current Russian economic growth, it clearly does have consequences for Russian individuals and households. Poverty has also grown rapidly, and the consequences for ordinary lives have been devastating. Millions have lost their lives through premature mortality, and infectious disease has reappeared.[46] A whole generation has lived through a period of great instability and anxiety.

It may be that rapid change in economic fortunes keeps open the possibility for households and individuals to secure a better future at some point, but there is evidence that a significant layer are now stuck in longer-term poverty. This itself can amplify the accumulation of personal misfortunes, and give little prospect of relief through personal efforts. The impact of government social and regional policies and spending is at best neutral as to its impact on this group, and more likely worsens inequality through poor targeting and financial restraint.

Notes

1 R. White and J. Donoghue, 'Marshall, Mannheim and Contested Citizenship', *British Journal of Sociology*, 54, 3 (2003) 391–406.

2 S. Kuznets, 'Economic Growth and Income Inequality', *American Economic Review*, 45, 1 (1955) 1–28.

3 P.A. Hall and D. Soskice (eds), *Varieties of Capitalism: the Institutional Foundations of Comparative Advantage* (Oxford: Oxford University Press, 2001).

4 O. Kislitsyna, 'Income Inequality in Russia during the Transition. How can it be Explained?', Working Paper series No. 03/08 (Moscow: Economics Education and Research Consortium, 2003), p. 11.

5 N. Birdsall, 'Why Inequality Matters: the Developing and Transitional Economies', paper to conference on The World Economy, Massachusetts, 18–19 Feb. (2000), pp. 13–14.

6 B. Milanovic, 'Global Income Inequality: What it is and Why it Matters' (World Bank, 2006), p. 16.

7 N. Manning, 'Diversity and Change in Pre-accession Central and Eastern Europe since 1989', *Journal of European Social Policy*, 19, 3 (2004) 211–32.

8 T. Mroz, L. Henderson and B. Popkin, 'Monitoring Economic Conditions in the Russian Federation, the Russian Longitudinal Monitoring Survey 1992–2004', University of North Carolina at Chapel Hill (2004).

9 P. Mitra and R.Yemtsov, 'Inequality and Growth in Transition: does China's Rising Inequality Portend Russia's Future?' (World Bank, 2006), draft.

10 A.Y. Sheviakov and A.Y. Kiruta, 'Economic Inequality, Standards of Living, and Poverty in Russia: Measurement and Causal Dependencies', working paper (Moscow: Economics Education and Research Consortium, 2003), p. 7.

11 H. Theil, *Economic and Information Theory* (Amsterdam: North-Holland, 1967).

12 Milanovic, 'Global Income Inequality'.

13 T. Smeeding, 'Globalisation, Inequality and the Rich Countries of the G-20: Evidence from the Luxembourg Income Study (LIS)', Center for Policy Research Working Papers No. 48 (New York: Syracuse University, 2002).

14 B. Janovich, 'Russian Roller Coaster: Expenditure Inequality and Stability in Russia, 1994–98', *Review of Income and Wealth*, series 47, 2 (2001) 251–71.

15 Mitra and Yemtsov, 'Inequality', Table 8, p. 29.

16 B. Milanovic, 'Explaining the Increase in Inequality during the Transition', World Bank Research Working Paper No. 1935 (World Bank – Development Research Group (DECRG), 1998).

17 Mitra and Yemtsov, 'Inequality', pp. 40–1.

18 Ibid., pp. 42, 47–9.

19 Ibid., Table 13.

20 Kislitsyna, 'Income Inequality', Table 8.

21 D. Popova, 'The Impact of the Gender Composition of Households on Inequality and Poverty: a Comparison across Russia and Eastern Europe', *Communist and Post-Communist Studies*, 35 (2002) 395–409, p. 405.

22 Kislitsyna, 'Income Inequality', Table 6.

23 R. Yemtsov, 'Quo Vadis: Inequality and Poverty Dynamics across the Russian Regions in 1992–2000', Cornell/LSE/WIDER conference on spatial inequality, LSE, London, 28–30 June 2002.
24 N. Manning and N. Tikhonova, *Poverty and Social Exclusion in the New Russia* (Aldershot: Ashgate, 2004), p. 66.
25 M.J. Bradshaw and K. Vartapetov, 'A New Perspective on Regional Inequalities in Russia', *Eurasian Geography and Economics*, 44, 6 (2003) 403–29.
26 L. Fedorov, 'Regional Inequality and Regional Polarization in Russia, 1990–99', *World Development*, 30, 3 (2002) 443–56.
27 Milanovic, 'Explaining the Increase'; N. Barkhatova, P. McMylor and R. Melloe, 'Family Business in Russia: the Path to Middle Class?', *British Journal of Sociology*, 52, 2 (2001) 249–69.
28 R. Rose, *New Russia Barometer VII*, Studies in Public Policy 303 (Glasgow: University of Strathclyde, 1998).
29 P. Frijters, I. Geishecker, J.P. Haisken-DeNew and M.A. Shields, 'Income and Life Satisfaction in Post-Transition Russia: a New Empirical Methodology for Panel Data', mimeo (RWI Essen, 2003).
30 M. Lokshin and M. Ravallion, 'Rich and Powerful? Subjective Power and Welfare in Russia' (World Bank, 2003).
31 T. Mroz, L. Henderson and B.M. Popkin, 'Monitoring Economic Conditions in the Russian Federation: the Russia Longitudinal Monitoring Survey 1992–2004', Report submitted to the US Agency for International Development, Carolina Population Center (North Carolina: University of North Carolina at Chapel Hill, 2005).
32 Frijters et al., 'Income'.
33 Lokshin and Ravallion, 'Rich and Powerful?'.
34 M. Suhrcke, 'Preferences for Equality: East vs. West', Innocenti Working Paper No. 89 (Florence: UNICEF, 2001).
35 Janovich, 'Russian Roller Coaster'.
36 J. Mack and S. Lansley, *Poor Britain* (London: George Allen and Unwin, 1985).
37 A. Macauley, M.A. Mozhina and L. Ovcharova, *Poverty: Alternative Approaches to Definition and Measures* (Moscow: Carnegie Centre, 1998).
38 Manning and Tikhonova, *Poverty and Social Exclusion*.
39 Ibid.
40 Ibid., pp. 227–57.
41 Ibid.
42 D. Cox, Z. Yezer and E. Himenez, 'Economic Support of the Family by Private Individuals in the Period of Transition to the Market Economy', in D. Klugman (ed.), *Poverty in Russia: Public Policy and Private Responses* (Washington and Moscow: World Bank, 1998); R. Rose, 'Getting Things Done in an Anti-modern Society: Social Capital Networks in Russia', *Studies in Public Policy*, 304 (Glasgow: University of Strathclyde, 1998); S. Clark and V. Kabalina (eds), *Employment and Household Behaviour: Adaptation to Conditions of Transition to the Market Economy in Russia* (Moscow: ROSSPEN, 1999).
43 Manning and Tikhonova, *Poverty and Social Exclusion*.
44 N.L. Rusinova and J.V. Brown, 'Social Inequality and Strategies for Getting Medical Care in Post-Soviet Russia', *Health: an Interdisciplinary Journal for the Social Study of Health, Illness and Medicine*, 7, 1 (2003) 51–71.
45 White and Donoghue, 'Marshall, Mannheim and Contested Citizenship'.
46 Manning and Tikhonova, *Poverty and Social Exclusion*, Ch. 1, *passim*.

10

Inequalities in Health and Health Care in Post-communist Europe[1]

Peggy Watson

Introduction

With life expectancy in virtually all of the post-socialist accession countries much lower than the average for the previous EU15, health has assumed a critical economic and political significance in Europe. The achievement of greater health equality within and among European member countries has become a key policy aim.[2] By emphasizing health and linking it to citizenship, the EU seeks to reconnect with its citizens, thereby enhancing the credibility of the EU. In this, the EU espouses the 'new universalism' which now informs the global discourse of health rights. This principle accepts a narrowing of the scope of health care to which universal rights will apply and is based on the argument that, if the needs of the vulnerable are met, limited universal health rights can be reconciled with equitable health care.[3] The aspiration is that even if social rights to health care are limited, equity in care can still be achieved, among others through the promotion of social cohesion and active citizenship.

Far from giving rise to political credibility, however, the transformation of health care has been among the most problematic sites of the transition to democracy after communism.[4] At the same time, in contrast to the volume of social science research focusing on other aspects of transition, health and health care in transitional Europe remains a field about which little is known.[5] The present chapter outlines the East–West health inequalities that now define the EU, and considers how increasing inequalities within eastern European countries are implicated in the continuing European East–West health divide. It goes on to discuss the extent to which health care reforms, rather than preserving equity, are themselves implicated in escalating inequality and the unequalization of post-communist citizenship. The chapter does this with particular reference to Poland, which accounts for over half of the population in transitional Europe, drawing extensively on the findings of the Nowa Huta Study, a programme of research into health and social change in Nowa Huta, now a part of the city of Kraków and once a Stalinist new town.[6]

Health inequalities and the East–West mortality gap in Europe

Since 2004, the EU has been characterized by an East–West health divide. The reasons for this division are partly historical: before the end of communism adult mortality rates in eastern Europe had been rising steeply, in contrast to the West. By the time communism ended, the mortality rate of men in all eastern European countries exceeded that in any western European state.[7] Moreover, since the end of communism adult mortality rates in eastern Europe have in general been slow to improve. For example, while rates of mortality among adult men rose sharply in Poland in the decade preceding the end of communism, they showed only modest reduction during the subsequent ten years, with the consequence that death rates among Polish men remain about twice the average in the previous EU15 (see Figure 10.1).

The slowness of life expectancy to improve in eastern Europe is linked to rapid increases in health inequalities in these states. For example, Estonian data have shown that while mortality has declined among men with higher education since 1989, it has increased markedly among those whose education is limited to primary school.[8] For Poland, the Nowa Huta Study has followed a cohort of the workforce employed at the Nowa Huta steel plant in 1973 to establish mortality in contrasting social groups over time.[9] The study has shown increasing inequalities in adult health. While the mortality of the manual and non-manual male workforce was approximately the same until 1992,

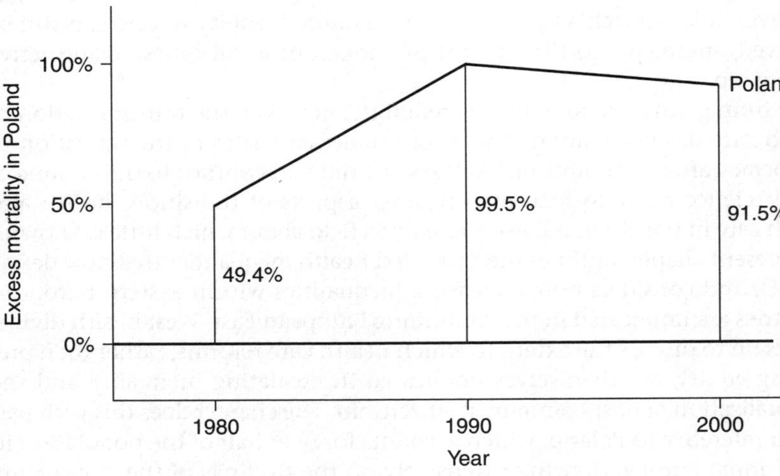

Figure 10.1 Mortality among working-age men: Poland, EU
Source: WHO HFA database

mortality inequalities subsequently came into being to the advantage of non-manual men (see Figure 10.2).

There are some data to suggest that increasing health inequalities in eastern Europe are associated with increasing social inequality. For example, while increases in health inequality have not been observed in the Czech Republic, which has among the lowest levels of social inequality in eastern Europe, clearly diverging mortality trends have been observed in Estonia, where social inequality is highest.[10] In Poland, alongside rising adult mortality differentials since the end of communism, poverty and social inequalities have also substantially increased. While in 1989 it was estimated that 14.8 per cent of Poles lived below the social minimum – a level of minimal adequacy defined by food expenditure accounting for 60 per cent or more of household income,[11] by 2001 the figure had reached 54 per cent.[12] The Polish Social Diagnosis Survey found 25 per cent of respondents living in poverty in 2003 (http://www.diagnoza.com), and the extent of poverty continues to increase.[13] The 'new poverty' in Poland is associated with the collapse of employment, the pauperization of public sector workers, the loss of income among small farmers, as well as the low level of social benefits.[14] Currently almost 50 per cent of the working age population in Poland is not working, and official unemployment has risen from zero to about 17 per cent. Between 1997 and 2003, rises in unemployment were concentrated among people with secondary education or less, as well as among the young, constituting an increase of

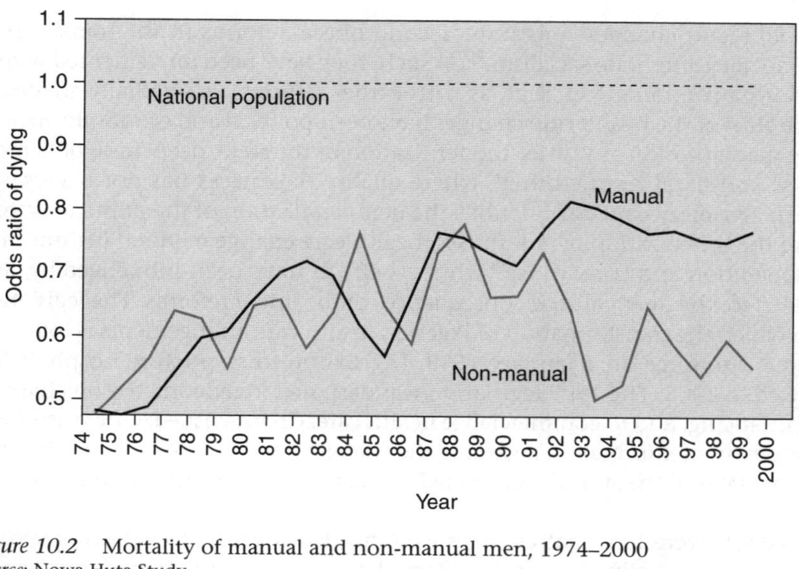

Figure 10.2 Mortality of manual and non-manual men, 1974–2000
Source: Nowa Huta Study

unemployment of 25 per cent among this social grouping, while rising by only 1 per cent among people with a university degree.[15] About one in seven of unemployed persons have guaranteed income support; for most of those in work wages are low.[16] The average wage of Polish enterprise workers in August 2005 was 2480 zloty – about £425 per month.[17] Social inequalities have grown. While between 1995 and 2000 the official monthly income of employers doubled from 2307 to 4538 zloty, for small farmers, whose income had already collapsed, it fell from 230 to 211 zloty per month.[18]

At the same time, privatization initiated a process of dependent development in Poland, and has not led to the economic miracle it was claimed it would.[19] With the exception of 1990, the year in which extra taxes to finance privatization were raised from state enterprises, the Polish budget has been in constant deficit.[20] With national GDP now below 50 per cent of the EU average, Poland is classified, in contrast to Hungary or the Czech Republic, as a low-income country,[21] where health care is considered to have heightened importance for health.[22] Meanwhile, health care reforms in Poland have brought high levels of dissatisfaction in opinion polls,[23] significant increases in direct costs to patients, industrial action, hunger strikes, and challenges in court. Radiologists, anaesthetists and other health professionals have taken industrial action, while nurses have engaged in hunger strikes. Ongoing changes have led to a situation said by the incoming Minister of Health to be 'ready to explode'.[24]

Transforming health care in Poland: the Bismarck social insurance model and the desocialization of care

Social sector changes constitute 'second phase' reforms in the transition to democracy after state socialism.[25] As such, they have been implemented within a normative framework that, as with earlier reforms, was globally shaped.[26] The aims of the health care changes have been political and economic, including marketization as well as 'modernization of the state, deepening of democracy, and fiscal restructuring', where quality of services has not necessarily been a primary concern.[27] Unlike the democratization of the political system and the privatization of enterprises, health care change required institutional cooperation and consensus,[28] while its effects have been influenced by, and added to, the unequalizing consequences of the initial reforms. The legislation on which the transformation of Poland's health care arrangements is founded, came into force on 1 January 1999. Legislation to restructure hospitals followed in 2005. The 1999 legislation was designed to redefine the mechanism of financing, and to commercialize health care. Chaos ensued. One reason was the dearth of information regarding the changes involved. Referring to the publicity material that was disseminated at the time, one health journalist wrote:

> People were told that changes were needed because 'the existing system was structurally inherently inclined to wastefulness, it had the wrong

structure of goals, the structure of the health service system was wrong, the structure of medical education was wrong, the financing structure was wrong and the structure of work remuneration was wrong'. And how would the patient benefit from the new system? Ah well, the patient would be the central link of the new system. I try to imagine what a pensioner waiting to see her doctor would learn from this.[29]

The reform substituted central state funding with a social insurance scheme based on the Bismarck model, thereby facilitating the language of solidarity and equity in health care.[30] However, the context differed greatly from the one that obtained when the Bismarck model was originally devised. The situation in nineteenth-century Germany had been one of rapid industrialization where social relations were still influenced by a spirit of feudalism, and where the idea of the individual was late to take hold.[31] A powerful nation state faced by the spectre of socialism, drew on pre-existing traditions and increased provision in order to preserve the social order and integrate manual workers into the state.[32] Integral to the transformation of social relations in Poland, however, has been the transcending of state socialism and the marginalization of sections of the populace. Here, the Bismarck social insurance model has been part of a reform where health care has been desocialized. This has been achieved by redefining responsibility for health in terms of the individual – thereby detaching responsibility from power, by framing reform in terms of abstract fiscal discourse – thereby eliding questions of social justice, need and equality, as well as by cutting health care finance.

An internal market was introduced where services were to be purchased from competing providers by 16 local sickness funds, one in each voivodeship region, using revenue from personal contributions originally set at 7.5 per cent of taxable income and increasing each year.[33] In 2003 the sickness funds were replaced by a central National Health Fund, with a corresponding branch in each voivodeship. The decision to set social insurance contributions at a level of 7.5 per cent of taxable income was critical and represented a substantial cut with respect to earlier funding levels, and the suggested level of 10 per cent. The issue was hotly disputed throughout the first half of 1998; the action committee KOROZ (The Committee for the Defence of Health Care Reform – Komitet Obrony Reformy Ochrony Zdrowia) was formed at this time.[34] Nevertheless, on the intervention of the Minister of Finance, the politician who had done most to promote economic shock therapy in the wake of communism, a funding level of 7.5 per cent prevailed. The decision ensured that the social insurance scheme had a deficit which took the form of limits to funded services beyond which payment was required. To illustrate the extent of the funding deficit involved – in the year 2000, the number of gynaecological consultations that could be planned and funded in the Mazowiecki region was only 40 per cent of the number of visits that had taken place in 1996, the equivalent of one consultation per woman every 7–8 years.[35]

Between 1998 and 2000, access to alcohol addiction treatment fell by 20–25 per cent.[36] In addition, the Polish Social Diagnosis Survey found that between 1998 and 1999 the percentage of respondents having dental care fell from 46 to 26 per cent, while those seeing a laryngologist declined from 35 to 18 per cent, falling to 15 per cent by 2005 (http://www.diagnoza.com).

'Once we saw patients eight hours a day', a laryngologist from the town of Slupsk complained in a 2005 newspaper interview.

> Now it's only four or five. The limits have greatly decreased (...). There's no one who will pay us for the patients that we see over and above the limits. Letters to the NFZ (The National Health Fund) have no effect. In urgent cases we try to see patients, especially children, but we can't do much more. Patients hold it against us, but it's not our fault.[37]

The partial coverage built into the social insurance scheme coupled with the failure to make the cuts explicit have undermined in practice the solidarity and equity to which the insurance scheme laid rhetorical claim. An increased level of co-payment, the amount paid by people directly for health care, and hence a selective reduction of access to care, have been the result of the reform. A survey conducted in November 1999 found that one in six respondents paid privately for medical services they would previously have received free of charge.[38] Overlaying this has been the increased extent to which physicians exact informal payment for services covered by public funds.[39] For these reasons, although health care has theoretically remained available to all, the changes have been 'leading in one direction only – to huge increases in inequalities in society'.[40]

Privatizing pharmaceuticals: new costs and inequalities

While legislation imposed financial limits to care, the privatization of Poland's pharmaceutical industry had introduced new health costs including the profits of pharmaceutical firms. Where Poland was once a major – non-profit – pharmaceuticals producer, currently about 90 per cent of its pharmaceuticals market – the sixth largest in Europe – is accounted for by firms of Western origin (http://www.biotechnologia.com.pl). A further consequence has been that the proportion of the pharmaceutical market accounted for by generic medicines has systematically declined in favour of more expensive patent-protected drugs.[41] This process has been mediated by the EU. For example, in 2003 the European Commission required Poland to lift fines imposed on Western drug companies for excessive prices, on the grounds of discrimination against the firms,[42] while a pre-accession requirement to conform to rules extending the life of patents effectively structured Poland's pharmaceutical market in favour of the more expensive drugs.[43] In consequence, just over one-fifth of the Polish health budget is now accounted for by the costs of reimbursed drugs, while the balance – 33.4 per cent of the total costs of reimbursed drugs – is currently paid for directly by patients themselves;[44] in 1990 the corresponding figure had been 6 per cent (http://www.ckzeto.com.pl). Patients are charged either a nominal flat fee, or 30–50 per cent of the full price of drugs, depending on drug category. There are very few exemptions from prescription fees. The exempt include the army, war and army invalids, regular blood donors, as well as a 'victim of political oppression' category.[45] A select group of state dignitaries and their families are also exempt, and hospital medicines and medicines for some diseases are free of charge for everyone. However, some exemptions are capped, as are reimbursements, including reimbursements for flat-fee life-saving drugs. Capping levels for some drugs were reduced in 2005, meaning the level of co-payment was effectively increased.

The new costs have excluded patients already pauperized in the course of transition, from care they had once had. The Polish Social Diagnosis Survey found in 2003 that income was positively correlated with use of health care, and that between 2003 and 2005 the proportion of people without earned income who had been prevented by costs from seeking medical care had increased by over 13 percentage points (http://www.diagnoza.com). Another 2003 survey found that while 4 per cent of respondents with higher education said they often had no money to buy essential drugs, among people with primary education the figure was 38 per cent.[46] A nurses' leader who had taken part as a Solidarity representative in the Health Care Round Table discussions in 1989 indicated how far the changes that had taken place had diverged from what had been hoped for when communism came to an end:

> It began not too badly, because it began in a very human way to make order, to begin to build some foundations, so that there could be something rational, economic, not necessarily that health (would be) a commodity like any other but ... patients' rights were introduced, standards started to obtain, it started well, but later (...) successive political teams introduced such chaos that (...) there are a lot of people, and I don't know whether I will soon be one of them, who say that during the period of totalitarianism there was both more common sense and more humanitarianism.[47]

Neo-liberalism and the redefinition of responsibility

Observers noted the ideological changes taking place. As one wrote: 'while the Polish economy at the beginning of the 1990s underwent a transition from socialism to capitalism, (...) the health service is going from communism to capitalism. That means that the scale of the changes, in the sphere of consciousness too, have to be more radical in health services than in the case of industrial enterprises.'[48] Ideological transformation was entailed in the creation and prioritization of interests defined as private, the shedding of the notion of the social responsibility of the state and a reliance on 'victim-blaming' instead.[49] 'Why do you keep going on to me about the social interest (*interes spoleczny*)', a high-ranking official in a Sickness Fund said during one exchange. 'That was under communism – now all there is, is business (*interes*)!'[50] At a recent meeting of the Polish–English Chamber of Commerce in Kraków the Director of the National Health Fund similarly declared, 'healthcare should be run on business principles and if these conditions were met, health care would be a very profitable business'.[51] The day before, he had been asked in an online medical journal interview, for his position on the high level of co-payment in health care.[52] His response had been to suggest that for increasing health care charges, people should hold, not decision-makers, but themselves, to account:

> You have to look at co-payment from several points of view. In the first place, the state of our health is fifty percent dependent on us ourselves, and only partly – less than 15 per cent – on the health service. So if we agree that our goal is to extend life expectancy and to raise health standards, then we should be motivated to look after our own health. So you have to look at co-payment in the following way: am I not, through my behaviour, myself generating the additional costs of my treatment?

In contrast, critics have seen the new level of co-payment as an act of assault. Indicating the low level of most earnings, one wrote: 'In such a situation forcing people to make use of paid services, which most people simply can't afford, is no longer discrimination, but more like extermination.'[53]

Experiences of health care reform

Health care change in post-communist Poland has been a site of gain, among others by 'public sector capitalists' and pharmaceutical firms. Meanwhile social surveys have consistently shown negative evaluations of health care after the reforms. Most recently, a CBOS (Centrum Badań Opinii Społecznej) survey showed that only 19 per cent of respondents were satisfied with health care in Poland.[54] However, the lack of clarity regarding rights that people have in practice after the reform coupled with a lack of detailed research, means that the way health care change has been experienced in practice has become a 'grey area' about which little is known. The Nowa Huta Study has provided a forum within which people have formulated their perceptions, among others, of health care reform.[55] The paper draws on a focus group study carried out between 1998 and 2000, where the participants included current and former employees of the local steel plant, and on individual interviews between 1998 and 2003. Although the Nowa Huta population was largely constituted by industrial manual workers, mortality was lower there than in any other district of Kraków, a town where mortality was already relatively low.[56] At the time of the focus group research the enterprise was halving its workforce in a restructuring process designed, as an outcome of pre-accession negotiations, to protect Western producers from competition from Polish steel.[57] The steel plant health service had employed 821 people by the time it was privatized at the end of 1995, a privatization bitterly contested by the Solidarity Healthworkers' Union. The then Director of the Health Centre later recounted how, despite being recognized as better than health facilities elsewhere, she was told it had to be closed down. 'I was told that there could not be an island of happiness in a sea of unhappiness', she explained.[58]

How, then, has health care change been experienced in Nowa Huta and what are the implications for the understanding of citizenship? Among the participants of the Nowa Huta study, stress was seen as the most important influence on health in post-communism.[59] Along with unemployment, social inequality and financial strain, health care reform was perceived as a major cause of stress, and seen in terms of loss. There was a perceived lack of care, and quality of care, to which people still felt an entitlement. As a retired worker put it:

> (After the threat of unemployment) the next thing that has an effect on stress (...) is medical care. You used to go to the doctor, and then you knew that you were going to that doctor, and no-one was doing you a favour. True, you had to wait in queues, but (that's the case) today too, in spite of the reform, but well, you went to the doctor, he listened, and whatever was needed, you were supplied with it.[60]

Rights to health care were in practice being undermined by increasing costs. Rather than confidence and safety, these changes had given rise to uncertainty and fear which were seen as having negative implications for physical and mental health. The views of the participants of two focus groups quoted below quantify the impact of the increased prices of medicines. The first quotation comes from a retired male manual worker, the second from a woman who had worked at the steel plant in the 1970s, and was now retired:

> Before, last year still, it would happen that I got prescriptions ... for medicine ... sometimes two prescriptions, completely free-of-charge, because I've had two heart attacks, I've had my gall bladder removed, and I've got an artificial hip as well, an endoprosthesis, so I've already been (...) Well, today I don't get a single prescription, I have to pay for them all, and every month I pay 240, 260 zloty, month after month. (...) My pension, I've got group 1, because I've got disability, so (...) including that, I've got 1000 zloty (about £170 a month).

> I can confide to you ladies how much pension I really get for 27 years' work – 480 zloty and 50 groszy. I'm afraid it's true. That's less than all

> those social benefits; well I can show you the slip because I've got it here. (...) You've been talking about reaching seventy. Well, I'll be 70 in two years' time. Well, I'd like to live to see it, but in the present conditions I don't really know ... if it weren't for my husband – my husband is seriously ill too, because he's got diabetes and coronary problems, and I'm not very... either ... And the medicines you are talking about, well (...) my pension doesn't cover the medicine, and to pay the bills and live off the other (...) I once said to myself that I can't go on any longer, (...) I think whether to have the treatment or not, because if you just have to live like this from one day to the next in fear ... is it really worth it? (...) And it's those nerves, those stresses which lead to various unnecessary illnesses. Because those heart problems, (...) it has a big effect ... all those depressions, well, it's really ... terrible.

Although health care reform had been contributing to increasing poverty, the retired people in the Nowa Huta Study were all in receipt of a pension, and therefore not among those living in the extremes of poverty. On the other hand, their call on health care was significant by virtue of their age and work history. Moreover, the effects of rising health care costs were magnified by the fact that other essential monthly outgoings, notably housing charges and utility bills, were increasing at the same time. The respondents held to a notion of the social responsibility of the state, and expressed the view that elected politicians, instead of representing social interests, were betraying them. A former manual worker offered an example of this when he recounted an exchange on a radio phone-in programme between a caller and the Minister of Health:

> The thing is that people are hopeless, because they've got no perspectives. A moment ago, before I came here, I heard a discussion on the radio on the Third Programme, about taking away from December 25th, the allowances for that illness ... Alz(heimer's) ... They used to have pads free of charge, ... Now it turns out that people who are ill, phoning the programme, wept openly, where would they ... get (it) from ... and the Minister who was taking part in the discussion so beautifully, so convolutedly, well because she had an education – from the previous system, by the way – and today she can sell out work-weary people (*spracowani*) ... They phoned in and wept, literally (...) well because they've got nothing to pay for it with ... and (the person who was phoning in) said – 'how can the Minister, a representative of our government, instead of raising our spirits, tell us that she's taking away the last ... when we go round institutions begging' (...) There's not a few that say that it's better that they finish (their lives), and not look at what's going on today. Because that is how the government is (...) and now they've made that revolution in the health service. Well that's the worst thing. (...) I used to come to the doctor in this building when there

> were 200–300 people in the morning. Today (...) you come here and there's absolutely no-one, you can't see any patients, people don't want to go off ill, the ones that work, because they're sure they'll be fired (if they do). Because even that isn't being supervised. There's no-one to supervise it. They only look after their own positions, their seats (*stolki*).

The undermining of confidence and safety that had accompanied health care reform, and the sense of persecution that could result from this, was reflected in the comments of an electrician who had worked at the steel plant since the 1960s, and was now retired. Unusually, he implicated European politics in this process:

> It's not for nothing that I heard that there have been instructions from Brussels, that Polish society should number – not 40 or 38 million or whatever ..., but 24 million people. Well ... and that can be done very neatly. Medicine has gone up. You must have heard more than once that older people leave the counter window in the chemist's (empty handed). Because they can't afford the medicine. And (it's) basic medicine, which is supposed to help them, (it) costs this much and this much, and (so) they want to give up on the medicine. – Just the vitamins, and what good will that do them? And what's it about in my opinion? It's so that older people, who in effect are not needed any more, why should they take benefits – disability or retirement – when you can get rid of them – and (then) more money will be left in the state budget. And so – simply put up the medicine (...) Put up the medicine, the disability and retirement (benefits) don't go up at all – and (that way) the old people will be finished off by themselves. (...)[61]

The individualistic ideology underpinning liberal democratic citizenship had yet to be embraced by the participants in the research. Rather than interpreting their health problems in terms of 'behaviour', they interpreted them in terms of work – the social meaning of which was the basis of their sense of entitlement. Under communism, the health hazards of work at the steel plant had been explicitly recognized in law, and had been built into administrative structures of social entitlements and rates of pay. For example, people working in 'harmful conditions' were entitled to special meals, early retirement and regular sanatorium stays. The connection that people continued to make between the hazardous work conditions at the steel plant, their current state of health and by implication their right to care, is reflected in the exchange between two women participating in a focus group. The first had been in charge of a cleaning brigade for 25 years in one of the dustiest departments in the steel plant; the second had been an overhead crane driver, retiring in the 1970s on grounds of ill health:

> The department (where I worked) was really dirty, and so what (happened)? You worked, and you got ill (like the others), because everyone knows ... in

that department ... Medicines non-stop, I buy eye drops non-stop, because I've got that ... glaucoma. I spend 20 zloty a month on drops, that's non-stop. Every month just one little bottle and ... And still ... you buy other medicines – and expensive ones at that ... Well my pension is 820 zloty, well it isn't high, you pay (your bills), well sometimes you take a little loan from Huta, because I still belong to the fund, well you have to pay that back, and sometimes there's literally only 300 zloty left to live on for the month.

I, for example had an eye operation, I had a lens inserted, well (the previous speaker doesn't) spend much, because I spend 50 zloty a month, because I've got two kinds of drops – one for the healthy eye, and one for the bad one. (...) Twenty five zloty Betoptic costs, and where did I get my bad eye from? – From that dust, from that ... gas where one worked. After all, in (that) department (...), after all, there was a terrible noise there, unbelievable dust, you breathed all that in and it's no wonder that I've got angina pectoris, diseased coronary pathways, so that I couldn't walk here. And then there's the inhaler for the bronchial pathways – because it's those bronchial pathways most of all ... No, our government doesn't know how to govern, that's what I say. Here you have to say that they are doing people harm (*krzywdza ludzi*).

Financial strains were often experienced in terms of the formation of new inequalities and as such, unjust. As a retired engineer described people's reactions when unable to have health care because of inability to pay, he contrasted the language of democracy and choice, with the economic limits to democracy that he experienced in practice:

They curse. They curse terribly ... And they compare ... oh ... with what is written here (opening a newspaper and indicating the salary of an official quoted there) ... They wait until (the symptoms) pass, and if they don't pass, well, you know what they're waiting for (laughs softly) – but we've got democracy. And democracy means that we have a choice (hint of sarcasm), except that we have nothing to choose with ... It's changed for the worse. During communism people didn't vegetate like now. Let's say there was a general poverty. Everyone lived very modestly. On a low level. But now there has been a terrible polarisation (*rozwarstwienie*). Some live very well, they're rich. For others, it's worse and worse. (Opens the newspaper again.) That is the salary our representatives are getting ... that is the salary the representatives that we voted for, are getting. I don't get that kind of pay in a year, even though they say I'm a Croesus among pensioners. My wife (who had worked for 25 years at Huta) wouldn't get in three years what the Member of Parliament here gets in one month.[62]

Discussion

The discourse of citizenship and equality that informs the new European health programme is derived from the sequence of historical development in the West. Because liberal democracy was 'a fairly late product' of market society,[63] it presupposed capitalism even as it sought to transcend its effects. Liberal democracy is thus 'democracy conceptualized and structured within the limits of liberalism',[64] where liberalism's founding notion is the 'individual' that is socially abstract. In the liberal West welfare rights have historically been understood in terms of the progressive expansion of citizenship rights; as social (rather than liberal) rights they have been seen to limit the effects of class inequalities already in place.[65] Thus health care rights have been seen as bringing to an end the adverse social consequences of ill health among people who, in a class society, are poor.

The implications for social relations of the transition to liberal democracy after communism cannot be constructed in this way. In this transition, relative equality and universal citizenship are the starting point rather than the stated goal of change.[66] State socialism was based on the principle of social equality, and this was achieved to the extent that private property and class differences were brought to an end. This had been accomplished through the creation of a social order where liberal rights had no place. The key ideological category was 'society', rather than the 'autonomous individual' as the bearer of rights. As an explicit aspect of the exercise of power, the non-profit, non-private property economy represented a core element of the party/state that defined its role as acting on behalf of society as a whole. Limits to political liberty applied to all of society, which came to be defined in opposition to the state. Because relative equality and universality of citizenship existed before the transition to liberal democracy in Poland, the transition to liberal democracy after communism cannot be framed in terms of the equalization of rights as it was historically in the West. Liberalization, rather than the equalization of rights, has been central to the transition to liberal democracy after communism. As rights were liberalized they became 'conditional capacities' rather than social entitlements under state guarantee.[67] Among the new liberal rights, the right to private property was key.

In the engagement with citizenship in Western political sociology, issues relating to the political effects of capitalism have been put to one side.[68] In political theory, a similar observation has been made.[69] Current approaches which emphasize the cohesive potential of social rights, exclude the overriding political implications of a capitalist social order and hence the terms on which cohesion might occur, from the analysis of citizenship. This exclusion naturalizes class inequalities, the effects of which social citizenship was designed to limit in the first place. Developments since the end of communism bring into question the assumptions through which such occlusions have been sustained. Liberalism and the idea of the capitalist economy as a quasi-natural phenomenon, were kept buoyant by the ideology of the Cold War. With the rise of neo-liberalism after communism, they have become a primary issue for critique.

Health care change in Poland has been integral to the transformation of the social order, a primary feature of which has been the creation of these new power asymmetries based on poverty and wealth. The commodification of health care has rendered it a means through which these new social relations and subjectivities are being put in place. By inscribing in them new differences of security in health, health policy contributes to the 'cumulative causation' of class.[70] The implications of health security differences are diverse. The selective withdrawal of access to health care transforms illness into a mode of exclusion as well as heightening dependency and hence exploitability in the labour market.[71] When state socialism was being constructed, the health policy of the time was seen as instrumental in producing a new, more equal society and a new kind of citizen.[72] After communism, the transition to liberal democratic citizenship has been inseparable in practice from liberalization, the privatization of property rights, and the instantiation of capitalism, and has devolved upon the differentiation, on this basis, of de facto rights. In practice, the extent to which people are able, at a time of ill health, to have specialist care, basic medicine or even nutritious food, is defined in terms of location with respect to the new social order, indeed defines that location and order, even though constitutionally the right to health care for everyone is still guaranteed.[73]

The unequalization of the social order within Poland has been part of a broader transformation of global relations of power. The new EU health programme deploys the language of citizenship to articulate a horizon of greater equality in health. However, as the Nowa Huta interviews have shown, 'the vulnerable' are not a transhistorical category, in terms of which the adequacy of health care provision might be assessed. Rather, they show that health care change – along with other contextual changes – are integral to the production and social structuring of vulnerability itself. The contradiction of this health and citizenship discourse after communism lies in its depiction of a safer, healthier and more confident future for all, a prospect whose credibility depends on leaving out of the picture the unequalizing social order both within Poland and among the countries of Europe, which the EU itself has – through setting the terms of accession – played a critical role in bringing about.

Acknowledgements

This chapter draws on research funded by the ESRC (Grant No. R000222627), the Isaac Newton Trust, the Wellcome Trust and the British Academy. Thanks go to all those who were interviewed.

Notes

1 This chapter draws in part on material published in P. Watson, Unequalising Citizenship: the Politics of Poland's Health Care Change', *Sociology*, 40, 6 (2006) 1079–96.

2 European Commission, *Healthier, Safer, More Confident Citizens: a Health and Consumer Protection Strategy* (Brussels: European Commission, 2005); K. Judge, S. Platt, C. Costongs and K. Jurczak, *Health Inequalities: a Challenge for Europe* (London: UK Presidency of the EU, 2005).

3 WHO, *Making a Difference. World Health Report 1999* (Geneva: WHO, 1999); C.J. Redden, *Health Care, Entitlement and Citizenship* (Toronto: University of Toronto Press, 2002).

4 P. Mierzewski, 'Commentary: Patients' Empowerment – the East Side Story', *British Medical Journal*, 331 (2005) 226–7; A. Fandrejewska-Tomczyk, 'Przyczyny Niskiej Akceptacji Spolecznej Reformy Powszechnych Ubezpieczen Zdrowotnych w 1999r.' in L. Kolarska-Bobinska (ed.), *Cztery Reformy: Od Koncepcji do Realizacji* (Warsaw: Instytut Spraw Publicznych, 2002); P. Krasucki, *Optymalizacji Systemu Ochrony Zdrowia: Koszty i Korzysci* (Warsaw: CeDeWu, 2005); CBOS, *Opinie o Opiece Zdrowotnej w Polsce, Czechach, Slowacji i na Wegrzach* (Warsaw: CBOS, 2005).

5 World Bank, *Growth, Poverty and Inequality: Eastern Europe and the Former Soviet Union* (Washington, DC: The World Bank, 2005); C.W. Afford, *Corrosive Reform: Failing Health Systems in Eastern Europe* (Geneva: International Labour Office, 2003); K. Fister and M. McKee, 'Health and Healthcare in Transitional Europe – Evidence-based Policy-making and Greater Participation are Needed', *British Medical Journal*, 331 (2005) 169.

6 The Nowa Huta Study was initiated in 1992, and has involved, among others, the creation and tracing of vital status in a historical cohort comprising the entire workforce of the Nowa Huta steel plant in 1973 (approximately 35,000 persons), as well as a study of the perception of health risk among cohort survivors. More information is available at the website: http://www.nowahutastudy.info

7 P. Watson, 'Explaining Rising Mortality among Men in Eastern Europe', *Social Science and Medicine*, 41, 7 (1995) 923–34.

8 M. Leinsalu, D. Vågerö and A. Kunst, 'Estonia 1989–2000: Enormous Increase in Mortality Differences by Education', *International Journal of Epidemiology*, 32 (2003) 1081–7.

9 For more details, see P. Watson, 'Health Difference in Eastern Europe: Preliminary Findings from the Nowa Huta Study', *Social Science and Medicine*, 46, 4–5 (1998) 549–58.

10 For comparisons of social inequality in eastern Europe, see B. Heyns, 'Emerging Inequalities in Central and Eastern Europe', *Annual Review of Sociology*, 31(2005) 163–97.

11 L. Beskid, 'O Materialnym Rozwarstwieniu Spoleczenstwa Polskiego' in H. Domanski, A. Ostrowska and A. Rychard (eds), *Jak Zyja Polacy* (Warsaw: IFiS PAN: 2001).

12 J. Glowczyk, *Spoleczno-ekonomiczne Skutki Transformacji Ustrojowej w Polsce* (Warsaw: Fundacja Innowacja – Wyższa Szkoła Społeczno-Ekonomiczna, 2002).

13 World Bank, *Growth, Poverty and Inequality: Eastern Europe and the Former Soviet Union* (Washington, DC: The World Bank, 2005).

14 Cf. L. Beskid, 'O Materialnym Rozwarstwieniu Społeczenstwa Polskiego', in H. Domański, A. Ostrowska and A. Rychard (eds), *Jak ŻyjąPolacy* (Warsaw: IFiS PAN: 2001).

15 OECD, *2004 OECD Economic Survey of Poland* (Paris: OECD, 2004).

16 Ibid.

17 http://www.stat.gov.pl. Enterprises with ten or more employees.

18 J. Glowczyk, *Społeczno-ekonomiczne Skutki Transformacji Ustrojowej w Polsce* (Warsaw: Fundacja Innowacja – Wyzsza Szkoła Społeczno-Ekonomiczna, 2002), p. 148.

19 J. Staniszkis, *Władza Globalizacji* (Warsaw: Wydawnictwo Naukowe Scholar, 2003).
20 J. Glowczyk, *Społeczno-ekonomiczne Skutki Transformacji Ustrojowej w Polsce* (Warsaw: Fundacja Innowacja – Wyzsza Szkola Spoleczno-Ekonomiczna, 2002).
21 OECD, *New GDP Comparisons Based on Purchasing Power Parities for the Year 2002* (Paris: OECD, 2005).
22 G. Bloom, 'Equity in Health in Unequal Societies: Meeting Health Needs in Contexts of Social Change', *Health Policy*, 57 (2001) 205–24.
23 CBOS, *Opinie o Opiece Zdrowotnej w Polsce, Czechach, Słowacji i na Wegrzach* (Warsaw: CBOS, 2005).
24 Zb. Religa, *Wywiad z prof. Zbigniewem Religą*, 14 October 2005, http://www.mp.pl (accessed 18/11/2005).
25 J.M. Nelson, 'Linkages between Politics and Economics', in L. Diamond and M.F. Platner (eds), *Economic Reform and Democracy* (Baltimore: Johns Hopkins University Press, 1995).
26 B. Deacon, *Global Social Policy: International Organizations and the Future of Welfare* (London: Sage, 1997).
27 R.R. Kaufman and J.M. Nelson (eds), *Crucial Needs, Weak Incentives: Social Sector Reform, Democratization, and Globalization in Latin America* (Washington, DC and Baltimore: Woodrow Wilson Center Press/Johns Hopkins University Press, 2004), p. 511.
28 J.M. Nelson, 'Linkages between Politics and Economics', in L. Diamond and M.F. Platner (eds), *Economic Reform and Democracy* (Baltimore: Johns Hopkins University Press, 1995).
29 E. Cichocka, 'Chaos Informacyjny na Temat Reformy', in B. Chołuj (ed.), *System Opieki Zdrowotnej-Efekty Zmian w Polsce i Krajach Sąsiednich* (Warsaw: Scholar Wydawnictwo Naukowe, 2002), p. 90.
30 The Bismarck model of social insurance is classified as solidarity-based insofar as contributions are scaled to income, and services used according to need.
31 T. Veblen, *Imperial Germany and the Industrial Revolution* (New York: B.W. Huebsch, 1915).
32 J. Tampke, 'Bismarck's Social Legislation: a Genuine Breakthrough?', in W.J. Mommsen and W. Mock (eds), *The Emergence of the Welfare State in Britain and Germany 1850–1950* (London: Croom Helm, 1981).
33 S. Golinowska, Z. Czepulis-Rutkowska, M. Sitek, A. Sowa, C. Sowada and C. Wlodarczyk, *Opieka Zdrowotna w Polsce po Reformie* (Warsaw: CASE, 2002). K. Tymowska, 'Health Care under Transformation in Poland', *Health Policy*, 56 (2001) 85–98.
34 A. Fandrejewska-Tomczyk, 'Przyczyny Niskiej Akceptacji Społecznej Reformy Powszechnych Ubezpieczeń Zdrowotnych w 1999r.', in L. Kolarska-Bobińska (ed.), *Cztery Reformy: Od Koncepcji do Realizacji* (Warsaw: Instytut Spraw Publicznych, 2000).
35 M.M. Lech, 'Potencjalne, Negatywne Skutki Reformy Ochrony Zdrowia dla Stanu Opieki Polozniczo-Ginekologicznej w Polsce', in B. Chołuj (ed.), *System Opieki Zdrowotnej – Efekty Zmian w Polsce i Krajach Sąsiednich* (Warsaw: Wydawnictwo Naukowe Scholar, 2002).
36 'Narodowy Program Profilaktyki i Rozwiązywania Problemów Alkoholowych na lat 2000–2005' (Dokument Zatwierdzony do Realizacji na Posiedzeniu Rady Ministrów w dn. 6 września 2000).
37 Drenowanie Kieszeni Pacjentów, *Głos Pomorza*, 30 March 2005 (http://www.nfz-wroclaw.pl/prasowka).

38 A. Fandrejewska-Tomczyk, 'Przyczyny Niskiej Akceptacji Społecznej Reformy Powszechnych Ubezpieczeń Zdrowotnych w 1999r.', in L. Kolarska-Bobińska (ed.), *Cztery Reformy: Od Koncepcji do Realizacji* (Warsaw: Instytut Spraw Publicznych, 2000).

39 A. Kubiak, Pacjenci i Lekarze o Korupcji w Publicznej Służbie Zdrowia. Raport z Badań (Warsaw: Fundacja Batorego, 2001).

40 E. Cichocka, quoted in C. Włodarczyk, 'Cele Reformy Opieki Zdrowotnej', in L. Kolarska-Bobińska (ed.), *Cztery Reformy: Od Koncepcji do Realizacji* (Warsaw: Instytut Spraw Publicznych, 2000), p. 167.

41 This trend was reversed in 2004.

42 J. Bielecki, 'Bruksela Domaga się Darowania Kar', *Rzeczpospolita*, 4 June 2003.

43 R. Sołtyk, 'Nowe Leki Dluzej Drogie', *Gazeta Wyborcza*, 12 September 2003. This prompted an unprecedented protest by the Health Ministers of the accession countries.

44 Najwyzsza Izba Kontroli, *Informacja o Wynikach Kontroli Funkcjonowania Systemu Tworzenia Wykazu Leków Refundowanych* (Warsaw: NIK Departament Pracy, Spraw Socjalnych i Zdrowia, 2004).

45 'Ustawa o świadczeniach opieki zdrowotnej finansowanych ze środków publicznych, Dz.U.04.210.2135 z dnia 27 sierpnia 2004 r'. (http://www.nfz.gov.pl).

46 W. Górecki, 'Dostępność Leków', in T. Borkowska-Kalwas and M. Paczkowska (eds), *Dostępność Świadczeń Zdrowotnych w Opinii Polaków 1998–2003: Raport z Badan* (Warsaw: Centrum Systemów Informacyjnych Ochrony Zdrowia: Zakład Analiz Socjologicznych, 2004).

47 Interview with A.G., Kraków, 17 October 2003.

48 W. Misiński, 'Mity Rynku Uslug Medycznych', *Służba Zdrowia*, 40–41(2000) 8–10.

49 R. Crawford, 'You are Dangerous to Your Health – Ideology and Politics of Victim-Blaming', *International Journal of Health Services*, 7 (1977) 663–8.

50 P. Krasucki, 'Siła Przyzwyczajenia', *Służba Zdrowia*, 65–68 (2000) 14.

51 'Stop Protecting Public, Let Private Thrive – a Call for Private Health Care', British–Polish Chamber of Commerce Business Breakfast, Kraków, 28 January 2005. http://www.polishmarket.com, accessed 16 February 2005.

52 Interview with Jerzy Miller, 27 January 2005 (http://www.mp.pl/kurier/index.php?aid=25553), accessed 15 February 2005.

53 P. Krasucki, 'Knajpa bez Kelnera', *Służba Zdrowia*, (2000), 20.

54 CBOS, *Opinie o Opiece Zdrowotnej w Polsce, Czechach, Słowacji i na Węgrzach* (Warsaw: CBOS, 2005).

55 P. Watson, 'Nowa Huta: the Politics of Postcommunism and the Past', in J. Edmunds and B.S. Turner (eds), *Generational Consciousness, Narrative, and Politics* (Lanham, Md.: Rowman and Littlefield, 2002); P. Watson, 'Stress and Social Change in Poland', *Health and Place*, 12 (2006) 372–82.

56 P. Watson, 'Health Difference in Eastern Europe: Preliminary Findings from the Nowa Huta Study', *Social Science and Medicine*, 46 (1998) 549–58.

57 P. Keat, 'Penalizing the Reformer: Polish Steel and European Enlargement', *Communist and Postcommunist Studies*, 33 (2000) 201–21.

58 Interview with K.M., Kraków, 23 November 1998.

59 P. Watson, 'Stress and Social Change in Poland', *Health and Place*, 12 (2006) 372–82.

60 Interview with J.L., Nowa Huta, 6 December 1999.

61 Interview with J.M., Nowa Huta, 9 May 2003.

62 Interview with M.S., Nowa Huta, 6 December 1999.

63 C.B. MacPherson, *The Political Theory of Possessive Individualism. Hobbes to Locke* (Oxford: Clarendon Press, 1962).
64 B. Parekh, 'The Cultural Particularity of Liberal Democracy', in D. Held (ed.), *Prospects for Democracy: North South East West* (Cambridge: Polity Press, 1993), p 165.
65 T.M. Marshall, *Citizenship and Social Class and Other Essays* (Cambridge: Cambridge University Press, 1950); K. Polanyi, *The Great Transformation: the Political and Economic Origins of our Time* (Boston, Mass.: Beacon, 1957).
66 P. Watson, 'Re-thinking Transition: Globalism, Gender and Class', in J.W. Scott and D. Keates (eds), *Going Public: Feminism and the Shifting Boundaries of the Private Sphere* (Urbana and Champaign: University of Illinois Press, 2004).
67 J.M. Barbalet, *Citizenship* (Milton Keynes: Open University Press, 1988).
68 M. Burawoy, 'For a Sociological Marxism: the Complementary Convergence of Antonio Gramsci and Karl Polanyi', *Politics and Society*, 31 (2003) 193–261.
69 W. Brown, *States of Injury: Power and Freedom in Late Modernity* (Princeton: Princeton University Press, 1995); *Edgework: Critical Essays on Knowledge and Politics* (Princeton: Princeton University Press, 2005).
70 N. Brenner, *New State Spaces: Urban Governance and the Rescaling of Statehood* (Oxford: Oxford University Press, 2004).
71 G. Esping-Andersen, *The Three Worlds of Welfare Capitalism* (Cambridge: Polity, 1993).
72 Zs. Ferge, *A Society in the Making: Societal Policy in Hungary* (Harmondsworth: Penguin, 1979).
73 M. Palska, *Bieda i Dostatek: O Nowych Stylach Życia w Polsce Końca Lat Dziewięćdziesiątych* (Warsaw: IFiS PAN, 2002).

11

Mass Privatization and the Post-communist Mortality Crisis

Lawrence King and David Stuckler

The massive economic contraction that followed the disintegration of the Soviet system has attracted a great deal of scholarly attention. What has been relatively neglected is the most troubling aspect of the transitions, the explosive rise in 'violent mortality', or epidemic levels of cardiovascular disease and 'external' causes of death, such as alcohol poisoning, homicide and suicide.[1] Countries in the 'mortality belt', spanning from Estonia in the north to Ukraine in the south, experienced life expectancy declines of up to six years within the first half-decade of reform – a peacetime mortality crisis unparalleled in modern history.[2] To put this in perspective, eliminating all common forms of cancer corresponds to a life expectancy increase of approximately three years, a little less than half of the magnitude of Russia's mortality experience.[3] The United Nation's MONEE project tabulates that the excess mortality during the 1990s, or deaths that would not have occurred if mortality had remained at 1989 levels, totalled over 3.2 million.[4] This crisis is in no respects over; 15 years after transition 11 out of 25 of the post-communist countries have failed to recover to pre-transition levels of life expectancy,[5] and public health professionals fear chronic disease epidemics and resurgent infectious disease crises such as AIDS and drug-resistant TB.

While the generalized economic crisis that has been labelled the 'Post-communist recession' obviously contributed to this increased mortality, it has not followed the typical patterns of development and health, and can at best be considered only a partial explanation. During the initial stages of reform from 1989 to 1994 the correlation between the logarithmic change in gross domestic product per capita and the logarithmic change in life expectancy was substantial ($r = -0.60$). Over the next six years, however, the unadjusted relationship weakens considerably ($r = -0.13$). Several countries, including Russia, exhibit the anomalous experience of declining mortality in the midst of economic recovery. Another enigmatic aspect of the excess deaths has been the disproportionate impact on working-age men, rather than vulnerable groups such as the very young and elderly that historically have borne the health brunt of rapid economic destabilization. Infant mortality levels in Russia, aside from an immediate and transient spike following the 1992 reforms, have steadily declined against a background of 'epidemic' levels of chronic disease.

Epidemiologic analyses clearly show that the increase in mortality is due to a rise in cardiovascular disease and 'external causes' like alcohol poisoning, violent deaths, homicide, suicide and accidents. Psychosocial stress levels and alcohol consumption have occupied central roles in these explanations. Yet, even in the most comprehensive analyses a sizeable residual remains unaccounted for.

We will advance a sociological theory of post-communist mortality that complements the public health literature. We find, all things held equal, that those countries that implemented the neo-liberal inspired mass privatization programmes had greater declines of life expectancy than countries that pursued different types of privatization. This explains a substantial part of the variation, although the magnitude of the effect and the variance explained is sensitive to the type of statistical test employed. Our most conservative estimate of the decrease in overall life expectancy as a result of implementing a mass privatization programme is 0.86 years, with the highest estimate of 5.14 years.

This chapter has four sections. In the first, we review the findings from the public health research and discuss different explanations. In the second we discuss the neo-liberal analysis, and develop a 'neoclassical sociological' theory of post-communist mortality that supplements the public health account. We then generate our hypotheses. In the third we discuss our methods and data. In the fourth we present our results, and in the conclusion we discuss the implications for public policy and future research.

Explanations of the post-communist mortality crisis

There are several explanations of the post-communist mortality crisis. One is the state collapse thesis. Logically, a collapsed medical care system, unable to provide preventive medicine, or to adequately treat the ill, could account for this rise in mortality.[6] Furthermore, the marketization of health care, combined with a growing lack of purchasing power among the poor, could account for increased mortality.

Similarly, a change in diet affected by the changes in the supply and price of food, especially the increased availability of alcohol, could also have a substantial impact on post-communist health.

However, the most significant findings, mostly from the public health literature, focus on increased levels of psychosocial stress and the related increase in alcohol consumption and other risky 'coping' behaviours.

Stress (the anxiety/fear caused by a person's perception of a challenge and the perceived inability to meet those challenges) has long been recognized to be associated with cardiovascular disease. The stress response is necessary for all life to respond to various stimuli in the environment, but damage to health comes when stress levels are maintained for long periods of time[7] because the body cannot adequately recover normal levels of the hormone cortisol. Elevated cortisol levels have been linked to impaired cognitive performance, suppressed thyroid function, blood sugar imbalances, decreased bone density and muscle tissue, higher blood pressure, suppressed immunity, increased stomach fat (which in turn is linked to a variety of cardiovascular diseases). Thus, multiple mechanisms have been found by which psychological and social stressors 'get under the skin' to affect a wide range of pathologies.[8]

Such stress may also reasonably be assumed to be a cause of some of the massive increase in the suicide rate in the post-communist world, in addition to killing through other types of 'violent mortality'. Stress can of course lead to poor health through an increase in 'risky' behaviour, such as using alcohol or drugs as a coping mechanism.

Thus, the major finding of the public health literature is that an increase in stress and an increase in alcohol consumption has had a prominent effect on the post-communist mortality crisis, but that these factors leave a large amount of variance between countries and variance within countries over time unexplained. Comparative data on life expectancy and region are shown in Table 11.1. Moreover, this finding forces us to ask, what explains variation in stress and risky behaviour both over time and between countries? We provide a first attempt to answer this by investigating the effect of implementing large-scale privatization programmes on mortality.

Policy choice and the mortality crisis

What remains mostly unasked is how does 'transition policy' relate to the post-communist mortality crisis. Overall, the neo-liberal policy package termed 'shock therapy' – combining rapid and comprehensive liberalization and privatization with strict monetarist stabilization policies – won the day. Although implementation of the 'three shocks' varied, the full policy package was implemented in Russia by 1994, and most other countries implemented some or all of its components by the mid-1990s.

Neo-liberals expected that the transition from the planned to the market economy would catalyse the 'epidemiologic transition' as found in Western societies, in which modernization leads to declines in overall mortality and a decrease in its variability until it reaches a low and stable level.[9] In the mid-1990s Sachs theorized that 'liberalization' would lead to increases in life expectancy, while Prichett and Summers believed it would lead to lowered infant mortality rates and longer life expectancy.[10]

Neo-liberals have never suggested that actually implementing their prescribed policies might have contributed to the public health crisis, and in fact offer no structural account at all. They ultimately resort to will-based, or voluntaristic, explanations to the mortality crisis: poor health is related to poor personal choices. Therefore the policy advice is that individuals must decide to make better choices and take better care of themselves (and perhaps to

Table 11.1 Mass privatization and life expectancy by country and region

Region	*Country*	*Mass privatization*	*Date*	*Life expectancy change (1989–2002)*[a]
Balkans	Georgia	Yes	1995	1.04/1.43%
	Armenia	Yes	1994	2.81/3.89%
	Azerbaijan	No	–	−5.11/−7.35%
Baltics	Lithuania	Yes	1993	1.29/1.83%
	Estonia	No	–	1.71/2.46%
	Latvia	Yes	1994	1.53/2.21%
Central Asia	Kyrgyz Republic	Yes	1994	−3.52/−5.14%
	Uzbekistan	No	–	−2.50/−3.61%
	Kazakhstan	Yes	1994	−6.66/−9.79%
	Turkmenistan	No	—	−1.25/−1.90%
	Tajikistan	No	–	−3.99/−5.68%
Central Eastern Europe	Czech Republic	Yes	1994	3.50/4.88%
	Slovenia	No	–	0.94/3.73%
	Slovakia	No	–	2.73/1.30%
	Poland	No	–	3.55/5.00%
	Hungary	No	–	3.09/4.44%
Former Soviet Union	Russia	Yes	1992	−3.57/−5.16%
	Ukraine	Yes	1995	−0.59/−0.86%
	Belarus	No	–	−2.20/−3.13%
SEE	Romania	Yes	1995	0.56/0.80%
	Bulgaria	No	–	0.31/0.44%
	Bosnia	No	–	0.96/1.31%
	Macedonia	No	–	1.60/2.22%
	Croatia	No	–	1.80/2.50%
	Albania	No	–	1.85/2.56%
	Moldova	Yes	1994	−0.55/−0.81%
Total Δ		Avg. Δ Privatization		−0.38 years/−0.61%
		Avg. Δ Non-privatization		+0.23 years/0.36%
Average difference	Δ Privatization – Δ Non-privatization =			−0.61 years/−0.97%
Average LE difference[b]	Avg. LE privatization – Avg. LE non-privatization			−0.90 years

[a] When available, otherwise longest difference available. (Equivalent to the unadjusted estimate of LE on mass privatization.)

[b] Correlation coefficients: $R_{LE} = -0.29$, $R_{LEmale} = -0.33$, $R_{LEfemale} = -0.20$.

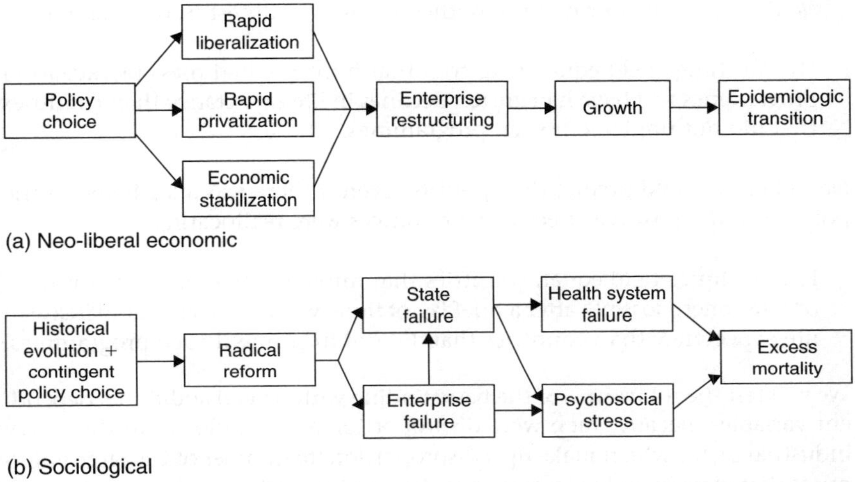

Figure 11.1 Neo-liberal economic (a) and sociological (b) theories of post-communist health experience

support educational campaigns). A recent study conducted by the World Bank on the Russian mortality crisis concluded that 'Russians must ease back on the bottle, cut down on smoking, watch their diet and lead healthier lives if they are to reverse population decline and maintain economic growth ... Though the report referred to the Russian's legendary fondness for vodka, it also cited excessive smoking, poor diet and low personal fitness as contributory factors.'[11]

We consider this a non-explanation. It begs the question, *why did people all over the post-communist world start making worse personal choices, and why much more so in some countries rather than others?* Such decisions could in no sense be considered 'rational' in the medium or long term – so why did people decide to start discounting the future so heavily? There must be a change in people's environment to trigger this behaviour. We seek an answer to these questions by providing a sociological analysis of the effects of the most contested of all transition policies, mass or 'shock' privatization.

Our causal model identifies supply and demand shocks from mass privatization programmes that undermine economic organizations, producing a decline in economic activity and a rise in barter, both leading to declining state revenues, producing a decline in its capacity. The state can no longer supply the inputs necessary for medium and hi-tech production, including skilled labour, creating a vicious circle of declining enterprises and a failing state.[12] The generalized organizational failure resulting from these processes increases physical and emotional stress for all involved, and diminish the organizational strength of care-giving institutions. These two social facts combine to increase mortality. Figure 11.1 compares the neo-liberal with the sociological causality.

We thus generate our main hypothesis that we will test in the chapter:

> H_1: All things held equal, countries that implemented mass privatization programmes will have had greater declines in life expectancy than countries that did not implement such programmes.

Neo-liberals would predict the opposite, even if there was a lag between the policy and the positive effect while resources were reallocating.

> H_2: All things held equal, countries that implemented mass privatization programmes, possibly after a brief lag of time, will have a greater increase in life expectancy than countries that did not implement such programmes.

We will test the robustness of the basic finding with several additional dependent variables. Because men were disproportionately employed in the heavy industrial sector which make up a disproportionate number of the large enterprises that were included in mass privatization programmes, we would expect men to suffer from more psychosocial stress than women. We look at the difference between male and female changes in life expectancy as one test for robustness. Thus, contingent on H_1 being supported, we test:

> H_3: All things held equal, mass privatization programmes will have a larger negative effect on male life expectancy than female life expectancy.

To further test for the robustness of our psychosocial stress mechanism, we compare the effect of mass privatization on the rate of two causes of death which we can reasonably assume are to a significant extent the result of increased psychosocial stress – alcohol-related deaths and suicides. As a final variable to test for the psychosocial stress mechanism, we add ischaemic heart disease (IHD) or coronary artery disease, which has been shown to be related to anger and socio-emotional distress.[13]

> H_4: All things held equal, countries that implemented mass privatization programmes will have higher increases in the rates of alcohol-related deaths, suicide and ischaemic heart disease than countries that did not implement such programmes, and
> H_5: The increase in these rates will be greater for men than for women.

The sociological explanation for the post-communist collapse emphasizes that the economic crisis that contributes to the psychosocial stress will also undermine state capacity, and thus medical provision, further contributing to the mortality crisis. In the analysis we use a variety of measures of health provision (per capita number of physicians, nurses, dentists, hospital beds, inpatient admissions, as well as public health spending as a percentage of GDP and finally the log of absolute levels of public health spending). Thus we generate additional hypotheses.

> H_6: All things held equal, countries that implemented mass privatization programmes will have declining health provision (hospital beds, physicians, nurses, dentists, public health spending, inpatient admissions), and
> H_7: This decrease in health provision will increase mortality.

Data and methods

We construct a panel using the January 2005 mortality data from the WHO Mortality Database and the January 2006 European Health for All Mortality Database for 26 transition countries in central and eastern Europe including the Baltics, Russia and other members of the former Soviet Union.[14] Economic and social variables are derived from the World Bank's World Development Indicators (2005), the European Bank for Reconstruction and Development (EBRD) *Transition Report* (2003), the TransMONEE database (2003), and the World Bank/EBRD Business Environment and Enterprise Performance Survey (1999). Econometric analyses are conducted using LimDep version 8.0 and Stata version 9.

Modelling framework

The most appropriate statistical estimator is the fixed-effect model.[15] Differences in changes in life expectancy that arise from differences between countries are excluded from the analysis. In essence, this is like putting in a set of country dummy variables. This allows us to isolate the effect of our policy variable (mass privatization), without worrying about differences between countries or country-specific factors that might impact on changes in public health. This estimation is by far the most conservative estimate.

The model

Our basic model is that life expectancy can be explained by the effects of implementing a mass privatization policy, economic growth, and the standard control variables used in demography:

$$\begin{aligned} \mathrm{LE}_{it} = \alpha + \beta_1\,\mathrm{MPRIV}_{it} + \beta_2\,\mathrm{GDP}_{it} + \beta_3\mathrm{DEP}_{it} + \beta_4\mathrm{FERT}_{it} \\ + \beta_5\mathrm{URBAN}_{it} + \beta_6\mathrm{EDUC}_{it} + \theta\lambda_{it} + \varepsilon_{it} \end{aligned} \tag{11.1}$$

where *i* denotes country and *t* time; MPRIV is coded as 0 for years preceding mass privatization (initiation of a programme that privatized at least 25 per cent of large SOEs with a combination of vouchers and insider giveaways) and 1 for years following the implementation of mass privatization (the coding is taken from country descriptions in the EBRD's *Transition Report* for 1996 and 1999). GDP is the log of per capita GDP in constant US$. DEP is the dependency ratio (the fraction of the population composed of elderly persons and children). FERT is the fertility rate in expected births per woman; URBAN is the percentage of the population living in urban settings.

Appendix 11.1 defines all variables and presents descriptive statistics.

Main results

The result of the basic equation is presented in model 2 of Table 11.2.[16] Mass privatization knocks 0.86 years off overall life expectancy. Time dummies for each year, not presented, did not significantly modify the direction or magnitude of the covariates, indicating the results were not artefacts of period effects. The impact of GDP per capita on health is, as expected, positive, by which an order of magnitude increase in GDP per capita corresponds to a 1.4 year increase in life expectancy. The 'break-even' effect of the health benefits resulting from increased economic performance relative to the adverse effect of mass privatization would require a 4.2-fold increase in GDP to achieve offsetting life expectancy gains of 0.86 years.

We tested a variety of public health indicators to try to capture the effect of state collapse on the mortality explosion (results not shown). Surprisingly, per capita numbers of doctors, nurses, hospital beds, as well as health expenditures as a percentage of GDP and log of total health expenditures in constant dollars had no significant effect.

We must interpret this with caution, however. In turbulent periods money flowing towards health systems may not be a suitable indicator of health system performance, particularly with the documented rise of informal health care payment mechanisms.

The only finding that may indicate that shrinking health care capacity is contributing to life expectancy trends is the positive effect of the number of dentists per 100,000 (an increase of the rate of 1 increases life expectancy by 0.05 years). During periods of economic flux, dentists, substituting for surgeons, may play a more prominent role in ensuring population health (for example, due to the diverse nature of their abilities, many military establishments favour the enlistment of dentists to physicians). Another interpretation of this finding may relate to the migration experience of dentists relative to physicians. The period of transition was marked by high levels of cross-country migration, particularly for the specialist classes. The promise of better compensation under market-driven health-financing reforms may have lured dentists away from countries with bleaker economic outlooks, whereas physicians may have had less opportunity to benefit from emigration. The positive effect of dentists on life expectancy may therefore indicate that countries which retained dentists fared better socially and economically during transition than others, possibly accounting for the observed effect in a manner unrelated to health care delivery. At any rate, one statistically significant effect out of eight indicators is not very strong – and is moving dangerously close to being indistinguishable from a result of chance.

Table 11.2 Impact of mass privatization on life expectancy in transition countries

Covariates	*Model 1: POLS*	*Model 2: Fixed effects*[a,b]	*Model 3: 2SLS (IV)*[a]	*Model 4: Treatment effects (IV)*[c]	*Model 5: Random effects (IV)*[a,c]	*Model 6: Fixed effects (IV)*[a,b]
Mass privatization	*−1.79 (0.32)***	*−0.86 (0.22)***	*−1.17 (0.43)***	*−3.34 (0.40)***	*−5.14 (0.53)***	*−0.91 (0.35)***
GDP	−0.33 (0.11)**	1.38 (0.24)**	0.08 (0.16)	−0.35 (0.11)**	−0.37 (0.14)**	1.38 (0.24)**
Urbanization	−0.02 (0.02)	−0.00 (0.07)	−0.04 (0.02)	−0.01 (0.02)	0.00 (0.02)	0.00 (0.07)
Dependency	−0.22 (0.04)**	0.15 (0.04)**	−0.12 (0.04)*	−0.17 (0.04)**	−0.15 (0.05)**	0.15 (0.04)**
Fertility	−1.15 (0.60)*	−0.77 (0.32)*	0.22 (0.53)	1.07 (0.54)*	0.35 (0.74)	−0.79 (0.33)*
Price liberalization	0.48 (0.19)*	−0.02 (0.11)	0.01 (0.12)	0.72 (0.20)**	1.11 (0.26)**	−0.01 (0.13)
Education	0.03 (0.01)*	0.07 (0.01)**	0.02 (0.01)	0.06 (0.01)**	0.02 (0.02)	0.07 (0.01)**
Lambda	–	–	–	1.55 (0.24)**	3.24 (0.33)**	0.04 (0.20)
Number of observations	313	313	313	313	313	313
Number of countries	26	26	26	26	26	26
R^2	0.37	0.93	0.36	0.46	0.62	0.94

Notes: Hausman $\chi^2 = 44.27$, $p < 0.001$; favours FEM; constant not reported; one-way fixed effects with country-specific effects presented, period effects do not alter results.

[a] Prais-Winsten transformation to calculate AR(1) error structure.

[b] Mass privatization and GDP significant at $p < 0.05$ using White robust covariance matrix.

[c] Standard errors adjusted for selection.

* $p < 0.05$.

** $p < 0.01$ (two-tailed tests).

The basic finding, that mass privatization decreases life expectancy, also holds when we put in (very imperfect) controls for nutrition: the availability of fruits and vegetables, the availability of protein, and the availability of alcohol (results available on request from the authors).

Thus, if we can rule out health resources, and nutritional changes, we are left with psychosocial stress. We do a series of tests of the robustness of this explanation. First, since men were disproportionately employed in the big enterprises subject to mass privatization, we would expect a bigger effect on men than women. As can be seen in Table 11.3, mass privatization knocks 1.99 years off male life expectancy, far more than the 0.7 years for women. Urbanization exerts a strongly negative effect on life expectancy (−0.5), but only for men. Fertility also exhibits a larger effect on men, roughly fourfold higher than the non-significant effect on women. Fertility declined in nearly all of the post-communist countries, in some plummeting to dangerously low sub-replacement levels with profound demographic implications. Using the main specification to regress fertility on mass privatization roughly suggests that mass privatization suppressed fertility by −0.20 births per woman (results not shown). This follows a rich body of literature that finds fertility is determined by a panoply of social and economic factors,[17] primarily those which shape a household's desired number of children.

We look at three other variables associated with psychosocial stress: alcohol-related mortality, suicide, and ischaemic heart disease (Table 11.3). Mass privatization programmes increased rates of alcohol-related mortality causes by 41 per 100,000 in males and 6.68 in females – approximately a six-fold difference. These results are similar in magnitude to the health-promoting effect of a 10-fold increase in GDP. We find the same patterns of findings for fertility and urbanization as in model 12 and 13. Higher education levels significantly decrease alcohol mortality, but only among females.

Mass privatization explains an increase of 5 suicides per 100,000 people for men, quite large given the rare nature of a suicide. By rough comparison, in the US in 1996, suicide claimed the lives of 10.8 males per 100,000 population (US Public Health Service, 1999). The effect for women is only 0.25 years, and it is not statistically significant. Mass privatization also increases the rate of ischaemic heart disease by 20.49 for men and 7.24 for women. The effect on both genders are statistically significant and large, but they are three times larger for men (20.49 to 7.24).

Of the covariates, it is noteworthy that the direction of the effect of fertility reverses, corresponding to decreases in male suicide. This may relate to the psychosocial benefits of family size in face of economic stress, possibly indicating a role of fertility experience as a coping mechanism for men. Increased levels of education also appear to buffer against suicide risk and ischaemic heart disease – and this effect holds for women as well, although the effect is much smaller. This variable may capture the ability of people with higher education to find new, better jobs in the private sector.

Table 11.3 Effect of mass privatization on violent mortality in transition countries, by gender and disease

Covariates	*Model 19: Male LE*	*Model 20: Female LE*	*Model 21: Male Alcohol MR*	*Model 22: Female Alcohol MR*	*Model 23: Male Suicide*	*Model 24: Female Suicide*	*Model 25: Male IHD*	*Model 26: Female IHD*
Mass privatization	*−1.99 (0.33)***	*−0.70 (0.25)***	*41.19 (11.78)***	*6.68 (2.56)***	*5.29 (1.08)***	*0.25 (0.25)*	*20.49 (4.33)***	*7.24 (1.54)***
GDP	1.98 (0.36)**	1.16 (0.28)**	−42.16 (13.26)**	−10.74 (2.88)**	−3.97 (1.16)**	−0.30 (0.27)	−37.54 (4.63)**	−10.54 (1.65)**
Urbanization	−0.51 (0.11)**	−0.04 (0.08)	13.22 (3.63)**	0.02 (0.79)	1.43 (0.34)**	0.08 (0.08)	11.67 (1.35)**	3.67 (0.48)**
Dependency	−0.01 (0.06)	0.08 (0.05)	−2.46 (2.08)	−0.41 (0.45)	0.29 (0.19)	0.02 (0.04)	−1.29 (0.75)	−0.24 (0.27)
Fertility	−1.65 (0.59)**	−0.44 (0.45)	42.42 (17.68)*	7.66 (3.84)*	−4.61 (1.66)*	0.07 (0.38)	10.77 (6.62)*	3.94 (2.35)
Price liberalization	0.18 (0.17)	0.02 (0.13)	−14.42 (5.99)*	−2.26 (1.30)	1.45 (0.56)	0.04 (0.13)	−1.55 (2.23)*	−0.57 (0.79)
Education	0.04 (0.02)**	0.06 (0.01)**	−0.94 (0.49)	−0.38 (0.11)**	−0.26 (0.05)**	−0.07 (0.01)**	−1.01 (0.18)**	−0.25 (0.07)**
Number of observations	235	235	275	275	297	297	297	297
Number of countries	25	25	24	24	25	25	25	25
R^2	0.93	0.91	0.86	0.92	0.97	0.95	0.93	0.93

Notes: Models 21–26 mortality rates per 100,000; constant not reported; fixed effects with country effects presented, period effects do not alter results; Prais-Winsten transformation used to accommodate AR(1) error structure.

Finally, we turn to the effects of mass privatization on the supply of health care, even though we have already seen that we have only very weak evidence of the decline of health services having a statistically significant impact on the rise in mortality (results not shown). Mass privatization has a very modest, but statistically significant, negative effect on the number of physicians per 1000 people (−0.15), dentists per 100,000 people (−3.92) and hospital beds per 100,000 people (−0.72). In fact, it seems that mass privatization increases the relative and even the absolute levels of health care spending – possibly through an increase in the number of paying customers as a result of the negative effects of the associated stress on health, and/or as a result of an increase in cost of the health care that is available (so that more money may well be spent on less health care). Indeed, mass privatization increased both the relative and absolute levels of spending on public health. Thus, countries that mass privatized had an increase of 0.6 per cent of GDP spent on health care. They also experienced a large (20 per cent) and statistically significant effect on absolute levels of spending.[18]

Returning to our hypotheses – we can safely accept H_1 (all things held equal, countries that implemented a mass privatization programme will have had greater declines in life expectancy than countries that did not implement such programmes) and reject H_2, the neo-liberal alternative (all things held equal, countries that implemented mass privatization programmes, after a brief lag of time, will have a greater increase in life expectancy than countries that did not implement such programmes).

We also find strong evidence in favour of accepting H_3, 'All things held equal, mass privatization programmes will have a larger negative effect on male life expectancy than female life expectancy' and H_4, 'All things held equal, countries that implemented mass privatization programmes will have higher increases in the rates of alcohol-related deaths, suicide and ischaemic heart disease than countries that did not implement such programmes', and H_5, 'The increase in these rates will be greater for men than for women.'

We find mixed evidence on H_6, 'All things held equal, countries that implemented mass privatization programmes will have declining health provision (hospital beds, physicians, nurses, dentists, public health spending, inpatient admissions).' We have modest negative effect on the availability of physicians, dentists and hospital beds per capita. It also increased relative and absolute spending on health care.

Surprisingly, we find only very weak evidence for H_7, 'The decrease in health provision will increase mortality.' Only one of seven indicators (number of dentists) had a statistically significant effect – and this might be picking up differential opportunities for emigration.

We must use caution when interpreting this final negative result. It might be the case that informal networks are able to compensate for the reduction in health resources somehow. It might be a problem in measuring health resources in the chaotic and highly informal post-communist economies that results in this weak finding. It also might well be, that even if 'civil society' has somehow been able to mitigate the effects of declining official resources, this does not mean it will be able to do this in the future. Russia, for example, faces looming epidemics in HIV and drug-resistant tuberculosis. Russia will need substantially more resources to deal with these problems.[19]

Endogeneity

The major remaining objection to our findings, and one immediately raised by most economists, is the problem of endogeneity. That is, there might be some set of conditions (such as a terrible political and economic crisis) that both causes the adoption of mass privatization policies and would have caused the post-communist mortality crisis anyway. Perhaps the very worst off countries to begin with, facing the greatest economic challenges with the least going for them, adopt mass privatization as a measure of desperation. If this were the case, it is perfectly possible that the statistical estimations of the effects of mass privatization on life expectancy are spurious, since life expectancy was going to fall no matter what policy was adopted.

We can address this problem statistically.[20] We show the results of a probit model on predicting the adoption of mass privatization in Table 11.4. The

Table 11.4 Determinants of mass privatization

Covariate	*Probit*[a]	*Probit ME*[a]
log(GDP)	0.43 (0.28)	0.08 (0.06)
log(FDI)	−0.35 (0.35)	−0.65 (0.61)
log(IMF)	0.03 (0.02)	0.01 (0.00)
Urbanization	−0.04 (0.05)	−0.01 (0.01)
Dependency	0.09 (0.06)	0.02 (0.01)
Fertility	−3.46 (0.99)**	−0.65 (0.25)**
Education	−0.11 (0.03)**	−0.02 (0.01)**
Political freedom index	−0.35 (0.20)	−0.07 (0.04)
Price liberalization	1.44 (0.25)**	0.27 (0.10)**
Years central planning	0.04 (0.04)	0.01 (0.01)
Ethnic minority	1.48 (0.46)**	0.28 (0.13)**
FSU	4.81 (1.10)**	0.79 (0.14)**
CEEB	0.77 (0.86)*	0.17 (0.22)
Number of observations	313	313
Number of countries	26	26
χ^2	196.83**	196.83**
Pseudo-R^2	0.56	0.56

[a] Clustered standard errors for intra-group correlation. Prais-Winsten transformation to accommodate first-order autocorrelation; discrete marginal effects given by $\partial F/\partial x = F(x_1{}^*\beta) - F(x_0{}^*\beta)$; continuous marginal effects evaluated at $\bar{x}$.
*$p < 0.05$.
**$p < 0.01$ (two-tailed t-test).

biggest determinant of implementing a mass privatization programme is being a member of the former Soviet Union (FSU) (such countries were roughly 79 per cent more likely to implement such a programme). We think this demonstrates a large 'policy diffusion' effect or 'mimetic isomorphism'. That is, countries looked to the policies of powerful neighbours when formulating policies. There are other important determinants as well.

The relative size of the second biggest ethnic group is also a highly significant predictor of privatization experience. The data are divided into three groups, so that each third (~20 per cent difference) increases the chance of implementing a mass privatization programme by about 28 per cent. What we think is happening is that newly independent political elites of the FSU use mass privatization to remove the ethnically Russian population that had immigrated to the 'near abroad' to fill positions in new industries. Thus, the elites of the new countries that emerged from the disintegration of the Soviet Union could have used mass privatization policies as a vehicle of removing the Russian managers in charge of large industrial enterprises that were established by Soviet industrialization.[21] Therefore, the bigger the ethnic minority, the greater the chance mass privatization will be employed.

Countries that introduced price liberalization (measured on the EBRD's 1–4.3 point scale) were more likely to implement mass privatization programmes by 27 per cent for each point. Presumably, this represents a general neo-liberal ideology on the part of policy makers. Crucially, levels of external debt, long-standing debt, IMF credit, and IMF credit to external debt ratios did not enter significantly into the model of mass privatization. Thus there does not seem to be an economic factor that could have provoked the mortality crisis even in the absence of shock therapy or mass privatization.

Several socio-demographic variables were also predictive. Higher levels of fertility corresponded to lower probabilities of mass privatization. To the extent that fertility is a proxy for each country's stage in the demographic transition, these findings suggest that less advanced countries (i.e. with higher fertility) were also less likely to rapidly privatize SOEs as a reform strategy. This fits our theory, as our domestic mechanism, ethnic political competition, only becomes salient where there was a large inflow of ethnic Russians, which was a by-product of Soviet-led industrialization. Tertiary education also decreased the likelihood of mass privatization – such that each percentage point of higher education reduces the likelihood of implementing a mass privatization programme by 2 per cent. This could be capturing a large specialist/expert class, which might favour privatization via management and employee buyouts or via FDI to mass privatization.

Using each cross-sectional observation to predict the likelihood of a country having adopted a mass privatization programme correctly predicts 87 per cent of the actual outcomes (results available on request from authors).

When we use the techniques that account for endogeneity, we find that the effect of mass privatization is actually magnified. That means that those countries that implemented mass privatization had characteristics that indicated they would have had an increase in life expectancy with the transition (models 3–6, Table 11.1). In model 5, for example, the effect is magnified, estimating that mass privatization knocks off 5.14 years of life expectancy. The selection parameter λ indicates that countries that had mass privatization programmes have better health-promoting conditions (by 3.24 years), and that the effect of mass privatization programmes was adverse to health independent of these conditions. Finally, when we include the selection effect in the fixed effects model (model 6), the estimate increases slightly to 0.91 and the selectivity coefficient falls from significance. This suggests that the factors that predisposed countries to differentially adopt mass privatization programmes were relatively time-invariant, and that either fixed effects or differencing models annihilates this bias.

Let us summarize the interpretation of the selection models. The method of privatization tends to be 'politically' rather than 'economically' determined. In fact, the biggest factor in explaining intra-FSU variation is ethno-national structure – which is historically determined. Mostly, it was affected by the timing and extent of industrialization. Those regions that were industrialized under the Soviet Union had a large ethnic Russian population that staffed many of the specialist occupations of the new enterprises. Thus, the countries that mass privatized were also likely to be the more industrialized ones. More industrialized countries should have had fewer very poor people, and thus we would expect that any given economic shock will be less likely to push people below some (socially understood) basic level of consumption to maintain good health. They also will have a more highly educated labour force, and are thus more likely to have the professional expertise to implement improved public health measures (e.g. the presence of Russian-educated doctors in the universal Soviet-sponsored health care system). Thus, our analysis suggests that to the extent countries that mass privatized differed significantly from countries that did not mass privatize, this difference suppresses the effect of mass privatization on mortality.

Conclusion

Overall, our primary findings are quite clear and robust: the implementation of mass privatization policies substantially decreases life expectancy via the mechanism of psychosocial stress, and that this explains part of the distribution of mortality experiences across gender and accounts for the unique patterns of violent mortality. We are not claiming that this is the only cause of declining life expectancy, only that is a major cause. This analysis goes beyond the existing understanding of both the public health literature and the economics literature – that the post-communist mortality crisis can be explained by unhealthy and risky lifestyles (especially drinking) as well as psychological stress – by identifying one of the policies that induced this stress.

Mass privatization goes a long way to explaining the mortality differences between central eastern Europe and the 'mortality belt' in the FSU. Only the Czech Republic implemented a large enough mass privatization to count by our operationalization, but even this programme was far smaller in scale and scope than the Russian version. Importantly, the best quantitative[22] and qualitative[23] evidence shows that mass privatized firms had worse performance than other enterprises. It is likely that the Czech Republic's extremely low unemployment rate and the provision of social democratic welfare benefits probably mitigated the increase in stress associated with mass privatization.[24]

An alternative explanation for our findings would be that mass privatization proxies for the propensity of countries to implement radical policy reforms more generally and that it is not mass privatization per se that directly impacts on life expectancy. Future work needs to operationalize these other transition policies and see their individual and combined effects on life expectancy, and to test whether the sequence of reforms is important. We wish to stress that these are just a set of first findings relating economic policies to demographic outcomes. Much more work needs to be done. This includes expanding the list of policies to include price, trade and foreign exchange liberalization, as well as stabilization programmes. We believe this will explain even more of the variation in mortality patterns in the post-communist world, such as the spike in Russian mortality following the 1998 default and devaluation (as this was a result of the IMF condition of funding government spending with special bonds (the super high-yield GKOs), creating a huge financial pyramid (and a stock market bubble) on top of a crumbling real economy, combined with current account convertibility). If the mechanism is economically induced psychosocial stress, these other policies might reasonably be expected to have similar effects as mass privatization.

We must emphasize that the neo-liberals' political prediction – that delays in large-scale privatization will result in lack of 'transition progress' or even a reversal of reforms – has been shown to be false. Both Poland and Slovenia greatly delayed large-scale privatization, but have not suffered economically or ended up any less 'Western'. In fact, they have the highest overall growth rates in the post-communist world (excluding East Asia). Ironically, by increasing stress to catastrophic levels, mass privatization is likely to do more harm than good for the long-term prospects for capitalism in the region. Mass privatization is not the second or third best way to privatize, as key members of the World Bank thought, but very likely the second worst way. The worst is to directly transfer the nation's most valuable enterprises to cronies in a flagrantly corrupt manner in exchange for political support (e.g. Russia's infamous 'Loans for Shares programme').

The policy implications are clear. Any macroeconomic and microeconomic reforms must consider the potentially gigantic effects these policies can have on public health. These externalities must be internalized in the design of economic policy. This will likely involve two policy solutions. First, implementing economic reforms which do not shatter the existing organizational base of the economy, but instead build on existing institutions. This does not necessarily mean slower reforms, for simple management and employee buyouts in which the non-managerial employees have a legal device to centralize their shares (an ESOP) can be *even faster* than mass privatization programmes.[25]

Second, when disruptive economic reforms are deemed necessary, they must be accompanied by social policy that shields the population's health from associated shocks. Finland and Cuba are examples in these regards. The Finnish economy was hugely reliant on trade with the Soviet Union. Therefore, the collapse of the Soviet economy was experienced as a massive exogenous economic shock. However, an inclusive social policy was able to detach developments in mortality entirely from the health of the economy.[26] Similarly, Cuba suffered enormous external supply and demand shocks from the collapse of the Soviet Union (and the intensification of the US economic sanction regime), and yet its health care system was able to handle this, avoiding a mortality crisis. Cardiovascular disease showed no spike during this period, and actually improved.[27]

Some might question where the revenue for these programmes would come from. But arguing that these policies are too expensive is merely delaying this expense – for the economic consequence of the public health crisis will be paid eventually – only in the future they are paid for in lives in addition to money. If the predicted epidemic of drug-resistant strains of TB and other diseases occurs, and if it is globalized, the cost to the world will be exponentially higher still.

Therefore, it would be appropriate for the Bretton Woods global institutions (the IMF and WB), whose role in the global economy is now subject to furious calls for a fundamental reconstruction from both the left and right,[28] to consider making non-conditional grants for such social programmes in countries in need of economic reform.

Appendix 11.1 Definitions of variables and descriptive statistics

Variable	*Definition*	*Mean*	*SD*	*Min*	*Max*
Health outcome					
Life expectancy	Life expectancy at birth	69.96	2.86	61.67	75.91
Male CVD	Deaths per 100,000 due to myocardial infarction (heart attack), ischaemic and haemorrhagic stroke, coronary heart disease	554.45	201.05	171.52	969.79
Male IHD	Deaths per 100,000 among working age population (15–64) due to heart attacks and coronary heart disease	131.63	55.05	30.26	285.37
Female IHD	Deaths per 100,000 among working age population (15–64)	40.27	19.61	5.19	100.21
Male suicide	Deaths per 100,000 due to suicide and other intentional causes of death	30.48	21.70	1.03	87.43
Female suicide	Deaths per 100,000 due to suicide and other intentional causes of death	6.07	3.56	0.17	16.16
Male alcohol-related mortality	Deaths per 100,000 from combined, selected causes of death known to relate to alcohol. Includes alcohol dependence syndrome, liver cirrhosis and chronic liver disease	221.16	94.92	65.81	546.40
Female alcohol-related mortality	Previous for females	66.46	28.68	18.75	152.73
Policy variables					
Mass privatization	0 prior to implementation, 1 thereafter	0.32	0.47	0.00	1.00
Log GDP	GDP per capita, current US$ 2000	23.11	1.47	20.38	26.97
Political freedom	Heritage Foundation Political Freedom Index, from 1 to 7	3.55	1.99	1.00	7.00
Price liberalization	EBRD Liberalization Index, scale of 1–4.3	3.15	0.93	1.00	4.30
Years of central planning	Number of years under planned economic regime	56.72	13.08	41.00	74.00
Foreign direct investment	Log FDI as a percentage of GDP	0.28	0.37	−0.50	0.28
IMF credit/external debt	Percentage of IMF credit to external debt level	8.80	10.67	0.00	53.56

Sociodemographic					
Urbanization	Percentage of population living in urban areas	56.70	12.44	25.13	75.20
Fertility	Fertility rate (births per woman)	1.85	0.75	1.07	5.04
Dependency	Percentage of population youth + elderly	53.85	10.60	39.49	88.33
Education	Percentage tertiary enrolment	23.38	12.04	2.60	69.30
Ethnic minority	Percentage of population in second largest nationality; country levels ordered by thirds: 0, 1 and 2	0.80	0.88	0.00	2.00
Health resources					
Physicians	Number per 1000 people	3.05	0.85	1.28	5.19
Nurses	Number per 100,000 people	680.54	229.58	143.40	1244.20
Dentists	Number per 100,000 people	33.66	22.45	1.20	83.00
Hospital beds	Number per 100,000 people	8.49	2.68	3.02	13.71
Bed occupancy rate	Hospital bed occupancy rate (%) in acute care facilities	73.17	14.98	25.60	97.00
Health investment	Health expenditures as a percentage of GDP	3.92	1.72	0.20	7.40
Log health investment	Log of health expenditures in current US$ 2000	24.33	1.79	20.04	28.23
Inpatient care	Inpatient care admissions per 100	16.67	5.82	4.57	30.02
Dietary and nutritional inputs					
Alcohol consumption	Pure alcohol consumption (litres per capita)	6.08	3.83	0.17	14.33
Fruit and vegetables	Availability of fruits and vegetables (10 kg)	151.31	42.53	56.40	304.60
Calorific intake	Average number of calories available per person per day	2831.23	393.64	1675.10	3767.90
Protein	Percentage of total energy available from protein	11.92	1.18	9.37	17.00

Appendix 11.2 Competing explanations of post-communist mortality experience

Variable	*Effect size*[a]	*Standard error*[a]	*P-value*[a]	*Unadjusted* R^2	*Change of variable in Russia (1991–94)*	*Magnitude of effect on life expectancy in Russia (1991–94)*
Alcohol consumption	−0.128	0.052	0.015	0.118	+0.950	−0.122
Alcohol-related deaths	−0.015	0.002	<0.001	0.368	N/A	N/A
Cardiovascular disease (male)	−0.010	0.001	<0.001	0.000	+216.088	−2.161
Chronic disease (male)	−0.004	0.001	<0.001	0.035	+223.201	−0.893
Ischaemic heart disease (working age)	−0.041	0.005	<0.001	0.518	+64.040	−2.626
Fruits and vegetables	−0.007	0.003	0.010	0.325	−16.200[b]	+0.113
Calorific intake	0.000	0.000	0.305	0.134	+8.800	0.000
Protein intake	−0.104	0.105	0.324	0.139	−2.630	+0.270
Suicide	−0.202	0.021	<0.001	0.069	+16.070	−3.246
Homicide	−0.011	0.009	0.233	0.270	+17.320	−0.191
Age-dependency ratio	0.142	0.034	<0.001	0.216	+0.275	+0.039
Fertility	−0.744	0.319	0.021	0.146	−0.332	+0.247
Mass privatization	−0.984	0.224	<0.001	0.035	+1.000	−0.984

[a] Fixed effects model adjusted for log(GDP), EBRD Price Liberalization Index, Political Freedom Index, age-dependency ratio, fertility rate, and percentage population with tertiary education.
[b] Denotes $X_{1994} - X_{1992}$.

Notes

1 World Bank, *Dying too Young: Addressing Premature Mortality and Ill Health due to Non-communicable Diseases and Injuries in the Russian Federation* (Washington, DC: The World Bank, 2005); E. Brainerd and D.M. Cutler, 'Autopsy on an Empire: Understanding Mortality in Russia and the Former Soviet Union', *Journal of Economic Perspectives,* 19 (2005) 107–30.
2 It is noteworthy that cardiovascular diseases generally require decades of risk accumulation over the life course before their clinical manifestation as heart attacks and strokes.
3 Swiss Re, 'Special Report: Mortality Risk', *The Review,* (2004) 24–6.
4 UNICEF MONEE Project, 'A Decade of Transition' (Florence: UNICEF, 2001).
5 In 2006 Russia's life expectancy was 159th in the world, one place worse than Guyana, and 11 places worse than Bangladesh.
6 M. Field, D.M. Kotz and G. Bukhman, 'Neoliberal Economic Policy, "State Desertion", and the Russia Health Crisis', in *Dying for Growth: Global Inequality and the Health of the Poor* (Monroe, Me: Common Courage Press, 2000).
7 S. Levine and H. Ursin, 'What is Stress?', in M.R. Brown, G.F. Koob, C. Rivier (eds), *Stress: Neurobiology and Neuroendocrinology* (New York: Marcel Dekker, 1991), pp. 1–21.
8 M. Kristenson, H.R. Eriksen, J.K. Sluiter et al., 'Psychobiological Mechanisms of Socioeconomic Differences in Health', *Social Science and Medicine,* 58 (2004) 1511–22.
9 A.R. Omran, 'The Epidemiologic Transition: a Theory of the Epidemiology of Population Change', *Milbank Quarterly,* 49 (1971) 509–38.
10 Jeffrey Sachs, 'The Transition at Mid-Decade', *American Economic Review,* May 1996; L. Pritchett and L.H. Summers, 'Wealthier is Healthier', *Journal of Human Resources,* 31 (1996) 841–68.
11 Reuters, Moscow, 8 December 2005.
12 L. King and P. Hamm, 'Privatization and State Capacity in Postcommunist Society', William Davidson Institute, Working Paper No. 806, 2005; Lawrence P. King, 'Postcommunist Divergence: a Comparative Analysis of Russian and Polish Capitalism', *Studies in Comparative International Development,* 37, 3 (Fall 2002) 3–34. Lawrence King and Ivan Szelenyi, 'Postcommunist Economic Systems', in Neil Smelser and Richard Swedberg (eds), *Handbook of Economic Sociology,* 2nd edn (Princeton: Princeton University Press, 2005).
13 P.P. Chang, D. Ford, L. Meoni, N. Wang and M. Klag, 'Anger in Young Men and Subsequent Premature Cardiovascular Disease', *Archive Internal Medicine,* 163 (2002) 901–6.
14 The panel is unbalanced because not all data for the regressors are available in the same years.
15 A much longer paper available from the authors includes a full discussion of the various econometric issues raised by our analysis. A Hausman test indicates that fixed effects were preferable to random effects.
16 Model 1 treats each year from each country as an independent case, and utilizes ordinary least squared regression.
17 T.P. Schultz, 'An Economic Model of Family Planning and Fertility', *Journal of Political Economy,* 77 (1969) 153–80.
18 Log transformations of the mortality rate variables, not shown, do not alter the significance or direction of these results.
19 The government will have to spend some of its massive windfall oil revenues (which it is currently stockpiling [as of June 2006]) to deal with this. It is hard to

see where resource-poor transition countries will find similar resources. Harvard Medical School and Open Society Institute, *Review of Tuberculosis Control Programs in Eastern and Central Europe and the Former Soviet Union* (Boston: Harvard Medical School and Open Society Institute, 2001).

20 It could be addressed historically for each case with a detailed political analysis that carefully constructs plausible counterfactuals. We believe that such an analysis in Russia would clearly show that alternatives to mass privatization were quite possible, but this is well beyond the scope of this chapter.

21 Within Russia we think a similar process occurred, as mass privatization was used to oust managers loyal to the all-Soviet side. B. Kogut and A. Spicer, 'Taking Account of Accountability: Academics, Transition Economics and Russia', INSEAD Working Paper, 2005).

22 J. Hanousek, E. Kocenda and J. Svejnar, 'Ownership, Control and Corporate Performance after Large-scale Privatization', William Davidson Institute Working Paper No. 652, 2004; E. Kocenda and J. Svejnar, 'The Effect of Ownership Forms and Concentration on Firm Performance after Large-scale Privatization', William Davidson Working Paper No. 471, 2002.

23 G.A. McDermott, *Embedded Politics: Industrial Networks and Institutional Change in Postcommunism* (Ann Arbor: University of Michigan Press, 2002).

24 Poland had a much smaller programme (about 10 per cent of small and medium enterprises) implemented only in 1995, mostly because of worker resistance. Here too, it is important that enterprises privatized in this way seemed to have poor performance as well (see the case study and statistical evidence summarized in Lawrence P. King and Aleksandra Sznajder, 'The State Led Transition to Liberal Capitalism: Neoclassical, Organizational, World Systems, and Social Structural Explanations of Poland's Economic Success', *American Journal of Sociology,* 12, 3 (November 2006) 751–801).

25 Such reforms, by giving the de facto ownership rights of employees *de jure* status, have the massive economic benefit of eliminating principal–agent problems that devastated so many post-communist firms. Mass privatization programmes also transferred shares to employees, but ESOPs were *de jure* or de facto prohibited. Without a legal device to coordinate worker control, workers' shares quickly move to managers and/or politically connected business groups or banks.

26 M. Jantti, P. Martikainen and T. Valkonen, 'When the Welfare State Works: Unemployment and Mortality in Finland', in G. Cornia and R. Paniccia (eds), *The Mortality Crisis in Transitional Economies* (Oxford: Oxford University Press, 2000).

27 R. Cooper, P. Ordunez, M. Ferrer, J. Munoz and A. Epsinosa-Brito, 'Cardiovascular Disease and Associated Risk Factors in Cuba: Prospects for Prevention and Control', *American Journal of Public Health,* 96, 1 (2006) 94–101.

28 Ngaire Woods, *The Globalizers: the IMF, the World Bank and Their Borrowers* (Ithaca: Cornell University Press, 2006).

Part IV

Alternative Scenarios: Reform without System Change?

12
Belarus: Prototype for Market Socialism?

Mario Nuti

Introduction

Following the break-up of the Soviet Union in December 1991, Russia on 2 January 1992 liberalized most prices, raising them by a large multiple to equilibrium level. This unilateral move forced all other FSU [former Soviet Union] republics to follow Russia, in order to avoid an accelerated drainage of their goods supply towards Russia and those other republics where they fetched highly inflated, liberalized, rouble prices. Russian monopoly of rouble currency issue caused a generalized cash scarcity in other FSU republics and forced them to issue bank-money, which they could still use in settlement of transactions with Russia. But the Russian Gosbank first in June 1992 set a ceiling to these republican issues of non-cash roubles, then disowned them outright. The other republics were forced to transform the republican subsidiaries of Gosbank into proper republican Central Banks, and to issue first their own rouble substitutes then their own republican currency. If the split of the rouble area had preceded Russian price liberalization in an orderly fashion, instead of following it chaotically, the republics could have chosen from the beginning their own independent monetary policy and inflation path. As it happened each republic received an initial inflationary shock from Russian inflation, before following its own macroeconomic path.

Monetary disintegration, both within the FSU rouble area and – officially from September 1991 but in practice from early 1991 – within the Comecon (Council of Mutual Economic Assistance or CMEA) transferable rouble area, disrupted traditional trade flows between FSU republics, and any residual form of planned trade between Comecon partners, exposing state enterprises to market forces. Intra-FSU trade, which represented over 60 per cent of total Soviet trade, collapsed as a result of trading at new relative and absolute prices, very different from the old ones, now settling transactions in hard currencies or barter, and losing credits and budgetary transfers available before the break-up. Both international agencies and the objective state of economic crisis exercised pressure to transform the old centrally planned, state ownership system, towards a private enterprise market system open to international trade and investment. But the similarity in the development of different FSU republics ends here. Individual Comecon countries and – once they had absorbed some of the Russian inflation in the delays of establishing a domestic monetary system – individual FSU republics were now absolutely free to shape their own economic system and policies according to their own wishes. They could have privatized or retained state ownership; liberalized domestic prices or retained subsidies and/or administrative controls, even to the point of recreating a monetary overhang; opened trade or maintained barriers, made their currency convertible or maintained overvalued multiple rates, or they could have moved at different speeds towards different target degrees of system change.

They could follow individual paths, and did. By and large former Comecon member states and FSU republics moved, at different speeds in different fields, towards the introduction of capitalism – for some of them its reintroduction, or restoration. But even 15 years later a small number of FSU republics have made very little progress, both in economic and political terms, towards the new system: Belarus, Uzbekistan, Turkmenistan, until fairly recently Ukraine. In these countries the declared transition intentions are still very far from implementation.

Undoubtedly Belarus is the most glaring laggard, not to say non-starter, both politically and economically, *the* outlier. Arguably it would not have been called a transition economy except by assimilation to the parallel more significant change of other east European and former Soviet countries. Politically Belarus is broadly unchanged, with communist monopoly of power and an authoritarian political system. Economically it is a 'command economy without central planning',[1] in view of the persistent dominance of administrative controls over prices, outputs and foreign trade. Yet Belarus' economic performance – though inferior to that of leading reformers such as the new members of the enlarged EU – has been superior to that of much more committed reformers of the FSU.

A number of questions arise. What impeded Belarus' transition to date? Is Belarus' intermediate regime between socialist planning and capitalist markets a temporary, non-replicable, non-sustainable system, or is it a durable, general, resilient alternative system? If the latter, in what conditions might it operate successfully? Could that system have been successfully adopted by other FSU republics and other members of the bloc, or indeed by the whole Soviet economy avoiding disintegration and collapse?

The answers given in this chapter are that the Belarus economy remained centralized because of the party leadership's fear of losing or weakening their power, and because its economic performance – after an initial drop in GDP relatively small in FSU terms – was not as bad as in other transition economies and notably in Russia. The Belarus model is perfectly feasible and sustainable as long as (1) there are no endemic shortages on the Soviet scale; (2) administered prices are not too far from international relative prices; (3) state enterprises are given significant managerial autonomy and are subject to competition; (4) there is continued access to energy and materials (from Russia in Belarus' case) at prices lower than those paid by its competitors. A corollary of this proposition is that the entire ex-Soviet area could have maintained a command economy if Gorbachev had understood the need to have market clearing prices regardless of the economic system selected, if he had accepted greater enterprise autonomy and opening to foreign trade, as long as Russia's natural resources lasted and Russia continued to support the Union's other republics.

Belarus political and economic system

Belarus politics is broadly unchanged with respect to Soviet days, with communist virtual monopoly of power and a political system that has been called 'quasi-democracy' or 'demagogical democracy'[2] or 'isolationist authoritarianism'.[3] In 1994 Alexander Lukashenko was elected the first president of the new independent republic; he extended his own powers in 1995–96 and 2004, abused them after 1996 and even more so after 2006. A first referendum in May 1995 restored Soviet symbols and established equal status for the Russian and the Belarusian languages. Following a referendum in 1996 Lukashenko replaced Parliament with an appointed/co-opted Palace of Representatives and extended his five years' tenure to seven, thus cancelling the presidential elections due in 1999. Only pro-Lukashenko official parties were allowed into the Palace of Representatives elected in 2000 and 2004. In 2001 Lukashenko was re-elected and in 2004 amended the Constitution eliminating the maximum two terms of presidential tenure, so as to be re-elected in 2006.[4]

In 1996 Lukashenko and Yeltsin joined their countries into a Community, that became a Union in 1997–98 and the 'United State of Russia and Belarus' in 1999; Lukashenko reportedly aspired to preside over it.[5] After Putin's election in 2000 relations with Russia worsened: Putin's idea of a joint state was adding the six Belarus regions to the Russian Federation; plans for a joint currency area – questionable from the start[6] – were shelved; the price of Russian oil and gas exports to Belarus was raised in 2004 and 2007, and Gazprom gained control over the pipeline that crosses Belarus into central Europe. Relations with the EU have been practically frozen since 1996, in spite of Belarus' formal inclusion in the European Neighbourhood Policy towards states bordering with the EU that are not candidate members. The United States have taken a more hostile approach through the 2004 Belarus Democracy Act.[7]

Officially the Belarusian economy is designated as a 'social market economy', a 'Third Way' follower like Uzbekistan, China or Vietnam, but behind this facade we find an almost unchanged incarnation of the old system. Of course none of these countries are conventional Soviet-type economies. Macroeconomic stabilization has been slow and delayed, but has taken place. There is no longer a Central Planning Commission, there are no annual or even five-year plans, there is no longer Comecon nor the transferable rouble within it, no foreign trade planning. There are still administered prices for many goods but by and large these are available at those prices; shortages are still present but are occasional rather than large scale and endemic as they used to be in the Soviet days. State enterprises are still subject to the authority and the orders of sector Ministries but have a greater scope for autonomy. The exchange rate regime has been largely unified and a degree of currency convertibility is in operation. Trade with Russia is now trade with a market economy, and access to foreign trade is the ultimate guarantee of economic decisions being decentralized to the level of state enterprises, which now operate next to new private enterprises.

Of course the social market economy of these countries has nothing in common with the German model that goes under the same label, and their 'Third Way' does not correspond at all to that followed recently, at different times, by various 'progressive parties' in Europe.[8] Specifically, Belarus and the other transition laggards do not recognize, unlike their west European counterparts, the supremacy of markets domestically and internationally; the disadvantages of public ownership and enterprises; the importance of tight budget constraints at all levels.

The best definition of the post-Soviet Third Way was given by Uzbekistan President Islam Karimov,[9] as a system where 'the state is collective entrepreneur, production regulator and public investor in priority sectors'. In truth this is the absolute negation of a market system, where entrepreneurship is not collective but diffused in capillary fashion, where the state regulates markets – if anything – but never production, where public investment takes place almost exclusively in infrastructures, and there are no priority sectors.

The Belarus-type economy can be characterized by ten fundamental economic features:

1 Administrative controls – actual and potential – on prices on a vast scale, for goods of 'social importance' and other goods at central and local level. The share of administered prices in the Consumer Price Index, both in 2000 and 2005, was 27 per cent, with a fall in-between to 21 per cent in 2003. These controls are implemented through product subsidies, price limits, statutory criteria for price fixing, an obligation to communicate and justify price increases, controls on natural monopolies, controls on military supplies, centralized wage-fixing. At least until recently the maximum monthly rate of inflation was decreed by the President. As a consequence, production often has low profitability and there is an incentive also to export goods in short supply. There are some shortages, but nowhere near the large-scale and endemic shortages of Soviet days, and relative prices are closer to international relative prices than they used to be.
2 A small share of the private sector in GDP and employment. Belarus has the lowest private share in GDP among post-communist countries,

25 per cent in the EBRD estimate, which is probably overoptimistic. (Uzbekistan's share comes second, estimated to be 45 per cent, though it is surely exaggerated by the large size of the agricultural sector, formally private but subject to restrictions and central controls on prices, sales and allocations, and on landownership.) Private enterprises are subject to bureaucratic controls, repeated registrations, often punitive fiscal pressure, restricted access to credit[10] – though business registration was simplified in April 2006. Private enterprise credit in the last ten years has been, and still was in 2005, under 10 per cent of the total. The transformation of state enterprises into companies has progressed, but the majority is still in state ownership. The actual privatization of state enterprises is not very advanced, often it is limited by the sale of minority share stakes, or by the government retaining a controlling 'golden share' (abolished in August 2006 in the banking sector) or by sales to 'insiders'. In August 2006 a presidential decree renationalized 82 formerly privatized loss-making enterprises. *Cumulative* privatization revenue was a negligible 3.1 per cent of GDP in 2005, and the early attempts at mass privatization led to the issue of *vouchers* not covered by assets for sale. Landownership is subject to restrictions.

3 Industrial policy is directed at particular sectors, products and even enterprises, with ad hoc regimes of taxes, subsidies and credits; output, employment and the wage bill, and exports, are subject to direct commands, or to *recommendations* – such as recommended price increases or recommended interest rates on bank lending also for private enterprises and banks. Small and medium enterprises (not defined) are supposed to rise between 44,000 and 46,000 in the 2006–10 Development Plan – as if the demography of private firms could be planned.
4 Fiscal policy appears to be inspired by principles of austerity, more than in other transition economies. The consolidated budget recorded a surplus of 2.2 per cent of GDP in the first half of 2006. However such features of fiscal policy are offset by quasi-fiscal net liabilities that do not appear in the budget, being delayed and/or contingent or located in independent institutions. The overall fiscal picture is much less under control than it might seem.
5 Monetary policy has been expansionary, with negative real interest rates, and credits directly assigned to sectors such as agriculture, construction, mining and metallurgy. However, monetary policy has been successful in lowering both interest and inflation rates gradually and steadily over the last six years, down to one-digit inflation in 2006 (estimated at around 7 per cent).
6 In the 1990s the economy was relatively demonetized, and still was in 2000–4 with a ratio between M3 (the more inclusive definition of the quantity of money) and GDP around 15–18 per cent, though it went up to 19.7 per cent in 2005. Dollarization, rampant in the 1990s, has receded.

State banks have a large and increasing share of capital and assets (75 per cent in 2006), although there are signs of increasing competition. More importantly, the share of non-performing loans has been falling steadily and surely from 15.2 per cent in 2000 to 1.9 per cent in 2005.

7 The exchange rate regime, until the early 2000s typically overvalued and segmented into various official and informal sections, is now effectively unified and convertible at a crawling rate, though still subject to limitations. In foreign trade there are still quotas and custom barriers.

8 Foreign direct investment is relatively low, around $300 million in 2005 and 2006 or only about 1 per cent of GDP. In July 2006 the Investment Code was amended, abolishing some preferential treatment for foreign investors, including the freedom to set prices and a moratorium on legislative changes affecting business with foreign capital during the first five years after registration.

9 Domestic and external debts are relatively low – not least because of the unwillingness of potential lenders – though rising and probably underestimated. Belarus still does not have a sovereign rating, but state-owned Belarusian banks are rated by Fitch; in February 2006 the largest state banks were upgraded from CCC+ to B−. The newly amended Banking Code strengthens the supervisory role of the National Bank and bans direct financing of the budget, except in special cases by presidential decree.

10 In 2005 the external sector recorded a surplus for the first time, of 1.5 per cent of GDP, though a record deficit is expected in 2006 when official reserves fell drastically, from as little as 0.7 months' worth of imports in 2005 (0.5 months in 2000–4, instead of the IMF-recommended prudential level of 3 months' worth of imports).

The Belarusian economic system is reminiscent of the Polish system of 1985–89, based on 'permissions and negotiations', with enterprises exercising discretion limited by parameters fixed on a case-by-case basis, negotiated by the enterprise and state organs or among enterprises. Subsidies on products or on enterprises (which in Belarus represent almost 20 per cent of GDP), taxes, prices, quantities, foreign exchange transactions, are all contracted but are diversified and therefore do not have the efficiency implications of market negotiations. The system is 'parametric' but the parameters are multiple, specific and centrally fixed. Inevitably, corruption takes the place of arbitrage.

The later start, slower progress and lower achievements of Belarus' transition are summarized in Figure 12.1, where eight transition indicators estimated by the EBRD (European Bank for Reconstruction and Development)[11] are plotted for Belarus, for the whole of the CIS (except Turkmenistan) and for the Baltic states (that joined the EU on 1 May 2004), for the period 1991–2005. The indices, on a scale from 1 = little or no change, to 4+ = OECD standards, summarize large- and small-scale privatization; enterprise restructuring and corporate governance; trade and foreign exchange liberalization; competition

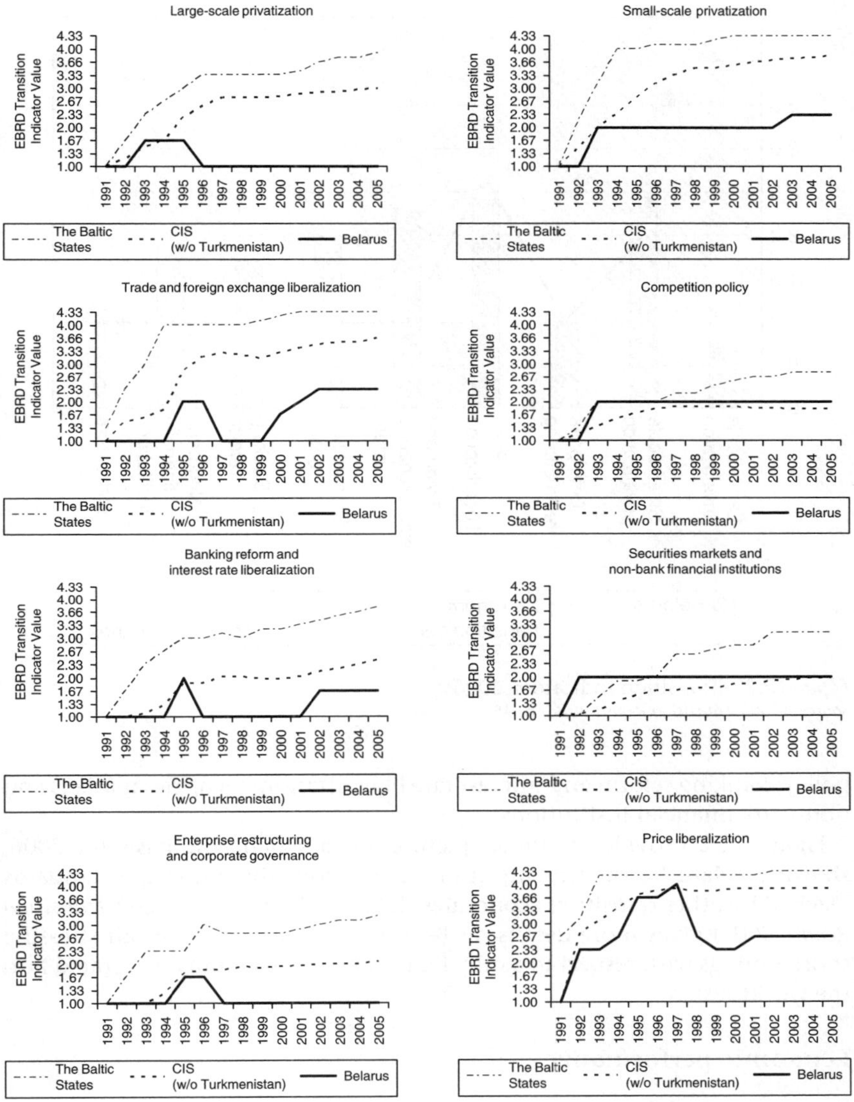

Figure 12.1 Belarus and other FSU countries: transition progress, 1991–2005
Source: EBRD *Transition Reports* 1994–2006.[11] From Yerashenkava[12]

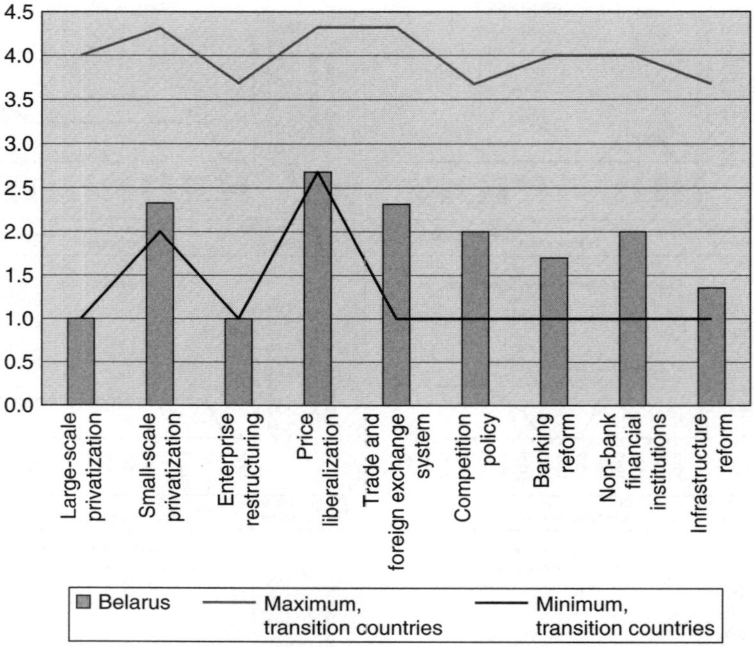

Figure 12.2 Transition indicators, 2006
Source: EBRD *Transition Report 2006*, p. 95

policy; banking reform and interest rate liberalization; securities markets and non-bank financial institutions.

Figure 12.2 provides a similar picture, on a synchronic basis for 2006, showing Belarus' achievements at or barely above the minimum standards reached by other transition economies. Table 12.1 (from the EBRD *Transition Report 2006*) gives more details on Belarus' economic policies, all stressing shortcomings with respect to a fully fledged market economy integrated into the world system.

Economic performance

Belarus' macroeconomic performance, for all the system's shortcomings with respect to a fully marketized system, has been surprisingly good (see Figure 12.3). GDP has fallen less than in any other CIS (Commonwealth of Independent States = former Soviet Union – Baltic states) country and has recovered faster, regaining the 1989 level in 2003 and reaching 120 per cent of it in 2005. Growth has speeded up in Lukashenko's second term (2001–6), at over 7 per cent real growth per annum, with the average monthly wage

Table 12.1 Belarus economic system and policies

Liberalization and privatization	*Business environment and competition*	*Infrastructure*	*Financial sector*	*Social reform*
Current account convertibility – **limited**	Competition Office – **no**	Independent Telecom Regulator – **no**	Capital adequacy ratio – **8%**	Share of population 2002 living in proverty < **2%**
Controls on inward FDI – **yes**	Quality of insolvency law – **medium**	Independent Electricity Regulator – **no**	Deposit insurance – **yes**	Government expenditure on health – **5% GDP**
Interest rate liberalization – **limited de facto**	Secured transactions law – **malfunctioning**	Separation of railway infrastructure/ operations – **no**	Quality of securities market laws –**low**	Government expenditure on education – **6.4% GDP**
Exchange rate regime – **crawling peg**	Quality of corporate governance law – **very low**	Independence of road directorate – **no**	Private pension funds – **no**	Household expenditure on power and water – **4%**
Wage regulation – **yes**		Quality of concession law – **very low**		
Land tradability – **limited *de jure***				

Source: EBRD *Transition Report 2006*, p. 96.

rising from $70 to $270. The World Bank[13] firmly asserts that the progress is not delusory but real. In terms of purchasing power parity US dollars, Belarus GDP per head has gone from $4310 in 1990 to $6970 in 2004 (in the same period Russia has gone from $8340 to $9902, Ukraine from $6930 to $6390, and Poland from $5980 to $12,974).[14]

We have already noted Belarus' excellent performance in bringing down inflation and interest rates, public deficit and current account deficit in the previous section. Unemployment peaked at only 4 per cent in 1996 and in 2004 was down to 1.9 per cent (while the Czech Republic has 9.5 per cent, Hungary 8 per cent, Poland 19.1 per cent, Slovakia 10.6 per cent, and even Russia and Ukraine have 2.6 per cent and 3.5 per cent). Inequality in income distribution – measured by the Gini coefficient, equal to 0 for absolute equality and 1 for absolute inequality (one person takes all) – has barely moved from 22.9 per cent in 1989 to 24.8 per cent in 2004, while rising from a similar start to over 35 per cent and over 40 per cent in many other transition economies. Less than 2 per cent of the population lives below the poverty line (half the median income).

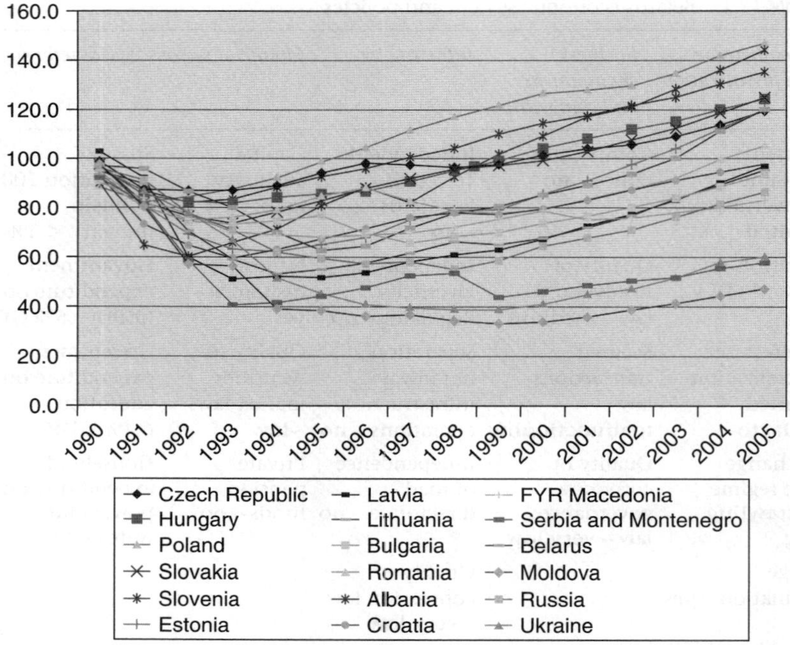

Figure 12.3 Real GDP index (1989 = 100)
Source: UNICEF transMONEE data bank, 2006. See note 14

Clearly the system is not particularly brilliant, nor efficient, but it has a considerable flexibility. Commands are not used all the time, or even very often, but are always a possibility of last resort and therefore a threat. The system has a good capacity of reproducing itself, of re-establishing activity levels already reached in the past after they have decreased for any reason, of growing quantitatively if not qualitatively.

By avoiding drastic transformation Belarus and similar countries have avoided the disorganization and chaos of a systemic vacuum. With respect to Russia, they have maintained law and order, avoided the dissipation of state assets, the disadvantages of insider privatization, fiscal collapse, insolvency on public debt. In this way the deep and protracted transformation recession experienced by all transition economies has been partly avoided or alleviated.

An assessment

Belarus and the other transition laggards have changed little their economic system for several reasons. The Communist Party has maintained its political monopoly and the transition is viewed as a threat to such a monopoly.

Russia has given a bad name to the transition, and the unfavourable developments of the Russian economy (such as corruption, undue appropriation of state assets by *nomenklatura* and insiders/managers, lack of corporate governance mechanisms) are wrongly attributed not to the Russian government mistakes but to transition *tout court*. With a later start than Russia, their policy choices were heavily influenced by the Russian experience.

These countries believe they are different, and in the name of their reputed diversity have chosen a strategy of 'gradualism', that in their case stands for broad inaction. They have not learned from Gorbachev's economic failures, they know that transition/stabilization/liberalization involves immediate disadvantage the immediate political consequences of which they fear, they are not far-sighted enough to anticipate subsequent advantages. Above all, they do not realize the threats to the sustainability of their system.

Many of the changes that Belarus and other laggards wish to avoid are in reality simple and unavoidable consequences of being a monetary economy involved in foreign trade, and sooner or later efficiency requirements will impose them; the alternative is extinction. But it is perfectly feasible that the further evolution of this system might not stop for some time, well before transforming into normal market economies.

For all their similarities with the old Soviet-type system, we need to stress the differences, already anticipated above: decentralization of many enterprise decisions, an absolute price level near-market-clearing (with only brief and sporadic shortages), relative prices not so distant from relative international prices, also thanks to trade with Russian companies which are now market-driven. Lack of market-clearing prices, and the consequent monetary overhang, or repressed inflation with shortages and queues, was lethal to the Soviet-type system because it disabled any attempt to activate a market mechanism to accompany public ownership in order to set up some form of market socialism.[15] The attenuation of such a monetary overhang is an essential feature of the Belarus model and an indispensable ingredient of its feasibility and possible sustainability.

Last but not least, Belarus has – until 2007 – had access to Russian materials and energy at privileged prices, as well as Russian credits, assistance estimated to correspond to about 30 per cent of GDP,[16] thus enjoying a rent with respect to its competitors. A rentier does not have to be as efficient and hard-working as non-rentiers in order to survive.

Not only can the Belarus economic system, if propped up by a share of Russian oil rent, survive indefinitely. So too the entire Soviet economy could have survived, on the strength of its availability of energy and materials, remaining in existence and moderately prospering – especially with oil at $60 a barrel but also at much lower prices even more than two-thirds lower – avoiding both the collapse of its economic system and the transformational recession associated with it. If, and only if, Mikhail Gorbachev had understood that not even the most powerful monopolist in the whole world can determine both quantity and price of its products; that no economy in the world, characterized by division of labour and exchange whether planned or market-oriented, can function efficiently and smoothly at prices kept artificially low, below exchange equilibrium. Once these glaring defects of the Soviet-type system were eliminated, some enterprise autonomy, competition and access to international markets could have implemented a more efficient allocation of resources without shifting the balance from state to private ownership, just as has happened in the case of Belarus.

Notes

1 Mario D. Nuti, 'Belarus: a Command Economy without Central Planning', *Russian and East European Finance and Trade*, 26, 4 (July–August 2000), also in Mario I. Blejer and Marko Skreb (eds), *Transition – the First Decade* (London: Kluwer, 2000).
2 Elean A. Korosteleva, Colin W. Lawson and Rosalind Marsh (eds), *Contemporary Belarus: Between Democracy and Dictatorship* (London and New York: RoutledgeCurzon, 2003); Elena A. Korosteleva, 'Why Belarus is Unique: Explaining Institutional and Electoral Allegiances', paper presented to a Foreign and Commonwealth Office conference, October 2003.
3 Andrew Wilson, 'The East Europeans: Ukraine, Belarus and Moldova', in S. White, Judy Batt and Paul Lewis (eds), *Developments in Central and East European Politics*, Vol. 4 (Basingstoke: Palgrave Macmillan/Duke UP, 2007).
4 Ibid.
5 See Anastasia Nesvetailova, 'Muddling through Crisis: Economic Underpinnings of the Russia–Belarus Union', paper presented to a Foreign and Commonwealth Office conference, October 2003.
6 See John Odling-Smee, *Monetary Union between Belarus and Russia: an IMF Perspective* (Washington, DC: IMF, 2003); Mario D. Nuti, 'The Belarusian Alternative: Transition or Solely Reform', *Belarus Economic Trends*, Quarterly Report No. 2 (April–June 1999) 14–20.
7 Wilson, 'The East Europeans'.
8 See Mario D. Nuti, 'Making Sense of the Third Way', *Business Strategy Review*, 10, 3 (Autumn 1999) 57–67.
9 Islam Karimov, *Building the Future: Uzbekistan – Its Own Model for Transition to a Market Economy* (Tashkent: Uzbekistan Publishers, 1993).
10 See World Bank, *Belarus: Improving the Business Environment* (Washington: January 2003).
11 EBRD – European Bank for Reconstruction and Development (1994–2006), *Transition Reports*, various years, London.
12 Alena Yerashenkava, 'State Enterprises Restructuring in Belarus', degree thesis, Faculty of Economics, University of Rome 'La Sapienza', 2006.
13 World Bank, *Belarus: Window of Opportunity to Enhance Competitiveness and Sustain Economic Growth*, Report No. 32346, Washington, November 2005.
14 See UNICEF-ICDC, transMONEE data bank, Florence, 2006 http://www.unicef-icdc.org/resources/transmonee/
15 See Mario D. Nuti, 'Hidden and Repressed Inflation in Soviet-type Economies: Definitions, Measurements and Stabilisation', *Contributions to Political Economy*, 5 (1986) 37–82; Mario D. Nuti, 'Managing Transition Economies', in White et al., *Developments*, pp. 245–63.
16 Wilson, 'The East Europeans'.

13
Transnational Ties and Transformation of Cuban Socialism

Susan Eckstein

Cuba's world changed dramatically between 1989 and 1991 when the former Soviet bloc countries suddenly transitioned to market democracies, most of all when the Soviet Union joined the dustbin of history. At the time, trade accounted for approximately half of the island's gross national product, and Soviet allied countries for 85 per cent of that trade. Allies of 30 years left Cuba to fend for itself with no forewarning. Under the circumstances, Cuba's economy contracted, over 30 per cent in four years.[1]

Even with the Cold War's end, Washington remained, in the main, committed to bringing Castro's regime to heel. It sought to do so by obstructing island efforts to reintegrate into the world economy, including by strengthening the embargo that for three decades prohibited US trade with, and investment in, Cuba.

The US Congress launched its post-Cold War drive to fuel Castro's demise with promulgation of the Cuban Democracy Act in 1992. The new legislation was designed to destabilize Castro's rule by constricting third-country dealings with Cuba, and by restricting cross-border people-to-people ties. It prohibited foreign-based subsidiaries of US companies from trading with Cuba, called for the withholding of US aid to countries that traded with Cuba, banned ships that landed in Cuba from US ports for six months, and limited émigré family rights to income-share with, and visit, island family.

Four years later Congress passed the Cuban Liberty and Democracy Solidarity (Libertad) Act, which allowed US citizens (mainly Cuban émigrés) to sue international investors who 'trafficked' in property they claimed theirs from prerevolutionary days. The 1996 legislation also specified that Washington could deny such investors visas to visit the USA.

Then, in 2004 the George W. Bush administration tightened the so-called personal embargo, restricting family rights to bond and income-share across borders. It permitted no more than a maximum of one émigré visit to island family every three years, and visits only to immediate kin, to parents, children and siblings, not to grandparents, aunts and uncles, cousins and more distant relatives. It also allowed Cuban Americans to send no more than $300 quarterly to island relatives, and only to the same limited range of kin they could visit. Washington imposed no visitation and remittance restrictions on other Latin American immigrants, who, left to themselves, remitted on average $200–$250 monthly at the century's turn.[2] Although dollars the Cuban diaspora remitted helped families cope with the economic crisis, the White House wished to restrict diaspora cross-border income-sharing to keep Castro's government from accessing the foreign currency.

In that Washington stepped up the screw on Cuba while strengthening ties with communist China and communist Vietnam, its motives were not morally driven by a commitment to democracy over dictatorship. Nor were its motives driven by national security concerns, for Cuba's military prowess never was a match to that of the US, and Castro dramatically downsized his military when faced with the fiscal crisis that the ending of Soviet aid and trade caused. Rather, Congress and the White House responded to the wants of Cuban American lobbyists when formulating Cuba policy, as a quid pro quo for campaign contributions and help in delivering the ethnic group's vote in the largest partisan swing state, Florida, where most island diaspora lived. The lobbyists were unrelenting opponents of Castro who had fled the revolution early on. Having lived the American dream economically, they put money where they wished bear influence. Through PACs (Political Action Committees) that they formed, they channelled campaign contributions to candidates who furthered their anti-Castro mission, which they defined to include a tightening of a socially constructed wall across the Florida Straits at the people-to-people as well as state-to-state level.[3]

A 1994 US–Cuba accord gave 20,000 Cubans annual entry. But the wants of the early émigrés' lobbyists, and of the post-Soviet era arrivals who never knew life before Fidel, differed and conflicted. The New Cubans, as they are called, experienced a different Cuba, the revolution and its unravelling, and they moved to America mainly to improve not only their own lot but that of family they left behind. Even if not fans of Fidel, they in the main perceived themselves more as economic immigrants than political refugees. In contrast to the first ones who fled the revolution, the New Cubans covet ties with their island family. Yet, poor and politically uninvolved, they exert little influence on US policy.

Anti-Castro lobbyists met with some setbacks in their effort to strengthen the wall between the states, although not because of New Cuban influence. For brief periods in non-election years, when the matter of 'the Florida vote' was relegated to the back burner, first the Clinton and then the Bush administration loosened travel and remittance restrictions slightly. Anti-Castro lobbyists faced their biggest setback, however, in 2000, when Congress lifted the embargo on sales of US food and medicine to Cuba. Once freed from fear of criticism of being soft on communism, the agribusiness and the pharmaceutical industry, richer and more powerful than Cuban American lobbyists, fought for access to the untapped island market miles offshore.[4] Profits, not sympathy for communism, led them to press for the partial, one-way embargo opening. But Cuban American lobbyists were sufficiently influential to get Congress to prohibit Cuban government access to US trade financing, without which, they thought, the cash-strapped government would be unable to import US goods. Wrong they were. Within two years the US came to account for nearly one-quarter of island agricultural imports.[5] Castro put his opposition to the US aside to take advantage of the opportunity to lower island import costs.

The European Union (EU), as it became a force unto itself, did little to help Cuba adapt to its post-Soviet crisis when Washington made conditions more difficult for Fidel. The EU's reasons, like those of the US, were political, though not exile-driven. Particularly notable, Cuba's former communist ally the Czech Republic, after joining the European group, led an initiative to deprive the island of aid.[6] The new Czech government, deeply committed to market democracy and dismissive of its past, showed no residue of goodwill toward its former ally. Accordingly, in 1996 the EU adopted a 'common position' that made official EU assistance conditional on island political reform. It blocked Castro from receiving non-emergency humanitarian aid and barred Cuba's entry into the Cotonou Agreement, an EU trade and aid pact with developing countries. Under the influence of Spain's socialist government, however, the EU somewhat softened its stance in 2005. That year the EU suspended diplomatic sanctions it had imposed two years before to reprimand the Cuban government for its biggest crackdown on dissidents in 40 years.

Cuban government efforts to reintegrate into the capitalist world economy

Viewed from the vantage point of Cuba, the imports from the US represented one way that Castro sought to integrate into the market-based world economy. His government had no option following the Soviet bloc's demise, for it lost its main sources of aid, trade and investment. Cuba became a textbook Wallersteinian (and Trotskyite before him) case of the limits of socialism in one country in a capitalist world economy.[7]

Cuba faced difficulty reintegrating into the capitalist world economy partly because stronger states used their political muscle to limit Cuba's economic options. Cuba faced difficulties even after the turn of the century when Venezuela, under left-leaning Hugo Chavez, and communist China, driven at least as much by pragmatic as socialist solidarity considerations, came somewhat to Castro's rescue.

To finance imports and investment, as well as to service a foreign debt dating back to the Soviet era, Cuba needed foreign capital. Needs notwithstanding, Cuba, for one, attracted little foreign aid, especially on a per capita basis (see Table 13.1). Washington not only refused to extend bilateral assistance to Cuba but also used its influence to keep Cuba from accessing multilateral

Table 13.1 Official hard currency sources: aid, investment, exports and tourism in Cuba, the Dominican Republic and El Salvador in selected years

	Cuba	*Dominican Republic*	*El Salvador*
(1) AID			
(a) multilateral aid (millions of dollars)			
1999	8.7	126.4	68.3
(b) net official development assistance or official aid			
(1) millions of dollars			
1994	47	60	305
2000	44	62	180
2004	90	87	211
(2) aid per capita (dollars)			
1994	4	8	55
2000	4	8	29
2004	8	10	31
(2) Tourism (millions $)			
1990	243	900	18
1999	1,714	2,524	211
2004/5	2,100	3,508	543
(3) Direct foreign investment (millions of dollars)			
1990	54.0[a]	133	2
1999	178.2	1,338	231
2000	399.9	–	–
2001	38.9	–	–
(4) Exports			
1990	5,100	2,170	582
1995	1,507	765	998
2000	1,630	5,200	1,164
2004	2,181	5,657	3,220
(5) Long-term foreign debt (US billion dollors)			
2001	10.9	3.3	2.9
2005[b]	12.6	5.8	5.5

[a]1993.
[b]Estimate.
Sources: World Bank (WB), *World Development Indicators 2001* (Washington: WB, 2001), pp. 210, 340, 348, 356; Euromonitor, *World Economic Factbook 1989/1999* (London: Euromonitor, 1998), p. 143; Economist Intelligence Unit (EIU), *Cuba Country Report,* May 2001, p. 20, August 2001, pp. 28, 30, August 2006, p. 28; WB, *World Development Report 1997* (New York: Oxford University Press, 1997), pp. 218, 242; EIU, *Cuba Country Profile 1997–1998*, p. 36 and *1998–1999*, p. 35; WB, *World Tables* (Baltimore: Johns Hopkins University Press, 1995), p. 77; US–Cuba Trade and Economic Council (UCTEC), 'Economic Eye on Cuba' (www.cubatrade.org), 7 July 2002, p. 9 and 26 January 2003, pp. 5, 6.

sources of aid. Cuba, in addition, had difficulty attracting foreign private investment. For the first three decades of rule Castro received no such capital by choice. He rejected it on nationalist and ideological principles. Following the Soviet pull-out the country could no longer, however, afford such moral purity. Yet, even when offering incentives, formalized in a new investment code, foreign capital only selectively and erratically came to Cuba's rescue. Moreover, with Cuba unable to provide a sufficiently attractive investment climate in many sectors of the economy, in 2002 more than half of the 700 joint ventures involving foreign private investors operated at a loss and total foreign investment dropped to less than one-quarter the level two years before. Then, between 2002 and 2005, one joint venture and two smaller ventures, on average, closed weekly, while negligible new capital came in.[8] Mainly small and medium sized firms shuttered.

Compounding problems, the country attracted little foreign bank capital. So short of foreign exchange was the government that it suspended servicing its Western debt in 1986, still during the Soviet era. Because Western banks, in retaliation, cut Cuba off from new credit lines, the country has accessed little other than short-term, high interest-bearing hard currency loans since then, and credit mainly only to finance imports. Yet, interest charges on the unpaid loans continued to mount, to the point that the island's debt rose from \$7.3 billion in 1989 to an estimated \$12.6 billion in 2005 (Table 13.1).[9]

Soviet debts incurred before the superpower's demise further constrain Cuba's capacity to adapt to the new world order. Russia took over Soviet debt claims, and demanded repayment of the roubles Cuba allegedly owed in hard currency. In 2006 Russia argued this debt stood at \$20 billion.[10]

Cuba's export problems had both domestic and foreign roots. The collapse of the sugar trade was at the heart of Cuba's post-Soviet-era export woes. Although sugar had accounted for approximately three-quarters of island trade earnings for most of the twentieth century, by 2005 it generated only 5 per cent of the island's dramatically reduced export earnings.[11] Low world market sugar prices, owing to the development of cheaper, alternative sweeteners, new total dependence on the open world market for sales (despite only 10 per cent of all sugar traded in the open market), and a plunge in production from over 8 million tonnes in the last years of the Soviet alliance to some 1.3 million tonnes in 2004/5, all contributed to the deep dip in sugar earnings. Yields dropped as the government reverted from mechanized to labour-intensive production once it was deprived of cheap Soviet oil, and as labour resisted the back-breaking poorly paid work. Production dipped so low that the government had to import sugar to meet both domestic demand and international delivery commitments.

Nickel sales partially offset the drop-off in sugar revenue. The country benefited both from favourable world market prices and stepped up output of the mineral. Foreign, together with state, investments built up the export-oriented mining industry. Nickel, however, provided no alternative to sugar as an engine of growth. Capital-intensive, it generated little employment and few domestic economic linkages, and the export earnings it generated paled to those of sugar in its heyday.

Meanwhile, government efforts to develop non-traditional exports for hard currency paid off little. Always assuming a minor role in island trade, in 2000 the value of these exports stood at half their level when Soviet trade subsided.[12] Large pharmaceutical companies blocked Cuba from access to international markets for medicines it impressively produced. And Washington's blockage of Cuban products from the US market led the island to attract few foreign investors to new free trade zones the government set up. As of 2001 foreign firms in the island's three zones generated merely $26 million worth of hard currency earnings.[13]

Cuba much more successfully developed tourism. Blamed for the decadence of the pre-revolutionary society, Castro had reined in the pleasure industry soon after assuming power. But moral principles here as well became a luxury the government could no longer afford in the post-Soviet era. With beautiful beaches and an appealing culture, the government quickly restored its former niche in the international tourist market. Tourism became the most vibrant economic sector and principal source of foreign exchange. Tourist revenue jumped from $243 million in 1990 to $2.1 billion in 2004 (Table 13.1), with the sector's contribution to total hard currency earnings catapulting from 3 to 58 per cent in the course of the 1990s.[14] Here too the embargo cut into Cuba's economic potential. Although Americans account for most Caribbean tourists, the embargo denies them rights to vacation in Cuba.[15]

With tourism, along with exports, in themselves generating insufficient hard currency for the economy to rebound to its Soviet-era level, much less forge ahead, the government parlayed its impressive human capital investment into a hard currency revenue source, to the point that professional services, according to one Cuban government source, accounted for 39 per cent of island exports of goods and services in 2005. Tourism dropped to 31 per cent.[16] Cuba's most ambitious post-Soviet-era overseas labour contracts entailed health care and education provisioning to Hugo Chavez's Venezuela. In an oil-for-social assistance swap Cuba reportedly provided the South American country with 15,000–20,000 doctors and nurses and 7000 teachers, plus sports trainers and other advisers. The Cuban government withholds information about its overseas service contracts, but unofficial estimates placed the country's earnings from the skilled cadre sent to Venezuela in 2005 at $500 million.[17]

On a more reduced scale Cuba sold human services to other countries as well. Castro created a demand for the services by charging bargain rates by international standards. The government maintained for itself most of the foreign exchange contracts generated. It paid the cadre sent abroad mainly in pesos, the value of which deteriorated in the post-Soviet era.

In comparison to other Latin American countries Cuba is well positioned to send teachers and health care providers abroad. At the century's turn it had, on average, one doctor per 170 citizens and one nurse per 135 citizens,[18] and 6 elementary-level students and 8 secondary-level students per teacher. Cuba possibly had the best student/teacher ratios in the region.[19] Castro had massively expanded access to education, along with health care, after assuming power in 1959, in conjunction with his commitment to the provisioning of cradle-to-grave benefits.

Comparisons with the Dominican Republic and El Salvador, two nearby countries with fairly similar-sized economies to Cuba's but contrasting political economies and contrasting relations with the US and the international institutions the US influences, highlight the difficulties Cuba confronted in attracting foreign capital and in breaking into export markets. In most post-Soviet years the Dominican Republic and El Salvador attracted more foreign aid, had stronger export sectors, and were weighed down with less foreign debt, and the Dominican Republic attracted substantially more foreign investment and tourist dollars (see Table 13.1). US policies that targeted the Dominican Republic and El Salvador helped the two countries while the aforementioned policies targeting Cuba contained island options under Castro.

Remittances: Cuban Americans to the rescue

As the Cuban government desperately and creatively sought to adapt to the crisis its former allies caused, ordinary Cubans independently sought their own solution to their sudden subsistence plight. Some of them fled to America, initially mainly illegally because Washington cut back legal entry following the fall of the Berlin Wall. Washington hoped thereby to induce distraught islanders to follow the example of their former east European comrades and press for a democratic market transition at home. Indeed, the subsistence crisis, against the backdrop of no easy option to flee, fuelled a brief uprising in Havana in August 1994. But Castro calmed the unrest by unilaterally opening up the option to exit. He allowed the departure of Cubans who wished to make their way across the Florida Straits without Washington entry permission. The island, as a result, experienced its second largest exodus by sea. Approximately 33,000 fled to Florida before US and Cuban authorities signed the 1994 bilateral accord that guaranteed legal entry to minimally 20,000 Cubans yearly.

More islanders, however, reached out to the diaspora for material help than emigrated. They did so even though not only had political differences between Cubans on the two sides of the Straits kept ties between them minimal for decades, but Castro's government also had ruled dollar possession illegal. The prohibition notwithstanding, the dollar became the islanders' currency of choice. The black market value of the US currency, relative to the peso, soared to 1:130 in 1993, all the while that the two currencies remained officially on a par. The black market in dollars fuelled a black market in goods that mushroomed alongside a dwindling supply of affordable goods through the ration system. Only those fortunate to have family abroad willing to send money could afford an adequate diet.

Remittances, people-to-people cross-border income transfers, surged to the point of infusing more hard currency into the island economy than any single island export, and approximately double and twenty times the amount foreign businesses invested in 2000 and 2001, respectively (see Tables 13.1 and 13.2).

Table 13.2 Family remittances from the US to Cuba, the Dominican Republic and El Salvador

	Cuba	*Dominican Republic*	*El Salvador*
(a) Millions of dollars remitted, in:			
1980	–	183	11
1985	–	242	126
1990	50	315	322
1995	537	794	1,061
1999	800	1,519	1,374
2000	750	1,689	1,750
(b) Average annual amount remitted (in dollars) per Cuban, Dominican and Salvadoran foreign-born living in the US in:			
1980	–	1,083	116
1990	67	882	681
1999	848	2,237	1,805
(c) Average annual amount remitted (in dollars) per home country resident, in:			
1990	5	45	64
1995	48[a]	99	177
1999	73	211	291
(d) Annual amount of total remittances as a % of GDP			
1990	0.5[b]	5.3	6.0
1999	4.5	15.2	16.9

[a] Based on mid-1995 population.
[b] 1991.
Sources: Central Banks for Dominican Republic and El Salvador (as compiled by Manuel Orozco, personal communication, and analysed in his 'Globalization and Migration: the Impact of Family Remittances to Latin America', *Latin American Politics and Society* (Summer 2001); on Cuba, Economic Commission on Latin America and the Caribbean (ECLAC)/United Nations, *La Economía Cubana* (Mexico, D.F.: Fondo de Cultura Económico, 2000), p. 220, Cuadro A-30; US Bureau of the Census, *Statistical Abstract of the U.S. 1992*, p. 42 and *2000*, p. 48; World Bank (WB), *World Development Indicators 2001*, pp. 12, 44, 362; WB, *World Tables 1995*, p. 249; WB, *World Development Report 1997*, pp. 220, 248; United Nations Population Fund (UNFPA), *State of the World Population 1990* (New York: UNFPA, 1990), p. 35; Economist Intelligence Unit, *Cuba Country Report*, February 2001, p. 22.

Only tourism, and subsequently service contracts if the Cuban government source cited above is accurate, brought more hard currency to the island. Remittances rose from an estimated $50 million in 1990 to $1 billion at the century's turn,[20] although they are believed to have dropped to about $800 million when President Bush clamped down on Cuban American travel and remittance sending rights.

The informal transnational ties on which remittance sending rests are weakening the wall between the states that Washington and Havana constructed. Cross-border visiting picked up in the post-Soviet era, as Havana lowered travel barriers (and until Washington imposed new barriers). Cubans who bond across borders tend, in turn, to income-share, informally above all. At the start of the new millennium some 65 per cent of remittance dollars reportedly were transferred in ways that bypassed both US and Cuban regulations:[21] on family visits, through informal middlemen who responded to the new desire to cross-border income-share by making a business of transporting money and goods illicitly across borders,[22] and, less frequently, through formation of neighbourhood 'mini-banks'. Unregistered Cuban émigré 'bankers' transmit money for a fee that a Cuban family can withdraw from island 'bank partners' almost immediately. Ironically, Cubans rely more on informal remittance channels than other Latin Americans in less regulated economies in the region.[23]

Like other Latin Americans, Cubans use remittances to finance family subsistence. Even though Castro's government remained officially committed to cradle-to-grave welfare provisioning, including the provisioning of affordably priced food for all through rationing, its allotments came to cover no more than about one-third of monthly family needs. Supplies available through rationing dropped as domestic production plunged and as the cash-strapped government imported insufficient food, as well as when Cubans from the point of production to final retail distribution siphoned off produce for their own family consumption and for sale in the profitable black market that scarcities fuelled. Only islanders with dollar access could readily afford non-rationed items, even as the value of the peso partially rebounded from its 1993 nadir.

The more dollars islanders accessed the more they used the hard currency to finance not merely subsistence but a materialist lifestyle, home improvements, and small business ventures, similar to remittance recipients in market economies worldwide. In the Cuban case, though, these usages defied moral precepts of the revolution and state regulations. The emergent transnational informal economy and society rests, on the US side of the Florida Straits, mainly on recent émigrés. Only a minority of islanders who fled the revolution early on have ever made return visits or sent remittances to family remaining on the island,[24] although some put political differences aside, as noted above, when island relatives' survival was at stake.

State versus society in its transnationalized form: government profiteering from remittances at senders' and recipients' expense

While islanders took the lead in reaching to the diaspora for dollars, the government increasingly exploited the generosity of Cubans abroad to its own advantage, for its own institutional use, at remittance recipients' expense. State and dollar-holder interests increasingly conflicted while simultaneously overlapping, with the state financially gaining the upper hand.

The government, for one, profited from sales at new official dollar stores it established nationwide after legalizing dollar possession in 1993. Maintaining a near-monopoly on legal sales of non-durables and non-perishable foods, it could set prices with high profit margins. Authorities justified what they claimed an ideal mark-up, 240 per cent above cost, on equity grounds:[25] a hidden tax on consumers purportedly to fund programmes for dollarless islanders. But authorities instituted no guarantee that profits would be channelled to such distributive justice, and there is no evidence that the profits were so earmarked.

The government, moreover, periodically raised prices, further advancing its economic interests at consumers' expense. Price hikes it initiated in 2002 contributed to an 8 per cent inflation in consumer prices,[26] while price hikes introduced two years later raised consumer costs, on average, an additional 15 per cent.

The government further profits from the money wire servicing it permits, in that it revenue-shares with the international remitters. Émigrés paid, on average, 19 cents in service fees for every dollar they sent to Cuba through formal remitting services, more than the rate charged other Latin Americans immigrants. The government accordingly received more and remittance recipients less of every dollar Cuban, in comparison to other Latin American, immigrants wired to their homeland.

After the government ruled, in 2004, that the dollar could no longer be used as domestic currency its profiteering at remittance recipients expense deepened. The required trade-in for domestic currency allowed the government to charge a 10 per cent service fee, an additional tax on remittances.

Government-incurred remittance costs: society undermines state moral authority and control of the economy

Remittances may appear a highly profitable and relatively cost-free source of revenue, but from the state's vantage point they prove a mixed blessing. They cause as well as resolve state problems. The problems that they have generated are social, political, cultural and normative, as well as economic, and unintended by the diaspora who generously share some of their overseas earnings. The early émigrés who oppose remittance-sending, because they believe Castro's government benefits from diaspora dollars, ignore how remittances simultaneously hurt the state. Quite independently of reasons why family abroad cross-border income-share, remittances erode state legitimacy, state political and moral authority, state control over the economy and society, and precepts of the revolution, all the while that they help keep the regime afloat.

Remittances, the main though not only source of hard currency islanders access in the post-Soviet era,[27] undermine state peso-based production and productivity and the delivery of services central to the government's socialist roots of legitimacy. In the new economy islanders assess their peso earnings in terms of their dollar equivalency. With few state jobs paying more than the equivalent of $20 a month, far less than the average amount hard currency remittance recipients receive with no work effort whatsoever, incentive to labour at peso-paying jobs has eroded. The government faces the problem that in the new economy earnings hinge more on who you know abroad than hard work, skill and merit. Labour motivation remains highest in those peso-paying state jobs that provide either access to dollars, informally and illegally if not formally, or to goods that can be pilfered for family consumption and black marketeering.

Growing disillusion with peso-paid jobs, in turn, has fuelled a domestic, along with overseas, brain drain. Professionals have left state jobs for low-skilled work in tourism, the main alternative to remittances to access dollars. Hotel workers and room-renters in tourist areas can earn more in a day and prostitutes more in an hour than most state employees can earn in a month. Meanwhile, the brain drain leaves the government with a deteriorating return to its investment in schooling, and with social problems to boot.

With peso jobs unattractive, the younger generation has lost interest in higher education. One of Latin America's most educated populations has deschooled and deskilled. The percentage of the school-age population enrolled in post-secondary studies dropped from 17 per cent in 1980 to 12 per cent in 1997.

Youth disillusion with schooling became so widespread, and jobless youth so troublesome, that Castro personally intervened to encourage young people to study. Post-secondary school enrolments rebounded, and then surged to 54 per cent in 2004; they reached only 33 per cent in the Dominican Republic and 18 per cent in El Salvador that year.[28] Castro recruited young people particularly for studies and careers in social work and social research, to train cadres who could participate in a range of government-sponsored campaigns to address problems the new economy generated. By 2006 more than 10,000 students had graduated from the School of Social Work, started six years earlier.[29]

The cash-strapped government also initiated some costly worker-incentive reforms, to improve productivity and to convince labour to toil in priority state sector jobs outside tourism. The most economically valued state enterprises began to feed, clothe and house their workers,[30] to offer performance bonuses, and to pay employees a portion of their salary in hard currency or so-called convertible pesos with domestic dollar worth. Bonuses at the turn of the century amounted to one to seven times monthly base peso wages.[31] The bonuses cost the state $228 million in scarce hard currency, one-quarter to one-third of the estimated total remittance intake at the time (and a higher percentage, according to the most conservative remittance estimates). The government also raised base-pay earnings to motivate labour who lost interest in working for local currency. Increases in 2005 just in the minimum wage cost the government 1753 million pesos.[32] Such earnings incentives were labour costs that governments in market economies, where most of the workforce is privately employed, need not assume. Remittances indirectly contributed to the pressure for labour concessions, although they were not the only force at play.

Meanwhile, the government faced difficulty in accessing dollars islanders did not immediately spend on consumption. The amount deposited in the new dollar savings accounts the government set up was estimated at a mere $50 million in 1998.[33] Most Cubans preferred to hold on to their extra dollars, hiding them under mattresses, burying them in their backyards, and the like. They were wary of possible government appropriation of their deposits, a fear with some historic base. Cubans also preferred authorities not to know the amount of their dollar holdings, often obtained in ways not fully compliant with the law.

Furthermore, the very consumer culture that dollar stores on the one hand, and hard currency income on the other, fuelled, contributed to crime. Aside from inducing black marketeering, the desire for dollars led islanders to engage in rent-seeking, corruption and theft, including pilfering of supplies at state jobs to sell illicitly in the dollar-based (or dollar-equivalent-based) black market. It also led to employer bribery, to gain access to jobs providing illicit money-making opportunities.[34]

So pervasive did economic crime and corruption become that the Party and government repeatedly launched efforts to rein it in, drawing both on repressive 'law and order' crackdowns and on moral campaigns. At the start of the post-Soviet economic crisis the government launched a draconian anti-corruption campaign. Police arrested 500 people, including officials in high positions.[35] It also tried to reinvigorate the largely defunct CDRs, the Committees for the Defence of the Revolution, the state-linked block organizations, to contain crime,[36] and it launched a so-called Battle of Ideas, in part to fight the corrosive effects of pilfering and illegal trade. The campaign brought back memories of the moral campaign of the 1960s to revolutionize society, although it resonated far less with the populace who by the 1990s had grown weary of unfulfilled utopian promises.

The remittance economy, in turn, fuelled new inequalities that eroded precepts of the revolution. Claes Brundenius estimates that the Gini coefficient rose from 0.22 to 0.41 between 1986 and 1999.[37] Cuba's new poor are the entirely peso-dependent. Remittance-rooted inequality is race-based, in that access to transnational income-sharing varies by skin colour. The diaspora on whose generosity the islanders depend is predominantly white. According to the 2000 US census, 84 per cent of Cuban Americans, including US born, identify themselves as white.[38] Blacks, who in pre-revolutionary Cuba were the most disadvantaged group, benefited most under Castro – relative to their situation in the pre-socialist era. For this reason few of them emigrated, especially before the 1980 Mariel exodus but even since. This put them at a decided disadvantage in the dollarized economy.[39] Unequal access to income-sharing transnational ties has contributed to racial inequalities returning with a vengeance.

The new inequality also takes regional form. This too defies an initial revolutionary concern. In his early years of rule Castro made a concerted effort to reduce pre-revolutionary regional as well as racial inequities.[40] But Havana residents, who constitute a fifth of the island population, receive approximately 60 per cent of remittances.[41]

Dollar-linked differences in lifestyles, in turn, are fuelling tensions between those with and without foreign currency access. The peso-dependent populace resents the absolute and relative deprivation they have experienced in the new economy. Labour union and public forums make the resentment apparent.[42] Worker dissatisfaction, according to one study, rose from 27 to 41 per cent between 1989 and 1999.[43]

Remittances and the remaking of Cuban norms and values

As islanders became enmeshed in ties across the Straits homeland norms and values changed. Cubans began to embrace, and openly so, the material lifestyle the United States epitomized and their overseas relatives personified. Cubans embraced the imported lifestyle to the point that previous stigma of it disappeared. Dollars earned informally through tourism and black marketeering, as well as through remittances, contributed to the cultural transformation. Only remittances, however, were embedded in cross-border people-to-people ties.

Overseas relatives and their remittances ushered in a mimicking of Miami materialism that led islanders to yearn for dollars for far more than basic subsistence. Cubans came to welcome first such basic items as toothpaste, soap, shampoo and detergent, but soon thereafter electric fans, televisions, VCRs, brand-name clothing and shoes, and other consumer goods, that the overseas family mailed from the US or brought with them on visits, or that could be purchased domestically with dollars. By the early 2000s Cuban awareness of US brand names had become among the highest in any non-English-speaking country.[44] Any remaining residue of 'Che' Guevara's utopian vision of the 'new man', who worked for the good of society, joined the dustbin of history. Differences between families on the two sides of the Florida Straits came to hinge more on their wallets than their values.

The decades-old taboo on American-style consumerism broke down to the point that Cubans began to flaunt materialism in their everyday life. Teenagers began to show off their Nikes and Adidas. 'The Miami Cuban culture promotes Lycra (spandex), puffy hair, lots of make-up, and gold', bemused a man I interviewed in Havana who works for a state agency engaged in hard currency economic activity.[45] With remittances from two sisters in the US he lives in a freshly painted house that he fenced in and furnishes with a TV, VCR, CD player, stereo, computer, wireless phone and beautiful artwork. Class distinctions, as he correctly noted and personified, have increased.

The government has become party to the new materialism, though not under conditions of its choosing. Paradoxically, it promotes consumerism more directly than governments in market economies, through the state-run dollar stores, the only places where islanders can purchase non-perishables legally.[46] Meanwhile, because the government restricts investment in private entrepreneurial ventures it indirectly encourages dollar-receivers to consume rather than invest.

Authorities promoted the new, largely remittance-based materialism, however, with ambivalence. The Party leadership spoke of dollars as ideologically contaminating, encouraging individualism as well as materialism.[47] Remittances, moreover, were antithetical to the purported basis of socialist reward: linked to work contribution, legitimated in terms of Marxist philosophical premises. Remittances depend on generosity of overseas relatives, not on work skills and effort.

Conclusion

The Cuban government weathered the storm the domino collapse of Soviet bloc communism caused, although the economy has yet to recuperate completely from the loss of trade and aid from its former allies. Formally, little has changed on the island since the Soviet era. Informally, however, the economy, society and normative order have quietly undergone transformation. Cuba has 'regressed' from the utopian project Castro initially took on. Yet, the government remained committed to a cradle-to-grave welfare state, even if not as fully and extensively as when the Soviets helped keep the regime afloat.

Sources of capital to fuel the economy have not been sufficiently forthcoming for a combination of reasons. In particular, Washington, desirous to bring Castro's government to heel, stepped up the embargo when Cuba most needed new market access and assistance. Yet, Cuba is also part of its own problem. The state economy produces few goods and services besides tourism and contract labour marketable abroad on sufficient scale.

Under the circumstances, ordinary islanders who reached to the diaspora for financial help contributed to a dramatic break with the past. In so doing they informally dollarized the economy, transformed island norms and transnationalized social and economic life. The government, desirous of hard currency for its own use, responded to islanders' cross-border reach by facilitating visits, in which cross-border income-sharing is embedded, as well as by facilitating remittance-sending and legalizing dollar possession. But it quickly took advantage of diaspora goodwill by introducing a number of measures that enabled it to benefit at remittance senders' and recipients' expense.

While islanders benefited from the dollars they informally accessed, even if less than had the state not appropriated so much of the money family abroad allot them, the impact of diaspora-attained dollars on the state has been mixed. Dollars the government appropriates provide revenue for the cash-strapped state, but the informal dollarization has eroded the socialist moral order and has had the effect of eroding productivity and undermining state control over production and distribution. The informal dollarization of the economy has adverse spillover effects in the peso economy. To address the emergent problems the government incurs fiscal costs.

Cuba's experience in the post-Soviet era thus reveals a regime weaker than models of strong states/weak societies under communism suggest. Ordinary Cubans have transformed and transnationalized the social and cultural along with economic base of island life. Yet, the political system put in place during the years of Soviet solidarity formally remains intact, the broad range of societal changes notwithstanding. Whether it will survive a leadership transition as Fidel leaves the political scene remains, however, to be seen.

Notes

1 Economic Commission on Latin America and the Caribbean (ECLAC), *La Economía Cubana* (Mexico, DF: Fondo de Cultura Económico, 2000), p. 220.

2 *International Herald Tribune,* 13 July 2001 (www.iht.com).

3 PAC is the name commonly given to a private group organized to elect or defeat government officials, in order to promote legislation typically supporting the group's special interests.

4 While liberalizing trade to Cuba, Congress continued to prevent Castro's government rights to export to the US, which could generate needed hard currency, including to cover import costs.

5 US–Cuba Trade and Economic Council (UCTEC), 'Economic Eye on Cuba', 20 October 2002: 18 (www.cubatrade.org).

6 Economist Intelligence Unit (EIU), *Cuba Country Report* (*CCR*), May 2005, p. 7.

7 Immanuel Wallerstein, *The Modern World System* (New York: Academic Press, 1974), and *The Capitalist World-Economy* (Cambridge, UK: Cambridge University Press, 1979).

8 Omar Everleny Pérez Villanueva, 'The Cuban Economy Today and Its Future Challenges', in Jorge Domínguez, Pérez Villanueva and Lorena Barbería (eds), *The Cuban Economy at the Start of the Twenty-First Century* (Cambridge: Harvard University Press, 2004), p. 173; US Department of State, Commission for Assistance to a Free Cuba (CAFC), *Report to the President,* May 2004, p. 42 (www.state.gov); EIU, *CCR,* February 2006, p. 34.

9 See also Susan Eckstein, *Back from the Future: Cuba under Castro* (New York: Routledge, 2003), p. 247.

10 EIU, *CCR*, August 2006, p. 29.

11 EIU, *CCR,* May 2005, p. 28 and November 2005, pp. 20, 21.
12 Eckstein, *Back from the Future,* fn. 11, p. 305; Jorge Mario Sánchez Egoscu, 'Cuba: los desafíos de la inserción en el comercio Caribe-EE.UU', paper delivered at the Latin American Studies Association, Dallas, March 2003.
13 Omar Everleny Pérez Villanueva, 'El comercio exterior y la inversión extranjera en la economía Cubana en 1996', in *La Economía Cuba en 1996: Resultados, Problemas y Perspectivas* (Havana: University of Havana, Centro de Estudios de la Economía Cubana, 1996), pp. 25–33.
14 Moisés Pérez Mok and Alfredo García, 'Reformas Económicas en Cuba, Turismo: Retos, Posibilidades y Perspectivas', paper presented at the Latin American Studies Association, Miami, 2000, p. 5; EIU, *CCR,* August 2001, p. 28.
15 US-to-Cuba travel regulations have changed many times over the years, in the context of the embargo. Both Presidents Carter and Clinton relaxed non-Cuban-American travel (although Clinton suspended direct flights between the two countries between 1996 and 1998). President Bush introduced yet new travel restrictions, on group travel in 2003 and family travel the following year.
16 Ariel Terrero, 'Economía del conocimiento: inversión en células grises', *Bohemia,* Ano 98, 10 (12 May 2006). I am grateful to Paolo Spadoni for this reference.
17 EIU, *CCR,* May 2005, p. 31 and November 2005, pp. 27, 28. On Cuba's overseas human service provisioning, see also Julie Feinsilver, 'La diplomacia medica cubana: Cuando la izquierda lo ha hecho bien', *Foreign Affairs en Espanol,* 16, 4 (Oct.–Dec. 2006) 81–94.
18 However, in the early 2000s the doctors per population and number of graduates in medical studies declined somewhat.
19 Eckstein, *Back from the Future,* pp. 249, 250 and references therein.
20 For a discussion of ranges of difficulties in assessing remittances, see S. Eckstein, *Diasporas and Dollars: Transnational Ties and the Transformation of Cuba* (Cambridge: Massachusetts Institute of Technology, Center for International Studies, Rosemarie Rogers Working Papers Series No-16, 2003), p. 12. I am indebted to Manuel Orozco for the 2005 estimate.
21 Estimates by employees in wire service companies interviewed in the US and Cuba, and personal communication with Manuel Orozco. In December 2002, however, a new Canadian web-based money transfer service was introduced that reduced commissions and increased the speed of transfers. Cuban recipients who register for the service receive a card usable for cash withdrawals. In its first month of operation the service reported handling $320,000 of transfers and registering 10,000 users. EIU, *CCR,* February 2003, p. 28.
22 An estimated 10 per cent of Cuban-Americans visited the island annually, as of 2000. Dorothy Robyn, James Reitzes and Bryan Church, 'The Impact on the U.S. Economy of Lifting Restrictions on Travel to Cuba', paper prepared for the Center for International Policy, July 2002, p. 1.
23 An estimated 70 per cent of transfers to Mexico, in contrast, are made electronically. M. Orozco, 'Family Remittances to Latin America: the Marketplace and Its Changing Dynamics', paper delivered at the Inter-American Development Bank Conference, 'Remittances as a Development Tool', May 2001, p. 5.
24 S. Eckstein, 'Cuban Émigrés and the American Dream', *Perspectives on Politics*, 4, 2 (June 2006) 297–307; Florida International University (FIU), Institute for Public Opinion Research (IPOR), *FIU/Cuba Poll* (Miami: FIU-IPOR, 2004).
25 This means an item that cost $100 to produce or import, would carry a 140 per cent tax and sell for $240.
26 EIU, *CCR,* February 2003, p. 9.

27 Remittances account for an estimated 80 per cent of the hard currency ordinary islanders access. Paolo Spadoni, 'The Role of the United States in the Cuban Economy', in *Cuba in Transition*, Vol. 13 (Association for the Study of the Cuban Economy, 2003), p. 419. Other sources of dollars include money earned informally and illegally in tourism and black marketeering, and supplements to pesos earned at state sector jobs.
28 http://devdata.worldbank.org/data-query.
29 EIU, *CCR*, August 2006, p. 13.
30 Workers received debit cards usable only at designated stores. In this manner the government addressed consumer demand while minimizing the circulation of money that could fuel the black market.
31 US–Cuba Trade and Economic Council (UCTEC) 'Economic Eye on Cuba' (www.cubatrade.org), 17 March 2002, p. 12.
32 EIU, *CCR*, August 2005, p. 21.
33 The government accessed far more hard currency through consumption than savings. In 1998 dollar stores took in $870 million in revenue, and in 2003 $1.3 billion. EIU, *CCR*, August 2001, p. 20 and *CCR*, June 2000, p. 19; Lorena Barberia, 'Remittances to Cuba: an Evaluation of Cuban and U.S. Government Policy Measures' (Cambridge, Mass. David Rockefeller Center Series on Latin American Studies, Harvard University, 2004), pp. 372–3.
34 While scarcities alone might induce pilfering, the new dollar-based consumer culture made islanders covet more material goods at a time when peso earnings bought less.
35 EIU, *CCR*, 1 (1991) 17.
36 EIU, *CCR*, August 2006, p. 20.
37 Claes Brundenius, 'Whither the Cuban Economy after Recovery? The Reform Process, Upgrading Strategies and the Question of Transition', *Journal of Latin American Studies*, 34, part 2 (May 2002) 365–96.
38 My analysis of Steven Ruggles, Matthew Sobek et al., *Integrated Public use Microdata Series (IPUMS). Version 3* (Minneapolis: Historical Census Projects, University of Minnesota, 2003) (www.ipums.org). See also *Current Population Survey 1997* (March), Table 61: Selected characteristics of the foreign born population by year of entry. Washington, DC.
39 See Alejandro De la Fuente, 'Recreating Racism: Race and Discrimination in Cuba's Special Period', *Georgetown University Cuba Briefing Paper Series*, 18 (1998).
40 Eckstein, *Back from the Future*, Ch. 6.
41 UCTEC, 17 March 2002, p. 12 (www.cubatrade.org).
42 EIU, *CCR*, November 2000, p. 18.
43 EIU, *CCR*, February 2001, p. 11.
44 *New York Times*, Section 3 (26 May 2002), p. 4.
45 In conjunction with my study of Cuban transnational ties and transformations, I interviewed 130 rank-and file and well-placed Cuban-Americans in the US and 80 Cubans in Havana. For a more detailed discussion of my interviews, see Eckstein, 'Transnational Networks and Norms, Remittances, and the Transformation of Cuba', in Domínguez et al. (eds), *The Cuban Economy at the Start of the Twenty-First Century*, p. 320.
46 The government ultimately opened some peso-based stores, but the supply of goods in these stores is far inferior to that available in the dollar-based stores.
47 William LeoGrande and Julie Thomas, 'Cuba's Quest for Economic Independence', *Journal of Latin American Studies*, 34 (2002) 325–64.

14
Change and Continuity in North Korea

Soyoung Kwon

Rethinking system change of state socialism

A debate on convergence and divergence of post-socialist development is no longer relevant. Demonstrated by various paths of development in the former and present state socialist countries, conceptualizing transition from state socialism should move beyond a simple one-way trajectory of transition towards political pluralism, democracy and the market. It needs to encompass the perception of diversity, deviation and regression in the process of system change.

System change entails a comprehensive transformation of the main features of the political, ideological, economic and social dimensions of a society.[1] System change thus involves two consecutive, but to some extent autonomous, processes: the breakdown of the existing (declining) system and the subsequent formation and consolidation of a new one. In the transformation process, changes in the subsystems may not occur simultaneously and may proceed at different speeds and at different levels. If change occurs in one of the subsystems or at a policy level, it is a reform within the system rather than a system change. A complete departure from existing practice within all the political, ideological and economic spheres is what constitutes the first stage of system change from state socialism – the breakdown of the existing system. The second stage involves a transition progress of those countries that have abandoned the previous system of rule and adopted a post-socialist system with some form of democracy, free and multi-party elections, pluralization, a market economy based on private ownership, decentralization, civil liberties and autonomy.

While the first stage determines a trajectory of transformation (system disintegration), partial transformation (reform survival) and non-transformation (system survival) of the state socialist system, the successful and unsuccessful outcomes of transformation are shaped at the latter stage. Depending on the nature and the degree of transformation from the original state socialist system, generally four different sets of countries are distinguished as representatives of diverging outcomes of transformation.

Firstly, there are *cases of successful system transformation*, which include the post-communist countries that have relatively successfully extricated themselves from state socialism, and replaced it with a new set of political, economic, social and legal systems. Secondly, *cases of relatively unsuccessful transformation* show either retarded transitional progress in terms of political, economic, social and legal transformation or strong institutional legacies of state socialism. Thirdly, there are *cases of partial transformation,* which exhibit a distinctive evolutionary development of state socialism via a reform path. China and Vietnam are examples. Lastly, there exist *cases of system survival of state socialism* which feature a lack of significant institutional change in the state socialist system, and continuation of the following characterization of the state socialist system: (1) formal hegemony of single party control and absence of political competition; (2) official dominant ideology; (3) a dominant state sector and public ownership; (4) central planning and state control of the economy. These cases often feature coercive rule as well as a strongly repressed and controlled society. One representative case of this type is North Korea, formally known as the Democratic People's Republic of Korea (DPRK).

Whether the present North Korean regime represents a typical state socialist country is a matter of contention. A point of departure for the discussion is the premise that the North Korean system survived the domino-like collapse of the socialist bloc of 1989–91 and that it has not been replaced by a conspicuously different economic and political system, at least formally. The question remains: is North Korea simply lagging behind others in terms of transition or slowly evolving into a different system? This chapter attempts to address the issues of system survival in North Korea and the development within its system from the late 1990s, outlining noticeable changes in the political, economic and social subsystems.

Detailing the evolution of the North Korean system, the chapter argues that the impact of the fall of state socialism in the world was minimized in its domestic scene partly due to its early deviation from the typical socialist development, which effectively differentiated itself from other state socialist societies and eradicated the existence of alternative forces in the leadership and in the society. At the same time, other challenges such as the nuclear crisis, the death of the leader, and a grand-scale famine emerged almost simultaneously, which, in effect, helped North Koreans to divert their attention from questioning the existing system to struggling for their own survival. A process of change within the old system only manifested itself in the new century, as the North Korean leadership came to the realization that it had to transcend the 'old working style' and search for a new direction to revitalize its system. North Korea finally gave in to a new pragmatism and took reform initiatives from 2002. The economic and social subsystems were consequently affected, but featured change within the existing system that is clearly distinguished from system change of state socialism.

Formation of the North Korean system and deviation

Deviation from the general path of socialist development had occurred in North Korea at the early stage of its regime consolidation process. The communist movement in Korea was intertwined with nationalism and anti-Japanese resistance during the Japanese colonization period (1910–45). With the termination of the colonial system on 15 August 1945, Korea was immediately occupied by the two allied powers in a form of trusteeship: the Soviet Union in the north and the United States in the south. Kim Il Sung, who took part in guerrilla resistance outside of Korea, became chairman of the unified Communist Party, and initiated radical socialist reform programmes within the coordinates of the Soviet model. Land reform and social welfare programmes were widely welcomed by the Korean people who had suffered and been deprived under the Japanese colonization. The Democratic People's Republic of Korea (DPRK or North Korea) was formally proclaimed in the northern half of the Korean peninsula in September 1948 with strong endogenous support. Nationalists, communists and intellectuals who believed in this new vision and system flocked to the North, endowing the new regime with solid legitimacy.

In the beginning, there were several competing political factions and power struggles among the communist leaders, namely the indigenous nationalists; the domestic Communists; returnees from China, called the Yanan faction; returnees from the Soviet Union, called the Soviet faction; and Kim Il Sung's personal followers who had participated in guerrilla activities, called the Kapsan faction. Policy disputes and theoretical controversy as well as polarization between the hard line and moderate line within the core leadership group on the issue of economic development strategies appeared in the pages of the Party newspaper, *Rodong Sinmun*, and other theoretical journals.[2]

The backwash of Khrushchev's denunciation of Stalin threatened to spill over into North Korea from 1956. At the third Korean Workers' Party (KWP) Central Committee meeting, the groups affiliated with the Soviet and Yanan factions attacked the growing personality cult of Kim Il Sung and his industrial policy which mimicked the Stalinist style. The intensity of criticism somewhat resembled the Stalin–Bukharin struggle in the Soviet Union of the late 1920s. Kim Il Sung counter-attacked, accusing his opponents of being anti-revolutionaries and sectarians, and eased them entirely out of power. Kim Il Sung continued to eradicate factional struggles and resentment over policy differences in the following decade, by purging most of his rivals including the domestic, Yanan, Soviet-Korea factions and even a number of people from his own faction.[3] The result has been a cohesive elite comprising the surviving loyal supporters of Kim Il Sung and the creation of an absolute monolithic totalitarian socialist state.

Kim Il Sung began to move away from communist orthodoxy. Building a theoretical rationale and device for legitimating Kim's power consolidation, the term *Juche* was introduced. *Juche* is commonly known as 'self-reliance', but depending on the context in which it is used, it can mean national identity, self-reliance, independence, national pride or national assertiveness.[4] In 1967 Kim Il Sung stated, 'our *Juche* ideology refers to the most correct Marxism-Leninism oriented philosophy designed to carry out our revolution and construction'.[5] This meant disconnecting the North Korean communist revolution from the Soviet or Chinese ones. *Juche* thought evolved through various phases, ranging from a mere political slogan to a system of values and the central guideline for policies in the fields of politics, economy, society, military and foreign affairs. North Korea concentrated on pursuing an independent line based on its *Juch*e (self-reliant) idea and distanced itself from the Sino-Soviet disputes. The status of the *Juche* idea escalated and finally superseded Marxism-Leninism, as shown in the DPRK constitution (article 4) adopted in December 1972, which takes 'the *Juche* idea as the guiding principle of the republic, the ideology that creatively applied Marxism-Leninism to our own situation'.

At the same time, the North Korean society was shaped into a unique entity where all individuals were bound by various organizations and all social organizations were systematically structured. Through strict media censorship by the state and the surveillance mechanisms, North Korea developed into a tightly controlled and repressed society featuring collective supervision and punishment. The state's monopoly of economic and public life left organizations outside the state with few resources with which they could increase opposition to the political leaders or be able to organize an opposition movement. With the country effectively sealed from outside influences, the North Korean people did not have an 'outside' frame of reference or connection with external forces that could support any dissident movement.

Kim Il Sung dedicated nearly two decades to building a monolithic *Juche* state, and sought a way to guarantee the continuation of his legacy after his death. From observing the factional struggles after the death of Mao and Stalin, Kim designated his son, Kim Jong Il, as the next leader, and gradually prepared him as heir apparent. The hereditary succession scheme was initially met with some opposition, but Kim Jong Il's opponents and those who were sceptical of the succession plan were removed from key positions in the Party, state and military.[6] After conducting intense campaigns to remove challengers and select reliable and loyal supporters of Kim's son, a cohesive support base of Kim Jong Il was formed at the Sixth Congress of the KWP in October 1980. Consequently, a gradual transfer of power from father to son took place without evident intra-elite struggle or opposing challenge. By the time the succession preparatory period was finalized in the 1990s, Kim Jong Il had already gained full control of the state, the Party as well as the military.

Assessment of the nature of development in North Korea brings out some important features that might have effectively prevented implosion within the ruling elite or spontaneous system collapse. Firstly, differentiation of the North Korean state socialist system based on its independent *Juche* idea minimized the impact of the breakdown of the Soviet Union on its own continuation. Secondly, building a closed but controlled society curtailed any possibility of a societal force being organized that could challenge the existing leadership. Thirdly, a lack of factional division prevented formation of an alternative to Kim's political power or possible conflicts within the leadership. Fourthly, a long-term preparation for the father-to-son leadership succession eradicated a possible power struggle surrounding the succession issue.

Whether it is 'transition from above' or 'transition from below', a prerequisite is the presence of an agent of transition in a form of an organized opposition force that has an alternative vision regarding how the system should be changed.[7] The primary actor in the process of regime breakdown is generally an organized group or a new ascendant class that is capable of challenging the existing leadership's confidence in its own ruling and the system it advocates. In the case of North Korea, this element was certainly missing. There was little change or differentiation in the ruling elite as well as absence of civic culture or distinct large social strata having their own peculiar social interests or established political–ideological views. These features are very much due to the unique development of the North Korean regime, in which the nature of the North Korean polity evolved towards monolithic and dynastic configuration and a society strongly controlled and repressed. In the absence of alternatives, survival of the existing leadership and its system of rule was guaranteed in North Korea.

Continuity and change in the North Korean system

Subsequent to the collapse of socialism in eastern Europe and the Soviet Union, the North Korean regime proclaimed the supremacy of 'socialism in our own style' (*Urisik Sahuijuyui*). Serving as an ideological base for safeguarding the North Korean regime, this concept represented a unique brand of socialism based on the independent line and isolation policy that was immanent in the *Juche* thought, which again differentiated itself from the socialism of other failed states.[8] Confronting the changing environment, the North Korean regime managed to persist not by adaptation to these changes but through an emphasis on the superiority and particularity of the North Korean regime, under the name of 'socialism of our own style' and 'the supremacy of the Korean nation'. Kim Jong Il blamed the collapse of the Soviet Union and eastern Europe on weak leadership, wrong decisions and loss of faith and demanded unity and stronger social and ideological integration.[9] In contrast with the assertion of 'superiority of our-style socialism', the North Korean political, economic and social systems were dysfunctional. The Party Congress did not take place, the economy recorded minus growth for nine consecutive years, food and energy shortages prevailed, and the public distribution of goods broke down.

With the collapse of the Soviet Empire and China's market reform, North Korea was left standing alone. Preventing the regime collapse was one thing, but revitalizing the failing system was another. It was not till the end of the 1990s that the Kim Jong Il leadership began to project an alternative vision of 'building a militarily strong and economically prosperous country'. By then, a militaristic make-up of the leadership had become apparent. Change in politics, ideology, economy and society respectively followed, conforming to the projected goal. The change was one of atypical post-socialist development with growing military-oriented features in politics and ideology and market-oriented characteristics in the economy and society.

A. Politics and ideology

For several years following the death of Kim Il Sung in July 1994, political development in North Korea showed both ambiguity and continuity. General elections to the Supreme People's Assembly scheduled for 1994 did not take place. With the excuse of the mourning period, Kim Jong Il did not officially assume the posts of General Secretary of the Party or State President, but remained as the supreme commander of the Korean People's Army and as the chairman of the National Defence Commission, the positions he took respectively in 1991 and 1992. The continuing leadership was in the driver's seat to steer the country, but there was no clear signal to which way the system should move despite economic decline.

An analysis of the Central Committee of the Korean Workers' Party confirms continuity of the leadership without any significant restructuring or reshuffling of the political elite in the 1990s.[10] The political elite group continued to become smaller and more exclusive, featuring a cohesive group bonded by personal relations and school ties. The number of Central Committee members reduced from 180 in 1990 to 129 in 2004. A majority of the political elite belonged to the ageing second generation, who were born in the 1930s and 1940s, and shared similar educational backgrounds with Kim Jong Il. Continuity of the existing membership with old cadres who were over the retirement age was manifested even in 2004 when the average age of the group was 76 whereas it was 57.3 in 1980. The political elite had been closed to recruitment or co-option since 1995, hampering elite circulation. As a result, younger-generation cadres who might possess different orientations and skills did not have access to the Central Committee to replace the deceased or dismissed members. Despite this general trend of continuity and cohesiveness in terms of social attributes of the political elite, there was a marked difference in the functional group representation of the Party Central Committee in the 1980s and 1990s. Whereas the composition of the 1980s showed a widening differentiation with an increasing number of people with technical and managerial skills, the political elite structure of the 1990s displayed a reverse of this pattern with an increasing representation of military and Party elites and a decreasing representation of state elites.

Rapid turnover and an accelerated diversification process of the political elite through infusion of younger elites from different backgrounds who advocate different interests, which followed the accession of Gorbachev in the USSR and Deng Xiaoping in China, did not take place in North Korea under Kim Jong Il. The overall features of the political elite in the Kim Jong Il leadership were those of concentration and limited differentiation, with declining representation of technocrats and increasing representation of the Party and military elites. A deliberate readjustment of the political elite directed towards minimizing elite differentiation and reinforcing elite integration became apparent in the North Korean leadership from the mid-1990s. The relatively compact size of the ruling elite enabled its members to act together in a conscious and cohesive manner, and thus manage and manipulate the political sphere – at least in the short run – to perpetuate its domination.

One noticeable feature of the North Korean leadership of the 1990s was a rise of the military. Among the newcomers to the Central Committee between 1990 and 1995, 50 per cent were military elites engaged in the defence and security sector.[11] Since this trend appeared following the collapse of the socialist bloc and at the time of rising tension with the US over the nuclear issue, an increasing number of military officials in the political elite group may reflect Kim Jong Il's effort to accommodate military power and support in managing the North Korean regime at a critical time. Kim orchestrated the political ascendancy of generals and apportioned senior military officers significant roles to play in the top councils of the Party, enabling them to participate in the political process and granting important responsibility to the military to play a leading role in state affairs. This also meant placing the military under Kim's tight control. In effect, bringing the military into the leadership and Kim Jong Il's power base minimized the chances of a possible military action (e.g. coup) or threat against the leadership at the time of crisis.[12]

Coinciding with the military-oriented readjustment of the leadership, a new ideological remoulding process began in North Korea with the concepts of 'military-oriented thought', 'army-centred politics', and 'military-first politics'. The 'military-first (*Songun*) politics' imply politics that put priority on the military and on strengthening the People's Army as the 'main pillar' of revolution and the 'driving force' of the North Korean brand of socialism. Although the term 'military-first politics' first emerged as a way to rationalize the role of the military in defending the regime from external threat, it later developed into an ideology that legitimizes a significant increase in the role and influence of the military over politics, economy and society of North Korea. Accordingly, the North Korean regime was transformed into a military-oriented state in which the 'military-first' thought provided a substantial rationality for its actions and changing political procedure.

Kim Jong Il officially assumed the post of General Secretary of the KWP in October 1997. The power of Chairman Kim Jong Il was greatly reinforced by allowing him to command both the Party and the military, making him the holder of real supreme power. At the Tenth Supreme People's Assembly meeting in September 1998, Kim Jong Il was re-elected as the chairman of the National

Defence Commission, the position recognized in the revised Constitution as the most senior position in the state hierarchy (article 100). On the occasion of Kim Jong Il's official succession to power, rhetoric of *Kangsong Daeguk* was introduced, signalling a new vision of the Kim Jong Il leadership. The term literally means 'a powerful and prosperous nation', but implies turning North Korea into a great country that is militarily strong and economically prosperous. It first appeared in a North Korean newspaper editorial of 9 September 1998 under the heading of 'Let's construct *Kangsong Daeguk* as led by the great leadership of the Party', with an emphasis on 'revitalising its economy and establishing a self-supporting economy as the primary task for building an ideologically, politically, militarily strong state'.

The new goal of building *Kangsong Daeguk* and this alternative vision of the Kim Jong Il leadership hinted at a break from the old Soviet-style management and the beginning of an era of economic change based on pragmatism. By proposing a new task of turning North Korea into an economically and militarily strong country, the leadership prepared a way to rationalize any change that would occur in the system. As a means to transforming the country into a 'strong and prosperous country', North Korea began to accentuate phrases such as 'renovation in thinking and in practice', 'IT science and technology-oriented economy', 'improvement of economic management' in the new century. Accompanying some market-oriented reform measures of 2002, the *Kangsong Daeguk* slogan with its synonyms *Buhung Kangguk* and *Kangsong Buhung* (resurgence of a strong country) prevailed in North Korea.

Concurrently, the military-first rhetoric was intensified. The hard-line stance of the Bush administration, re-emergence of nuclear crisis, Bush's 2002 remark on North Korea as a part of the 'axis of evil', and the US invasion of Iraq together brought back the security issue to the top of North Korea's priority list. Facing the security threat, a drastic rise of the 'military-first' rhetoric and an intensified tone became apparent in North Korean publications. The nation was to be a military camp where military requirements took priority over all else. In recent years, the 'military-first' ideology came to predominate over North Korean society and political rhetoric; its prevalence in all aspects of the present North Korean regime parallels the *Juche* ideology in the 1970s. Figure 14.1 clearly demonstrates this rising trend of the military-first ideology in North Korea.

Illustrating the overall change of ideology and legitimating value in North Korea, the figure displays the proportion of certain ideological terms appearing in the editorial headings of *Rodong Sinmun*, the North Korean Party newspaper, between 1980 and 2004.[13] It clearly shows that Marxism-Leninism (ML) is long gone as an ideological reference for the North Korean regime and the *Juche* ideology is on the decline. The red banner ideology symbolizing the Korean revolution for socialism based on unity, integrity and faith was stressed for a short period of time between 1996 and 1997, intending to call for unconditional loyalty to the new leader and to legitimize the leadership succession to Kim Jong Il. But the red banner ideology was insufficient to rationalize

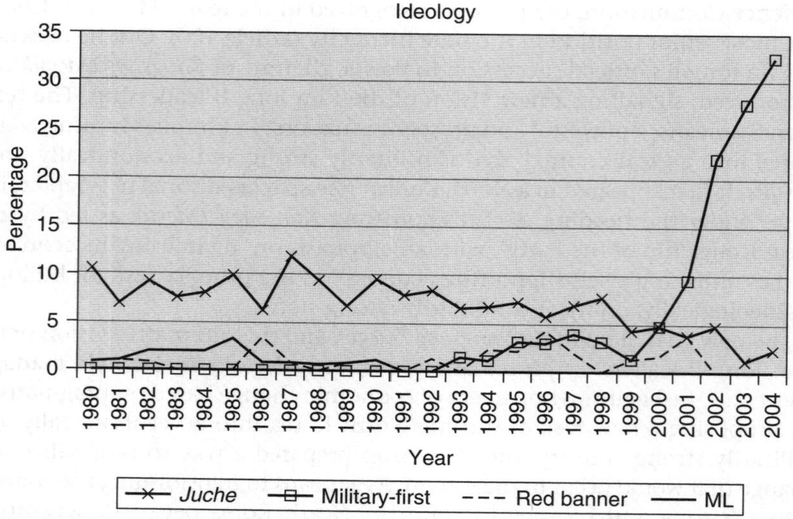

Figure 14.1 Changing ideology in North Korea

regime continuation in the rapidly changing environment or provide the ideological platform for Kim Jong Il's military-oriented ruling style. The 'military-first' ideology, on the other hand, has been sharply rising as a dominant rhetoric from 1999. The prevailing usage of the military-first rhetoric in North Korean politics and society indicates that it no longer represents a mere political slogan or a strategy for crisis management, but a system of values, social norms, and an effective system of authority under the Kim Jong Il leadership. It is premature to conclude whether the military-first ideology can successfully replace *Juche* ideology, which has been the backbone of the North Korean regime since the 1960s, in providing a new alternative value. What is clear is that Kim Jong Il is transforming Kim Il Sung's *Juche* state into a military-first state with his own ideological brand of *Songun*.

B. Economy and society

The impact of the fall of state socialism was greater on the North Korean economy than on its politics. Although construction of a self-supporting national economy and self-sufficiency was accentuated in Kim's economic planning[14] and development strategies in the midst of the Sino-Soviet conflict, economic exchanges with other countries were needed to import raw materials and advanced technological equipment. The massive economic and technical assistance provided by the Soviet Union, China and the eastern European countries certainly helped reconstruction of the North Korean economy and contributed to its record growth rates of 20–30 per cent in the 1950s and 1960s

Table 14.1 Economic assistance from the communist countries (million US$)

	1945–49	*1950–60*	*1961–69*	*1970–76*	*1978–84*
Soviet Union	53 (Loans)	514.8 (Grants) 198.5 (Loans)	196.7 (Loans)	906 (Loans)	0
China	0	336.0 (Grants) 172.5 (Loans)	105.0 (Loans)	1.6 (Loans)	258.7 (Grants)
East Germany	0	101.4 (Grants)	35 (Loans)	0	0
Other eastern Europe	0	326.3 (Grants) 3.9 (Loans)	0	0	0
Total	53 (Loans)	1,278.5 (Grants) 374.9 (Loans)	336.7 (Loans)	907.6 (Loans)	258.7 (Grants)

Source: Adapted from the Republic of Korea National Unification Board, *Statistics of North Korean Economy* (Seoul: National Unification Board, 1986).

(see Table 14.1). Figures vary, but it is estimated that total assistance equivalent to US$3.5 billion was provided in the form of grants and loans by the communist countries between 1946 and 1984, of which 45 per cent came from the Soviet Union.

Economic growth began to slow down substantially as economic assistance from its traditional allies fell during the Sino-Soviet rift. Although the economic performance failed to meet the plan target from the late 1960s, the North Korean economy was sustainable, at least till the 1980s. The North Korean economy of the 1990s, however, was on the verge of collapse, with continuing negative economic growth and declining foreign trade. System collapse of the socialist states led to actual abrogation of North Korea's long-term trade arrangements with these countries, which consequently led to a declining supply of equipment parts, petrol and raw materials that North Korea heavily depended upon as imports.

The fall of the Soviet Union adversely affected trade between Russia and North Korea, and the trade volume dropped drastically from $2.5 billion in 1989 to $33 million in 1993. The amount of heavy fuel oil imported from the Soviet Union was reduced from 855,000 tonnes in 1986 to 30,000 tonnes in 1992. Since the decline in economic relations between North Korea and Russia, China has stepped in, partially making up for the withdrawal of Soviet assistance. Trade with China rose from $48.3 million in 1989 to $89.5 million in 1993. North Korea received 72 per cent of food imports, 75 per cent of oil imports and 88 per cent of coal imports from China.[15]

In 1993, North Korea announced a three-year buffer economic plan to prioritize development of agriculture, light industry and trade. However, the attempt to revitalize the economy failed to produce tangible results due to lack of resources, technological backwardness, outdated industrial facilities linked to shortage of investment resources, and an imbalance in manufacturing industry. To attract foreign investment, North Korea announced the creation of a

Special Economic Zone (SEZ) in the north-east region of the Rajin-Songbong area in 1992. The SEZ effort was not successful since problems with infrastructure, bureaucracy, and uncertainties about investment security and viability hindered growth and its development.

The economic crisis worsened with a series of natural disasters including the record floods of 1995. In retrospect, food shortage and famine deaths were blessings in disguise. The international aid from the UN and NGOs as well as direct aid from individual governments flowed into the country from the mid-1990s, contributing to the weak survival of the North Korean regime. In 1995 alone, South Korea provided 150,000 tonnes of free grain and Japan provided 150,000 tonnes of free grain plus 150,000 tonnes on concessional terms. China became one of the largest donors of emergency food aid with 500,000 tonnes of free grain and an additional 30,000 tonnes on a concessional base.[16] Between 1995 and 2005, the World Food Programme (WFP) alone provided North Korea with nearly 4 million tonnes of food worth $1.7 billion. The South Korean government and NGOs provided aid that amounted to $747 million. In 2005, about 49 per cent of the food aid North Korea received was from China followed by 36 per cent from South Korea.

Additionally, the negotiation pact of 1994 between North Korea and the US as a solution to the first nuclear crisis, gave North Korea food and fuel aid from China, South Korea and the United States in exchange for freezing its nuclear programme. The package included annual delivery of 500,000 tonnes of heavy fuel oil, which continued till 2002. The new South Korean government from 1998 initiated an engagement policy towards North Korea, providing an extensive amount of food and developmental aid and facilitating trade with the North and inter-Korea economic projects. Since then, South Korea has emerged as a significant investor and supporter of the North Korean economy, compensating for North Korea's loss of old trade partners. In 2005, over $212 million of assistance in the form of food, fertilizer, health care, farming tools and others were sent to the North from the South. The volume of inter-Korean trade, which was $18.72 million in 1989, surpassed $1 billion in 2005.[17]

International humanitarian assistance, food aid from China as well as economic cooperation and assistance from South Korea, have helped to avert the worst effects of famine and economic collapse, and kept the regime on 'life support'. The North Korean economy was on the rebound from a desperate situation in the 1990s (see Tables 14.2 and 14.3). Nevertheless, the impact of the famine and a breakdown of the public distribution system left the North Korean people struggling to feed themselves. People began to engage in illegal transactions on the black market, resulting in the spread of farmers' markets. They were barely tolerated at first, but the state that could not provide basic needs to the people had no choice but to reluctantly acknowledge them. Responding to the disruption, the North Korean leadership came to take bold measures to restructure and improve its economy.

Table 14.2 Economic growth in North Korea

Year	*1990*	*1991*	*1992*	*1993*	*1994*	*1995*	*1996*	*1997*	*1998*	*1999*	*2000*	*2001*	*2002*	*2003*	*2004*
Economic growth (%)	−3.7	−3.5	−6.0	−4.2	−2.1	−4.1	−3.6	−6.3	−1.1	6.2	1.3	3.7	1.2	1.8	2.2

Source: Bank of Korea data (Seoul: Bank of Korea, 2005).

Table 14.3 Economic performance in North Korea

Section	*Unit*	*1995*	*1996*	*1997*	*1998*	*1999*	*2000*	*2001*	*2002*	*2003*	*2004*
GNP	$ Billion	22.3	21.4	17.7	12.6	15.8	16.8	15.7	17.0	18.4	20.8
GNP/person	$	1,034	989	811	573	714	757	706	762	818	914
Total trade volume	$ Billion	2.05	1.98	2.18	1.44	1.48	1.97	2.27	2.26	2.39	2.86
Export	$ Billion	0.74	0.73	0.91	0.56	0.51	0.56	0.65	0.74	0.78	1.02
Import	$ Billion	1.31	1.25	1.27	0.88	0.96	1.41	1.62	1.52	1.61	1.84
Foreign debt	$ Billion	11.8	12.0	11.9	12.1	12.2	12.5	NA	NA	NA	NA

Source: Bank of Korea data (Seoul: Bank of Korea, 2005); Ministry of Unification data (Seoul: Ministry of Unification, 2005).

From the late 1990s, the leadership sought new ways of economic management and cooperation aimed at improving prospects for expanded trade, foreign investment and development assistance. Kim Jong Il toured and witnessed China's economic miracles in the Fudong area in May 2000 and January 2001. What came next was a proposal of 'New Thinking'. Possibly having acquired an alternative vision of how to develop his deteriorating economic system, Kim Jong Il announced in January 2001 that 'there must be fundamental renovation in our way of thinking, ideological stance and work style to meet the demands of the new century' and that 'we should transcend the old working style and fixed economic framework of other countries in old times ... it is impossible to advance the revolution even a step further if we should get complacent with our past achievements or be enslaved to outdated ideas and stick to the outmoded style and attitude in our work'.[18] Achievements of the economic building in China and success stories of Chinese economic reforms were reported in an assigned special column in *Rodong Sinmun* from January 2001 as a frame of reference. Kim Jong Il's scheme of new economic development stressed practicality, information technology (IT) industry, science and technology-oriented economy. This signalled that North Korea has come to realize that the old style of economic development based on heavy industry is no longer valid as a developmental strategy for the new century.

A bold attempt to change the economic system took place in 2002 in a form of economic reform. Aiming at boosting production and improving living standards by introducing agricultural price incentives and stimulating the production of light industrial goods, the North Korean government implemented limited economic reform initiatives on 1 July 2002. The so-called 'Economic Management Improvement Measures' were implemented by the State Price Control Bureau 'to improve the management of the socialist economy' with some elements of pragmatism and markets. This meant that the state would continue to own the means of production, but factories and cooperative farms that the state lent to enterprises have a responsibility of their own to maximize profit. The measures included introduction of price and wage systems, legalization of the existing underground economy (i.e. farmers' markets), granting greater autonomy to farms and enterprises through reforms in industry and management, and reform of the foreign exchange system. The monetary reform package devalued its 'won' currency by a factor of 100 and raised wages by a similar amount. The old emphasis on equality was replaced by an emphasis on boosting production, maximizing efficiency, and incentives.

Subsequent reforms include new laws governing foreign investment, trade and development of special economic zones. Opening of the North Korean economy was promoted in 2002 with the designation of the Sinuiju special administrative district near the Chinese border, the Kumgang mountain tourist region, and the Kaesong industrial complex. Opposition by the Chinese government and arrest of the appointed first Chief Executive, Yang Bin, forced the North Korean Cabinet to officially withdraw its decision on the designation of the special economic zone in August 2004. However, the inter-Korean projects such as the Kumgang mountain tour and the Kaesong industrial complex have been progressing well since November 2003. Land development for the model complex in Kaesong City in North Korea for small and medium-sized South Korean companies was completed and is now in operation for manufacturing goods. Inter-Korean cooperation combining North Korea's cheap manpower and South Korea's investment, facilities and technology transfer in Kaesong has been promoting modernization of the North Korean economy to overcome long-term stagnation and development of labour-intensive light industry.

North Korea has taken the first tentative steps on the reformist path. The change accompanied side effects such as high inflation, a soaring exchange rate, social hardship, growing inequality, and the growth of informal sectors. Nevertheless, the reform initiatives induced significant changes in economic practice and within the society. Firstly, there has been a spread of markets and market activities in North Korea. The July 2002 economic package introduced the market at which farmers could sell their products, and subsequently expanded the farmers' market to be a synthetic consumer's market. In the middle of Pyongyang, there appeared 'Tong-il market' where market transactions take place legally, in which thousands of North Koreans sell and buy goods at largely free-floating prices. The markets in Pyongyang and in most of the major cities and towns have evolved into a large, covered, regulated market, complete with foreign exchange services with a wide variety of both domestic and imported consumer goods. Small family-sized businesses and street vendors became widespread even on rural roads. In addition to an increased number of small markets and selling points for agricultural products, more advanced forms of petty trade and services have developed. The most noticeable are small cooperatives, groups of a few people, which sell handicrafts and snacks or provide shoe and bicycle repair services. Foreign visitors and media increasingly see evidence of a grass-roots market economy.[19]

Secondly, the reform measures changed the survival mechanism of the North Korean people by lessening their state-dependent attitudes and encouraging market-oriented behaviour. The impact of the famine and food crisis of the mid-1990s disrupted the lives of the North Korean people. People left their jobs and assigned districts in search for food, creating a flock of economic migrants crossing the border to China or carrying out illegal transactions in the black market. A decade of struggles against hardship and adjusting to a new way of living resulted in some flexibility in the ideologically rigid and controlled social system in North Korea. It also gave isolated North Korea unprecedented exposure to foreign influences and to limitations of their command economy. With the establishment of 'general markets', people began to depend on these markets and private trading for their daily necessities rather than state provision. The change has facilitated people's awareness of money, materialism and commercialism, growing autonomy, and individualism associated with the new market mechanism.

Thirdly, the reform measures changed economic behaviour at the enterprise and individual level. There has been growing understanding of a market economy and rising working motivation owing to increasing market function and profit-based enterprise management as well as reduction of state planning and public assistance. A system of equal distribution of wages was replaced by an incentive system of labour wages and a distribution system based on performance, allowing the rise of actual income for some individuals among factory workers, employees in the service sectors, and farmers of collective farms. With the growth of management autonomy in factories and enterprises, the criteria for evaluating enterprises that used to be 'the volume of manufactured goods' shifted to 'profit'. Consequently, productivity has improved in some labour-intensive industrial sectors, such as agriculture and light industry. In the agricultural sector, crop productivity increased from 3.95 million tonnes in 2001 to 4.31 million tonnes in 2004 owing to the improvement of land utility and growing farming motivation. The growth rate of light industries marked a 2.3 per cent increase in 2003 and, in the commerce sector, the growth of wholesale and retail business reached 9.8 per cent in 2003, exceeding the total growth rate of 1.8 per cent.[20]

A shortage of investment resources, energy and raw materials hampers an increase of production in industry overall. However, the economic reform initiatives, though limited, opened up a new possibility of change in the North Korean system. The North Korean leadership is still carefully studying the transformation paths that other states have gone through to find a plausible way to accommodate partial changes without threatening regime continuation. During the EU high-level visit in May 2001, Kim Jong Il expressed his wish to introduce new economic policies, although not yet in a position to define them in detail, and stressed the importance of education and research development for the economy.[21] Since then, Kim has been sending a group of senior officials and managers to Europe to get acquainted with European economic policy models. He encouraged more extensive training of North Korean cadres in market economics and business management, and sent economic fact-finding missions to China and Vietnam to study their reforms. In January 2006, Kim Jong Il himself again toured in the southern part of China, including Wuhan, Guangzho and Shenzen, prior to sending an economic observation group comprising 30 inspectors to the same place to work out policy alternatives that could tackle the economic difficulties in North Korea.

North Korea invited the European Commission and EU member states to run some small-scale training and capacity-building projects mainly in the fields of economies in transition, international finance and trade, language courses, environment, etc. Representative examples are two rounds of EU–DPRK economic workshops in Pyongyang, in September 2004 and October 2005 respectively, where European experts discussed experiences of economic transition in other parts of the world and their views on doing business in the DPRK. Whereas the first workshop focused on giving a general overview of the economic transition process, the second dealt with more specific issues including strategies to attract foreign direct investment, restructuring the agricultural sector, and creation of small and medium-sized enterprises.[22] The workshop involved experts from Poland, Czech Republic and Hungary to outline a variety of ways of reform from which North Korea could seek its own path to improve its economy. Various EU–DPRK economic seminars were organized to present a variety of routes to economic and political development as well as modernization and of exploring how such alternatives might best be harmonized with specific conditions in the DPRK.

North Korea's economic structure is in many ways more similar to that in eastern European countries since it is more industry dependent than agricultural based. Although it is essential to modernize its agricultural sector to ensure food security for its population, agriculture is unlikely to become the motor of economic development. Significant effort had to go into reviving its industry and finding appropriate market niches to develop domestic and export trade in manufactured goods and to attract foreign investment. One advantage is that North Korea has a big pool of low-cost, educated labour, thus it should aim at an export-led growth trade strategy based on cheap labour assembling/outward processing. As a frame of reference, the Kim Jong Il leadership could perhaps look into the South Korean case at the beginning of the 1960s which had a strong military leadership, a well-educated and disciplined workforce, a low GDP and nationalism as the overarching force of integration. South Korea's economic success based on development of labour-intensive light industry, an export-led strategy combined with external inputs of significant amounts of capital, and state-directed economic planning could well be of relevance to present North Korea.

Conclusion

The main features of the old system were maintained in North Korea. However, continuation of the North Korean state socialist system in the 1990s was not a consequence of the superior functioning of its system to other disintegrated systems, but of lacking an alternative vision of how to restructure the existing system without risking regime collapse. The collapse of the socialist bloc left North Korea extremely insecure and paranoid both militarily and economically, as it lost its traditional allies and trade partners. The insecurity of the regime was manifested in its 'military-first' rhetoric of the 1990s and mirrored in the proposed vision of 'building an economically prosperous and militarily strong country'. If it were to survive, the leadership needed to find a way to adjust its system to overcome the challenges.

Only from the late 1990s did many significant changes take place in North Korea, signalling a Chinese-style reform within the existing system. Politically, leadership change from Kim Il Sung to his son, Kim Jong Il, brought about a different leadership style based on military-oriented features. Ideologically, the socialist ideology or revolutionary *Juche* idea that served as a dominant ideological platform in the past is declining, being replaced by rhetoric of 'building a powerful and prosperous nation' and 'military-first politics'. Economically, Kim Jong Il proposed a 'new way of thinking' and 'transcending the old working style', followed by economic reform measures on 1 July 2002. Introduction of prices and wages, working incentives, partial autonomy of enterprises and collective farms, and legalizing markets facilitated an unprecedented change in the North Korean economy and society. Moreover, an investment flow from South Korea through ever-expanding inter-Korean economic cooperation projects and from China gave special advantages to North Korea's economic development and modernization.

The evidence is that Kim Jong Il is prepared to step outside the political and economic limits laid down by his father Kim Il Sung's work. China and Vietnam's success in reform and openness may have provided Kim Jong Il with an alternative vision of a variant of market socialism (i.e. a gradual and controlled shift to open markets that allows the Communist Party to keep power). Yet, reforms hold both promise and peril for the Kim Jong Il leadership. The economic reform measures initially achieved only weak results, creating problems of inflation and social hardship. Opening up the country and allowing market activities accompanied relative loosening of political and social control of the population. Development of small-scale economic initiatives brought about a remarkable change of attitude and economic behaviour at the enterprise and individual level.

Present security issues and regime survival concerns plus economic sanction imposed by the US continue to dominate North Korea's policy choice and constrain the pace and nature of the reforms. The elite-led reforms, pursued by the existing cohesive political elite in North Korea, are likely to be limited. For significant long-lasting changes to occur in the North Korean system, it would require an elite change, a fundamental elite differentiation and the emergence of a new political generation or a rise of reform-oriented elites in the ruling group. Nevertheless, a long process towards a market economy has already started in North Korea.

The driving force of change is certainly coming from the leadership, and its strategy and management of the change will determine whether it will follow the Soviet or the Chinese path. North Korea today, therefore, stands at a critical juncture where it has to choose the right path of sustainable development while balancing change and continuity of the existing system. Learning from the experience of transformed societies, the Kim Jong Il leadership is likely to take careful steps towards economic reforms while protecting its political and ideological configuration. Although Kim Jong Il's blueprint for the future North Korea is hidden behind a veil at the moment, observation of the change in the North Korean system in the new century points to the path of the Chinese reform experience. While the pace of change is uncertain due to various internal and external variables, the direction towards modernizing the economy and opening up is clear and the process currently underway seems irreversible.

Notes

1 Taking 'system' as a generalized and comprehensive concept, Kornai defines system change as a process in which a society shifts away from the fundamental characteristics of one system and transforms itself into another system with a completely different configuration. J. Kornai, *From Socialism to Capitalism: What is Meant by the 'Change of System'?* (London: Social Market Foundation, 1998), p. 11.
2 I.P. Kim, *Communist Politics in North Korea* (New York: Praeger Publishers, 1975), pp. 65–76.
3 He eliminated the Yanan group in 1956, the Soviet group between 1957 and 1959, and his own Kapsan group in 1967. For the chronology of purges by Kim Il Sung, see I.S. Lee (ed.), *North Korea, the Land that Never Changes* (Seoul: Naewoe Press, 1995), pp. 17–19.
4 For discussion of *Juche* philosophy, see S.C. Kim, 'Juche Idea: Base of Regime Legitimation of North Korea in the Age of Decaying Socialism', *The Korean Journal of National Unification*, 1 (1992) 155–60.
5 For the original script see *Kim Il Sung Works*, Vol. 21 (Pyongyang: Foreign Languages Publishing House, 1985), p. 414.
6 The list of people who were purged by the charge of opposition to the hereditary succession plan is shown in the 'chronology of purges by Kim Il Sung', Lee, *North Korea,* p. 19.
7 Focusing on the agent of transition, there may be two major approaches to transition: the state-centred approach stresses institutions and elites as the major determinant of the transitional process and outcomes, and the society-centred approach regards modernization and mass political culture as important socio-economic and cultural preconditions for the societal force to induce transformation. See H. Eckstein et al., *Can Democracy Take Root in Post-Soviet Russia?: Explorations in State–Society Relations* (Lanham: Rowman & Littlefield Publishers, 1998), pp. 53 and 231.
8 Kim Jong Il, in May 1991, proposed the term and further developed the slogan in an address delivered before members of the Central Committee of the KWP. Kim Jong Il, 'Socialism of Our Style, Centered on the Masses, is always Victorious and Invincible', *Rodong Sinmun,* 27 May 1991.
9 'Historical Lesson in Building Socialism and the General Line of Our Party', Kim Jong Il, speech given on 3 January 1992, published in *Rodong Sinmun* on 4 February 1992, and broadcast on the same day by KCNA, transcribed by *FBIS*, East Asia, 92-024, 5 February 1992, pp. 11–24.
10 S. Kwon, 'Changes in the Composition and Structures of the North Korean Elite', *International Journal of Korean Unification Studies*, 12, 2 (2003).
11 Ibid., pp. 115–20.
12 There was a rumoured coup by a group of pro-Soviet military officers in North Korea in 1992. The rebellion was allegedly plotted by several generals of the People's Armed Forces, who had training in the USSR and aimed at overthrowing the North Korean leadership. It is said that the coup attempt failed and the coup participants were arrested and punished. For the details and the list of conspirators, see Kongdan Oh (ed.), *North Korean Policy Elites* (Virginia: Institute for Defense Analysis, 2004), p. II-28 footnote 28 and p. III 8-9.

13 The graph is based on my content analysis of 3364 *Rodong Sinmun* editorials between 1 January 1980 and 31 December 2004. As a part of the analysis, frequency counts of specific words or political symbols in all editorial headings that might mirror the substantial rationality of the regime were conducted. Change of ideology was illustrated on the basis of the analytical results. S. Kwon, 'Survival of the North Korean Regime and Changing Legitimation Modes', The Mario Einaudi Center for International Studies working paper series, No. 07-05 (Ithaca: Cornell University, 2005).

14 For details of the economic plans, see Table 1 in M. Noland, *Avoiding the Apocalypse: the Future of the Two Koreas* (Washington, DC: Institute for International Economics, 2000), pp. 66–7.

15 Quoted in the section 'relations with China' in ibid., pp. 99–101.

16 Ibid., pp. 187–9.

17 Data from the Ministry of Unification of Republic of Korea website: http:www.unikorea.go.kr

18 *Rodong Sinmun* editorial, 'Let us see and solve all problems from a new perspective and a new height', 9 January 2001. The so-called 'innovation in thinking and work attitude' in building an economically prosperous country, however, first appeared in a *Rodong Sinmun* editorial on 4 January 2001.

19 For reference, see the following articles: 'Shop till You Drop', *Hong Kong Far Eastern Economic Review*, 13 May 2004; 'Hermit Kingdom Peeps Cautiously out of its Shell', *Financial Times*, 12 February 2004; 'How N. Korea is Embracing Capitalism by any Other Name', *Guardian*, 3 December 2003; 'A Crack in the Door in N. Korea', *Washington Post*, 24 November 2003; 'Quietly, North Korea Opens Markets', *New York Times*, 21 November 2003; 'N. Korea Shifts toward Capitalism', *Washington Post*, 14 September 2003. For a detailed description of change inside North Korea, see also *North Korea: Status Report on Nuclear Program, Humanitarian Issues, and Economic Reforms* at the US Congress, 23 February 2004 and special report of FAO/WFP, *Special Report: FAO/WFP Crop and Food Supply Assessment Mission to the Democratic People's Republic of Korea*, 11 November 2004.

20 Y. Kim and S. Choi, *Understanding North Korea's Economic Reforms*, Analysis on North Korea 2005-02 (Seoul: Korea Institute for National Unification, 2005), pp. 45–6.

21 European Commission, *EC-Democratic People's Republic of Korea Country Strategy Paper 2001–2004*, p. 7 website: http://ec.europa.eu/comm/external_relations/north_korea/csp/01_04_en.pdf

22 Friedrich Naumann Stiftung, *Final Report on Workshop on Economic Reform and the Development of Economic Relations between the EU and the DPRK*, 1–3 September 2004, Pyongyang, DPRK. The Second EU–DPRK Workshop on Economic Reform was co-organized by the Friedrich Naumann Foundation with the support of the EU presidency, 12–14 October 2005 in Pyongyang. See the details of papers, speakers and programmes on the Friedrich Naumann Foundation website, http://www.fnfkorea.org

15
The Impact of the Demise of State Socialism on China

Jeanne L. Wilson

The demise of state socialism in eastern Europe and the Soviet Union in the late 1980s and early 1990s left China the most notable member of a dwindling cohort of Communist Party regimes. This chapter surveys the Chinese response to the collapse of state socialism throughout most of the former communist bloc as well as the Chinese assessment of these regimes in the process of transformation. I am primarily concerned to evaluate the Chinese Communist Party's (CCP) analysis of the relevance of these events for the Chinese leadership, in making policy decisions and interpreting the operation of the international system.[1] Two decades ago, Gilbert Rozman noted that the Chinese debate about Soviet socialism served as a surrogate means of discussing policy choices facing the Chinese leadership.[2] This tradition continues in China today.

This endeavour, however, faces certain methodological challenges. On the one hand, it is incontestable that the demise of state socialism has had a significant effect on the way in which Chinese leaders and elites view domestic and international events, which has subsequently been reflected in policy decisions. On the other hand, it is difficult, if not impossible, to determine the relative impact of the collapse of Marxist-Leninist regimes on the Chinese polity, compared with other causative factors, or to connect particular statements made by Chinese leaders to specific outcomes. Chinese leaders, like all political figures, carefully tailor their remarks to a specific audience and political context, which does not make for an absolute consistency of message.

Moreover, the Chinese assessment of the collapse of state socialism cannot be disassociated from the efforts of the Chinese leadership to come to terms with the Tiananmen incident in the spring of 1989. Both events, which overlapped temporally, challenged the stability of the regime and the legitimacy of Communist Party rule. These developments, moreover, evoked a crisis in the CCP, resulting in group infighting between reformists and their more conservative opponents over the appropriate response. Paramount leader Deng Xiaoping eventually managed to prevail over his adversaries, but debate still continues within Chinese political and intellectual circles as to the enduring significance of the collapse. Neither faction questions its relevance for China but they differ in their assessment of causes and policy implications. Generally speaking, the reform-oriented group within the CCP leadership has displayed more attention toward a factual investigation of the domestic and international factors that contributed to the collapse, while conservatives have been more likely to reference these conditions as a backdrop to a hortatory defence of domestic policies. This raises the question as to the extent to which the putative lessons of the collapse are rooted in an empirical assessment of events. Both sides, however, invariably evoke the experience as a platform for the promotion of their own domestic political agenda. Thus, a generic response by the CCP to the demise of state socialism does not exist.

China and the Soviet Union in the Gorbachev era

The Chinese leadership took careful note of Mikhail Gorbachev's ascension to the position of General Secretary of the CPSU in March 1985. Initial hostility to Gorbachev's efforts at domestic reform was replaced with an assessment that was cautiously affirmative, with analysts noting the similarities to China's own – albeit considerably more advanced – economic reform programme. At the same time, Gorbachev's promotion of glasnost or openness evoked envy among liberal Chinese and consternation among more conservative elements. In October 1988, Deng Xiaoping referred to Gorbachev as a 'comrade', signalling the impending normalization of relations.[3] Gorbachev's long anticipated trip to Beijing in May 1989 was, however, at best awkward. The Soviet leader arrived to a capital in tumult in the grip of the Tiananmen events. He was greeted as a hero by Chinese protestors who saw him as a representative of democratic forces. Several weeks later, the Tiananmen situation reached an ignominious conclusion as troops from the People's Liberation Army used force, killing at least hundreds of Chinese civilians, to clear the square and its surroundings.

The Tiananmen events evoked a crisis in the CCP, revealing the fissures created in Chinese society by a decade of reform. The student protests for greater democratization in Beijing and other urban areas were supported by a wider stratum of the Chinese social order (which was not, however, necessarily motivated by the same goals) that included intellectuals, workers and representatives of Chinese state and Party organs. Party conservatives viewed the continuation of the reform movement as a threat to political stability and to China as a Marxist-Leninist state under CCP leadership. The protests also raised the question as to China's appropriate relationship with the outside world. Many Party leaders were convinced that the West had played a decisive role in the instigation of the conflict, seeking to move China onto the path of a 'peaceful evolution' toward capitalism. While Deng Xiaoping remained the pre-eminent political leader, his prestige and authority were significantly undermined. Deng was a political conservative who shared the hardliners' concerns about preserving political stability and CCP primacy. But he was also an adherent to the cause of economic reform. As Deng noted in his June 1989 address to troops in Beijing: 'What about ... keeping to the policies of reform and opening to the outside world? Is that wrong or not? It is not wrong. How could we have achieved the success we have today without the reform and the open policy?'[4] In the short run, however, Deng was compelled to acquiesce to the conservative position placing reform on hold.

The policy debate within the Chinese leadership post-Tiananmen was inevitably affected by the simultaneous unfolding of events in eastern Europe, in which Marxist-Leninist regimes, like a series of falling dominoes, were sequentially replaced by multi-party governments committed to a capitalist future. The CCP observed this process with mounting concern, convening a series of high-level meetings and releasing a number of internal reports to analyse the situation. In the initial stages, the CCP was inclined to put the blame on Gorbachev personally for the troubles in the socialist bloc. In July 1989, China's leaders were reported to have censored publications dealing with Mikhail Gorbachev as politically too explosive.[5] Leading figures within the Party, including Jiang Zemin, Deng Xiaoping and Chen Yun, directly criticized Gorbachev for his role in encouraging 'bourgeois liberalization' and allowing events in eastern Europe to career out of control. The United States and its allies were also seen as active players in plotting the downfall of state socialism. As Deng noted in June 1989: 'The Western imperialists are trying to make all socialist countries abandon the socialist road, to bring them in the end under the rule of international monopoly capital and set them on the road to capitalism.'[6]

The formal Chinese response to the demise of socialism in eastern Europe was to adhere to China's long-touted policy of non-intervention in the domestic affairs of other states. The CCP, however, was clearly unnerved by the scale and rapidity of the events, publishing a series of internal documents that analysed their causes. These documents tended to emphasize that China was not subject to the maladies (i.e. bureaucratism, corruption, presence of bourgeois ideology) that had permeated the regimes of eastern Europe, weakening them to the point of dissolution. The inability of the Marxist-Leninist parties to staunch the political demands of demonstrators was taken as a vindication of the CCP's response to the Tiananmen crackdown.

The Chinese leadership's attention to eastern Europe, however, was soon diverted by the accumulating signs of political disintegration in the Soviet Union. The prospect of the collapse of state socialism in its birthplace posed a far greater challenge to the CCP than in eastern Europe, raising questions as to the legitimacy and sustainability of Marxism-Leninism in China itself. Chinese leaders watched with mounting revulsion the political changes sweeping the Soviet Union, the steady erosion of CPSU authority, the intensification of ethnic demands for political autonomy, and the utter failure of Gorbachev's efforts at economic reform. As with the events surrounding the collapse of communism in eastern Europe, CCP leaders were inclined to place much of the blame for the Soviet deterioration on Gorbachev personally, and his 'New Thinking', that led him to advocate a humanitarian and democratic socialism that ran counter to fundamental principles of Marxism-Leninism. A number of leaders, including Wang Zhen and Deng Liqun, pressed for the public repudiation of Gorbachev and the cessation of links with the Soviet Union, a policy that was steadily rejected by Deng. Eventually, CCP internal analyses came to the dispiriting conclusion that an endorsement of Gorbachev was the lesser evil compared to the truly unpalatable alternative represented by Boris Yeltsin and the only pragmatic option given the lack of support for figures on the political left.

The Chinese leadership was brought to a point of crisis by the failure of the August 1991 coup attempt in the Soviet Union and the subsequent dissolution of the CPSU. Formally, the CCP issued a dispassionate statement stressing that changes in the Soviet Union were 'its own internal affair'.[7] Behind the scenes, the CCP began a process of agonized appraisal of its options. In the wake of the coup, the Politburo, meeting in emergency sessions, set forth Deng Xiaoping's 24-character principle to summarize the Chinese reaction: 'observe coolly, stand firm, tackle calmly, hide our capacity, be good at maintaining a low profile, and never try to take the lead'. This prescription, however, did not reflect a consensual view. Party conservatives argued that the dismantling of Marxism-Leninism in the Soviet Union necessitated a more aggressive response, in which the CCP would assume leadership of what remained of the communist bloc, and export revolution abroad. Party leftists also urged a reversion to Maoist era practices on the domestic front, embodied in the intensification of efforts to combat peaceful evolution through class struggle. Deng Liqun, in particular, advocated extending class struggle to the intellectuals, a decision that was justified in part by the contributory role that intellectuals had played in the overthrow of Marxist-Leninist states in eastern Europe.[8]

Led by Deng Xiaoping, the reformist wing of the CCP was constructing its own agenda, which sought to reinvigorate the stalled economic reforms. In April 1991, Deng managed to secure the appointment of Zhu Rongji, widely known as 'China's Gorbachev' for his liberal economic views, to the position of vice premier. In January, 1992 Deng embarked on his celebrated 'Southern Tour' preaching the message of economic reform. Deng reiterated the perspective that he had steadfastly upheld over the years: reform and opening up to the outside world were imperative, and a matter of China's survival. In his attacks on Party conservatives, Deng made it clear that the greater danger to China originated from the left rather than the right.[9] With the critical support of the military, Deng was able to prevail over his opponents, some of whom lost their positions as a consequence.[10] The Fourteenth Party Congress, held in October 1992, was a landmark event for the 88-year-old

Deng Xiaoping and his supporters who managed to set China irrevocably upon the course of reform, as well as to lay down the framework for the institutionalization of political succession in the PRC. The factional struggles that had racked the CCP since the Tiananmen events were not extinguished, but they were greatly diminished.

In the short run, at least, the CCP had demonstrated its capacity to survive in the face of the disappearance of most of the communist bloc. There is no doubt that the demise of state socialism was a serious blow to the CCP. Yet, paradoxically, it also provided some positive benefits. The collapse of the Soviet Union removed a formidable military presence to the north. The political violence that accompanied the overthrow of Ceauşescu in Romania and the tumult that gripped the Soviet Union in its death throes were unattractive to Chinese across the political spectrum, leading many, including former dissenters, to accept the Party's rationale for its violent suppression of student demonstrators in 1989. Political stability through the governance of the CCP seemed preferable to the political disarray and economic decline prevalent throughout the states of the former communist bloc, and the only realistic option for China. The conservatives within the CCP were also discredited by their inability to construct an approach that did not seem fundamentally retrogressive in its retreat to the discredited and anachronistic policies of the Maoist past. The rejection of the reform course promoted by Deng seemed to leave China, especially in a world without visible remaining alternatives to integration into the global market economy, in an untenable position, reminiscent of a renegade state like North Korea.

The demise of state socialism: implications for China

Many Western assessments of China in the post-Soviet era take the eventual collapse of the CCP as a given, assuming that state socialist regimes have become societal anachronisms, soon to be relegated to the dustbin of history.[11] Nonetheless, the CCP has shown little interest in a deliberate policy of self-annihilation. Since 1992, the Chinese leadership has viewed the collapse of state socialism in eastern Europe and the Soviet Union as a cautionary lesson for China, which merits continuous examination, with consequent policy implications. To these ends, the CCP formed a number of working groups to issue reports and called upon Chinese academics with a specialization in eastern Europe and the former Soviet Union to redirect their research to the topic.[12] The Central Party School of the CCP added a course on lessons for China from the Soviet Union's collapse to its curriculum. The Chinese leadership's reaction to the collapse of communism in eastern Europe and the Soviet Union can be broadly grouped into two – albeit interrelated – categories: (1) critiques supportive of the reform programme outlined by Deng Xiaoping, and continued by his predecessors; (2) critiques promulgated by the left wing of the CCP that attributed the demise of communism to the revisionist domestic policies of Communist Party regimes – especially in the Soviet Union – which were further weakened by the onslaught of external pressures applied by the imperialist states.

This categorization, however, does not reflect the full range of Chinese reactions to the failure of state socialism. In the 1990s, Chinese intellectual thought became increasingly heterodox, exploring modes of thinking and ideological approaches that deviated from traditional assumptions of Marxist-Leninist analysis.[13] These included neo-conservatism, neo-statism and the emergence of the so-called 'new left'.[14] Certain themes were common to many of these approaches: a strongly nationalistic orientation, the need for strong state intervention in a market economy (akin to the experience of other East Asian states), and a scepticism if not outright hostility to China's increasing integration into the world market economy. Shortly after the failure of the Soviet coup attempt, for example, a group of intellectuals associated with *China Youth Daily* wrote a report, 'Realistic Options and Strategic Options for Chinese after the Soviet Upheaval', that was generally considered to reflect the opinions of Chen Yuan, the son of party elder Chen Yen, and other members of the so-called 'princeling faction' of the CCP, a group of middle-aged well-connected cadres with political ambitions and an unorthodox interpretation of Marxism-Leninism that fell into the range of neo-conservative discourse.[15] The authors maintained that China needed to maintain Party control over the economy, place more emphasis on patriotism and nationalism in the struggle against peaceful evolution, and apply realist principles to China's foreign policy behaviour as a means of preventing a Soviet-style debacle. While this perspective was touted with the Party itself, the adherents to new left discourse largely remained distanced from the corridors of political power. According to Wang Hui, the co-editor of *Dushu* (Reading), a repository along with *Tianya* (Frontier) of new leftist thought, global capitalism had advanced to a new historical stage with the disintegration of the Soviet and eastern European socialist systems, impelling the emergence of neo-liberalism as the global hegemonic ideology.[16] For Wang, moreover, in a reversal of commonly assumed causal linkages, the Tiananmen events loomed as the determinant factor in initiating the demise of state socialism: 'the Tiananmen incident that took place on 4 June 1989 shook the world and in its wake initiated the collapse of Eastern Europe and the Soviet Union'.[17] This rather grandiose and Sinocentric assessment implicitly dismissed the premise, upheld by the CCP leadership, that there were lessons to be learned from studying the Soviet and eastern European experience.

Reform as the predominant lesson of the Soviet collapse

In the 1990s, CCP General Secretary Jiang Zemin turned to Chinese academics, mostly located within the Chinese Academy of Social Sciences (CASS) in Beijing, to provide an intellectual justification of his reform polices and to counter the attacks of his opponents. Liu Ji, a close friend of Jiang, and the Vice-President of CASS from 1993 to 1998, was instrumental in aiding Jiang in this endeavour.[18] During the course of the decade a series of publications appeared extolling the virtues of Jiang and his reform policies, some of which addressed the issue of the socialist collapse. These assessments of the causes of the demise of the Soviet Union tended to emphasize structural factors, in particular the deficiencies of the Soviet economy. In 1966, Liu arranged for the publication of *Heart to Heart Talks with the General Secretary*.[19] Written by a group of young scholars, the work commended Jiang's vision of reform based on a 1995 speech, and was notable in its identification of Leonid Brezhnev, not Gorbachev, as the chief culprit responsible for the demise of the Soviet Union. In this view, the stability of the 18 years of Brezhnev's leadership was not a genuine stability but a form of stagnation that provided the preconditions for the Soviet Union's eventual demise, and ensured the failure of Gorbachev's efforts at reform. The authors acknowledged that reform resulted in the 'smashing of equilibrium' but also argued that the lesson of Brezhnev was that 'not to push reform, not to persist in reform, not to carry reform through to the end means only that the party, state, and socialism will not be able to have genuine security, and that the final result will be a thorough instability'.[20]

This theme carried over to assessments of Soviet foreign policy, with the 1998 publication of another reformist tract, *China Will Not Be 'Mr. No.'*[21] The author, Shen Jiru, argued that the Soviet Union's pursuit of superpower status had come at the cost of creating unnecessary enemies and the loss of potential friends, leading to economic overextension and the exhaustion of its national strength. The Soviet Union's unwillingness to cooperate with other countries and to cling to a policy of economic autarky (Mr No is a reference to the long-standing Soviet Foreign Minister Andrei Gromyko) was a factor in its eventual demise. Shen's analysis implicitly evoked Deng Xiaoping's 24-character principle that 'China should hide its capacity, be good at maintaining a low profile and never try to take the lead', and served as a rebuke to Jiang's opponents who favoured a more militant foreign policy approach and found rapprochement with the United States unacceptable. Shen's major message, however, was that the Soviet collapse was a result of its dismal economic performance, which eroded popular confidence in socialism and aggravated ethnic tensions. In this regard, the Soviet Union held an important message for China.

In his first years as General Secretary, Jiang Zemin proved to be a cautious leader. By the late 1990s, however, Jiang, working in collaboration with Premier Zhu Rongji, began to step up the pace of reform in China. In February 2000, Jiang introduced the concept of the 'three represents' (*sange daibiao*), an effort to redefine the CCP's ideological legacy to correspond with contemporary conditions. According to Jiang, as long as the Party adhered to the development needs of the advanced forces of production, the forward direction of advanced culture, and the fundamental interests of the broad masses, it would be able to withstand future challenges. Jiang's speech was a signal – albeit a rather obtuse one – that China would intensify its movement toward market capitalism and integration into the global economy. In a subsequent speech, given in July 2001 on the Eightieth Anniversary of the Founding of the CCP, Jiang reiterated the three represents precept while urging that entrepreneurs be accepted into the Party.[22] The emphasis on developing the most advanced forces of production also provided the CCP with a theoretical justification for laying off workers in unprofitable state-run enterprises. Jiang's outline clearly exceeded the ideological parameters laid out by Deng. Whereas Jiang emphasized the importance of satisfying the interests of the 'broad masses', Deng was unyielding in his promotion of the dictatorship of the proletariat as one of his Four Cardinal Principles.[23] The three represents were formulated as a domestic agenda for China, but they also reflected the latest evolution in China's effort to deter a Soviet-style collapse. According to Luo Zhongmin, Dean of the Party History Research Office at the Beijng Party School, Jiang's answer to the question as to why the Soviet Union disintegrated was that 'it didn't represent the development of the most advanced forces of production, advanced culture, and the fundamental interests of the broad masses. It was backward. It felt it was the best and that it didn't need to change.'[24]

Jiang's promulgation of the three represents soon generated a profusion of articles which attributed the failure of regimes in eastern Europe and the Soviet Union to their inability to meet the needs of socialism, especially with respect to the development of advanced productive forces.[25] These analyses further tended to link the legitimacy of the CCP to its ability to represent the fundamental interests of the Chinese people, which more pragmatically meant the provision of tangible economic benefits. With China's entrance into the World Trade Organization in 2001 (a controversial move in China domestically as well as internationally), proponents of the CCP's reform path began to fault the Soviet model for its rejection of globalization. Previous critiques had criticized the Soviet Union for its adherence to the Soviet planning model and for its rejection of integration into the global economy, but these analyses went further in claiming globalization as an overall net benefit to socialist states. As an article appearing in a Yunnan CCP publication noted: 'the Soviet collapse demonstrates it is not possible to take an independent road that seals off contact from globalization. Of course, contemporary globalization is dominated by capitalism, but it is also a means of socialist development.'[26]

Jiang's embrace of globalization, and his implicit sanctioning of widening income inequality as an inexorable cost of growth, has been partially modified by his successor, Hu Jintao, who assumed the position of CCP General Secretary in 2002. In contrast to Jiang, Hu has displayed a greater concern over the adverse consequences of China's rising disparity between rich and poor, rural and urban regions, and the affluent eastern coastal regions compared with the impoverished western provinces. He has also targeted corruption within the CCP as a threat to regime legitimacy. Hu, moreover, has indicated some anxieties over the long-term effects of globalization for China. In 2003, for example, CCP authorities instructed CASS to establish a study group on neo-liberalism, a concept which had been a concern of the new left but had not hitherto been the object of particular attention by the CCP.[27] Hu's own contribution to the Chinese theoretical canon has been the notion of a 'socialist harmonious society', a slogan with overt Confucian overtones that places an emphasis on providing for the people's livelihood (an updated version of Sun Yat-sen's Three Principles of the People) and promoting social equity, justice and good governance. The construction of a 'socialist harmonious society' received a formal endorsement at the Sixth Plenary Session of the CCP Central Committee in October 2006. In fact, Hu has had good reason to seek to address issues of equity and corruption in China. The relentless movement to the market has exacerbated societal tensions to the point at which social unrest poses a danger to the Party's pre-eminent desire to preserve social stability. In the first ten months of 2006, for example, over 86,000 mass incidents and public disturbances were reported to have taken place.[28]

The struggle against peaceful evolution: views from the CCP left

The left wing of the CCP was dealt a decisive setback by Deng's success in reactivating China's reform programme in 1992 but it continued to fight a rearguard struggle against the reformers throughout the 1990s and into the 2000s. Fortunately for the reformers, the most powerful leftists were an ageing group, associates of Deng Xiaoping, many of whom like Deng, gradually faded from the political scene in the 1990s through death or ill health. Nonetheless, a substantial cohort remained, touting a political agenda that had not evolved in significant measure since the early 1990s. Leftist analyses were to be found in a wide range of journals and periodicals, but the leftist camp exercised editorial control over four periodicals in particular as a forum for their perspective: *Gao Xiao Lilun Zhanxian* (Theoretical Front in Colleges and Universities), *Dangdai Sichao* (Contemporary Trends of Thought), *Zhongliu* (Mainstream) and *Zhenli de Zhuiqui* (Search for Truth). The gist of the leftist position was that the reform programme was setting China upon a path away from the genuine practice of Marxism-Leninism toward outright revisionism. The movement away from the collective economy, the toleration and later encouragement of privatization, the implicit repudiation of class struggle and the acceptance of capitalists as members of the CCP paralleled the policies that had been pursued in eastern Europe and the Soviet Union with disastrous consequences. These measures were also considered to play into the hands of the imperialist forces which sought the peaceful evolution of socialist states into the capitalist fold.

Whereas the reformist wing of the CCP came to stress structural conditions as a critical factor in the demise of the Soviet Union, the leftists continued to ascribe much of the blame to Gorbachev as a key catalyst, castigating him for his 'humanistic democratic socialism' that led the CPSU away from its Marxist-Leninist roots. In the mid-1990s, several 10,000 character documents were circulated inside the CCP, prepared by members of the leftist faction. The second one of these to be released concentrated on the impact of external factors on China's domestic development. According to its author, Wu Yifeng, a professor at China's People's University, bourgeois liberalization in the Soviet Union had led to its demise, a fate that he also foresaw for China if current trends continued. In Wu's opinion, 'Moscow is a mirror to Beijing.' Following this logic, the capitalist system being developed in Russia as a consequence of the Soviet Union's disintegration was simultaneously appearing 'at an accelerated pace' in China, such that the 'bourgeoisie inside our country is joining forces with international capital practicing a strategy of peaceful evolution in China'.[29]

Shortly before Jiang Zemin delivered his July 2001 speech, an article appeared in *Zhenli de Zhuiqui* that also commemorated the eightieth anniversary of the founding of the CCP.[30] The author, Zheng Tianxiang, an influential member of the CCP's leftist leadership and the former president of China's Supreme People's Court, found it 'incredible' that within the Party 'there were those who advocated admitting capitalists'.[31] Zheng further argued that a new capitalist class in fact had already emerged in China, and that some theoreticians desired that China abandon socialism in favour of the development of a capitalist system like that of the United States. This, Zheng noted, was a steadfast aim of the imperialists, who 'daily pushed China toward capitalism and a capitalist transformation.... They have already managed to achieve capitalism in the Soviet Union. They also desire to promote this plan with China.'[32]

Jiang's July 2001 speech predictably aroused considerable opposition among the CCP left. Leftist ideologues circulated yet another 10,000 character document, more virulent than those issued in the mid-1990s, which contained a personal attack on Jiang Zemin. In response, Jiang instructed that those who voiced public opposition to his speech be denied access to the new Central Committee and barred from promotions to higher-level positions.[33] Jiang further ordered that *Zhenli de Zhuiqui* and *Zhongliu,* the two flagship publications of the leftists, be shut down.[34] Censorship of right-wing and ideologically liberal publications was, of course, nothing new to China, but the application of the same measures to left-wing magazines was unprecedented. If Jiang saw the three represents as a means of saving the CCP from the fate of its socialist brethren, the left wing of the CCP appeared to be equally convinced that such policies would strike a death blow for Marxism-Leninism in China.

Divergent outlooks and common ground

Reformist critiques did not forsake an obligatory recital of the myriad ways in which the Soviet Union and the eastern Europe regimes had deviated from a correct interpretation of Marxism-Leninism, seen in corruption, bureaucratism, and lack of democracy both within and outside the Party. Their analyses on the topic did not differ from the leftists in substance as much as degree. Both groups also shared a common concern with the maintenance of political order and stability. Nonetheless, reformist assessments tended to differ from the more traditional analyses of the leftists not only in their proposals, but also in their methods of analysis. The reformists were more inclined to emphasize the key role of structural factors in the demise of state socialism, and also more oriented toward empirical research in their publications. To put it bluntly, the reformists tended to be better scholars than the more pedantic ideological leftists, and also arguably better Marxists in their approach. As the Soviet Union spiralled toward collapse, virtually the entire CCP leadership criticized Gorbachev personally for his role in orchestrating events leading to the collapse of the socialist bloc. By the 2000s, however, reformist assessments had become nuanced in their treatment, placing more emphasis on the economic conditions which Gorbachev inherited and proved intractable to reform. Gorbachev, however, remained the object of leftist excoriation. The notion that leaders play a decisive role is a staple of bourgeois historiography – the Great Man Theory of History – but runs counter to Marxist explications of historical materialism. Similarly, the reformists' detailed examination of events led them over time to look more carefully at the nationalities issue as a factor in the disintegration of Yugoslavia and the Soviet Union. Although the CCP leadership was concerned about the potential impact of ethnic unrest in the Soviet Union spilling over into China, the internal documents released by the CCP did not devote widespread attention to the topic.[35] In contrast, a CASS-commissioned book, *Collapse of a Superpower*, published on the tenth anniversary of the Soviet demise, focused heavily on Soviet national minority policy, arguing that China could learn from the Soviet Union's failed experience. The final chapter of the volume listed 12 historical reasons for the Soviet disintegration, seven of which referred in one format or another to national minority issues. Blaming Great Russian chauvinism for the aggravation of minority tensions in a tightly controlled system, the authors cautioned for the need to give Chinese ethnic minorities greater autonomy in governance while simultaneously promoting economic development.[36]

China and the post-socialist states

Chinese analyses have been more concerned with the events surrounding the collapse of state socialist regimes than their subsequent evolution. The first issue has the most direct policy significance for China, and has thus aroused the most controversy. Nonetheless, Chinese leaders have continued to maintain a vigilant watch over processes of post-socialist transformation. Chinese pragmatism prevailed over ideological disdain as the Chinese leadership, at the urging of Deng Xiaoping, opted to maintain ties with the former socialist states. In effect, the Chinese leadership accepted the demise of state socialism as a fait accompli, redirecting its efforts to the survival of China as a Marxist-Leninism regime rather than its resurrection elsewhere. Chinese assessments of the post-socialist experience of eastern Europe have tended to focus on its economic performance with some attention given to the efforts of the emergent regimes to democratize. In contrast, China's interactions with Russia and the other former Soviet republics – especially the states of central Asia – have been highly motivated by strategic calculations, especially with regard to the implications of US involvement in the region. The eastern European reforms are seen to have direct policy implications for China. Scholarly assessments of the eastern European experience have tended toward a neutral recounting of the economic situation.[37] The negative effects of reform – rising levels of income inequality, unemployment, etc. – are reported but with little sense of triumphalism inasmuch as China is acknowledged to suffer from many of the same maladies. The Russian experience with reform, however, has been so dramatically different from that of China that it is considered to provide few direct lessons, except as a negative example. For the Chinese leadership, Russia's economic travails in the 1990s were taken as a vindication not only of the Chinese incremental path to economic reform but also of the CCP's role in Chinese society.

The CCP's sense that it had successfully weathered the disintegration of the socialist bloc was shaken, however, by the onset of political unrest and subsequent leadership successions in Georgia, Ukraine and Kyrgyzstan, beginning in 2003. The 'colour revolutions' (*yanse geming*), as the Chinese labelled them, received considerable attention in the media, and provoked reactive measures by the leadership. The CCP perspective on the colour revolutions was notably similar to that of the Russian government under the presidency of Vladimir Putin.[38] Although internal factors were considered to play a role in the development of political instability, external actors, notably the Western powers and the US in particular, were considered decisive in inciting political unrest. In the Orange Revolution, for example, Viktor Yuschenko was viewed as prevailing in his quest for the presidency because of the strong backing and financial support that he received from the Western powers.[39] The US was seen to have several interrelated goals in its incitement of colour revolutions: it was a means of encircling Russia and constricting its power and it also provided a way for the US to establish control over central Asia through the installation of pro-US regimes.[40] Central Asia, in this assessment, was considered as a new global heartland, providing a base for fighting the war on terror, access to energy resources, and a strategic geographical position to pressure Russia and China.

In effect, the Chinese considered the colour revolutions as simply the latest tactic in the long-standing efforts of the US and its allies to carry out a programme of peaceful evolution. The emphasis of the Bush administration on democratization was viewed as a means of ensuring supportive regimes in the region. Colour revolutions differed from more overt policies of the imperialist powers in their reliance on the electoral process and instruments of 'soft power'. These included financial and public relations backing to opposition forces, manipulation of the media, and especially the use of non-governmental organizations (NGOs) as a front for Western interests. As one Chinese assessment put it: 'NGOs are an instrument that the Western states like to use. They are a "Trojan horse" planted by the Western intelligence agencies.'[41]

In the view of the Chinese leadership, the Western states were not content to foment regime change in the former Soviet Union, but also harboured the same goal for China. Chinese sensitivities were further heightened by the heavy-handed rhetoric of US officials. In a 2005 policy speech Robert Zoellick, the US Deputy Secretary of State, urged China to adopt democratic reforms and allow direct elections. In May 2005, Hu Jintao was reported to have issued an internal report to cadres calling for vigilance against US attempts to instigate a colour revolution in China.[42] Hu and his associates also turned their attention to CASS, instructing scholars to investigate colour revolutions (with the aim of preventing their spread to Xinjiang province) as well as suggesting they intensify their focus on the political situation in the region, with particular attention on Russia and central Asia. The CASS report also noted that the central authorities had instructed them to stop accepting external funds for research.[43]

The Chinese leadership also took steps to restrict the penetration of the foreign media. In November 2005, Beijing suspended plans to allow foreign newspapers to print in China. Shi Zhongyuan, head of the General Administration of Press and Publication, was candid in his explanation for the decision: 'When I think of the "colour revolutions", I feel afraid.'[44] Parallel efforts were also undertaken to step up censorship control over the domestic press and the Internet. In addition, the Chinese leadership sought to tighten its supervision of NGOs. A proposal to provide greater freedom of operation to NGOs was shelved, and the Ministry of Civil Affairs stopped processing applications for the registration of new groups. Foreign-funded NGOs were placed under close observation, with the government beginning intensive financial and security probes of their operations. Unsurprisingly, organizations funded by such non-profits as the International Republican Institute, the National Endowment for Democracy and the Ford Foundation came under particular scrutiny.[45]

Conclusion

The Soviet collapse was not an unmitigated disaster for China. It enhanced the credibility of the CCP's justification of the Tiananmen crackdown, and led many to conclude that strong authoritarian rule and political stability were far preferable to the political upheaval and economic dislocation in the former Soviet Union. But the demise of most of the Marxist-Leninist regimes posed a formidable challenge to the legitimacy of the CCP as well as its capacity to endure as a seemingly fading representative of a historically doomed movement. The steady embrace of market capitalism in the 1990s and

2000s, exemplified in the 2002 decision to admit capitalists into the Party, pushed China further away from its Marxist-Leninist roots. Regime legitimacy after 1992 was premised in large part on the commitment to increase the standard of living of the population, a promise that was increasingly threatened in the 2000s by persistent economic inequalities between regions and a dramatic rise in income inequality. Nationalism emerged as another pillar of regime legitimacy. Patriotic fervour was easier to mobilize in China with its predominantly Han population than in the ethnically diverse Soviet Union. Nationalism had always comprised an underlying component of the CCP's programme, but after the demise of the Soviet Union, it increasingly became a substitute for Marxism-Leninism, rather than coexisting in some uneasy synthesis.

Deng Xiaoping's answer to the Soviet collapse was to pursue a programme of economic reform under the sole direction of the CCP. Since Deng's death, Chinese reform has continued unabated, while the sanctity of Deng's Four Principles has been called into question. The Party is not about to jettison its adherence to Marxism-Leninism, nor abandon its claim to leadership, but its commitment to the socialist road and the dictatorship of the proletariat has been eroded by reformist policies. Without refuting the three represents, Hu Jintao's own contribution in the ideological sphere has been the promotion of a 'harmonious society', a phrase which deliberately taps into traditional Chinese cultural values, while simultaneously downplaying the relevance of societal contradictions under conditions of market socialism. The CCP conservatives who objected to Deng's reform programme as undercutting traditional precepts of the Chinese approach to Marxism-Leninism were undoubtedly correct, although it is difficult to believe that their approach – the rejection of market reform and a return to Marxism-Leninism–Mao Zedong thought as the sole criterion of truth – would have been more effective in preventing a Soviet-style collapse. By the 2000s, China's economy had modernized such that it required greater transparency and openness for optimal efficiency, demands that were incongruent with its political structures. The CCP leadership contemplated numerous measures aimed at democratization, but conservatives and reformers alike were wary of potential adverse consequences. In this respect, Gorbachev's attempts to install a humanitarian democratic socialism presumably served as a compelling negative example.

The extent to which the demise of state socialism can be attributed to external or internal factors has been a topic of enduring concern to the Chinese leadership. Deng's position was to acknowledge the presence of both as contributory but to stress the foremost importance of making domestic changes as a defence against external attacks. Conservatives and reformers alike accept the premise of peaceful evolution as a conscious explicit goal of the Western powers, and a key factor in the demise of the socialist bloc, although conservatives tend to place greater emphasis on the concept. To reformers, however, integration into the global economy is a necessary prerequisite of economic modernization. In contrast, members of both the old left and the new left have a much more sceptical attitude, concerned that China's actions are at the cost of the loss of state sovereignty and subordination to the hegemonic powers – i.e. the US in particular – that exercise a commanding control over the operation of the global economy. Whereas globalization presents an economic challenge, the colour revolutions indicate a threat of a different order, with the Western states practising a policy of subversion from within, building ties with opposition groups, making use of NGOs, and seeking to promulgate their message through both the foreign and if possible the domestic media. This is, as far as the Chinese leadership across the political spectrum is concerned, the updated pursuit of peaceful evolution in a new guise.

The Chinese situation differs from that of its former socialist brethren in eastern Europe and the western areas of the former Soviet Union insofar as it is simultaneously pursuing the dual task of economic modernization and the transformation from a command economy. China has benefited from some conditions not readily available to many other former socialist states, including an overseas diaspora with ample funds to invest, a seemingly unlimited supply of inexpensive labour, and stable governance. Still, the challenges facing China are enormous, and any prediction of China's eventual fate is a perilous undertaking. Nonetheless, over a decade and a half after the demise of state socialism in eastern Europe and the Soviet Union, the Chinese leadership has so far managed to chart a flexible course of adaptation so as to ensure regime survival.

Notes

1 For additional assessments, see Gerald Segal, 'China and the Disintegration of the Soviet Union', *Asian Survey*, XXXII, 9 (September 1992) 848–68; John W. Garver, 'The Chinese Communist Party and the Collapse of Soviet Communism', *China Quarterly*, 133 (March 1993) 1–26; Christopher Marsh, 'Learning from Your Comrade's Mistakes: the Impact of the Soviet Past on China's Future', *Communist and Postcommunist Studies*, 36 (September 2003) 259–72; and Christopher Marsh, *Unparalleled Reforms: China's Rise, Russia's Fall, and the Interdependence of Transition* (New York: Lexington Books, 2006).

2 Gilbert Rozman, *The Chinese Debate about Soviet Socialism, 1978–1985* (Princeton: Princeton University Press, 1987). For Rozman's study of Soviet scholarship on China, see *A Mirror for Socialism: Soviet Criticisms of China* (Princeton: Princeton University Press, 1985).

3 FBIS-CHI, 24 October 1988, 4.

4 Deng Xiaoping, *Selected Works of Deng Xiaoping*, Vol. III (Beijing: Foreign Languages Press), p. 302.

5 FBIS-CHI, 29 July 1989.

6 Deng, *Selected Works*, Vol. III, p. 302.

7 *Xinhua*, 30 August 1991.

8 Yeh Lu-ching, 'CPC Holds Up Communism on its Own, Launches Protracted War against Capitalism', *Tangtai*, 6 (23 September 1991) 13–17 in FBIS-CHI-91-187, 26 September 1991; and Hsi Wen, 'Special Topic: CPC's Internal Anti-subversion, Anti-Peaceful Evolution Materials: CPC again Mentions Need to Remold

Intellectuals', *Chiushih Nientai*, No. 264, 1 January 1992, 34–5 in FBIS-CHI-82-010, 15 January 1992.

9 Deng, *Selected Works*, Vol. III, p. 363.

10 At the Fourteenth Party Congress, the Central Advisory Commission, a haven for conservative party elders, was abolished, while a number of leftists in the CCP, including Song Ping, formerly a member of the Politburo Standing Committee and Gao Di the Director of *People's Daily,* were removed from their posts.

11 See, for example, Gordon C. Chang, *The Coming Collapse of China* (New York: Random House, 2001) and Jack A. Goldstone, 'The Coming Chinese Collapse', *Foreign Policy*, 99 (Summer 1995) 35–52.

12 Marsh, 'Learning from Your Comrade', pp. 264–5; and Marsh, *Unparalleled Reforms*, pp. 107–10.

13 For an expanded discussion, see Joseph Fewsmith, *China since Tiananmen: the Politics of Transition* (New York: Cambridge University Press, 2001).

14 Fewsmith, in *China since Tiananmen* (p. 114) indicates that he prefers the term 'postmodernists' to refer to this group, as the term 'leftist' has a negative connotation for most intellectuals in China. In a 2006 interview, Wang Hui reiterated that he disliked the term 'new left', preferring to be identified as a 'critical intellectual'. Pankaj Mishara, 'China's New Leftist', *New York Times Magazine*, 15 October 2006, 50.

15 David Kelly (ed.), 'Realistic Responses and Strategic Options: an Alternative CCP Ideology and Its Critics', *Chinese Law and Government,* (March–April, 1996) 13–31.

16 Wang Hui (edited by Theodore Hunter), *China's New Order* (Cambridge: Harvard University Press, 2003).

17 Ibid., p. 62.

18 Fewsmith, *China since Tiananmen*, pp. 167, 184.

19 Weng Jieming, Zhang Ximing, Zhang Qiang and Qu Kemin (eds), *Yu zhongshuji tanxin* [Heart to Heart Talks with the General Secretary] (Beijing: Zhongguo shehui kexue chubanshe, 2001).

20 Ibid., p. 19.

21 Jiru Shen, '*Zhongguo bu dang "bu xiansheng"*' [China will not be 'Mr. No'] (Beijing: Jinri Zhongguo chubanse, 1998).

22 This measure was adopted in 2002.

23 Deng's Four Cardinal Principles were (1) uphold the dictatorship of the proletariat; (2) adherence to the socialist path; (3) uphold CCP leadership; and (4) uphold Marxism-Leninism–Mao Zedong thought.

24 Susan V. Lawrence, 'Three Cheers for the Party', *Far Eastern Economic Review* (26 October 2000).

25 See, for example, Hou Wenhua, '"Sange daibiao" zhongyao sixiang yu tangde zhizheng zhiji – jiantan sugong miewang de lishi jiaosun' [the 'Three Represents' is an Important Ideology and a Cornerstone for the Maintenance of Party Rule – on Drawing a Historical Lesson from the Destruction of the CPSU], *Zhonggong shandongsheng weitangiao xuebao* (October 2003), 22–4; and Xia Meicai, 'Cong Su Dong jubian kan jianzhi "sange diabiao" de zhongyao xing' [On the Importance of Implementing the 'Three Represents' from the Observation of the Drastic Changes in the Soviet Union and Eastern Europe], *Chuxiong shifan xueyuan xuebao*, 18, 4 (2003) 57–9.

26 Jiang Zhiqiang, 'Quanqiuhua yu Su Dong jubian' [Globalization and the Great Changes of the Soviet Union and Eastern Europe], *Zhongyang Yunnan shengwei dangxiao xuebao*, 3, 2 (2002) 93.

27 Joseph Fewsmith, 'China under Hu Jintao', *China Leadership Monitor*, 14 (2005).
28 Willy Wo-Lap Lam, 'China after Hu Jintao: the Looming Class War in 2010?', Conference Summary, The Jamestown Foundation, 1 November 2006.
29 Chou Yingju, 'Political Situation as Viewed from Two "10,000-Character" Statements Circulating inside the Party', *Ching Pao,* 229 (1 August 1996) 23–6 in FBIS-CHI-96-170, 1 August 1996.
30 Zheng Tianxiang, 'Guangrong weida de licheng yu women mianqian de yanzhong wenti' [Our Glorious Great Past and the Serious Question before Us at Present], *Zhenli De Zhuiqui*, 6 (2001) 1–11.
31 Ibid., p. 4.
32 Ibid., p. 3.
33 *Singtao Rih Pao*, 1 September 2001.
34 According to a 16 August 2001 article in the Hong Kong newspaper *Ming Pao*, the directors of *Zhenli de Zhuiqui* and *Zhongliu* decided to halt publication themselves rather than endure the indignity of submitting their materials to the scrutiny of officials within the Central Propaganda Department.
35 PLA units in Xinjiang, Tibet and other border regions were reported to have been placed on special alert after the August 1991 coup attempt. Tsai Yungmei, 'Beijing's Reactions to Great Changes in the Soviet Union', *Kai Fang*, 15 (15 September 1991) 22–4; in FBIS-CHI-91-189, 30 September 1991.
36 Xu Xin, Chen Lianbi and Pan Deli (eds), *Chaoji taguode bengkui: Sulian jieti yuanyin shenzxi* [Collapse of a Superpower: a Deep Analysis of the Reasons for the Soviet Union's Disintegration] (Shehui kexue wenxian chubanshe, 2001), pp. 385–400.
37 For an account of Chinese media coverage of eastern Europe in the late 1980s and early 1990s, see Czeslaw Tubilewicz, 'Chinese Press Coverage of Political and Economic Restructuring of East Central Europe', *Asian Survey*, 37, 10 (October 1997) 927–43.
38 For comments by Putin directly on the 'colour revolutions', see Putin zaveril, chto u rossii net imperskii ambitsii [Putin Attests that Russia has no Imperial Ambitions], *Novosti*, 9 June 2005 at http://www.rian.ru/politics/russia and http://www.vesti.ru/files.html?id=5604.
39 Shih Chen-yu, 'The Orange Revolution: Introspection after the Dream Fell Apart', *Ta Kung Pao*, 5 December 2004. FBIS Translated Text.
40 Chen, Xiancai, '"yanse geming" yu MeiE zhanlue zhizheng' [Colour Revolutions and the Strategic Competition between the United States and Russia], *Anhui shifan xueyuan xuebao*, 33, 4 (July 2005) 333–86.
41 Pan Rulong and Dai Zhengqin, '"yanse gemin" yu guoji fei zhengfu zuzhi' [Colour Revolutions and NGOs], *Dianzi keji tasxue xuebao shekeban*, 7, 4 (2005) 78.
42 Frank Ching, 'Not Amused by Those Colour Revolutions', *New Straits Times*, 27 October 2005, at http://web.lexus-nexis.com
43 *Hong Kong Standard*, 4 June 2005.
44 *Financial Times*, 18 November 2005.
45 *Boston Globe*, 15 June 2006.

16 The Consequences of the Transformation on the Third World

Satoshi Mizobata

The socialist system and its transformation have played a role of navigation for state and institution building. The purpose of this chapter is to investigate the consequences of the transformation on the Third World, the evolution of the Third World in the period of the transformation, and factors involved in the changing of developmental strategy, based on the dynamics of the developing economies. In particular, the East Asian countries including the socialist regimes like China (socialist market economy) and Vietnam (socialist-oriented market economy) have clearly shown a mutual linkage between the transformation and development. The changes in the Third World have strongly influenced the socialist transformation and in turn the transformation has had an impact on development strategy after the 1990s. Through the experiences of the Third World, I will draw some lessons common to the transformation.

Changes in developing countries

The drastic changes that took place in the world's economic order after the first oil crisis brought about a continuous imbalance of international payments for developing countries and led to a polarization between different developing countries. The total external debt to developing countries increased from US$751 billion in 1981 to US$1351 billion in 1991.[1]

The debt crisis was inevitable in socialist countries, where the external convertible currency debt statistics were subject to considerable uncertainty. Initially, Poland went into crisis in the 1980s, when its debt reached US$26 billion in March 1981. According to the OECD, the total cumulative debt balance of socialist countries at the end of 1984 was as follows (US$, billion): 26.8 in Poland, 23.1 in the USSR, 11.3 in East Germany, 8.8 in Hungary, 6.3 in Romania, 2.1 in Bulgaria and 20.5 in Yugoslavia.[2] The Soviet Union was more than moderately indebted by international standards: estimates of its 1990 debt-to-exports ratio range from 135 to 166 per cent, and at the end of 1990, convertible currency debt stood at about US$55 billion. For eastern European countries, the external financing picture in 1990 and 1991 has been one of strong official commitments, but modest disbursements. The World Bank and the IMF accounted for three-quarters of net disbursements.[3]

The above results sufficiently indicate the failure of the socialist development strategy, fragility of 'the Soviet umbrella', lack of a cohesive force of the CMEA, and overbearing pressure from Western organizations and the IMF. For developing countries, the debt crisis in the socialist countries severely aggravated the crisis in the Third World and saw the potential alternative to the capitalist system fade away.

The debt crisis changed the actors of development policy making. In the 1980s, the IMF and the World Bank led the development policy which was focused on structural adjustment based on neo-liberalism with stabilization, liberalization and privatization where cross-conditionality for the revision of the economic policy and the local institutions were regarded as conditions for granting credits. Although the IMF conditionality included many criticisms and errors, it played a major role in helping countries cope with the debt crisis. After 1989, the IMF has played a main role in the assistance of market transition to the former Soviet Union and eastern Europe, it was the natural process of the international financial environment that the economic adjustment programme of the IMF has become conditional for transition economies.

Generally speaking, developing countries had the following characteristics of dirigisme, a planned economy, immature market mechanisms and government interference. Public enterprises were dominant in the national economy because of weak private capital formation, and the government had a strong hand in intervention, and the national development plan was drawn up. Habitual economics and politics were dominant; some countries introduced the Soviet-type economic regime as a result of a mounting liberalization movement backed by colonial memories. Therefore, the market-oriented development policy entailed the transition of the economic regime, and this target prevailed in Asian developing countries. In East Asia, dirigisme operated strongly in China and Vietnam, but was weaker in ASEAN countries. Therefore, the development policy oriented toward the market economy includes the tasks of economic system transformation. This measure, however, was suited only to middle-income countries where a market economy was already developed to a certain degree, which resulted in the disparity among developing countries becoming even wider.

Impact of the transformation: case of East Asia

The fall of the USSR and the CMEA did not noticeably affect developing Asian countries, because their changes (transformation) already occurred before 1989–91, and the degree and speed of changes appeared remarkably intense. The relative positions are shown in Figure 16.1. Vietnam and others broke the deadlock of the economic crisis by strengthening their foreign trade with the West in order to replace their weakened economic relations with the Soviet

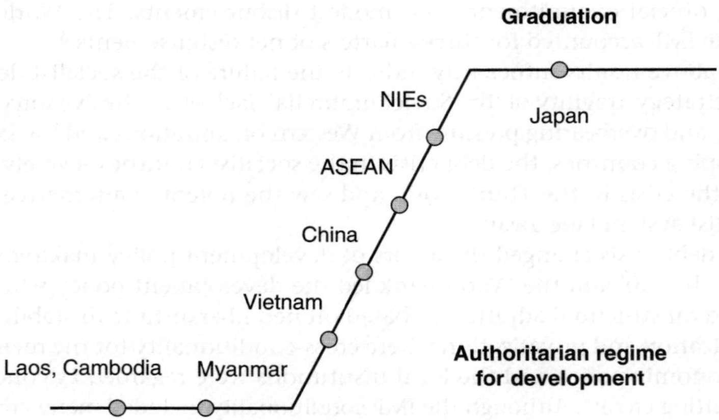

Figure 16.1 The catch-up (flying geese) model in East Asia
Source: K. Ohno and K. Sakurai, *Development Economics in East Asia* (Yuhikaku, 1997), p. 190

Union. Moreover, from the mid-1980s onward, economic policy once based on the development of autocracy shifted towards a much more liberal economic policy. Asian countries developed their economies through foreign direct investment (FDI), international finance and enlarged interdependence. These above trends demonstrate how withdrawal from the Soviet socialist model became a development strategy.

India followed the path of socialist-type development and built an economic system characterized by high saving, state intervention and economic planning. Failure of import substitution industrialization brought India into economic decline and an imbalance of international payments. This led India to 'modest liberal reforms'[4] and an export-oriented path from the beginning of the 1980s. With regard to foreign aid,[5] although the USSR's share was small (about 8 per cent),[6] it played a greater role in the establishment and development of key industries. In the 1980s, India adopted an economic liberalization policy based on the credit provided from the IMF and the World Bank,[7] and the growing amount of FDI. In India, the impact of the collapse of the USSR was minimized, and India accepted reform packages from the West prior to the transformation. Since 1991, India has improved its competitiveness by a consumption-led approach and entrepreneur-driven growth.[8]

Vietnam depended heavily on USSR- and CMEA-based import subsidies and export quotas. Until 1975, Vietnam received economic assistance and engineers, and three-quarters of imports seemed to take on some aspect of assistance.[9] In the period of the Second Five Year Plan (1976–80), foreign assistance, which the USSR took a leading part in, made up 40 per cent of the total budgetary revenue. The twin deficits, budget deficit and foreign trade deficit, were compensated for by foreign assistance. While this structure continued until 1991, by the year 1987 there were institutional restrictions that Vietnamese exporters could not export to other areas unless they satisfied their export quota to CMEA countries. Therefore, the deterioration of relations with the USSR and the collapse of the USSR and CMEA ought to have inflicted a great impact on the Vietnamese economy. However, improved foreign trade relations with the West and an inflow of foreign capital were effective enough to offset the shock of the transformation. During 1980–90, foreign trade denominated in roubles grew by 2.5 times, and foreign trade denominated in dollars increased by 4.1 times.

Furthermore, it was the failure to pay off financial debt (defaulting) that brought about drastic changes in the Vietnamese reform. The IMF froze credit to Vietnam and promoted economic reform, the so-called 'Doi Moi'. Vietnam agreed that a third of unpaid debt would be paid when it was able and two-thirds would be paid by foreign loans at the IMF's discretion. Vietnam accepted the IMF conditionality, abolition of subsidies, and rational measures like adjustment of the exchange rate and prices.[10]

The basis of the economic policy reform 'Doi Moi'[11] was promotion of various kinds of ownership and management, financial reform, introduction of market principles, and opening up the economy. These measures were particular to Vietnam, and were regarded as an attempt to integrate the backward developing country of Vietnam into the capitalist economic system. In December 1986, the Doi Moi policy was adopted, which meant moving away from reliance on assistance from the USSR and establishing economic independence. The Doi Moi policy was equivalent to acceptance of the policy in the IMF and the World Bank, and to acquisition of IMF financing. Therefore, the Doi Moi policy represented substantial system transformation, and the introduction of foreign capital and land privatization. At the very least, the collapse of the USSR and the transformation with suspension of foreign aid promoted the market transition in many ways.[12] In other words, the economic reform of Doi Moi and the introduction of foreign capital not only minimized all shocks, but transformed the development strategy in Vietnam.

Vietnam under Doi Moi gained foreign aid and foreign capital which far exceeded the previous assistance from the USSR and eastern Europe. In 1988–99, foreign capital amounted to 2800 projects, with a capital of US$37.1 billion, of which 14.3 billion (around 40 per cent) was directed to industry (3 billion in petroleum and gas). The growth of FDI exceeded that of GDP. At the same time, assistance from international organizations and foreign governments far outweighed that from the USSR and eastern Europe; in particular, the World Bank financed US$2.575 billion in 26 projects with Structural Adjustment Credit-1 of US$150 million from 1993 to May 2000. In 1999, Vietnam was the biggest host country in the world for IDA (International Development Association) loans.[13] In this way, Vietnam created its own marketization policy of a 'socialist-oriented market economy', with the transformation of the external economic policy having advantageous effects on economic growth

Table 16.1 Vietnamese economic performance

	1986	*1991*	*1996*	*2003*
Annual economic growth (%)	3.4	6.0	9.38	7.24
Budget deficit per GDP (%)	6.2	3.7	0.5	1.8
Exports (billion US$)	0.494	2.042	6.800	19.88
Imports (billion US$)	1.121	2.105	10.200	25.00
FDI (billion US$)	–	0.22	8.54	1.51
ODA (billion US$)	–	0.110	2.4	1.77

Sources: N.X. Oanh, *The Making of Doi Moi: the New Economic Policy of Vietnam* (Akasi, 2003), p. 98; UNDP, *Human Development Report 2006*; The Japanese Embassy in Vietnam, March 2006 Report. ODA = Official Development Assistance.

compared with the transformation in the socialist countries.[14] Table 16.1 indicates the economic performance in Vietnam in the transformation period. In spite of instability caused by the ending of socialist aid, Vietnam achieved high economic growth by FDI and foreign aid from international organizations.

In the end, North Korea was the only case that experienced a significant shock from the transformation. As North Korea depended on the Soviet Union for energy, technology and markets, the transformation spoiled the Third Seven Year Plan (1987–93). The average annual growth of GDP in North Korea declined from 4 per cent in 1975–85 to 2 per cent in 1986–89, and since 1990 negative growth has continued. In particular, the year 1992 recorded 7.6 per cent negative economic growth, which may have been directly influenced by the collapse of the Soviet Union. Economic growth in North Korea stagnated like other socialist countries, and the collapse of the Soviet Union hit its industry and overall had a dire influence. Foreign trade declined sharply by 42 per cent in 1991. Since that time Russia and eastern Europe have not been able to recover their position as a foreign trade partners. North Korean foreign trade became dependent on Japan (later declined), China and South Korea, and consequently the East Asian financial crisis spread to North Korea through South Korea. Even though North Korea adopted joint venture law and introduced foreign capital, it has not had the desired economic outcome. Introduction of foreign capital during late 1980s and 1990s was mainly based on overseas Korean capital, for example through the enterprises of Koreans living in Japan, and consequently this foreign capital could not stimulate economic growth. Although in December 1991 North Korea set up the Rajin-Songbong Economic Trade Zone, the Tumen River Economic Development Area,[15] it could not achieve its full potential due to a lack of infrastructure, an inflexible economic structure, Russia's negative attitude, and low confidence.[16]

The following factors act to minimize the shock of transformation (except in North Korea). First, the less developed countries transformed and liberalized by themselves prior to the socialist transformation. Consequently, the socialist model (myth) had already lost some of its influence on developmental policy. Secondly, due to the cumulative heavy debt resulting from the twin deficits, the IMF, the World Bank and USA became the best group to gain assistance from. The austerity economic policy and economic adjustment programme were accepted as cross-conditionality, and Asian countries accepted this conditionality in exchange for assistance. The Polish debt crisis in 1981 can be regarded as proof of the exhaustion of Soviet power, and the fact that socialist countries could not escape from the cumulative debt crisis. However, assistance and the introduction of foreign capital had enough influence to absorb all the transformation shock (in Vietnam). Thirdly, in the 1980s, almost all Asian developing countries changed their foreign trade structure towards export-oriented industrialization and strengthened their interdependence within the Asia-Pacific area. Additionally, export commodities changed from primary and light industries to machinery-based industries, from low- to high-level technology, which was supported by the growing interdependence of foreign trade in the Asia and Pacific area.

Impact of the transformation: case of Africa

Compared with Asian countries, the impact of the transformation on developing countries was much greater for African nations, which had accepted Soviet economic assistance, development model and control regime. After the 'lost ten years' in the 1980s, Africa experienced drastic democratization in the 1990s. In the second half of twentieth century there was explosive urbanization in Africa, and such structural changes affected democratization.

In the mid-1980s, in Africa,[17] there were 24 countries, 60 per cent of which were controlled by a military regime. Others were under one-party control, and only six countries had a multi-party system.[18] The political situation, however, changed drastically after that time. In the 1990s, there were 40 countries where revision of the constitution enforced the multi-party system and political competition, and in 47 sub-Saharan countries elections took place. Except in Angola and a few other African countries,[19] we could observe the democratization process in Africa.

Internal and external factors influenced the above process. The transformation inevitably affected democratization. The end of the cold war reduced the strategic importance of Africa. A decrease in Western assistance and the democratization demand of domestic politics played a significant role. As Western assistance was given to authoritarian regimes and ended in disaster, economic development was thought to be in need of a responsible regime and corresponding ability.

The impact of the developed countries and the international organizations included not only economic conditionality but also political conditionality. In 1990, the USA set the following requirements in order for developing countries (including Africa) to receive assistance: (1) promotion and reinforcement of democracy, (2) distribution of assistance according to the results of economic liberalization and democratization, (3) promotion of participation and democratization in all programmes including the local authority. The UK and France also acted together with the USA and the assistance programme clearly transformed itself. In addition to Europe and America, Scandinavian countries regarded oppression of human rights as an important reason to suspend assistance, and Denmark effectively froze the new assistance to Kenya in 1991. They adopted the socio-democratic welfare policy and social justice concept for developing countries.[20] Thus, in African developing countries, nobody could ignore the external pressure: the 'good governance' requirement from the World Bank and the IMF (SAP: Structural Adjustment Policy). The political transformation of the one-party system in USSR and eastern Europe,[21] and external pressure, therefore directly influenced the internal pressure for democratization.[22]

Democratization, however, was not advantageous to the economic reform. In Africa, they lacked the social foundations for a democratic system; 'tribalism' and habitual social bonds (patrimonial) like patron–client relationships determined traditional society. Small governments found it hard to survive. Moreover, even though the expenditure of the central government is generally large, the dependence on ODA (Official Development Assistance) is extraordinarily high in Africa. In Tanzania, ODA per GNP was 40 per cent (1993). As Table 16.2 shows, many African countries depend on ODA, and state expenditure has a major position in the economy. As ODA increased rents, rent-seeking and corruption could not be avoided. Unlike Asian countries, African countries have strong tribalism, and rents are liable to specific interest groups (elites) and consequently public policy is easily concentrated in specific regions.[23] In short, under the heavy dependence of the external environment, the disappearance of assistance from the USSR had actual economic effects.

For the developing countries in Africa, the transformation indicates that the economic structure sustained by the cold war could not continue and neither could authoritarian regimes due to the pressure of democratization and the reconsideration of development policy and cold war policy in America and Europe. Therefore, the transformation affected not only socialist countries but also non-socialist countries through a loss of vision and the waning of the existing economic foundation.

Some lessons of the transformation in the Third World

The transformation seems to include some valuable lessons for developing countries. The severe transformational recession and the policy choices that disregarded initial local conditions can be regarded as a lesson.[24] On the one hand, even with the severity of the transformation, the East Asian socialist economies and developing economies fully accepted advice from international organizations and adopted local-oriented measures through trial and error. Some of the Asian NIEs and ASEAN countries adapted themselves selectively

Table 16.2 Asian and African economy

	Total population (millions), 2004	*GDP per capita, 2004*	*Official development assistance (ODA) received (net disbursements)*			*Total expenditure (% of GNP)*	
			Per capita (US$), 2004	*As % of GDP*			
				1990	*2004*	*1980*	*1993*
Developing countries	5,093.6	1,685	10.5	1.4	0.5	–	–
East Asia and the Pacific	1,944.0	1,921	3.3	0.7	0.2	–	–
Malaysia	24.9	4,953	11.6	1.1	0.2	29.6	26.7
Thailand	63.7	2,539	–	0.9	–	19.0	16.3
Philippines	81.6	1,036	5.7	2.9	0.5	13.4	18.1
Vietnam	83.1	550	22.0	2.9	4.0	–	
Indonesia	220.1	1,184	0.4	1.5	–	23.1	18.9
India	1,087.1	640	0.6	0.4	0.1	13.2	16.9
Myanmar	50.0	–	2.4	–	–	15.9	12.1
Pakistan	154.8	632	9.2	2.8	1.5	17.7	24.0
Sub-Saharan Africa	689.6	731	33.0	–	–	–	–
Zimbabwe	12.9	363	14.4	3.9	4.0	35.3	36.2
Madagascar	18.1	241	68.2	12.9	28.3	–	16.1
Cameroon	16.0	897	47.5	4.0	5.3	15.5	18.3
Kenya	33.5	481	19.0	13.8	3.9	26.1	28.9
Guinea	9.2	421	30.3	10.4	7.2	–	21.9
Senegal	11.4	683	92.4	14.4	13.5	23.9	–
Nigeria	128.7	560	4.5	0.9	0.8	–	–
Rwanda	8.9	208	52.6	11.3	25.3	14.3	31.9
Côte d'Ivoire	17.9	866	8.6	6.4	1.0	33.3	–
Tanzania, United Republic of	37.6	288	46.4	27.5	16.1	28.8	–
Zambia	11.5	471	94.2	14.6	20.0	40.0	–
Mozambique	19.4	313	63.2	40.7	20.2	–	–
Central African Republic	4.0	328	26.2	16.8	8.0	21.9	–
Mali	13.1	371	43.2	19.9	11.7	21.6	–
Niger	13.5	228	39.7	16.0	17.4	18.7	–

Source: The World Bank, *World Development Report 1995*, pp. 180–1; UNDP, *Human Development Report 2006*, pp. 298–300, 322–34, 344–7.

to the international conditionality. They kept their industrial policy which, combined with liberal market policy, brought about high economic growth. On the other hand, in Africa, advice from the international organizations was linked with democratization, and suspension of assistance by political conditionality made economic policy inefficient. The conditionality effects were remarkably strong and had the following consequences for developing countries.

1. Development under an authoritarian regime produced economic growth, urbanization and improvement of the education level, and as a result weakened the authoritarian regime itself. Such a cause and effect may overlap with the experiences of the socialist system and its transformation. Globalization also influenced developing countries by determining the rules. However, authoritarian regimes have not been abandoned altogether, with China and Vietnam still operating under them.
2. In spite of the illusion of debt-led growth in 1970s, the debt trap became apparent in the 1980s.[25] Failure to pay financial debt has become the important turning point for all the less developed countries in Asia and Africa. Therefore, the conditionality of the international organizations included liberalization, stabilization and privatization, for all the developing countries and transition economies. In some countries, economic policy has also been influential. However, as theses countries have insufficient domestic capital, privatization continues to be the primary policy. The practical scale of privatization is large, and the method has its own style in each country. Privatization seems to determine its own market model.
3. Initial conditions and country traditions have strongly influenced the transformation,[26] and have played dual roles. They have become a barrier to marketization, but they may guarantee social stability in the short and medium term. In this way, the size of the informal sector is normally large, and the role of social capital prominently becomes important for developing countries and transition economies.
4. The emphasis on the local society and the deeply embedded habitual institutions has created an East Asian economic model different from that of the global model. The central government has some degree of authority, and industrial and income redistribution policies have been put into effect. This model is thought to be based on the successful model of Japan and NIEs. In other words, the transformation served as a model of how not to operate in East Asia. The appropriate policy was not shock therapy, but instead gradual and pragmatic policy based on the local society and initial conditions.[27]
5. For many developing countries, the exploitative (negative) state has been central.[28] Not only market failure but government failure is clear, and interdependence of the government and market is regarded as important. The institutions and governance are necessary, and the growth strategy is not

free from poverty problems. 'Good governance' becomes a necessary condition for economic growth policy, while corruption and opportunistic behaviour like tax evasion lead to government failure. According to Transparency International's Annual Report 2005, developing countries and transition economies rank at the bottom in the corruption perceptions index.[29]

6. Many developing countries have limited revenue, and they need disciplined revenue officers and a responsible tax system. As government expenditure is dominant in the economy of developing countries (see Table 16.2), this task is inevitable. Small government (laissez-faire) during market transition suggests that a budget deficit exists and that it will be hard to build the tax system. A lack of trust in government has brought about capital flight and tax evasion and such negative behaviour makes government credibility worse.
7. The transformation does not simply mean marketization. In comparison with Russia and eastern European countries, apart from the political aspect, the transformation of the socialist economy and the habitual (traditional) economy in East Asia included 'the dual transformation'.[30] The first transformation is modernization from underdevelopment, and self-support family management transforms into the modern industrial economy. The other is system transformation from the socialist planned economy to the capitalist market economy, which in a narrow sense of the word indicates the transformation. Therefore, for development economics, the transformation was from the traditional economy to the market economy.

In order to compare the evolution of the transformation in China and Vietnam, Hiroaki Kato analysed the transformation through two benchmarks: the first is the shift from the traditional economy to the modern economy. The modern sector is determined by the second and third sectors like industry and services, and the traditional one is determined by the primary sector. The employees in the second and third sectors/the employees in the first sector became the first indicator of the transformation (modernization). The second is a shift from the planned state sector to the market private sector. The employees in the non-state sector/the employees in the state sector became the second indicator of the transformation (privatization).[31]

The dual transformation did not follow a predetermined path. In China, modernization took place first, and was then followed by marketization. In Vietnam, marketization (state-owned enterprises' reform) started in its early stages of reform, but the modernization process was more moderate than in China. In Vietnam, there were fewer changes than in China, and between both countries we can observe the following differences: the role of the governments, non-agricultural activity within the villages, saving rates, the role of foreign investments, and so on. Both countries went in the same direction but followed different paths[32] (Figure 16.2).

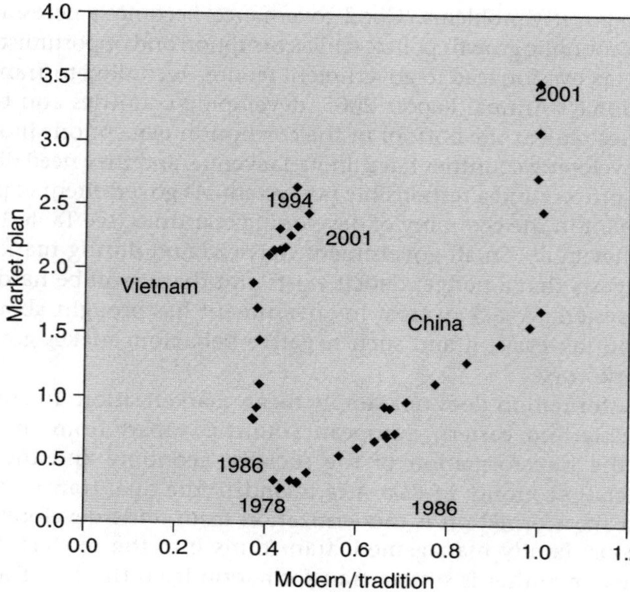

Figure 16.2 The transformation in China and Vietnam
Note: Non-state includes the collective. The employees in 1994 and 1995 are not continuous
Source: H. Kato, 'Market Transition in Developing Countries', in K. Uehara (ed.), *Rising China and Recovering Russia* (Kyoto: Takasuga-Shuppan, 2005), pp. 185–7. Originally from *Statistical Yearbook in China,* World Bank (1994, 1998, 2003)

When we compare the three countries (China, Vietnam and Russia) using these indicators (Figures 16.2 and 16.3), Russia had already achieved modernization prior to the transformation. In contrast to Russia, China and Vietnam have two targets in common, and development is an inevitable task for both countries. Moreover, the second indicator (privatization) is not so large, in comparison with China and Vietnam, because Russia has a strong state sector in the energy and resources sector and the regional and local areas have kept their power under the transformation. Therefore, the three countries are different from one another in the two indicators.

In particular, Russia has its own evolution process. In the early period of the transformation, 1990–94, the modernization indicator shows a slight decline. After 2000, modernization has shown a radical increase in energy sector development. Taking into account the age structure and quality of machinery in Russia, the Russian modernization level may be overestimated. The privatization indicator also increased radically after 1992, and after 2000 both indicators grew. In Russia, however, we cannot neglect the regional gaps. Moscow and St Petersburg achieved the highest modernization, they show isolated

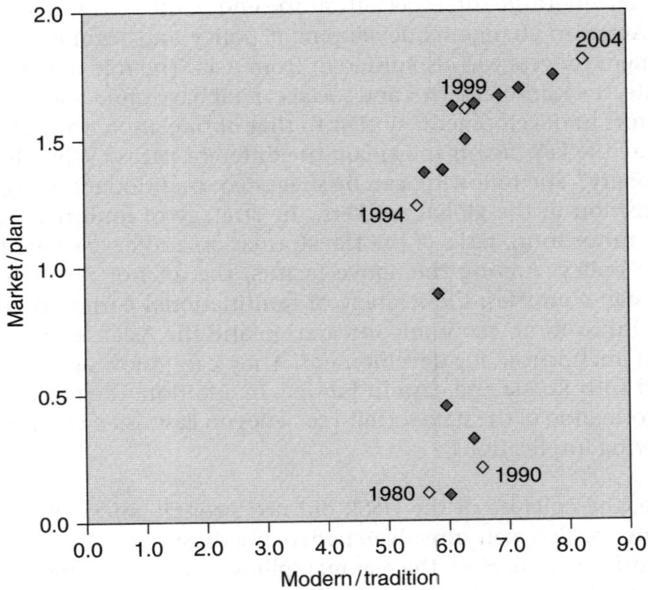

Figure 16.3 The transformation in Russia
Source: Rosstat, *Trud i zanyatost v Rossii*, 1999, 2001, 2003, 2005; Rosstat, *Rossiiskii statisticheskii ejegodnik*

modernization and continued after the transformation to raise the modernization level. In contrast to the two big cities, other regions, not only agricultural areas but the surrounding areas of big cities, show a relatively low level. With regard to the privatization indicator, though almost all regions appear to follow a similar trend, some local cities like company towns and energy-resource centres have followed the marketization process at a slower speed. At the very least, the Asian socialist countries have a different task and path in the transformation.

Conclusion

The transformation and the political changes occurred in the developing countries with the coming of globalization and the debt crisis. Based on the severity of the debt crisis, the influx of multinationals, and the dependence on ODA and foreign aid, the changes from country to country in the Third World were quite different. The Asian countries promptly shifted their development strategy towards export promoting and the flying geese model. They accepted the conditionality of the IMF and the World Bank, and had even begun changing policy prior to the system transformation. Africa showed a much different picture. It experienced a severe impact from the transformation, and due to the external environment, especially at the end of the cold war, it was necessary for Africa to change its development policy and regime. However, its development process was also different from Asia. The role of the state, trust in the state, the informal sector and social capital have often appeared as dominant factors in development, similar to that of transition economies.

What are the key factors to explain the different paths? What divides core and periphery? The following can be suggested: traditional linkage and economic position in the global markets, the strategy of multinationals, technological innovation, tasks of the transformation and development and the economic policy. Among the above factors, the anchor factor is decisive. In East Asian countries, the strategy of multinational corporations (MNCs) based on innovation, economic integration and the Asian economic model played an anchor role for development. They can enjoy significant profits compared with Russia and eastern Europe. In addition, the consequences of the transformation of the state socialist societies on East Asian countries include the following implications.

1. In Asia, the collapse of the USSR did not strongly affect the developing countries, which were already experiencing drastic changes in advance of the transformation. Here, the regional spillover effect is strong. But in Africa this is not the case. Vietnam and China have challenged the dual transformation in advance of Russia and eastern Europe, by following the industrialized Asian countries.
2. The transformation must be measured by various yardsticks like marketization, democratization, modernization and participation in the international division of labour. As the EU plays a role of anchor for the transformation, joining in the international integration has become critical. Above all, all the transformation processes are inevitably connected with the international division of labour, and regional economic integration.

   After the second half of the 1980s, the second wave of regionalism took place.[33] Enlarging and deepening the EU, NAFTA, APEC and others are such groups. Regional integration includes spillover effects, and integration extended not only to the economic dimension but also to the political one. Regional integration has spread through a learning process and imitation, and has locked in the effect of institutions.[34] In addition, FDI has strengthened regional interdependence and reorganized the regional division of labour. As a result, in contrast to the EU where regional integration expands intra-regional foreign trade and the CMEA where the manipulated regional integration collapsed, in East Asia the share of intra-regional foreign trade has increased, and regional integration has developed spontaneously.
3. The gradual and incremental transformation based on the non-Anglo-American model has been effective in East Asia, and the transformation is closely linked with the international development strategy. Even in Africa the policy is based on the local society.

The development and the transformation seem to raise a new vision that the transformation may be assessed from the viewpoint of a global position and economic integration.

Notes

1 The World Bank, *World Debt Tables 1991–92*, Vol.1 (1991), p. 13.
2 OECD, *Statistics on External Indebtedness* (1985).
3 The World Bank, *World Debt Tables*, pp. 10–11.
4 G. Das, 'The India Model', *Foreign Affairs*, July/August (2006) 5.
5 In 1958, the World Bank established the Aid India Club with developed countries (V.N. Balasubramanyam, *The Economy of India*, translated by M. Koga (Tokyo University Press, 1988), p. 197).
6 The USA supplied more than half of the assistance. As for economic assistance from the socialist countries, the USSR accounted for an absolute majority, and concentrated on state heavy and chemical industries.
7 In 1981, the IMF loan required liberalization of foreign trade and economic stabilization.
8 Das, 'The India Model', pp. 6–7.
9 In order to win the war and to succeed in industrialization at the germination stage, Vietnam needed aid from the USSR and China. USSR assisted with 400 million roubles every year, and the total aid amounted to 60 per cent of state revenue in the early 1970s (N.X. Oanh, *The Making of Doi Moi: the New Economic Policy of Vietnam* (Akashi, 2003), pp. 29–33).
10 See K. Fujita, 'Restructuring of Vietnam', in K. Nishiguchi and N. Nishizawa (eds), *East Asian Economy and Japan* (Minerva, 2000).
11 It is regarded as a hybrid of capitalism and socialism.
12 See Oanh, 'The Making of Doi Moi', p. 91.
13 See Fujita, 'Restructuring of Vietnam', pp. 119–21.
14 See S. Ishikawa, *Study on International Development Policy* (Toyokeizaishinposha, 2006), Chs 5 and 6.
15 The UNDP initiated discussions in 1991 leading to agreement among five north-east Asian countries to cooperate in economic development (http://www1.korea-np.jp, 26 August 2006).
16 See M. Pei, 'The North Korean Economy and the External Economic Relations', in Nishiguchi and Nishizawa (eds), *East Asian Economy*.
17 See K. Aoki, 'Democratization and the Tasks of African Countries', *International Affairs*, 460, July (1998).
18 Botswana, the Gambia, Mauritius, Senegal, Swaziland and Zimbabwe.
19 The opposition party turned to guerrilla warfare, insisting the election was unfair. See Aoki, 'Democratization', p. 4. There were some cases in which the democratic system was overturned by the military authorities.
20 See Ishikawa, *Study*, pp. 159–60.
21 They lost the legitimacy of the one-party system and the centralized political regime.
22 See Aoki, 'Democratization'.
23 See M. Takahashi, 'Rethinking the Contemporary African "Tribalism" ', *International Affairs*, 460, July (1998).
24 From the initial condition, the aim of development strategy is different between Asia and Africa. Asia has a target of catching up and egalitarianism, and Africa is forced

to focus on poverty (K. Ohno, 'Seeking the Development Cooperation Concept by East Asian Experience', *International Affairs*, 506, May (2002)).

25 H.W. Singer, Lessons of Post-war Development Experience: 1945–88', in S. Sharma (ed.), *Development Policy* (The Macmillan Press Ltd, 1992).

26 'The success stories of the East Asian NICs have not depended on the initial conditions of the 1940s, but rather on the adoption of appropriate policies during the 1960s and since' (G.M. Meier, 'Do Economists Influence the Developing World?', in Sharma (ed.), *Development Policy*, p. 20).

27 See Ishikawa, *Study*, p. 40.

28 Meier, 'Do Economists', p. 23.

29 www.transparency.org, 29 August 2006.

30 See Ishikawa, *Study*.

31 See H. Kato, 'The Transformation of Developing Countries: China and Vietnam', in K. Uehara (ed.), *Advancing China and Recovering Russia* (Takasugashuppan, 2005).

32 Ibid.

33 The first wave of regional integration occurred in Europe, America and Africa in the 1950–1960s.

34 See Y. Yamamoto, 'The Political Economy of the Regional Integration', *International Affairs*, 452, October (1997). Less globalized regions could not develop regional integration. In Asia, the regional integration in Tomangan of Russia, North Korea and China led by the UNDP with cooperation with South Korea and Japan was localized and it did not intimate relations with other regions.

Index